ONE-NINER

A Marine Infantry Chaplain's Struggle with PTSD and Depression in Viet Nam 1968

RICHARD STUART LIPPERT

PAGE PUBLISHING, INC.
New York, NY

First originally published by Page Publishing, Inc. 2018

ISBN 978-1-64138-702-6 (Paperback)
ISBN 978-1-64138-703-3 (Digital)

Printed in the United States of America

This book is dedicated to all who suffer from PTSD, both civilian and military. And to my brother Marines, I am eternally grateful for granting me the privilege of serving with the Marine Corp.

"…for he who sheds his blood with me shall forever be my brother."

Henry IV

Preface

There has been nothing definitive yet that has come out about Vietnam and our involvement there. This book is no exception. There is one thing, however, that I do know that is definitive and absolute about Vietnam and the combat veterans this war produced—something that every parent and every spouse knows.

Every one of us who faced daily combat never came back.

PROLOGUE

A stiff, chilly wind is blowing down the San Gabriel and San Bernardino mountain passes onto the flat coastal plains below the urban sprawl of Los Angeles. This offshore breeze is then propelled out into the vast, dark expanse of the Pacific Ocean, an earth process that is fundamental to patterns of wind and weather since the tectonic plates of the Pacific Ocean violently created the mountains of Southern California. These winds are also crucial to the development and form of coastal waves that are generated from giant ocean swells thousands of miles away in the southern or northern Pacific.

In the dark of early morning, Richard Strom slips into his winter wetsuit, still damp and cold from having been left outside overnight, shivering as the wetsuit slides up his body. His cold, stiff fingers then grasp the nylon string attached to the zipper on the back of his suit and slowly pulls it up, fastening the Velcro strap over the clasp. He gingerly attaches the leash to his longboard, then fastens the opposite end to his left ankle. Picking up his board, the seventy-year-old surfer carefully navigates around the rocks, walking the remaining fifteen yards to the water's edge.

The wind is brisk and cold. Although dark, he is able to see his breath when exhaling, reminding him of all those cold mornings in rural Minnesota when surfing and the Pacific Ocean were remote childhood fantasies. He winces as he steps into the knee-deep, fifty-five-degree water, then drops his waxed surfboard onto the swirling foam. Pushing off the rocks underneath his feet, he softly lies on his board and begins the paddle to his favorite surfing spot—the sandbar off *the point* at San Onofre. The frigid water numbs his hands and feet. He cannot see more than a few yards ahead but can hear the pounding surf one hundred yards away. Pushing through the first wall of whitewater the chilly water rushes over his bare head, producing an instant headache. Each successive wall of white water bleeds through the wetsuit and chills the body to the bone as Richard paddles on—a cold, difficult, arduous encounter with the power and vastness of the Pacific.

Exhausted he finally reaches the calmer waters beyond the impact zone and now sits quietly on his surfboard, awaiting the next set of waves. Just south seventy-five yards away, he sees three other surfers who have also braved the cold and dark of a California winter morning to rendezvous with this primitive passion that all surfers share.

He glances over his left shoulder toward the east as the early morning light now outlines the hills of Camp Pendleton. He suddenly experiences a moment of amusement, remembering his mom's comments about his surfing passion, saying that the many years in the saltwater and the multiple bumps on the head from his surfboard have surely caused brain damage.

Rapidly a giant five-wave set is bearing down on him. Quickly he lies down on his board and paddles furiously to the outside, adrenaline instantly pumping through his body, generating both fear and excitement.

Barely making it over the ten-foot wall of the first wave, he can make out the second and third waves close behind. Paddling over the crest of each massive wall, they both "feather" at the top, blowing salty spray thirty feet in the air generated by the brisk offshore wind. The fourth wave is a giant fourteen-foot wall of energy generated from a storm far away in the Aleutian Islands.

Instantly he whips his board around to face the shore and takes two strokes. As the surfboard shoots down the face of the wave at a steep angle, he instinctively jumps into a crouched position. Slashing across the powerful double-overhead wave, the space-time continuum ceases to exist, merging his body and the immense, raw power of the Pacific into an alliance of balance and unity, each encounter a reminder that the ocean has been one of the divine interventions that has saved his life.

Turning back toward the west and the thousands of miles of ocean between him and Asia, he flashes on those months and years after he returned from Vietnam when he truly believed that he was emotionally and psychologically scarred, maybe for good.

I

Beautiful words are not truthful;
truthful words are not beautiful.

Lao Tsu

NEW REALITIES

Flatly, mechanically, the battalion chaplain climbs aboard the chopper that will transport him from Echo Company back to battalion field headquarters. He slumps into the webbed seat, not bothering to utilize the seat belt, dumping his pack and communion kit on the deck, then leans back, eyes closed, hoping this will blot out the collage of images going through his head. Last night's encounter with the horror of battle and the sleepless, anticipatory paranoia of more battle to come has left him bereft of energy. There are no emotional reserves left. He is close to physical and mental collapse, his thinking is blurred and fuzzy, and the only feeling that blasts out of his innards anymore is a crushing, shattering, all-encompassing primal fear when in combat. All other life feelings have been squeezed dry.

Just as the sun was setting, within twenty minutes of Chaplain Strom's landing last night near the command post, the enemy unloaded on the isolated Marines of Echo Company. Enemy mortars, then small arms fire—the bullets and shrapnel whizzing through the trees and undergrowth, stopping only when hitting a solid object like wood or flesh and bone—fusing life and death together in a crap shoot. Living and dying becomes a game of chance dictated by inches and fractions of seconds, and the natural instinct of the species to gain control of this kind of environment is a deadly game of illusion.

Of the remaining seven people left in the company that Richard knew—his good friend Sergeant Mac went home seven days ago—four had been killed. First platoon had essentially been wiped out in an ambush two hundred meters away from the company CP, losing its platoon leader, a squad leader, and two veterans with less than three weeks left before being rotated back to the States.

At the time the devastating attack took place, Richard Strom was walking toward first platoon to speak with the new lieutenant about having church services the next morning before he left for battalion. The mortars hit first, shrapnel slashing into the platoon leader and four other nearby Marines. Then the small arms fire erupted throughout the area for the next five minutes, an ongoing wall of lethal bullets shattering any object in its path. The chaplain had immediately hit the deck and crawled toward two fallen Marines hit by shrapnel, lying motionless on the ground, one of them being tended to by a corpsman. Shortly Richard was holding the dying Marine in his arms as the veteran corpsman Jacobi crawled off to another body lying on the wet ground.

The battalion chaplain pushes the images of last night from his consciousness, focusing instead on the smells and sounds and interior of the CH-46 helicopter. He has trained himself to quickly use distraction, a process he learned months ago after combat when his negative ruminations and ugly feelings become too much. He continues to marvel at the endurance and stamina of the line grunt whose horror and depravation far surpasses anything he has experienced. Now he attempts to think as little as possible about anything.

The chopper is now descending and he looks out the window on his right as they slowly circle down toward a clearing that is billowing yellow smoke. "What's the smoke about?" Richard thinks to himself as the chopper lands in a swirl of yellow haze. "What the hell is going on?" He is aware that smoke is not normally used if a landing zone is benign and no hostiles are around.

The aircraft lands quickly without the slow, soft touch of most landings. The chaplain quickly picks up his gear and moves out the aft section. Immediately the chopper lifts off the deck, does a starboard turn, and forthwith heads on a southerly direction toward An Hoa and headquarters of the Fifth Marine Regiment. At once he can hear the distinct sound of mortars and small arms fire to the east a few hundred meters away. Richard instinctively throws on his pack, slings his communion kit over his shoulder, and walks quickly toward the battalion command post fifty meters away, his fight-or-flight mechanism now mobilized. The overwhelming fatigue he was feeling is now a fleeting memory—only the mordant, combat-driven, caustic anxiety that always gnaws at his innards is now present.

Upon reaching the command post, he drops his gear on the deck. The commanding officer, Lt. Col. Huggins, is on the radio and the operations officer, Major Copeland, turns to face Strom. "Damn, Chaplain," he begins anxiously, "we've got Charlie runnin' around all over the place. Glad you're back, heard you caught some shit up the hill."

"Yes, sir," Strom replies, "what's going on with Hotel Company?"

"Just stay here and don't be running off," he replies tersely, then whirls around to converse with the new assistant ops officer, Captain Vic Ciribello.

Richard is stationary for a few seconds, then picks up his gear and walks away toward the battalion aid station a few meters away disregarding the major's directive. He is met by an unfamiliar face, which for the chaplain is now routine. There isn't a person in the battalion with more time in-country than he. A young man in his twenties extends his hand. "You must be Chaplain Strom," he says as Richard drops his kit and extends his hand. "My name is Jim Lippert, I'm the new battalion surgeon replacing Dennis Jonsen."

"Where's my assistant Bob Marshall and the new chaplain?" is Richard's immediate curt response, disregarding the introduction and quickly looking around for his assistant. "And Smitty. Where's Smitty?" he continues with a look of alarm on his face.

"The new chaplain and, ah, your assistant left this morning for An Hoa," he says tentatively, feeling somewhat taken aback by the chaplain's abruptness. "Father Porter said he needed to get some supplies and equipment."

"Yeah, and where's Smitty?" the chaplain impatiently requests.

"He and Perkins went to Hotel when the firefight started," he replies. "They needed some more corpsmen because of the casualties."

Strom immediately turns and quickly heads back to the CP. He is suddenly aware of the silence of mortar explosions and AK-47 rifle fire that had permeated his consciousness upon arrival less than three minutes ago, his personal antennae always tuned in to the sounds or lack of sounds of battle. He walks back into the makeshift CP.

The commanding officer is now off the radio and moves next to his chaplain.

Huggins looks tense, releases a deep breath, places his hand on Richard's shoulder, and says in a quiet voice, "Hotel got whacked pretty bad a few minutes ago. I need you to go down there and see to the wounded troopers, Padre."

"How bad?" is Strom's immediate response, shifting his communion kit to his other shoulder.

"Bad enough, Chaplain Strom," he replies, "got an emergency medevac on the way. Sorry to get you involved like this." He turns toward Copeland, motioning for his S3 to come closer, as he continues to talk to Richard. "Father Porter went back to An Hoa to get some stuff he needed for the field, sent your man with him as well."

"Yes, sir," the chaplain responds quickly. "Could you get me a couple of Marines to go with me?"

The colonel whirls around and yells out, "Captain Ciribello, get the chaplain here some security!"

Within five minutes Strom has reached third platoon, which bore the brunt of the attack. Eleven troopers are strewn about, being tended to by corpsmen and Marines. Most of them were cut down by withering small arms fire. He stops by the first body he comes upon, two Marines by his side, a bullet hole through his right cheek exiting out his left ear. They look up sadly at Richard as he kneels down, placing his hand on the Marine's lifeless chest for a few seconds. Still kneeling, he says nothing, then slowly gets up and declares flatly, "I'll be back as soon as I check on the others."

He walks quickly by another prone Marine with a bullet wound in his leg, being attended to by a company corpsman. Richard is feeling the numbness again, pushing down any feelings of revulsion or sadness. He continues onto a small clearing away from a line of bamboo trees. "Hey, Chaplain," comes the sudden, anxious call twenty-five meters away from a trooper hovering over two occupied corpsmen working desperately on his grievously injured friend, "Foley's been hit really bad." He gestured frantically with his arm. "Please, sir."

Strom responds mechanically, like a robot, to the young Marine's request. He slowly drops his gear next to the busy corpsmen. "Oh God, Chaplain, do something, he's hurt real bad," he continues while grabbing Richard's arm. The corpsmen are fighting a losing battle because the critically wounded Marine is bleeding to death from bullet wounds to the neck and abdomen. In spite of their heroic efforts, Richard understands the scenario. He has witnessed the dying process far too many times: first the deep shock and then the slow release into unconsciousness and death.

Chaplain Strom now gently grabs the young man's arm and turns him away from his dying friend. "What's your name, son?" he says softly while continuing to hold his arm.

"He's dying… isn't he?" the young Marine questions, quickly turning back to his bloodied comrade on the deck.

With purpose but gently, Richard turns the trooper back around to face him and repeats his question: "Your name, son, I want to know your name."

"Turner, sir, Pfc Wally Turner," he replies, then turns again toward his friend, M-16 still in hand. The chaplain notices he is shaking badly.

Strom now moves directly in front of the young Marine. "Wally," he begins, then is quickly interrupted by one of the corpsmen.

"Chaplain, sir," Richard hears from behind as he gazes into the sad, anxious face of Turner, "I think you're needed here."

Strom, still holding Turner's arm, turns back toward the dying Marine and sees both corpsmen stand up, then the closest one shakes his head slowly. "Sir," he says gently, then steps back as Strom and Turner walk the remaining steps to the prone Marine. The chaplain kneels down next to the blood-soaked body as does Turner, still holding his rifle. Strom then gently takes Turner's free hand and places it on the motionless left hand of his friend. Slowly his consciousness fades, then momentarily he takes two shallow breaths. Within five seconds he has surrendered all and is dead. No family present to mourn, no heroic moments to recollect, no famous last words for posterity. Just a fading away witnessed by four individuals whose lives continue to diminish with each horrible encounter.

Richard lifts his hand and places it on Turner's shoulder, his other hand on the bloodied forehead of Pfc Eddie Carlton. "Lord, now let your servant, this young Marine, depart in peace," he begins softly, "according to your word... for we have seen your salvation, you have prepared a home for us and for all people." There is a long pause as the chaplain can hear helicopters in the background, then continues. "Our prayers are for his family, for his friend here Wally Turner, for the bravery and hard work and safety of our corpsmen." There is another pause as Turner weeps silently. The chaplain places his arm around the young man and pulls him close to his left side. "Keep us together as a family of Marines, watch over us, comfort us, Lord." Making the sign of the cross, he continues, "In the name of the Father, Son, and Holy Spirit. Amen.

PFC Turner remains kneeling by the side of his best friend. Richard stands, pats the young man softly on his back, then whirls to see an inbound helicopter coming into the open field less than one hundred meters away. He is struck by the fact that the helicopter is hardly making a sound and appears to be coming in for a landing in super slow motion, like he's watching a movie, as if his sensory processes are muted and distorted. Slowly, methodically he does a complete three-hundred-sixty-degree turn around, to orient himself to where he is, to get grounded and rooted in the reality of the present, to shake off the deep, moribund detachment and numbness he is presently experiencing. He is feeling lost, cut off from his surroundings and even from himself, a spooky, alien awareness that he is a completely withdrawn observer instead of a participant in the surrounding, unfolding drama. There is a dim awareness that Gunnery Sergeant Carter is walking toward him.

Richard James Strom is frozen in time and place, incapable of any kind of physical or mental response requisite to standing in the middle of a combat zone. Very slowly a consciousness of another time and place begins to seep out of his psyche, a gathering and mobilization of the senses, pushing the distraught chaplain into another world...

The phone is ringing inside the house as Richard Strom hastily unlocks the front door and steps into his home out of a murky New Orleans fall afternoon rain. A part of him wants to disregard the ringing phone and concentrate instead on the contents of a long-awaited letter from the Department of the Navy he has just retrieved from a wet mailbox.

However, having sufficiently conditioned himself into believing that the well-being of his small part of the world rests on answering all phone calls, Richard puts the letter aside and responds instead to his clergy instincts. This is a reaction that essentially has its roots in seminary theological training, which, among other things, taught the budding young clerics that they are indispensable to world order. This inevitably leads most of them to the conclusion—or compulsion—that any cleric worth his white collar would never let a ringing phone go unanswered.

He quickly moves into the kitchen and picks up the phone and is immediately jolted to a reality of hysteria and panic on the other end of the line. "Okay now... ah, okay," he stammers, attempting to make some sense out of the emotional volcano at the other end.

"Let's, ah, relax a bit here... and go slowly..."

"Oh my God, no, I'll never relax again... it's awful... oh God, I'm going to get sick," the caller moans. It isn't an urgency that Richard is hearing in her voice but rather pure terror. "You're... oh God... you're supposed to get over here right now," she says in a halting voice punctuated by the sounds of gagging, a preamble to her actually getting sick. Abruptly, as adrenaline rushes into his system, his level of anxiety elevates. Then quite spontaneously, he experiences a sick feeling in his stomach and the premonition that something dreadful has transpired. Richard is completely unaware of who this person is and what has happened to precipitate this crisis at which his presence is apparently a matter of life and death.

Within two minutes Pastor Strom has deciphered a parishioner's frantic call and is speeding down Chef Menteur Highway toward an apartment complex three miles away. The rain has increased in intensity and the drive seems forever as his mind races back and forth over the past two encounters he had experienced with Frank after he began attending church four months ago. Since his return from the central highlands of Vietnam as an army infantryman, Frank was having a difficult time adjusting to civilian life and had made passing references to nightmares and some paranoia.

After driving at an unsafe speed in the downpour, Richard finally turns off the highway into a large apartment complex and a parking lot filled with puddles of water. Two police cars have already arrived as he parks his car and sprints across the parking lot to Frank's ground-floor apartment. Both Donna and Jim, members of his parish, are huddled outside the front door next to a policeman, a look of terror frozen on their faces. A police sergeant emerges from the doorway, notices Pastor Strom immediately because of his clerical collar, and politely says, "Sir, he's in the bedroom."

"We couldn't get ahold of him this past weekend and he didn't show up for work this morning at the plant," Jim is able to murmur, "so we came here to check on him and the manager let us in." He shakes noticeably as he is talking. "What could I have done…" His voice trails off into silence as he places his hands over his face.

"It's okay, Jim," Richard tells him as he softly places his hand on his shoulder. "Please don't go anywhere. I'll be right back."

The young cleric nods to the sergeant and follows him through the kitchen into a dark hallway, past another policeman into the bedroom. There, slouched on the floor with his back to the wall corner, is Frank. A twelve-gauge shotgun is lying next to him and most of his head is splattered on the wall and ceiling behind his body.

A Paradigm Shift

Much of the time Richard James Strom feels as if he is walking dead, barely able to make it through his daily pastoral duties. The tragedy of a parishioner's suicide has thrashed him spiritually and emotionally. In spite of Frank's history of alcoholism and depression, he blames himself for having neither the insight into the magnitude of the problem nor the pastoral and psychological skills necessary to remedy Frank's pain. Still, two weeks past the funeral, he lies awake long hours into the night, the smell and sight of that bedroom scene flashing before him over and over again. Each night he prays for peace and sleep. Both elude him. These past two weeks have been the most difficult time emotionally and spiritually that he can ever remember.

Four years in a private liberal arts college in Minnesota and four more years in a Midwestern Lutheran Seminary has filled his head with information on English literature, world history, Old Testament patriarchs, New Testament missionaries, twentieth-century theologians, and the scholarly skill of conjugating even the most exotic Greek verb. However, it has done little to prepare a young clergyman for experiencing this type of tragic life experience, where the textures of life and death are mixed together in the market place called the real world. Corruption, infidelity, suicide, alienation, addiction, despair—such words are abstractions that can somehow be made palatable by applying theological theory or moving through an ancient religious ritual.

Although he has navigated unscathed and hopeful through the normal issues of parish politics, ideological squabbles, administrative headaches, and counseling families with a myriad of problems,

Frank's suicide has shaken Richard's belief system, a system wherein he experiences the world as essentially safe and predictable. The family and community milieu in which he grew up reinforced that experience, a view based upon a Scandinavian, upper Midwest work ethic and sense of orderliness. The gruesome suicide of a parishioner has stopped him in his tracks. He feels like a big Mack truck has driven right over him. For one of the few times in his life, he is experiencing sustained self-doubt, an ebbing of that certainty of self and resolution of purpose that has permeated most of his life. At this point, he isn't so sure anymore about safeness and predictability.

Richard is generally optimistic and usually looks forward to each day and what the future will bring. Mostly, he doesn't dwell on past events and what could have been. He is somewhat surprised, therefore, that again and again over the past week he finds himself drifting back to a rush of earlier experiences, back to the rich black farmland of south central Minnesota, almost as a way of soothing himself, needing to return to a safer and less complicated time…

… Remembering as a young boy, having grown up in a bilingual home, that he believed all older people had Swedish accents when they spoke English, that is until he took his first trip to Minneapolis at age four and encountered older folks speaking "regular English," a surprising event that began to crack the shell of insular, parochial experiences…

… Right after the church potluck supper, throwing a hard-packed snowball at a passing car and cracking its windshield, remembering the panic at discovering that it was the police car—the town had only one—then, shortly thereafter, being busted by the pastor's wife, who had observed this fiasco…

… Laughing softly to himself, recalling the day the Boy Scouts visited worship services at his church, assuming all Christians thought and worshipped as he did, then having an acquaintance sitting next to him, a Baptist, says to Richard, "Your church is different and you do funny things, especially the preacher who dresses in weird robes"…

… Going to school in a two-story brick building with four rooms and six grades, where everyone knew everybody else and also knew stuff about you or your family that you didn't want them to know...

... Shoveling snow at seven in the morning when it's still dark, shivering cold, wondering what people in southern California do in the winter at seven in the morning, then running out to the local pond just outside the city limits, skates and sticks in hand, to scrape new snow off the surface and get a good hockey game going with your friends...

... Watching the farm animals bearing their newborn, never giving it a second thought, accepting this process as naturally as watching the weather change or going to school each weekday...

... Remembering the distinct smells and sights of each room of the big white two-story farmhouse on the outskirts of the small town they grew up in, smiling softly at memories of his brothers and the good times they had as well as the suddenness of a fight between two or more boys, like "a brigade of ornery Marines," his dad would say on occasion.

Turning onto Gentilly Highway to head into the city, Richard is flooded with more recent memories. He remembers his graduation from seminary and subsequent ordination a month later at Christ Chapel overlooking the lush green Minnesota River Valley and directed to organize a new mission congregation. Thereupon, he is sent to the eastern fringes of a New Orleans swamp called Michoud, in the middle of a Yankee ghetto filled with NASA engineers, where the most prominent subject of conversation is how soon they, the Yankees, can "get the hell out of here" and move back to Seattle or Detroit. The rudeness of native New Orleanians toward nonnatives, suffocating heat, armies of mosquitoes, and closet mildew are the environmental issues "the Northerners" find most irritating.

Now, as he drives south on Canal toward the Mississippi River and a ten o'clock appointment at the Eighth Naval District for his physical, Richard is again having doubts about himself, about his direction, about his capacity to function at a brand-new and completely different type of ministry. The Bureau of Naval Personnel has accepted his request to go on active duty, which means that he will need to contact his synod bishop and let him know that resignation from his parish is imminent. These are all big decisions, and coming on the heels of the recent suicide of a parishioner, Richard is now tentative and unsure of himself. He has prayerfully asked the Lord to direct him daily on this matter, expecting both spiritual and emotional resolution. However, resolution has eluded him, which in turn creates more doubt and anxiety about his decision-making capacity and also his ability to carry through in this new venture and ministry.

Richard has selected the naval service because of its diversity and desire to be assigned to a ship, hopefully in the Atlantic Fleet. Instead, he is to be given orders to report to the Fifth Marine Division at Camp Pendleton in Southern California after attending chaplain school in Newport, Rhode Island. He isn't quite sure but has speculated to his wife and friends that in all likelihood he will probably end up in Vietnam within the year.

So as he parks his car at the district headquarters and gathers up his orders for his medical physical, he isn't sure at all that he wants to go through with this new venture. In the back of his mind Richard knows that he can get out the assignment simply by asking Bishop Wahlberg to withdraw his petition for transfer out of his parish to active duty in the military. It has been a passing thought on many occasions, especially since receiving a communication from the chaplain division that he will receive orders shortly to the Marines!

The headquarters building is adjacent to the river, and since he is a few minutes early, he walks to the top of the levee to observe the Mississippi. A stiff, cold wind is blowing. As he watches a ship slowly move up the river, his thoughts go back to his arrival in New Orleans three years ago, remembering that the house the national church had purchased for the parish was not ready for occupancy. So the Stroms lived in a cheap motel on the east side of the city for three weeks during which time a murder, two rapes, and a fire occurred at the thirty-unit premises. Then two days after they finally moved into the newly finished house, Hurricane Betsy hit with the force of 165-mile-per-hour winds, causing sixty-five deaths and massive destruction throughout southern Louisiana, including some damage to their house. It was an inauspicious start for a young ideologue.

As he gazes across the river from Algiers and the West Bank, Richard is aware that some erosion of idealism and energy has taken place since those eventful times. He recalls wistfully all the early Sunday mornings that first year, cleaning up the beer cans and cigar butts at the union hall so the congregation could hold worship services, the excitement and dedication of the parishioners as they moved into their new church and school building a year later, the shock and sadness the church council expressed the evening he announced that he would be going on active duty right after the Christmas holiday.

Richard turns away from the river, walks back down the stairway to the parking lot, then around to the front of the district headquarters, enters the building and walks toward the main reception desk attended by two enlisted personnel. The awesome finality of his decision to go on active duty—especially with the Marine Corps—stops him dead in his tracks, as if something way down deep in his bowels is giving voice to the thought "Run—right now. Get the hell out of here!"

Richard isn't very good at listening to these kinds of messages coming up from deep within himself. Rather, he pushes down any thoughts of indecision, any feelings of anxiety, and responds instead to the need to be on time for his ten o'clock appointment.

"Yes, sir, can I help you?" asks the young sailor behind the counter at the reception desk.

LEAVING ST. TIMOTHY

The Christmas holidays have always been special for Richard Strom, growing up in a tradition-filled family and community. Church, food, and secular Scandinavian celebrations culminated in Christmas Julotta, an early morning candlelight worship service that was held in the Swedish language. Even as a child, it was always an inspiring experience to come into a darkened, candlelit church and leave ninety minutes later to walk out into the cold and snow, the sun just beginning to rise in the east. The anticipated presents that awaited the Strom children under their Christmas tree no doubt contributed heavily to that inspiring experience as well.

This holiday season is devoid of the traditional celebrations Richard is used to, mainly because most of the members of his parish are not from the upper Midwest or from German or Scandinavian traditions. The majority of his parishioners are from other Protestant denominations with a smattering from Roman Catholic backgrounds. However, because of the new mission's inauspicious start and humble beginnings, the hard work and devotion so many parishioners put into the church, a close bond of caring and fellowship exists throughout the congregation. This bonding is a result of their mutual experiences at St. Timothy, not because of tradition or ethnic similarity.

It is now Christmas Eve and the congregation and Pastor Strom are encountering their last moments of worship and fellowship together, a bittersweet experience for all. Richard has nurtured this new mission church since its beginnings three years ago in a smelly union hall. The cycles of birth and death, serenity and despair, chaos and order, love and hate, misdeed and spiritual renewal—this is the montage of life itself as well as the living foundation of this family called St. Timothy.

Shortly the parish and its pastor will be forging new directions separately, a differentiating process that is both disquieting and filled with hope and opportunity. For many this has been their first exposure to church life since childhood and Strom's leaving is a somber experience, given the close bond the people have formed with him and one another.

Some of these fine folk have expressed their fear that when he leaves, and before they are to get a new pastor, the congregation will fall apart. Aware of their concerns but also a strong believer that prayer and hard work will continue to make their ministry strong and vibrant, Pastor Strom focuses again and again in his sermons on a very poignant scripture passage in II Timothy: "For God did not give us the spirit of fear, but of power and of love and of sound mind." It is a spiritual declaration he wishes to carry with him in the military, especially if he ends up in Vietnam.

Richard is now standing in the front doorway of the church, saying good-bye to all these good folks. They share their mutual tears of sadness as they pass through a final grasp, each member a last glance, a flash on the difficulties and sacrifices and good times and spiritual growth they've shared together.

Pastor Richard James Strom is now closing the door to his office for the final time at 1:30 a.m. after everyone has left for home. He feels a profound momentary rush of loneliness, of painful sadness. But only for a moment as he suddenly thinks about the Hebrew patriarch Abraham and his nephew Lot, of Lot's wife who turned into a pillar of salt because she was unable to focus her energy forward and could only look back. "Just close the door now. Turn and walk out of the building. That's all there is to it," he thinks to himself as he pulls the key out of his pocket to lock the door for the final time. "Nothing to it," he tells himself through burning, streaking tears of loss and grief.

THE MILITARY

Empty your minds now, if you will, of whatever projections you might have of clergymen. Instead, just imagine what it was like to have spent four years in college and another four years in seminary preparing for a holy calling, then spending a minimum of three years in a parish or synagogue, after which you are sent to an eight-week advanced sea scout training program called Officer's Training Program for Navy Chaplains run by a young navy lieutenant, a gunnery sergeant from the Marine Corps, and two navy chaplains with the rank of captain.

Richard's class of twenty-one chaplains, between twenty-eight and forty years old, do important things like memorize military jargon; learn what is proper to talk about in the wardroom of a naval ship (politics is forbidden); practice the sanctifying skill of packing a communion kit in less than three minutes; participate in a short cruise on a navy frigate, the USS *Bainbridge*, which makes most of them sick; are taught close order drill, which the gunny describes as looking like a group of stumbling catatonics; and study many other obtuse and banal things that have little relationship to the experiences most of them are about to face.

They even learn how to appreciate Beatle music by listening one whole day to the *Sgt. Pepper's Lonely Hearts Club Band* album. That would tell them about the younger generation they are about to face as chaplains.

So in order to make it through that kind of stuff day after day, some of the chaplains spend lots of time hanging out, sharpening their skills at such things as pool, table tennis, cribbage, and drinking scotch and soda at the officers' club.

After seven weeks of learning about things that most of them will never experience or use again, they all become full-fledged active-duty chaplains in the naval service. Two chaplains go to a destroyer division out of Norfolk, and two of them even get shore duty on the West Coast. The rest of the poor devils get the Marines!

Which is why Lieutenant Richard James Strom, USNR chaplain Corps, finds himself in Southern California one week after graduating from chaplain school, orders in hand, standing in front of "Foxhole Kelly," the division chaplain of the Fifth Marine Division. Father Kelly had that name tagged on him when he was serving with the Marines on Guadalcanal during World War II. It was his claim that he was able to "intuit" incoming and was always the fastest to get to his foxhole before the incoming hit.

He motions with his hand for Richard to sit down, slowly takes a seat behind his desk, and says, "I'm told that on your entrance form at chaplain school, you said that since you we're going to go to the Marines, you would rather be with the grunts. That right, Chaplain?"

"Yes, sir, I believe I did say that," the young chaplain responds.

"We're gonna send you out into the back country to San Mateo, out with the Twenty-Eighth Marines. The third battalion needs a chaplain, so that's where you can report for duty tomorrow when you get your living quarters squared away," he continues. "I hope you're in good shape. Plan on doing a lot of duty out in the field."

As quickly as that, Chaplain Strom is a part of the United States Marine Corps and subsequently sent out to the grunts. As he leaves the division chaplain's office, he remembers the admonition of Gunnery Sergeant Rodine back in chaplain school: "Any of you chaplains going with the Marines, especially if you end up with the grunts, when you start out with your new command, you have no status. You guys are considered aliens from another planet. You must earn your way into their confidence."

San Mateo is located in the northeast part of Camp Pendleton. There is a lot of room for the grunts to run around in the hills and play their military games, isolated and far removed from the amenities found at division headquarters and base command. The Twenty-Eighth Marines is the last infantry regiment of the Fifth Marine

Division left stateside as the other two regiments have been recently shipped over to Vietnam.

Chaplain Strom's initial experience of the Marine Corps is an overwhelming montage of introductions to his battalion staff, meetings, equipment procurement, advice on rules and regulations, new names and faces, visiting other tactical and medical commands on base, and memorizing acronyms and procedures that seemed endless and useless. There are some experiences, however, that did initially stand out as hallmark encounters for him, experiences that are central to the paradigm shift that is beginning to take place inside his head, events that disrupt his somewhat naive, parochial worldview.

The first of these experiences happens when he receives the following advice about how to get along with the Marines from a senior-type chaplain at his initial division chaplain's meeting at Camp Pendleton: "First, make those above you look good. Second, leave yourself room for maneuverability. And third, never get into a pissin' contest with a skunk."

The second encounter that makes an impact on him is listening to a colonel, with the richness of four-letter syntax that only a well-seasoned Marine could deliver; tell Richard, right to his face, why he thinks all chaplains in the Marine Corps are worthless.

The third is watching a married regimental chaplain, a lieutenant commander, get messed up one night at the officers' club, then observe him picking up on a woman at the bar and taking her home.

Within a month of his assignment to the Third Battalion, Twenty-Eighth Marine Infantry Regiment, Chaplain Strom encounters his first military operation called Beagle Leash, a combined navy and Marine amphibious and air assault that would take them from the beaches to the far back country of Camp Pendleton at a place called Casey Springs.

Initially the battalion is transported by the huge CH-53 helicopter to the USS *Monticello*, an amphibious assault ship that has a deck for landing helicopters as well as a dock in the aft section that allows landing craft into its interior. The Marines spend three days onboard going over plans, maps, radios, rifles, gear, stealing anything onboard that wasn't bolted down, a genetic behavior believed by the amphibious navy to be indigenous to the grunts. And then, when the navy is really fed up with the Marines onboard, the entire battalion is loaded into landing craft that will shortly take them to Red Beach at Camp Pendleton.

Climbing down the nets into the waiting, constantly pitching landing craft is not an easy task, especially with all the heavy gear each Marine is carrying. Shortly they are out into the ocean, getting sick from the sea and the exhaust of the boats going round and round in circles, finally to head directly to the beachhead itself. At this point, the landing craft on which Richard is located finally makes it to the beach, it's gate splashing down into about three feet of water. The battalion chaplain and his companions clamor down the gate into the water and forward toward dry land. "Just like in the war flicks," Richard muses to himself. When he steps on dry land, he looks up and to his left and see this small hill overlooking Red Beach. On top of this hill some bleachers are filled with spectators, mostly in uniform. They are watching the maneuvers through binoculars as the battalion slogs past them to their rendezvous point a mile away. It is at this moment that Richard feels a bit foolish, flashing on the time years ago when he was in the Boy Scouts playing capture the flag. Only these are grown men he is running around with, not a group of adolescent boys.

The next four days appears to Chaplain Strom like the first chapter on a how-to book by the Three Stooges. It becomes apparent to him that chaos and misdirection is standard operating procedure, as if everyone is in the dark as to the larger picture of what is to take place and how to proceed. The majority of the time is spent waiting and milling around. Then they would eat and do some more milling around waiting for new orders or for something to happen. It appears to the new chaplain that learning to mill around creatively in the Marine Corps is a valuable tool.

"Hey, Sergeant," the chaplain says to a Marine sitting next to him eating some sliced peaches from his C-rations, "this sitting around, wondering what is going on—is this unusual for Marine Corps operations?"

The sergeant, with two months left in the service, snickers and answers him: "Chaplain, all Marine Corps operations are run just like this one. It makes no difference whether it's in Vietnam or here. They're all classic FUBARs!"

Richard thoughtfully considers what the sergeant has said, then asks, "What's a FUBAR, Sergeant?"

"Well, ah, let's see, how can I put it," he says slowly and thoughtfully. "You take the first letter of the words 'fouled up beyond all recognition,' put them together, and you get the word 'FUBAR.'" He hesitates, then continues, "Most Marines don't use the word *fouled*. You probably can figure out what word they use, Chaplain."

The chaplain smiles, then replies, "Yeah, I think I can figure that one out, Sergeant."

On the last day of the operation, in the rain and in the middle of the night, the battalion humps the remaining distance up to Casey Springs located at an elevation of over four thousand feet. When they reach the final rendezvous point, Chaplain Strom flops down under a tree at 0530, wet, hungry, and exhausted. The battalion sergeant major is seated next to him. With a smile on his face, he leans over and says, "So, Chaplain, how do you like being a grunt?"

Richard slowly shakes his head and says, "How do those young Marines do it, carrying their own equipment as well as mortars, machine guns, and all that heavy gear? How do they do it?"

"That's why they call us grunts, Chaplain," he responds with a laugh. "We grunt all the way up the hill!"

Later that morning when Chaplain Richard Strom returns from Operation Beagle Leash to his battalion office in San Mateo, a large manila envelope is awaiting him from the Bureau of Naval Personnel in Washington. He has a sinking feeling that he knows what it contains.

A HOLY CALLING

Now the Lord God said to Abraham: 'Go from your
country and your kindred and your father's house to
the land that I will show you...' So Abraham went as
the Lord had told him.

Genesis 12:1–3

It was Richard Strom's original intention that upon going on
active duty he would be assigned to some kind of ship or destroyer
squadron. Instead, right out of chaplain school in Newport, Rhode
Island, he is sent to Camp Pendleton to run around the southern
California hills with Marines, then given orders to pack his bags,
"gird" his loins, and "tighten up your act, mister, because you're
going to Vietnam." A holy calling indeed!

The orders to the First Marine Division aren't unexpected,
given the huge buildup going on in Vietnam. This is especially true
with the Marines who essentially are in charge of operations in the I
Corps sector, the area of Vietnam from the DMZ south to Da Nang.
However, Chaplain Strom is finding some emotional and intellectual
difficulties arising within himself because of the war. He is beginning to question the morality of the conflict in Southeast Asia and
he does have some ambivalence about going to Vietnam. However,
because he will go there as a noncombatant and his task is to bring
spiritual nourishment and counsel to the Marines, at this juncture
he is able to separate his raison d'être from that of the combatant.
Nevertheless, reflecting on his own spiritual and emotional capacity
to be functional, given the parameters of being both a religious and
secular operative under the same hat, his question to himself over

and over is quite simply stated yet profound in its implication: "How will I resolve any conflicts that arise from the wearing of the cross on my left collar and the lieutenant bars on my right." It is a question as old as the military chaplaincy itself.

Richard was raised in a home where his mother nurtured her children in the scriptures, where the Bible was ready every night after the evening meal. His father's focus was on modern idealists, getting healthy doses of the teachings of Mahatma Gandhi and Martin Luther King. His dad had insisted that Richard, in his senior year in high school, read what he considered to be the single most important piece of current literature on the moral obligation of Christians to be called to action: "Letter from a Birmingham Jail," by Martin Luther King. In the seminary, this influence prompted Richard to read the writings of Dietrich Bonhoeffer, a Lutheran pastor implicated in the plot to kill Hitler and subsequently murdered by the Nazis just days before the Americans liberated Flossenburg Prison. *The Cost of Discipleship*, his most powerful book, was direct and to the point. When asked what he got out of the book, Strom would state simply, "You are or you aren't. You do or you don't. There is no free lunch!"

Having been detached from the Twenty-Eighth Marine Infantry Regiment at Camp Pendleton, Richard is now spending his two weeks of leave with his wife, three-month-old son, and his parents at a mountain cabin above Sonora, California, in the central Sierra Nevada. It is here, among the sugar pine and away from the raging debates going on in Washington and throughout the country about Vietnam, that Richard endeavors to resolve his own personal issues about this war.

His dad is against the war and has been vocal about it. When Richard raises the issue about his own personal ambivalence, his dad stares at him for a few seconds as he always did when he has something important to say, then shifts in his chair, leans forward, and says, "Idealism has no place at all where people are killing people in the name of peace or in the name of anything else. Killing is killing. War is war. Peace is peace."

Then he says something that makes no sense at all to Richard, confusing him even more. "There was an irascible American debunker and cynic, H. L. Mencken, who once said this a number of years ago about idealists: 'An idealist is one, who upon noticing that a rose smells better than cabbage, concludes it makes better soup as well.'" With that his dad gets up from his chair and says, "Time to go to bed, you'll work it out. Whatever you decide, I'll always support you. You know that." He gives his son a hug and walks off to bed.

Richard Strom goes to bed that night believing that his ambivalence about the morality of the war will resolve itself just in the process of life itself. He will accept his fate—the idealistic priest, prophet, and navy religionist armed with neither the surname of a nomadic patriarch from another time and nation or even sure that this is the will of God. He smiles to himself as he thinks about Jesus hanging out with thieves, prostitutes, sinners, lepers, and the common folk with whom he manifested the majority of his ministry. The smile comes because of the parallel he is drawing between the Marines of his ministry and the "untouchables" of the Gospels.

The time spent in the mountains with his family is relaxing and mostly carefree. Yet an underlying, subtle tension is now present and grows each day in magnitude until the day they leave for Sacramento and Travis Air Force Base. This is a reality the entire family does not want to face. Yet that day has arrived and they begin the sad, painful journey down the mountain and up Highway 99 toward an unknown destiny. It is a quiet journey, no one wanting to open up to whatever feelings are going on, everyone wanting to be "strong" for everyone else. As he turns the car into the main gate at Travis Air Force Base, Richard's dad hopes no one notices the tears running down his cheeks, at least for now, as he continues on toward the main air traffic terminal.

The time has now come to say good-bye to his parents, his wife and small son, and two of his brothers. He is at a loss for words. He just stands there in the terminal—no tears, no fear, no joy, no sadness, no excitement. He hasn't arrived yet in Vietnam and already he feels cut from his feelings.

He is just standing there, as if some kind of surreal movie is going on in front of him, observing it all, watching the show as they all say good-bye for a year, lifetime, eternity—who knows? Richard is saying good-bye to his family as if he is leaving shortly to go down to the supermarket and will be back shortly.

They're all crying except Richard as he is getting a last hug and kiss and hold and look—just a last look for all of them to remember. Their guts are shredded now, and Timothy, his young son, has picked up the energy and is crying very hard. Richard continues to just stand there, brushing off a fly that has landed on his mother's shoulder, as if the brushing off of that fly is the main event.

And then they are gone, a reality that suddenly hits Richard. As he turns to walk to the departure area in the terminal, his legs are shaking, his lips are quivering, his stomach is churning, his eyes are watering, his breathing is short, and he feels overwhelming loneliness. Two hours later his universe is the whine of jet engines and the pressure of his seat belt across his lap as the lights of the United States fade into the blackness of the Pacific Ocean.

"I'm on my way," he thinks to himself. "Sure as heck not like the war movies I've seen. Doesn't seem at all exciting or romantic, just sad and lonely."

THE BEGINNING

Richard is eagerly scanning the ground below him as the 707 circles west of Kadena Air Force Base and begins a slow descent. The terrain is lush and green as the plane finally lands and rolls to a stop at the passenger terminal. The troops are asked to depart the plane and immediately are herded into waiting blue buses, the kind of buses you see picking up kids for school in rural Minnesota. Only this is not Glencoe; this is Okinawa and there is a war raging to the west.

As Chaplain Strom boards the blue bus and begins the journey to Camp Hansen an hour away in the central part of the island, his thoughts again go back to his roots in Minnesota. He is amazed at his journey from the innocence of childhood to this time and place, knowing that a two-hour trip won't get him back to his family or back to the country that raised him. "Here I am," he thinks to himself, "a young, naive Lutheran cleric on a stopover in a strange country, on my way to another strange country and an even stranger reality. Soon I'll be a part of that living/dying experience in Vietnam, a reality of real guns, real bullets, and real dead people."

As the bus passes through the countryside, he recalls reading about some fierce battles when this island was under siege, when Americans and Japanese were dying as fast and inglorious as anytime, anywhere during World War II. He sees many people on the road, working their fields, living their lives—wondering what it was like for them so many years ago, when all that death and destruction and upheaval surrounded them and cast them into their present fate.

This in turn leads him to ponder the unfortunate people of Vietnam who travel their roads and work their fields and just want to live their lives—"What is happening to them in the midst of their dying and upheaval and destruction? What fate awaits them?"

That night, Richard gets a Marine "buzz," has dinner at the officers' club, drinks two beers, goes back to the officer's quarters, and sleeps twelve hours straight, a feat he has never done in his life. When he gets up the next morning, his thoughts are that maybe he has some resting up to do, that perhaps this will be the last peaceful rest he will experience for a long, long time.

After mustering at 2300 and another hour trip back to Kadena, the flight leaves for Vietnam at 0300 and is scheduled to arrive early morning in Da Nang. Richard looks like all the other Marines in the chartered 727 jet, all dressed in starched utilities, staring straight ahead—a very quiet, subdued group of men, unusual by Marine Corps standards.

Surrounding this group solemnity, as if the whole group of Marines are going to a business meeting in Chicago, the airline stewardesses are doing their thing, serving coffee and sodas, handing out pillows, chitchatting with the Marines and telling them how wonderful they all looked in their starched uniforms. Halfway to Da Nang, they are served a meal. Richard thinks to himself, "This is like Passover and I'm having my Last Supper."

Later when the pilot announces to the passengers that he is beginning his descent into Da Nang, Richard can make out on the port side where he is sitting the coastline of Vietnam. To him, it looks just like any other coastline that he has seen from an airplane. As they continue their descent, he continues to look for signs of battle—explosions, smoke, jet fighters—but sees nothing unusual and doesn't even know what to look for.

With the exception of a harder than usual *thump* upon landing, there is nothing to indicate that they are now in a war zone. As they taxi to the main terminal on the air force side of the base, the stewardess are going through their usual deplaning exercise. Whereupon an attractive blonde hostess then picks up the microphone and with her very best and flashiest smile says to the plane full of Marines, "Thank you very much gentlemen for riding with us on American Pacific Airlines. On behalf of Captain Maxwell and our entire crew, we hope you have enjoyed your trip to Da Nang from Kadena Air Force Base. And we hope you all have a good year."

Chaplain Strom thinks the statement lacks some reality and immediately hears a Marine in the seat just in back of him say out loud, "Have a good year my ass!" Arriving in the terminal, the Marines are told to exit south to the awaiting trucks, which will then take them to the Marine Corps side of the airbase. Richard picks up his valpac, typewriter, and duffel bag and walks through the terminal and notices rows and rows of vending machines and a hot dog stand just as he exits. To him it looks like most any air force terminal he's been through back in the States except they are now in a war zone. Outside as he walks down the sidewalk he is confronted by numerous Vietnamese that are hawking just about any kind of food, drink, or junk item that any good hawker would push at a big sporting event. Only here the prices are higher. Richard has visions of Da Nang being under siege and in contact with the enemy and here he is being confronted by a bunch of vendor trainees from Dodger Stadium.

This is not what he expects upon arrival in Da Nang. When he reaches the big transport trucks parked at the end of the sidewalk, he throws his gear in the back of the first truck, jumps in, and sits down at the back end of the long bench that runs the length of the truck. This way, in case of a rocket attack, he can perish falling out of the truck in the midst of morning prayers instead of dying ingloriously inside a flaming truck full of Marines yelling obscenities about the act of procreation.

After a ten-minute ride, Richard's truck arrives at the Marine Corps side. They unload and walk into a rather shabby-looking building that is obviously the Marine Corps' answer to an air terminal reception area. Even if one didn't see the yellow lettered signs on bright red background—the hallmark of Marine artistry—one could tell it is the right place by the number of personnel milling around aimlessly.

After aimlessly milling around himself looking for a phone to call division, a PFC tells him that the phones on this side—the Marine Corps side of the base—do not connect to division and that he will have to go back to the air force side to call the division chaplain. This, of course, makes lots of sense to the new incoming chaplain, having finally understood, after a few weeks with the Marines, why the term *military intelligence* is an excellent example of an oxymoron.

He now finds himself in a place cut off from communication, hauling around all his heavy stateside gear, looking for some way to get to the division chaplain's office. Parked next to the building are three jeeps, one of which has a driver sitting inside the vehicle. He goes back outside now intent on "hustling" a ride to division, wherever that is.

Up to this point, Richard Strom has not honed the fine skill of what many chaplains in the Marine Corps called the "benign hustle," a process that any chaplain worth his salt needs to perfect when serving with Marines. Since chaplains are not usually included in the fiscal budget at the level of battalion or regiment, and because they received little or nothing regarding logistical support, individual battalion chaplains are left to beg, borrow, scrounge, and hustle for what little they did need to do their job. Perhaps because they are disregarded in the budgetary process, chaplains on the other hand are many times given some leeway and leverage within Marine Corps rules and regulations, allowing them to perform their ministry as they see fit. For those chaplains who have gained the respect of their commands, the "hustle" for supplies, transportation, and the like is both expected and accepted.

Richard, gear in hand, walks to the back of the jeep containing the driver. He throws his baggage in the back. With that the driver jumps out of his jeep, a startled look on his face, as the chaplain says, "Okay, Corporal, let's go. They're waiting for me at division, should have been there and hour ago."

Chaplain Strom climbs into the back of the vehicle while the bewildered Marine looks at his trip ticket, then turns toward the officer in the back of his jeep and says, "Ah yes, sir. I mean, I think there's a problem here, sir."

"Really? I don't think there's any problem, let me see the ticket," Richard requests with a look of consternation on his face.

The young Marine then says, "Sir, I was supposed to pick up a navy captain and bring him to III MAF across the river. It doesn't say anything about going to division."

"Oh, I see what the problem is," Richard replies, now thinking fast. "See," he says, pointing to the ticket, "they've made a mistake. It really means navy chaplain, they just misspelled it as captain. Easy mistake, happens to me all the time."

The driver is now closely scrutinizing the paper, then replies, "But it says III MAF as the destination, sir."

Richard draws a big breath, stalling for time, then replies, "Ah, yeah, that's easy to explain. There's a reason for that as well, because coming over here all chaplains are attached to the Third Marine Amphibious Force, that's where they go when they haven't been given an assignment. I already know my assignment, First Division, so I don't need to go over there." He knows this is true for only a few of the navy chaplains and hopes the Marine will believe his generalization from the truth.

The driver gives Chaplain Strom a long stare, then looks again at his trip ticket, then looks back at Richard again skeptically and drawls, "I don't know, sir. I could get in deep trouble leaving a navy captain without his transportation."

The chaplain places his hand on the corporal's shoulder and says, "I will sign your ticket, and if there is a chance, a very, very slim chance that this wasn't meant for me, then I'm the one who is in trouble, okay?"

The young Marine reluctantly nods, sits back down in his jeep, starts the engine, makes a U-turn, then turns left on the main highway toward division headquarters.

As they make their way west on Highway 1, the main highway around Da Nang and north to the northern provinces and the DMZ, the road brings them past this incredibly dirty, junkie gathering of huts and hooches. These so-called buildings are made out of wood, plywood, smashed tin cans—anything that can be plastered together to make a dwelling.

The filth and smell by the side of the road is the worst squalor Richard has ever seen. "Making the slums of Tijuana, Mexico, look like a middle-class suburb," he thinks to himself. There are children, Marines, motorcycles, trucks, chickens, civilians, and Vietnamese buses all vying for position and attempting to move on this narrow two-lane road.

Right now they are moving through the notorious area outside Da Nang called Dogpatch, where skirts, drugs, and anything going on the black market can be procured for a price. These refugee cities did not exist prior to the war and are a result of the destruction of the countryside, the peasants being removed from their ancestral lands to the cities and the insidious and corrupting influence of American servicemen seeking drugs and prostitution with their endless supply of money and influence.

As the vehicle takes them further away from the airbase and Dogpatch, the road takes them through more open, rural country-side that is lush and green. To the left is the small mountain range just to the west of Da Nang. On their right are a number of rice paddies, small villes, and open fields. There are some farmers tending their fields with water buffalo. Shortly, they come to a large group of buildings surrounded by three different strands of rolled barbed wire encompassing the entire compound. They pass an entrance off the highway and Richard notices a sign that says, "First Medical Battalion." This is the field hospital for the First Marine Division. He makes a mental note to himself that more than likely he'll get to know that place quite well. Chaplains are expected to visit their wounded and sick troops as often as possible, given the logistic possibilities.

Continuing down the road, they pass the "praying mantis" helo base where large strange-looking helicopters are based that are devoid of the normal "body" for carrying troops and supplies. These heli-copters are used instead to externally transport large artillery pieces or heavy equipment from one LZ to another. Next they pass First Reconnaissance Battalion, division headquarters, division surgeon, and finally on their right, just above a large rice paddy, Richard sees a driveway leading up to three buildings—two Quonset huts that house the offices of the division chaplain and the third building, the division chapel. The chapel is nothing fancy, just a plain screened building like all the other buildings around division. They pull into the driveway and park in front of the Quonset hut next to a sign that says, "DIVCHAP."

Chaplain Strom signs the trip ticket as promised and assures the driver that everything is cool. A Marine PFC emerges from the office building, salutes Chaplain Strom, then asks Richard if he wants his baggage brought inside the office building. Richard nods, introduces himself, then follows the PFC into the building. He is then escorted to a large office in the back of the second hooch and sees a balding, somewhat overweight, red-faced Irishman sitting back in his chair with his feet on his desk drinking a beer.

"Father McConnell, this is Chaplain Strom, he just arrived in-country this morning," reports the young chaplain's clerk, who then turns and leaves the room.

"Chaplain Strom, am I glad to see you," he exclaims as he immediately rises up from his chair. "We heard you were on the way." They shake hands and he continues. "Sit down, sit down." He walks to the refrigerator, gets a cold beer, which he hands to Richard, then says casually, "You Lutherans are beer drinkers, aren't you? Or are you one of those stogy Norwegians?"

"No, I'm a stogy Swede," Richard answers, "but I'll still have a cold one." He is aware that it is only midmorning, wondering what time they started drinking beer over here. He then picks up the church key and opens the beer, lifting it to his lips to take a sip.

Krump! Krump! The sounds of two loud explosions are heard outside and to the east of them. The division chaplain looks at Richard with a startled look for a split second, leaps out of his chair, grabs his helmet and flak jacket next to him, and runs for the door, yelling, "Incoming!"

Richard's body is frozen in position, beer can at his lips, not sure exactly what is happening but aware that he is in a rather precarious position. Since the division chaplain and his clerk are already out the door and most likely heading at flank speed for a safer place, he is faced with the decision as to what he should do with himself. Right now! He hasn't the slightest idea where he is supposed to go or what he's supposed to do. He doesn't even have a helmet or flak jacket. He is so new in-country. And he hasn't been in Vietnam long enough to feel panic—only confusion!

Richard runs out the door, dropping the full beer can, and sees two chaplains roaring past him, both with their helmets and flak jackets. He yells at them, "Where in the hell do I go?" but they are oblivious to his entreaty as he watches them disappear into a small, enclosed bunker located adjacent to the chapel entrance. Shortly he finds himself inside a bunker shared with five other people.

He makes out the smiling face of the division chaplain next to him in the darkened bunker and asks, "How close was that stuff, whatever it was. How close did it come to our compound?"

"Close enough, Chaplain Strom," he says good-naturedly as he pokes Richard in the ribs. "That's the VC giving you a personal welcome to the Republic of Vietnam. Welcome aboard!"

While they wait for the siren to go off, which signifies the all-clear, the division chaplain introduces Richard to the personnel in the bunker: Commander George Williams, the assistant division chaplain; Lieutenant Commander Bernie O'Hearn, the newly arrived chaplain at First Medical Battalion; and Lieutenant Commander Gerald Jacobsen, the regimental chaplain with the Fifth Marines out in An Hoa.

"Jerry here tells me that your buddy from chaplain school, Richard Harrigan, just left on an operation with the second battalion," Father McConnell says to Richard. "He should be out in the bush for about three weeks. I just pray that all you guys will be all right."

The sirens suddenly go off and they all amble back to the offices in the Quonset huts. Strom and McConnell find themselves back at his office and resume their conversation.

"Ah, Father," Richard begins, "where will—"

"Listen, Strom," McDonnell interrupts with mock seriousness, "the first thing you've gotta know about this outfit is that you call me Spike. Understood?"

Richard smiles back and replies, "Okay, Spike it is. Now, about my assignment, you said back there in the bunker that all the infantry slots were filled. Does that mean I'll be with a rear unit right away?"

Richard was disappointed by his reply: "I waited as long as I could. I really wanted you to go with the Fifth Marines, but they need a chaplain immediately. The infantry has top priority and I will not leave them without coverage. So I sent your Irish buddy from Boston instead. Don't worry, though, you'll get your infantry later on. In the meantime I have an assignment for you that I believe you'll really enjoy."

Spike opens up another beer, takes a sip, then says, "I'm having you assigned to First Reconnaissance Battalion just down the road from us. The commanding officer, Lt. Col. Don Cherrington, is a good friend of mine. I've already built you up with him as a good infantry type who spent the past few months running around the Camp Pendleton hills with the Twenty-Eighth Regiment. My sources tell me you have all the makings for a good, energetic, hard-nosed Marine infantry chaplain," he now says, looking through Strom's personnel file, "someone who isn't intimidated by this separate species of *Homo sapiens* called Marines. I've heard some reports about how well you do with them."

"Ah hell, Spike," Richard shoots back, "you're just trying to brownnose me so I'll accept this assignment gracefully. Guess I don't have a choice, do I? I was just hoping for an infantry outfit right away so I could coast my last six months here."

"Listen, Rich," he quietly counsels the new chaplain, "this outfit you are going to is an infantry outfit, only better. These recon boys are the best the Marine Corps has to offer! These are the real tough guys who go out into the boonies without any support and gather intelligence. They're real animals, Rich."

Then, in a soft fatherly tone he quietly says to Chaplain Strom, "Now listen to me, Rich, I do not—I repeat, *do not*—want to hear of you going out on any of those intelligence inserts those boys make. Is that clear?"

Richard shrugs his shoulders and replies, "Well, Spike, what can I say? You want a promise from me?"

Spike immediately says, "All I want from you is that I hear no reports that you went on an insert, but then, you know"—he winks—"you've gotta minister to your men as you see fit. What you decide to do you're going to do anyway. I just don't want to hear about it, understand?" He looks at Richard in mock seriousness.

Slowly, a smile on his face, Richard answers, "Ah, yeah, I think I get the picture, Spike." Father Spike McConnell reiterates a basic principle Richard is beginning to learn about serving with the Marines. Pay attention to what the rules and regulations say and make an effort to stay within their bounds. However, should you choose to put aside the rules to make your ministry more humane and effective, then keep your mouth shut or learn to talk fast if you get caught!

Richard is told the commanding officer of First Recon is expecting him that evening. So he is sent to division supply to pick up his combat gear. An hour later he piles his gear into Spike's jeep and within five minutes the driver has him at the entrance to First Reconnaissance Battalion.

RECON RAIDERS

Recon Marines are definitely the glory boys of the Marine Corps. First, these are tough, highly trained infantry grunts, most of whom are cross-trained to handle any type of weapon in the infantry arsenal. Second, most of them are scuba- or jump-trained as well. Their essential mission is to be dropped by parachute or inserted by chopper behind enemy lines to collect intelligence on enemy troop movements or supply concentrations. There is absolutely no doubt in their minds that they are the best and the toughest of all the specialties in the military!

When not out in the bush on small patrols and inserts or manning forward outposts, recon Marines are usually found back at battalion headquarters running, fighting, drinking, or harassing each other. They truly are the guerrilla gorillas of the Marine Corps. "AARRUUUGHH!" is the sound a Marine must imitate in order to become a well-rounded recon type. It is also very similar in sound to what a male gorilla makes when attempting to bluff off intruders or what a bull sounds like when he smells a cow in heat.

It is now midafternoon and Richard is heading into the compound. It looks like all the other encampments he's seen thus far surrounding division. Hooches scattered about, three different rows of barbed wire surrounding the perimeter, a couple of smelly heads located at strategic areas, and always, Marines milling round the place. And everywhere, that musty odor coming up from the ground.

The division chaplain's clerk helps him carry his baggage through the compound, past a small amphitheater on their left where they show evening movies or have daytime training. Next to it, perched on a small incline overlooking a rice paddy is a hooch with a red sign that says, "Battalion Chaplain." This will be Chaplain Strom's home for a while. Next to his hooch is the chapel, the only white building in the entire compound. Walking up the five steps to his hooch, Richard wonders why the chapel is painted white, and wouldn't it stick out and make a good target?

The new battalion chaplain walks into his hooch and flips on the light switch. It is sparsely furnished. In the far left corner is a small field desk with two folding chairs next to it. To the rear a military cot with a thin mattress is covered by a frame and mosquito netting. Off in the right rear corner is a small military refrigerator eighteen by eighteen by twenty inches. The right wall has a small bookshelf containing a number of Bibles and interdenominational worship books as well as a box of rosaries and religious metals. There is also a sink and running water close to the entrance.

Richard drops his baggage, thanks the clerk for the help, then sees a note attached to his bed saying that the battalion adjutant, the chief administrative officer, needs to see him as soon as possible. He unpacks his belongings and places them in a footlocker next to the desk, grabs his orders, and heads for the admin office.

When he walks into the adjutant's office, he is met by a muscular, stern-looking first lieutenant. "Good to have you aboard, Chaplain, we've been expecting you," he says in a friendly voice, thick with a New York accent. "I'm Al Ursini." They shake hands, then he motions for Strom to sit down and continues, "When you need something, see me. When there's a problem, see me. When you get in trouble, see me. Need a bottle of Jack Daniels, see me. You Catholic by any chance?"

"No, I'm not a Catholic. I'm a renegade Catholic though, I belong to the Lutheran Church," Chaplain Strom responds with a smile. "Instead of turning water into wine, we turn it into scotch whiskey."

The adjutant laughs loudly, then says, "You and I are going to get along okay, Chaplain. Let me have your orders so we can get them processed and make you official."

For next two hours Al Ursini is the personal host for the new battalion chaplain, introducing him as the new "sky pilot" to all the available officers and staff NCOs on the compound. During this time, Richard is thinking to himself that the adjutant certainly has better things to do than to hang out all afternoon with him. Little did Strom realize that the boys in the rear who aren't fighting the battles against the Viet Cong, or North Vietnamese Army, are fighting another kind of battle—the battle of boredom, of repetition, of always doing the same thing day in and day out. Richard's entry into this battalion is the day's highlight for the adjutant. He also notices something else about Al Ursini this afternoon. Beneath the tough-sounding New York accent, underneath the sometimes harsh exterior of projecting a hard-nosed recon image, Richard experiences an officer interested in the welfare of the enlisted troops. It is a quality he would see over and over again with some of the Marine officers who are a cut above their peers. These commanding officers expected strict discipline and obedience. In return they are fiercely loyal to the troops under their command to the point that they will personally forfeit food and supplies for themselves to ensure that their enlisted personnel are always fed and clothed first.

When they pass the chapel, Richard turns to his host and says, "Al, I'm hot and sweaty and need a shower. Haven't had one since Okinawa. I'll see you later."

"Listen, Chaplain," he responds, "those two company commanders you met and I are going to the Stone Elephant tonight—that's the naval officers' club in downtown Da Nang. Why not join us for dinner and a few bottles of Mateus. We need to get you introduced to some of the finer amenities now that you're in Vietnam. Meet me at my hooch in an hour."

Within an hour the four of them are in a jeep winding their way through the traffic of Da Nang for the twenty-minute ride to the Stone Elephant. To Richard, Da Nang looks like a city under siege, with all the barbed wire and all the military checkpoints they encounter every three to four blocks. As they stop, then start up again through each checkpoint the chaplain wonders why, if the Americans are in such control of the situation in Vietnam, there is so much security about.

The thing that really struck him most about this city is the attitude of the South Vietnamese soldiers toward the Americans. Richard feels a coldness, a hostility from them that surprises him because his belief is that the Vietnamese want the Americans to be present in their country. This, of course, is what the government and most of the news media portrays. At each checkpoint manned by the Vietnamese soldiers that evening, to the club and back to the compound, Richard experiences that cold, hard stare. It is the look of deep dislike and malice.

When Richard comments to the adjutant about what he perceives to be hostile feelings emanating from the soldiers, he merely shrugs his shoulders and replies, "What'ya expect? We come here and screw their women, destroy their countryside, kill their people. How do you think you'd feel, Chaplain?"

This response took the chaplain by surprise, and of course, he didn't have an answer. It wouldn't be the only time he was confronted by this critical question concerning the American presence, a question most of the troops at some point will ask themselves: "If they despise us so much and hate our presence, why are we here in Vietnam?"

When they arrive at the Stone Elephant and step inside, Chaplain Strom is shocked by the fancy decor, the elaborate menu, and the number of civilians eating and drinking in the club. Al tells him many of the civilians are government contractors or are working for the CIA and have too much time on their hands.

"These bozos are a waste of the taxpayers' money and the government's time," he says in his tough New York accent, "and most of them are shit-faced most of the day. They oughta be forced to stay out at An Hoa for a month, the bastards!"

They continue through the club out into the back courtyard where they are seated and commence eating their steak dinner. The evening is what John Perriman, one of the company commanders in the group, calls a typical night "getting whacked at the Elephant." Al, John, and Markus end the evening by throwing their empty Mateus bottles against the back wall, which raises the level of anxiety for Richard, wondering who is in charge and who will be driving back to the compound. As they leave the club, he ponders the troubling thought about the hostile ARVN soldiers, hoping they don't shoot the inebriated Marines in the back as they pass through one of the numerous checkpoints.

Chaplain Strom awakens the next morning from a good night's sleep, throws some water on his face, changes into his combat gear, grabs his fully packed communion kit, and heads for the helipad located just below the chapel. Operations has arranged for Richard to get a ride out to Hill 429, a forward observation post located in the foothills overlooking the confluence of the coastal plane and the main mountain route back to the Ho Chi Minh trail and Laos. His excitement at going out to the field for the first time covers over any anxiety or fear he is feeling about this venture.

Soon, as he joins a group of four waiting Marines fully loaded with combat gear—rifles, grenades, and rocket launchers—Richard forgets about the headache that was cultured by too much Portuguese wine the night before and drops his gear on the dank ground. These four Marines are rotating back into the field after a few days back at battalion headquarters. Being back in the rear means three hot meals a day, a dry bed, and usually a much lower level of anxiety since no one is shooting at you all the time. These troopers are quiet and seem bored and energy-less. They've been through this before, being rotated in and out of the bush. It's unpleasant, leaving the compound, because "out there" the milieu changes significantly from one of relative safety to depravation, danger, and sometimes death. However, they eventually learn to put up with the changes, like one puts up with the flu or hemorrhoids. There is a dull resignation that one can't do anything about it anyway.

After two hours of waiting, and a trip to the mess for breakfast, two helicopters land. One shuts down completely and the crew walks to the mess hall. The other chopper dispatches a crew member out of the aft section, who waves the Marines and the chaplain onboard. Shortly Richard is on his way to one of four outposts manned by recon. He has been told that each of these outposts have come very close to being overrun by the enemy on numerous occasions. They alternate between being either the most boring or the most danger-ous place to be in Vietnam.

After being airborne for approximately twenty-five minutes, the chopper descends toward a narrow finger jutting off a mountain peak. The aircraft now hovers about three feet above a very narrow LZ. The Marines then jump out of the aft section onto the narrow strip of land and wait while four outgoing Marines clamber onboard the hovering craft, which then swiftly lifts off the hill and drops pre-cariously toward the valley below. The five incoming troops then move over a very narrow path to the heavily fortified compound, which measures about thirty by forty meters. The path drops off rad-ically on both sides. A slip would definitely ruin your morning.

The compound is fortified with three rows of razor-sharp barbed wire and strategically placed claymore mines, the kind of mines that explode only in one direction—outward like huge shotguns. Beyond the barbed wire the hill drops off dramatically on all four sides at about a seventy-degree angle. The only pathway that leads to this fortified outpost is booby-trapped and guarded by a mean, vicious German shepherd guard dog that is trained to smell the VC hun-dreds of yards away.

Inside the area of the compound there is a trench that is three feet wide and four feet deep on all four sides with covered observa-tional posts located at three of the four corners, the fourth comer being the entrance. At each corner an M-60 machine gun is posted, while the middle area contains three eighty-one-millimeter mortars.

The battalion chaplain is greeted by the young lieutenant in charge of the compound. Richard is told that most of the time is spent in observation or sleeping, that things have been quiet and mainly boring. "Hang out, Chaplain, and let us know what we can do for you," he says as they shake hands.

At this point it appears that everyone is either asleep or listen-ing to the armed forces radio station on their radios. While music is blaring from three different areas, Richard unpacks his gear, which consists of a box of C-rations, a poncho and liner, a dozen New Testaments, some rosaries, and two Hebrew psalm books. He will have no church services today. Richard only wants to hang out and meet some of the Marines.

Just as he finishes unpacking his gear, a staff sergeant begins to walk around the compound waking up the Marines that are asleep and telling the others to shut off their radios. Strom is incredulous at his action. These guys have been awake most of the night, they get most of their sleep in the morning when it's not too hot and humid, they're tired and burned out, and the sergeant does this to them… on behalf of the chaplain? Richard thinks to himself, "With friends like him, I should be able to alienate the whole battalion within a month. Damn!"

Richard can't figure out whether the sergeant did this because he thought this is the proper thing to do when the chaplain came, because he is angry at his men, because he dislikes chaplains, or because he is stupid. "Maybe," Richard considers, "it's all of the above!"

He spends three hours that afternoon chatting with a kid from Muscatine, Iowa, who hates the Marine Corps; a sergeant from Santa Ana, California, who wants to make a career of the military, "if I survive my time in Vietnam"; an angry young Navajo who believes his company commander hates him and "fucks me over all the time"; and a young lieutenant from Picayune, Mississippi, worried about his wife who is expecting twins any day. The rest of the contingent of twelve Marines either sleep or have nothing to say he while wanders around the compound.

That night, the chaplain is directed by "Mr. Personality," the sergeant who awakened everyone earlier in the day, to sleep under some corrugated roofing in the front trench facing the valley below, "in case it rains."

"Rains what?" Richard thinks to himself as their mortars start going off at dusk. It stinks in the trench, it's musty and wet, and the mortars are firing all night long. So he just lies there, wet, uncomfortable, sleepless, waiting for morning to come. At one point, about three in the morning, during a lull between mortars, he thinks about the consequences of being way out here in the boonies, completely isolated from the world except by radio, and what it would feel like being overrun by the Viet Cong. It brings up some very unpleasant, paranoid feelings.

Richard is lucky. He has a ride back to battalion in the morning. The rest of these poor devils have to stay up here day and night until their rotation time came. Then back out again. Two hours after sunrise, he is on his way back to Da Nang, less than twenty-four hours in the field. "Talk about being a weekend grunt," he thinks to himself.

Over the next week Chaplain Strom is beginning to feel a vestige of some acceptance. He is playing it slow and easy, wanting to get used to these recon Marines, as well as having them get used to him. They are the meanest, noisiest, nastiest bunch of people Richard has ever been around in his life, including some of his old Phi Alpha fraternity buddies back at Gustavus Adolphus College in St. Peter, Minnesota. Guerrilla gorillas indeed! Every night a good majority of the staff NCOs and officers seemed to be in various stages of inebriation. There is at least one major fight per evening that involves more than two Marines among the enlisted personnel. And always, day and night, from somewhere within the compound the sound of the recon trademark arises—*Haarruughhh!*—a sound that has to come from pre-neocortex times!

Richard's two worship services are well attended and he presides over a memorial service for two Marines killed on patrol. He is visiting wounded troopers in the hospital on a daily basis and is beginning to get the normal administrative and counseling stuff a chaplain sees daily—emergency leave back home, a lonely and depressed eighteen-year-old who just wants to talk, a Marine facing a court-martial. He's even has a couple of the battalion hustlers come in, classic malingerers who'd do anything or say anything, which always includes lying through their teeth, to get a no-duty chit so they don't have to go out in the bush. Each week they alter their stories dramatically!

The new battalion chaplain has the only hooch in the compound with running water, his commanding officer is very supportive, he is making personal friends among the officers and enlisted personnel, his body is beginning to acclimate to the Vietnamese environment, and he is now finding his work enjoyable. The CO even gives him his own jeep and driver, unheard of for chaplains at the battalion level.

Then secretly one evening, he prepares with the help of a company commander, a scheme to get inserted with a six-man team for a two-day intelligence gathering trip into the mountains west of Da Nang. Richard is beginning to feel comfortable and happy with his assignment, just as Spike had predicted.

However, Richard Strom has not taken into account a military phenomenon called the comfort syndrome. This simply means that the service has some magical, mystical way of knowing that you are comfortable with the assignment you've been given by giving you a change of orders.

GOOD-BYE, DA NANG

It is late afternoon and Richard is in his hooch asleep on his bed. Exhausted, he has just returned an hour earlier from staying out at a recon outpost for two nights and has slept very little during his stay. He is abruptly awakened by a loud voice saying, "Hey, dumb Lutheran, get your lazy butt outta bed!"

Richard opens his eyes, slowly turns toward the door, and makes out the short, mostly bald figure of the Monk, a Benedictine priest from New Hampshire, stepping inside his hooch. Vince Gerlitis is one of the three friends Richard had become close to at chaplain school along with Tom Bumpers, a Presbyterian who looked like Elmer Fudd, and Frank Doyle, another Catholic priest Richard had nicknamed Flash.

Vince Gerlitis is the battalion chaplain for first battalion, First Marine Regiment, an infantry outfit located about ten kilometers southwest of Da Nang. Aside from their field operations, their mission is to also guard the southern approaches and impede the flow of weapons and enemy into the suburbs and city itself. Beyond the First Marines and about ten kilometers west is the second line of defense where the Seventh Marines are located. The battalions of this infantry regiment are located further out in enemy territory where their function conforms more to the normal search-and-destroy missions of the Marine Corps. Another thirty kilometers southwest of Seventh Marine headquarters, positioned next to the mountains and at the confluence of two major rivers, is An Hoa and the home of the Fifth Marine Regiment. It has been said by many back at division that it is so bad out there—with all the incoming and combat going on—that their main mission is just to stay alive.

The Monk is dressed in neatly ironed, starched Marine utilities. He quickly walks toward the back of the hooch where Richard is lying down, attempting to get his foggy brain alert and his body moving. "It's afternoon, whatcha doing in bed, you lazy turkey?" he says with a big grin on his face.

Richard stumbles out of his bed, stands up, and greets him. "Good to see you, Monk. You're the first familiar face I've seen in a week even though you are the ugliest monk I've ever seen in my life!"

"Time to get moving," says the Monk, "we have to cross the river and be at III MAF in less than an hour." As he says this, Vince does a slow sweep of the room and continues, "Not only are you a dumb Protestant heretic but you're late and this place looks and smells like a pig sty. What are you going to do without your wife to feed and clothe you," he says with a smirk on his face, "and make you happy at night?"

"Same as you, Monk, take a cold shower," Richard responds.

As Richard looks for his trousers and boots, which are strewn about, he questions the Monk about the evening's activities. "What the heck are we going to tonight anyway, Monk," he asks as he steps into his boots, "the pope's coronation?"

Vince replies immediately. "No, we're going to fly to Germany and watch the Dominicans behead Martin Luther."

"Oh fine," he answers, "would you be so kind as to dispatch a few indulgences to my fearless leader as he goes to his eternal reward. And while you're at it, could I invite my friends Matthew, Mark, Luke, and John from the chapel next door? They're kind of into this religious stuff, you know. Hey, Vince, what the heck are we really going to tonight?" Richard puts on his clean, starched utilities as Vince replies, "There's going to be a new head chaplain taking over at III MAF headquarters, some senior-type desk-jockey navy captain from Washington who's probably bucking for admiral. They want as many chaplain faces as possible to say hello and good-bye. You know, get as many people out as possible, like the Russians do when they want to impress some boot dictator who visits their country."

"Damn, Chaplain Gerlitis," Richard responds with mock seriousness, "that sounds like sarcasm. Boy, you ain't been in the military long enough to be that jaded. You're supposed to communicate only those values that reflect the highest traditions of the Navy Chaplain Corps. So what's the matter, Vince, too many C-rations or are you wearing your utilities too starched!"

Walking out the screen door, down the two steps and onto the path leading to his vehicle, Vince smiles and says, "Chaplain Strom, after you've been in-country for one month, I'm going to do an attitude check on you."

Richard is now walking briskly to keep up with Vince and says, "Oh, how's that?" Vince continues to walk up to his jeep, turns, and looks at Richard with a somewhat doleful look and says, "We all change. Something happens, hard to explain." He then jumps into the front seat next to his driver, smile again on his face, and declares, "Get in, Strom, you've already made us late."

The jeep with the driver and two chaplains now heads south on Highway 1, past the area where weird-looking helicopters are based, on past First Medical Battalion and shortly through Dogpatch and into the suburbs of Da Nang before turning right to enter the bridge and crossing the river to the peninsula. As always, the road is crowded with Vietnamese civilians in buses, on small motorbikes and bicycles or walking with their loads of food or water or junk taken from nearby military dumps. After crossing the bridge and turning left, Richard sees the large navy hospital ship, the USS *Hope*, docked on the Da Nang side of the river. He wonders if the VC has ever shelled the ship, inadvertently or on purpose, especially since the recent rocketing of Da Nang over the past month. They continue to the end of the road, which ends at the beach facing the South China Sea.

This area south of Da Nang is also called China Beach and is a major in-country R&R center. Infantry units who have been out in the bush for extended periods of time are given a few days of rest, where they can hang out and drink beer, scuba-dive, eat, play baseball, or just sleep. Like most other Marine facilities in Vietnam, the buildings are shabby, dirty, and tacky. But it has enclosed hooches for sleeping and eating, something that most of the grunts haven't experienced in a long time. And they can shower at least once a day and are served hot meals twice a day. For a grunt out of the bush, this is luxurious living!

The chaplains arrive at the China Beach officers' club and walk into the building just as the dinner is starting. Most of the chaplains are milling about as the outgoing III MAF chaplain, a senior captain, attempts to herd everyone away from the bar and get them seated at the tables, which always seems to be a chore anytime one attends a Marine function.

After a long-winded prayer extolling the virtues of the military chaplaincy by Rear Admiral John Tjurnfjelt, the assistant chief of chaplains, a group of forty-two chaplains and Marine officers sit down to a five-course steak dinner served with wine. Chaplain Strom is surprised at the high quality of the food and also feels somewhat embarrassed at being served by local Vietnamese. He ponders what must be going through their minds seeing this abundance, contrasting it with the poverty they live with in their villages. This makes him uncomfortable but not enough to leave the table or to say anything to one of the senior officers who has planned this affair.

Momentarily he is distracted by introductions to the officers sitting close to him—Bernie O'Hearn the new Catholic chaplain at First Medical Battalion; Matt Horvatt, a Jesuit serving with the Seventh Marines; Paul Germani, a priest stationed at III MAF; and Warner Blackstone, a Southern Baptist serving with the Seabees north of Da Nang at Red Beach. Soon, Richard is eating a delicious meal, drinking a tasty Portuguese wine, and chatting with his new acquaintances. Any discomforting thoughts he has about the disparity the Vietnamese might be experiencing has drifted away.

Richard leans back in his chair, yawns, then whispers loudly to no one in particular, "Hey, when do we get out of here, I'm ready to leave."

Chaplain Horvath, seated across the table from Strom, whispers back, "No way, you're gonna pay for this. Nothing is free in life. Wait and see."

Which is right on the mark. The gathering sits through an hour of five very boring speeches, beginning with the assistant chief of chaplains and ending with a Marine officer giving a testimonial about the value of chaplains in the Marine Corps. For over an hour the speakers extolled the virtues and sacrifice of serving a tour of duty in Vietnam, reporting to them how much the chief of chaplains in Washington wants to be "in the trenches with the boys," informing them how much God loves Marines and therefore the chaplains who serve with them.

The next to last chaplain to speak is just new in-country and will soon take over as the head chaplain at III MAF, which makes him the most senior chaplain in the entire I Corps area. Toward the end of his speech, he suddenly throws in a parenthetical reference to the difficulty one encounters traveling throughout the Da Nang area by saying, "And I still want to find out which division chaplain stole my jeep last week and forced me to wait four hours at the airstrip before I could get transportation to III MAF. Somebody used guile to get my wheels and I am going to find out who that someone is!" Richard hopes his face is not turning bright red, slinks down further into his chair as the speaker goes back to his prepared text, and continues to drone on and on, followed at the speaker's dais by the III MAF chaplain who is being replaced.

So in order to get through that kind of banality after a big meal and a couple of glasses of wine, Richard considers a couple of options: "I could sleep inconspicuously with my head in my hand, pretending I was really listening, or I could do some guerrilla warfare and raise a little hell on the side."

Sitting next to Chaplain Strom is the Monk, his elbows on the table, his forearms pointed toward his head, face in palm, almost asleep. He looks very bored and sleepy. Richard remembers that when he giggles, he sucks air in his lungs in short bursts and sounds like a barking seal with laryngitis. So he leans toward Vince and softly whispers in his ear the punch line of a very funny joke the Monk once told him in chaplain school about the pope.

Immediately this big smile breaks out on Vince's face. Soon his body begins to convulse silently as he attempts to hold back his laughter. Then with his face still resting in the palm of his hand, he lets out this long series of short, jerky sounds: "*Haaugh, haaugh, haaugh.*" The scene surrounding this strange noise is a quiet, sleepy, inattentive, bored group of chaplains wanting this gig to be over. The baloney is really flying now as each of the senior-type chaplains, captain and above, are telling each other how wonderful each of them is and how wonderful it is to serve the Marines and how this has been the greatest year of their lives!

"*Haaugh, haaugh, haaugh.*" He breaks the silence again, bringing most of the sleepy audience to an aroused state. The senior chaplain at III MAF, who is rotating back to the States in two days, is again speaking but now stops in midsentence as if someone had just farted very loud during quiet prayers in the midst of Holy Communion.

The Monk is now laughing out of control. Horrible noises are emitting from him as a couple of the chaplains look at him with disgust while most of them seem to be enjoying this break from the tediousness of speech making. The speaker then begins anew with a loud voice, saying, "Freedom-loving peoples everywhere will look upon this time in America as her finest..."

At this point the Monk jumps up out of his chair, cups his hand over his mouth as if he is coughing, spins quickly, and swiftly begins to move toward the doorway leading to the back of the building and the kitchen. Just as he turns and makes his move, he runs head-on into a Vietnamese waiter carrying a full tray of desserts. The waiter spins and falls, crashing into the long table that runs perpendicular all the way to the head table where all the big shots are seated. As the waiter falls, he dumps the whole tray on the table and pulls the tablecloth and everything on it to the floor and onto the laps of many of the chaplains.

Above the sounds of breaking, crashing dishes and silverware, the loud guffaws of a few of the chaplains and the spreading chaos in front of him, the speaker still continues. "Ah, this has been our finest... what in the hell is going on in here?"

There is now total confusion in the place except for the repetitious litany of the speaker saying over and over, "What the heck is going on... what the hell...!" Officers are laughing, brushing off food, picking up broken pieces of dinnerware, some just sitting in stunned silence. The Monk, a half smile on his face, is now standing nearby in the hallway, leaning forward with his head against the wall, hands in pockets, just like Charlie Brown does when he leans against a tree trunk overwhelmed by the world.

It is right at this point in time that the First Marine Division chaplain walks in briskly, slows his walk as he does a double-take of the scene of destruction in front of him, then stoops down to slowly pick up what is left of a flower vase. As he places the broken pieces on the table and walks again toward the head table, he sees Vince coming back from the hallway, frowns, and says to him, "Looks like the VC overran this place. What happened?"

Vince has this big stupid-looking grin on his face and replies, "Oh nothing, nothing at all."

Spike shakes his head in confusion. When he reaches the shocked and bewildered chaplain who is the speaker, he engages him in a hushed voice as the chaos and noise begin to mellow out.

The two chaplains at the head table continue their quiet conversation as the Monk approaches Richard with that same grin he had in the hallway when he encountered Spike, that kind of smile that evokes the sense of being embarrassed out of one's mind! In a measured, hushed, but clearly distinct voice, he looks at Chaplain Strom directly in the eyes, points his finger right at his nose, and says, "I'm going to get you. I'm going to get you for this, Lutheran!"

"Ah, come on, Monk, just think of all the history that has been made here tonight, and you were a part of it. I'm sure your abbot will want to know how much we've enjoyed your noisy entertainment," Strom answers.

Richard and Vince turn toward the mess and help clean up the food and silverware still scattered about. The Monk is shaking his head like he can't believe this is happening, then says loudly to himself, "I knew I shoulda been a quiet Trappist!"

Their cleaning endeavors are interrupted by Spike banging a spoon on a glass. When the noise dissolves to quiet, he begins to speak: "Men, the reason I'm late for this event is because I just came from First Med where I've been for the past two hours. The battalion chaplain with *Two-five* was critically wounded this morning and just came out of surgery. He's going to make it they tell me but it was really touch and go for a while.

"Most of you don't know Dick Harrigan because he's only been here three weeks. He's a helluva nice guy and I really hate to see this happen to him or any of our guys in the Chaplain Corps. But those of you with the infantry know that your commanding officers want you out there where the fighting is going on, so as long as we minister to our troops in this way we're going to have casualties. Right now he's too banged-up to have any visitors. In a day or two his replacement, Chaplain Strom and I, will stop in to see him. If he stabilizers enough in the next few days he'll be medevaced to Japan. Please remember him in your prayers. *Two-five* hasn't been a very healthy place for our chaplains." Richard turns to Vince in shock and says, "Did he say Chaplain Strom is going to be his replacement? I did hear that, didn't I?"

"Afraid so, old buddy," Vince whispers with a mischievous smile on his face. "You wanted the grunts when you came over here and now you got them. I told you to be careful what you pray for, you might get it. See, prayer does work."

To himself and under his breath, Richard muttered, "You've gotta be kiddin' me, Lord!"

CARRIER LANDINGS

It is now two days past the announcement by Chaplain McConnell that *Two-five* will have a new chaplain. It is also Richard Strom's last night at recon battalion before traveling out to An Hoa the next morning. He is having dinner with two chaplains at the division mess hall across the road from recon. He saw them shortly at the chaplains' dinner two nights previous and both are friends from chaplain school in Newport, Rhode Island. One of them, a Southern Baptist from Mississippi, is stationed with the Seabees just north of Da Nang. The Monk on occasion would give Werner a hard time because he liked to have a couple of beers except when other Baptist brethren are around, at which time he would drink orange soda instead. The other fellow is Frank Doyle, a priest assigned to a supply ship now anchored in Da Nang harbor. Richard had nicknamed him Flash because of an incident that happened during chaplain school.

During a class lecture, a fire drill was initiated. Frank, as usual, was asleep at his desk and also slept through the ringing of the hall-way fire bell. The entire class minus Frank exited the building and assembled outside. About three minutes later, just when the bell rang again to signal a return to class, Frank slowly walked out the main entrance, yawned, approached LTJG Bennett, the instructor, and asked, "What's going on?" Bennett scowled at Frank, shook his head, and headed toward the entrance while the rest of the chaplains hooted and howled at Frank's impertinence and unconsciousness. After that incident, because of his slow, sleepy nature, the name Flash was synonymous with Frank Doyle for the remaining five weeks of school.

Since they all need to get back to their respective commands soon, Richard briefs them on the latest condition of their friend, Richard Harrigan, who had been critically wounded three days ago. Although still in serious condition, he is well enough to be transferred soon to a hospital in Japan, where he can recuperate and get the needed surgery on his leg, hand, and colon.

"Seeing you guys again is a boost to my morale," Richard says to them as they leave their table and walk out the door to the small parking lot next to Highway 1. "Thanks for coming over. I wonder what the heck happened to the Monk, why he didn't make it? Do you suppose his abbot heard about the destruction he caused at the dinner and had him exiled back to New Hampshire?"

"He should be excommunicated," Frank says with a scowl on his face, then laughs softly and continues, "It's been fun. Keep your head down and send me a postcard. And I hope you qualify tonight at recon's carrier landings."

Richard laughs loudly, shakes their hands, then heads across Highway 1 into the recon compound, through motor pool and toward the staff NCO and officers' club. There is a sudden touch of nostalgia as he thinks about detaching from his present outfit and leaving for his new assignment. When he approaches the club, he can hear loud, boisterous noises coming from within and hears someone yell distinctly, "It's time for some goddamn carrier landings!" Richard knows from past experience at Camp Pendleton that Marines do know how to party.

There is something very unique about fixed-wing naval aviators, a generic term encompassing both Marine and Navy pilots who sometimes train together, that always brings out their bravado in bars, bathrooms, bedrooms, and bullshitting contests! With some exceptions, and unlike the army and air force pilots, naval aviators must also be qualified for aircraft carrier landings. Being a qualified fixed-wing pilot on the flight deck of an aircraft carrier is one of those little one-upsmanship games that go on as a part of the interservice rivalry, and why naval aviators consider themselves—bar none—as the best pilots in the world!

However, there is another type of carrier landing that does not require the participant to be a trained, qualified pilot. Earlier, Richard was informed that he is expected to participate that evening in "carrier qualifications" since he is to be transferred the next day. When he walks into the dining bar area most of the staff NCO's and officers are in various stages of inebriation. It is at times like this that Chaplain Strom wonders who is in charge in case of an emergency, especially if some kind of attack were to begin—after all this is a war zone. But he thinks to himself, "so what does a greenhorn Chaplain like me know, I've only been in-country a little over a week."

The dining and bar area of the club is an enclosed hooch fifty feet long and thirty feet wide. The chairs and some of the Formica-top tables have been shoved to the side of the room. Running about two-thirds the length of the room is a long row of four-by-four tables that have been pushed together. At one end of the tables there are ten empty beer cans stacked on top of each other like a pyramid. Standing adjacent to tables running the length of the room are three Marines on each side holding open bottles of champagne. 1st Lt. Norquist, head of the motor pool, is standing in back of the beer cans at the end of the table and has been selected recovery chief. At his signal, the Marines next to the tables dowse the Formica tops with champagne. At the other end of the table Staff Sergeant Delkan, weaving badly, is attempting to stand at attention but is finding it somewhat difficult to even stand up.

The launch chief raises his arm above his head, drops his arm dramatically all the way to the floor, then yells, "Recover aircraft!"

Sergeant Delkan with as much dignity and form possible, given his state of inebriation, now takes a running leap and lands flat on his belly, his body stiff as a rod, arms by his side, and proceeds to slide across the tops of the tables head-on into the row of full beer cans. Bingo!

This is also called carrier landings.

What makes an aircraft landing on a carrier deck so dangerous are the many variables a pilot must take into consideration to make a safe landing. This is also true when one is participates in this type of carrier landing. When taking a flying leap, if you land with too much arch, it will knock the wind out of you; if you land on the tables too fast, your speed will carry you over the edge to land on your head in a big heap on the floor; if you aren't going straight, you will slide off the side and crash onto the floor; if you don't generate enough speed and stop short of the beer cans, a bucket of ice water is poured on you. The only way to remain unscathed is to generate the right amount of speed so your head knocks the cans off but you stop short of falling off the tables.

As Richard stands around watching this regimented, organized brawl, he knows that when Marines start drinking and getting rowdy, situations always get radicalized and carried to extremes. Because now he is observing the natural progression from empty beer cans to full beer cans to champagne bottles to beer cases with full champagne bottles stacked on top. In the latter game, your head is supposed to smack the beer case hard enough to slide through and past the falling full champagne bottles and hope they don't bust your head open. Of course, if you hit the case hard enough to do this, you are also going to fly off the table into a heap on the floor. When done correctly, it also brings the loudest cheers from the guerrilla gorillas of First Recon.

Lt. Col. Cherrington, the commanding officer, who himself is in a moderate state of inebriation, hears that Chaplain Strom is getting ready to leave the party and head back to his hooch. Cherrington yells for the group to be quiet, which is a major undertaking, then walks over to Richard, places his hand on his shoulder, then announces to the assembled group, "Our padre here is leaving us tomorrow to go with the Fifth Marines. Since they're ass-kickers like us, I think it's only appropriate that we get him qualified before he leaves us. What do you think, men?"

The whole room breaks into loud, boisterous yelling and cheering as well as that pre-neocortex emanation of sound unique to recon Marines—"*Aaaauuuugggghh!*"

Richard is not drunk, does not really want to pull off this so-called badge of courage, and would rather go back to his hooch and pack. However, the other part of him wants to respond to what his mother calls the "ready, fire, aim" part of his personality. "Okay, what the heck, why not," he says over the yelling and prompting of drunk Marines as he reluctantly walks to the launching area.

The colonel waves his hand to get the room quiet, and when the noise is down to a mild roar, he says, "Chaplain Strom, we're going to give you the toughest carrier landing of all, since you're going out to An Hoa where all those tough guys fight. Let's give him a night landing!" This was the most radical maneuver of all and brought the house down.

As Richard stands waiting to get launched, the adjutant wraps a towel around the Chaplain's head so he's devoid of sight. Marines dowse the tables with champagne and beer, a beer case is set up at the end, and loaded on top are four *full* bottles of champagne. The whole room is now chanting "*Go, go, go, go, go…*" as he is pointed toward the launch table ten feet away.

Richard takes a deep breath, thinking to himself, "I'm an idiot," then launches himself onto and across the tables, body rigid, arms like ramrods at his side. He slides the whole length of the tables without falling off the side, slams his head into the beer case, and off the table onto the floor. A bottle whacks him on the back of his head just as he hits the deck, stunning him momentarily as he struggles to his feet amid loud cheering and recon grunting.

1st Lt. Norquist removes the towel from Richard's head and then says, laughing hard, "Hey, Chaplain, you okay? That bottle hit you pretty hard when you fell on the deck?"

"Yeah, I'm okay. Thick-headed Swede like you can't hurt us there, you know," Richard responds to Norquist, lying about the pain.

It was about this time the battalion operations officer, Major Mario Vella, and one of the company commanders get into an argument about their relative sobriety.

"You know sumpin', Major? You're drunk," says Captain Markus.

"Buuuullshit," said the ops officer, "I could walk a straight line even if I want to!"

"Shit, Major, sir," replies Captain Markus, "right now you couldn't prime a piss ant's motor scooter… sir."

"Here's twenty dollars that sez I can," mumbles the major as he struggles to pull some money from his pocket.

The battalion adjutant, 1st Lt. Ursini, an accomplished artist at stirring up trouble, sees a good scene unfolding, so he eggs them on by saying, "Why don't you go outside and make that fifty yards of walking in a straight line?"

Most of the Marines now leave and gather outside the club to watch an incredible scene unfold as the major begins walking in a straight line, relatively speaking, for about fifteen yards, whereupon he encounters a hooch in his way. So now the major climbs over the porch and onto the roof, walks over the crest of the roof, trips and slides on his back the remaining distance on the roof to the eaves, falling all the way to the ground, landing with a big thump. Without batting an eye, he picks himself up off the ground, obviously dazed by the fall, staggers for a moment, then picks up his line again and starts walking/lurching forward at normal gait in a fairly straight line. After having walked for about twenty-five more meters, he suddenly disappears as if the ground has swallowed him up.

When Norquist and Ursini arrive at the spot where the major has disappeared, they see him sprawled out at the bottom of a five-foot-deep trench filled with half a foot of mud. He simply just lay there, passed out, snoring contentedly with his back against the side of the trench until he is shortly helped out by two passing Marines.

The major wins the bet and Richard will leave for the Fifth Marines the next morning, nursing a terrible headache resulting from the whack on his head while qualifying for a carrier landing.

AN HOA

It's morning, and Richard has just finished eating breakfast across the highway at division. Their food is always superior to recon's but that isn't saying a lot. The Marines are capable of messing up many things, especially good food. As he crosses the road back to recon, he sees and smells that heavy haze that hangs over the morning sky around division. The Marines called it shmaze and it is caused by a very unique process. This morning it seems to be particularly pungent and nasty.

Since all the Marines living around the division compound and throughout the command have no plumbing, the disposal of waste from the heads is accomplished in a very primitive way. Each head is an enclosed structure looking like outhouses still found in rural America. Most are two-seaters. Under each seat, a fifty-gallon drum has been cut in half, inverted so the opening faces the seat above. Into that drum about five to ten gallons of diesel fuel is placed. After two or three days, or when the drum is two-thirds full, it is removed. The mixture in the drum is stirred with long sticks, then set on fire and stirred again and again. Then the procedure is repeated until the mixture is gone. The burning is always done early in the morning, beginning at sunrise, by Vietnamese who have been hired as civilian workers.

When the chaplain reaches motor pool, he sees that the division chaplain has arrived and is waiting for him. "Hey, Spike, you're a little early," Richard remarks as he picks up his gear and loads it in the jeep, "been waiting long?"

"Long enough," he responds with his characteristic smile. "Let's get over to the hospital so we can see our boy." Richard hops into the backseat with Spike. They turn onto the highway and ride wordlessly the rest of the way—something unusual for both of them—until they arrive at the hospital parking lot.

"This is the part I hate the most," says Spike in a sad voice as they climb out of the jeep, "especially going into the intensive care unit." They now are walking toward the unit itself. "When you've visited this place a few times, it'll turn your head around. I've seen some bad ones, Rich, some kids who've had most of their arms and legs blown away..." His voice trailed off as they enter a Quonset hut adjacent to surgery.

When they enter the unit, they feel the immediate relief of air-conditioning and observe an aisle that runs the length of the room with five beds on each side. There are three corpsmen and a doctor present who are attending the badly injured Marines and monitoring EKG, respirator equipment, and the numerous IVs plugged into the gravely injured young men. When they reach the third bed on their left, the two chaplains approach an injured patient being worked on by the doctor. The patient has a colostomy bag by his bed and two IVs running into his body, his left leg is in a huge cast being supported by an overhead sling, and he has a nasty cut on his forehead above his right eye. The doctor is changing the dressing on his right hand, which looks more like a piece of raw hamburger than a normal hand.

"Hello, Doc, how's my patient?" says Spike as he looks across the bed to the person hunched over the severely injured hand.

The doctor continues wrapping the hand as he says, "He's doing much better today, Father, he may be ready for medevac outta here in three or four days."

"That's good to hear, really good to hear, Doc," comments Spike with a smile on his face as the doctor slowly closes the wrapping with tape, then excuses himself and walks to another bed across the aisle.

Chaplain Strom slowly takes Dick's uninjured hand in his as the injured chaplain looks up at him, his faced very flushed, and says in voice slurred and slowed by medication, "Hey, Rich, thanks for coming. You too, Spike. Shoulda been more careful out there..." His voice trails off.

71

"Lots of people, including chaplains, are getting hurt out there, Dick, that's the way it is," comments Strom, attempting to reassure him about his injuries and yet deal with his own feelings of inadequacy at that moment. "I'm really sorry to see you go," he says softly, "but when they get you to Japan, you'll get good care and needed rest."

"When Spike brought me communion yesterday, he said you will be going to *Two-five*, they're good people, Rich. You'll love 'em. I know you will," he says as his voice is now slurring even more.

"Our prayers are answered, Dick, that you're doing so good now," replies Spike in a soft, caring voice. "And you're also in good hands here, so we're going to go now. We just wanted to stop by a minute so Rich could say good-bye. He's leaving shortly for An Hoa and I'll be seeing you again, my friend."

The injured priest slowly turns his head again toward Chaplain Strom and squeezes his hand softly. There are tears in his eyes as he says, "God be with you my friend."

As he says this, Richard flashes on the day, which seems so long ago, just after their graduation ceremonies at Chaplain School in Newport, when they bade each other good-bye, their last words being, "See you in Vietnam." Chaplain Strom feels deep sadness for him and for all who are in this room as he responds softly, with a lump in his throat and near tears himself, "And with you too, Dick. You are in my heart and prayers each day. Get well and come back to us soon."

The division chaplain and Richard linger for a moment, cherishing that inner contact of spirit the three of them are finding. Strom gently lays Dick's hand back on the bed, they then turn and head back for the doorway. Richard finds himself not wanting to look at the injured or listen to the *hiss-thump… hiss-thump… hiss-thump* of the two respirators attempting to keep life in the bodies of two severely thrashed Marines on the other side of the aisle.

They walk out into the hot, muggy sun-filled day, quietly absorbed in their own thoughts as they cross the dusty road by the mess hall and climb into Spike's waiting jeep, sitting down in the back. "What's the prognosis?" Richard asks the division chaplain in a matter-of-fact way.

Spike turns to face Richard and says, "He has a compound fracture of the leg, shrapnel in his colon and abdomen, he may lose a couple of fingers on his right hand and he suffered a severe concussion. He's lucky to be alive, taking all the shrapnel he took!"

They slowly drive out of the hospital complex to Highway 1. As they turn right to head past division headquarters and toward the helipad that will take Chaplain Strom out to An Hoa, Spike continues, "Listen, Rich, that's a tough place out there with those Fifth Marines. You know that's where Congressional Medal of Honor winner, Chaplain Vince Cappodonna, got killed last year. For some reason we've had some back luck with our chaplains there, so be careful, Rich, please?" This is one of the reasons Richard respects the division chaplain so much, because as well as being a kind, sensitive person, he tells it like it is!

They are now passing recon battalion on their right as Spike places his hand on Richard's shoulder, saying, "You're commanding officer out at *Two-five* is a real tough Marine, from the old school, so you're going to have to keep a low profile at first. Just do your job and he'll come to respect you."

Strom again feels a tad of sadness passing by the recon entrance—his home for the past week—remembering the friends made and the relationships established during that short time he was assigned there. He glances back at Spike and says, "Thanks for the tip. And don't worry, Spike, I'll be real careful. I used to run the one-hundred-yard dash in ten flat!"

"Yeah, I know you will," he replies, then nudges Richard in the ribs with his elbow. "You're too damn ornery to have anything happen to you anyway." He laughs.

"Thanks, Spike, you sound like my mom, at least the ornery part," Richard jokes. In order to get to the main helipad for transportation to the various field commands, the drive takes you on a road past division supply on the left, then weaves through a couple of small villes, turns left past an artillery battery toward a flat area adjacent to a number of temporary military buildings. As they drive up to the matted helipad, Spike is telling Richard that this particular valley facing this helipad is one of the main areas through which the VC and NVA infiltrate into Da Nang. Some big battles have been staged just a few kilometers up the facing valley.

They now climb out of the jeep and Chaplain Strom helps the driver unload his baggage by the side of the helipad. About ten meters away five Marines are lounging about on their duffel bags. Spike turns to Richard and says, "Listen now, Rich, you stop by and see us when you make your hospital runs, okay?"

"Will do, if we can have communion over a beer and a peanut butter sandwich," Richard replies as he shakes his hand and continues, "You're one hell of a monsignor, Spike, whatever monsignors are. Anyway, thanks for all your help, especially your friendship."

"God be with you, my friend," he says, then turns and climbs into the front seat of his vehicle next to his driver.

The jeep backs up, turns, and heads back up the road as Richard smiles and waves at the division chaplain. "You're all right, even for a Catholic," he yells at him as his jeep speeds away. Spike turns back with a laugh and waves as the jeep rounds a curve and disappears from view.

Chaplain Strom now turns and walks toward the group of five Marines hanging out next to the helipad. They looked bored and unfriendly as he asks a question to no one in particular: "Is this where I catch a ride out to the Fifth Marines?"

A young corporal carrying only his rifle and sitting on his helmet replies, "Yes, sir, we've been waiting here for about three hours."

"Three hours… jeez, that's a long time to be waiting," Richard says incredulously.

"Must be your first time out to An Hoa, Chaplain," the young corporal responds, then continues, "Sir, the choppers are never on time, especially going out to An Hoa. They tell you to go to such and such a place and all you do is just wait around. There aren't no schedules," he explains, "but if you do miss them and you get to An Hoa a day late, the first sergeant will kick your ass—ah, your butt, sir, I'm sorry." He looks embarrassed at having used an offensive word in front of a chaplain.

With a touch of embarrassment himself, Richard adds, "Oh, I see… Ah, yeah, I'm pretty new in-country myself. I don't know much about these things yet."

Two of the seated Marines smile politely as he continues, "Any of you with *Two-five?*"

"I am," replies the young corporal, "I'm returning to An Hoa from division. I had to deliver some papers and special effects of some Marines killed last week. Are you the new chaplain replacing Father Harrigan?"

"That's me," Richard responds, reaching over to shake the corporal's hand. "I'm Chaplain Strom."

Richard places his helmet on the deck and sits down on it next to the young Marine. "You must work for S1 and personnel, that right?" he questions.

"Yes, sir," he replies, "and you'll be assigned to H&S Company like all the other navy and staff personnel. Right now the battalion is out on operations. Our colonel always wants his chaplain out with them, so I'll help you get your file and stuff in order."

"Tell me what happened to Chaplain Harrigan," Richard then asks.

"Yes, sir," he replies, "the battalion was on operations out by Phu Lac 6, where the main bridge crossing is located across the Song Tu Bon River. The first sergeant said he tripped a booby-trapped sixty-millimeter mortar round. At first they thought he was dead but one of the corpsman helped revived him. I guess the colonel was really pissed—ah, sorry, Chaplain. Anyway it's bad for morale when the chaplain gets hit. Sergeant Rooney said he's lucky he ain't dead."

Richard nods slowly in response, then turns to the other four Marines, who are still lying on their gear and asks what they've been up to. One of the Marines, a sergeant, turns to him. "We're all just back from R&R in Bangkok," he says as he slowly kicks some small rocks away from his flak jacket and helmet. "It's a real bummer coming back, Chaplain," he says as he lays his head back into the palms of his hands and closes his eyes. "It was so nice not being shot at all the time."

Softly, in the background, an approaching helicopter can be heard in the distance as a Marine next to the sergeant slowly raises his body to a sitting position, opens his eyes, and says with a voice filled with disgust, "Ah, shit. Back to the real world of killing gooks. I hate it!"

The sound of the chopper is getting louder as they all struggle to get their baggage off the deck and their gear slung on their bodies. Richard sees a twin-engine CH46 Sea Stallion, the workhorse of the Marine infantry, approach from the direction of division. It slows its forward speed and begins to descend slowly to the helipad.

The helicopter touches down, the gate is lowered in the aft section of the aircraft, and a crewman walks out of the opening toward the group of waiting Marines. The corporal from *Two-five* runs to meet the crewman and yells loudly over the sound of the engines for a few seconds. The crewman runs back onboard the craft for twenty seconds, then again runs out the back, stops, and waves to the waiting Marines to board aircraft. Under normal conditions, when not under enemy fire, it is standard operation procedure to check with the pilot regarding the number of passengers. Weight is critical because heat and altitude must be factored into the flight for safety purposes.

Chaplain Strom puts on his helmet and flak jacket and picks up his valpack and typewriter, while the corporal grabs the duffel bag. They then run to the waiting chopper and climb onboard. The pilot revs up the engines, and the helicopter slowly becomes airborne, does a half circle turn, picks up forward speed, then lifts up in a lazy spiral into the late morning sky.

The chaplain and the Marines are seated in the standard webbed seats one finds on most military aircraft. It's not a very comfortable kind of seating arrangement, especially on longer trips. Aside from the two pilots in the cockpit, there is a crew chief standing directly in the doorway leading to the cockpit, who is in constant communication with the pilots and the other gunner. He also serves as the gunner on the starboard side of the craft. The machine gunners are located at the side entrances of the helicopter and stand ready to fire at anything deemed hostile or unfriendly.

Shortly, the chopper is moving at one hundred knots at about seventy-five feet above the rice paddies. Soon they are passing division on their right, past the chapel, First Recon, the funny looking helicopters, finally passing First Med as the chopper bears right around the mountains into the broad plain of the Song Cau Do River delta. It is a wide, lush coastal plain made up mostly of rice paddies, tree lines, and small villages.

Richard looks out the window next to him as they gain altitude and the view gives way to a larger context of the river delta meandering through a beautiful patchwork of green and brown below. The bright morning sun gives the scenery below an almost fairyland quality about it. Continuing in a southwesterly direction and up into the patchy clouds above, the chaplain makes out the silvery silhouette of a jet making a run on a tree line far below the helicopter and to its right. As the jet passes this tree line, there is a bright orange explosion followed by the grayish white billowing smoke. Then a second jet follows in on the same trajectory and drops two silver canisters that slowly tumble over and over in the air until they too hit the same tree line. This time there is a large, spreading glow of orange fire followed by gray-black billowing smoke. Richard is seeing his first live demonstration of "snakes and nape," two-hundred-fifty-pound bombs followed by napalm. This is a view and perspective that few grunts will ever see, from an aircraft above and away from the dangers inherent in this kind of close air support.

The craft is airborne twenty minutes before they begin a slow, spiral descent toward a very large complex of buildings surrounding an airstrip. As Richard continues his observation out the window, he notices the helicopter heading for a large matted square area, about the size of a football field, adjacent to the airstrip. There are approximately one hundred buildings and tents scattered about the area with a village on both the north and south sides of the complex. He can also see the Son Tinh Yen River slowly winding its way from the south around the western part of An Hoa, then heading north and finally east toward the South China Sea.

Within the square mile complex itself, there is very little greenery and the ground is covered with a light reddish-orange clay dirt that is found throughout the area of the foothills surrounding the mountains. Just to the south of An Hoa is a jutting mountain strip that runs twenty kilometers almost to the coastal town of Hoi An south of Da Nang. To the east are high triple-canopy mountains that run all the way to the Laotian border. Triple canopy has a thick layer of ground undergrowth, a second layer of trees reaching thirty to fifty feet, and a third layer of trees usually over one hundred feet high. Very little sunlight filters down to the ground level where it is extremely wet and humid, especially during the rainy season. This also makes great cover for enemy troops and supplies.

An Hoa is strategically situated at the juncture of one of the main infiltration routes of the NVA from the mountains into the heavily populated coastal regions surrounding Da Nang. It is also the home of the Fifth Marine Infantry Regiment, two batteries of artillery from the Eleventh Marines, an infantry battalion from the Twenty-Seventh Marine Regiment, plus two companies of tanks. In all, it's home for about five thousand Marines.

The chopper hovers above the matted deck for a moment, then very slowly lands in the center of the helipad. The crew chief directs everyone out of the aft section as the young corporal and Richard slowly make their way south toward a group of hooches and buildings located adjacent to the tarmac. Just before they reach the edge of the helipad, four very loud, large explosions take place to the south and east—*kwaap, kwaap, kwaap, kwaap*... The chaplain turns toward the sound of the explosions just as Corporal Brown runs by him, yelling, "Rockets, Chaplain!"

They both drop the gear they are carrying and throw themselves into the ditch surrounding the pad. The ditch isn't deep, perhaps two feet, but offers some protection as they literally dive into the depression like they are going to belly-flop into the neighbor's pool. Only this isn't a pool, the neighbors aren't very friendly, the rockets are getting closer as more explosions go off, and there is about six inches of scummy mud at the bottom of the ditch in which they are lying. Richard is lying there, face in the mud, wondering whether he wants to die from suffocation or the shrapnel from the rockets when three more explosions go off just to the east of the runway. The sounds are even louder this time.

"The bastards have us zeroed in," he thinks to himself as he slowly lifts his face out of the mud. For now the rockets have stopped and he can hear the sound of a siren going off someplace, much yelling coming from the area of the hooches just south of where he is lying, and for the first time can hear the *thump, thump, thump* of his own heartbeat. Richard feels vulnerable, frightened, and nauseated from the stench of the rancid mud on his face and body. Slowly, he lifts his head up to see smoke billowing from two areas of the compound. He also notices that his portable typewriter is lying on the matting in three different pieces.

"Hey, Corporal, what do you think?" the chaplain asks as the sound of a siren continues, now without the accompanying sounds of exploding enemy fire. Right at that moment, the artillery batteries open up—the 105s, 155s and also those huge eight-inch guns that shake the whole area when they go off. The young Marine motions for Richard to stay down, which he finds it difficult to do because of the rancid-smelling mud they are in.

Chaplain Strom's gear is scattered or broken all over the place. He is lying in rancid mud, confused and frightened. He doesn't know where he is supposed to go if things get any worse and the rockets land any closer. Suddenly Corporal Brown jumps up and yells at the chaplain to follow him. Richard blindly responds to this timely instruction running after him to a sandbag bunker about forty meters off the helipad. When they get to the entrance, the bunker is jammed with a number of Marines, so they must push their way inside. It stinks in there, it's hot and humid, and Richard assumes he smells from the rancid mud. "Like a dog who just rubbed himself in a pile of dog crap," he thinks to himself. He turns to Corporal Brown and mutters more to himself: "Welcome to An Hoa and the grunts, Chaplain Strom!"

GETTING READY

Richard Strom awakens to the sounds of loud voices passing by his hooch, a large CH-53 helicopter overhead and the constant *boom* of outgoing artillery in the background. As he rolls over in his cot, he is amazed that he slept through the night with all the noise, which goes on twenty-four hours a day, seven days a week.

Getting out of bed his thoughts go back immediately to yesterday afternoon—the rocket attack that greeted his arrival in An Hoa, the half hour spent inside the smelly bunker scraping mud off his body while awaiting the all-clear signal, throwing his thrashed typewriter in the garbage can, running into a corpsman he knew at Camp Pendleton who showed him to the second battalion chaplain's hooch which had been locked since Harrigan had left for the field a week ago, then being told the showers were out of order for a couple of days.

Richard's meeting with the executive officer hadn't gone well either. After finally getting a Marine from supply to break the padlock so he could enter the chaplain's hooch and finally stow his gear, he gets a message that he is to report immediately to Major Moran for a briefing. He was baffled by that message, thinking to himself, "Why would anyone want to brief a chaplain? On what?"

That meeting he had yesterday afternoon with the XO was even more baffling than the earlier message. Moran is a short, wimpy, cigar-smoking officer whose singular intent is to survive his remaining fifteen days in-country before being shipped back to the States. Richard was first asked about the denomination to which he belonged, then was treated to a twenty-minute monologue about the major's eighteen years in the Corps and why chaplains don't belong out in the bush with the grunts. The meeting stopped abruptly when the major receives a message that a palette of beer had just arrived for the battalion and was being "liberated" by the corpsmen at the battalion aid station. His fleeting message to Richard was, "I've got an important matter to take care of. See you tomorrow, Chaplain."

Strom is now wandering around his small hooch, a fourteen-by-ten-foot room, looking for his shaving kit and towel, which he had stashed somewhere in the midst of unpacking yesterday. He has strategically placed his helmet and flak jacket by his combat boots next to his bed in case of another attack. Adjacent to his boots is a bottle of Chivas Regal that he had taken a whack at prior to his going to bed. He is somewhat startled by a knock at the door of his hooch.

He is wearing only his skivvies and a T-shirt. He hurriedly slips into his boots and walks to the door. Richard opens the door to find the corporal he had met yesterday on his trip out to An Hoa. He invites him inside, then says, "Sorry, I'm not more presentable. Guess I'm a little disoriented and somewhat muddled. What can I do for you? Ah, sit down." He motions for the young Marine to sit down on the footlocker since there are no chairs.

"Thank you, sir," he says quietly, "but I only need to give you these two letters that are addressed to the chaplain. The adjutant wants you to get these before you leave for the field."

Richard is now pulling on his utility pants, turns, and says, "You know something that I don't know, Corporal? What this stuff about going out in the field?"

"Yes, sir," he responds. "Ah, it's just that the colonel always wants the chaplain out in the bush with the battalion." Then he hands the two letters to Richard.

"Thanks for your help," says the chaplain to the young Marine as he opens the door and leaves.

It is now 0800 and the chaplain's curiosity is raised by the two letters addressed to the battalion chaplain. The first letter is from a high school senior from somewhere in Arkansas who wants to know why her boyfriend can't come home and marry her before *their* baby is born. Richard makes a mental note to ask the S1 about this partic-ular case and what kind of proof is needed to get him home on emergency leave. He is well aware that oftentimes this has been used as a ruse to get Marines out of Vietnam. But since he is new in-country and rather tentative as to how his command works with this kind of situation, he will seek counsel with the S1 and check it out.

The second letter is from a mother in Connecticut who is worried because she hasn't heard from her son in over two months. The mother isn't freaked out, nor is she demanding. She just wants to know why her son isn't writing and if he is okay. "Some very natural concerns," Richard thinks to himself as he writes down the names of the two Marines and the line companies to which they belong.

He finishes dressing, shaves with his electric razor, and as he is preparing to head to the mess tent for something to eat, sees the young corporal returning to his hooch. As Richard walks out the door to greet him, he salutes and says, "Sir, Major Moran would like to see you right away. I think it's something about the colonel wanting you out in the field right away."

"All right, thanks," he replies, then as Corporal Brown turns to go away, he continues, "Listen, can you find out where these two guys are?" He hands the corporal the piece of paper with their names on it. "I want to talk to them if they're around."

"Yes, sir," he says, reading the names to himself as he turns to head back toward his office nearby. "I'll let you know where they are, Chaplain."

When Strom arrives at the exec's office the major is on the phone talking to regiment about flight schedules out to the bush. When he finishes his conversation with them, he turns to Richard and says, "Look, Chaplain"—he takes a big hit on his cigar—"it's time to get your shit together because shortly you will be going out to Hill 52 to be with the big boys." The big cigar he is smoking looks as fat as his neck is round. Richard thinks to himself that he looks more like someone hired to clean up horse crap on the street after the town parade than a tough Marine, sitting here on his butt while the real action is going on out in the field.

"The chopper is scheduled to leave at 1300, so be sure you get your butt down there on time," he declares in his squeaky voice, again attempting to project a tough-guy attitude. "If you need some help regarding what to bring to the field or how to pack," he drones on in his wimpy voice, "check out the battalion doctor. Old Bernie can give you some pointers," he adds.

Richard thanks the major, walks out the door, and heads south to find the hooch where the two battalion doctors are quartered. The usual protocol when the battalion is out in the field on maneuvers is to have one doc out and one back in the rear to handle sick call for the troops in An Hoa.

Richard walks quietly to the hooch and sees an enclosed porch with a doorway leading back into the living quarters. On the porch, sitting in a chair leaning back against the wall, completely engrossed in the magazine he is reading, is a kind of chubby fellow with wire-rimmed glasses. He is shirtless, barefoot, and is wearing shorts.

Richard knocks twice before he gets a response. "Yeah, whatta ya want?"

"Could you tell me where I can find the battalion doctor?" he asks.

"That's me," he replies in an irritated voice, never taking his eyes off his magazine. "Sick call was earlier this morning."

Richard opens the door and walks onto the porch and approaches the doctor. He has not moved nor has he taken his eyes off his magazine as the chaplains says, "I don't need to go to sick call. I'm the new battalion chaplain. I just came by to meet you." Richard extends his hand to greet him.

The doctor pauses for a moment, closes his magazine while keeping his thumb on the page he was reading, looks up at Richard, then shakes his hand with an almost brusque manner and says, "Hi, Chaplain, I'm Bernie. Make yourself at home." Then he returns to his reading material. Richard is surprised, though not shocked, to see that Bernie is reading a pornographic magazine and is making no attempt at all to hide it from him. This of course did not fit the image the chaplain had of a physician, even one who is attached to the Marines, sitting on a porch, shirtless, on a very muggy morning, sipping beer, completely engrossed in some hardcore porn!

Bernie didn't look up from his magazine and appears somewhat irritated at being interrupted, grunting twice when Richard informed him he would be leaving shortly to go out in the field. At this point, Richard excuses himself and leaves quietly, feeling foolish and also somewhat taken aback at his meeting with the doctor, especially because he would likely be working closely with him over the next few months. Chaplain Strom remembers hearing stories at Camp Pendleton about some of the weird doctors in the navy and how most of them found their way into the Marine Corps.

It will be two hours before his scheduled chopper ride, so Richard decides to check out those names he gave to the young corporal and get that business taken care of before heading out into the field. When he arrives at headquarters, he is greeted by the adjutant, John Kelly, a first lieutenant who has come up through the ranks as a "mustang." These are former career enlisted men selected to become officers. Kelly has been in the Corps over twenty years and is an old school Marine, raised in Boston, tough and profane, yet treats the chaplain with dignity and respect.

"Chaplain Strom, welcome aboard," Kelly declares in his loud Bostonian accent. "Sit down and have a beer with us."

He shakes Richard's hand, turns toward the refrigerator, and pulls out two beers, handing one to the new chaplain. Richard, not wanting to offend his host, opens the beer and sets it down on the deck by his feet. However, drinking beer before noon, let alone before late afternoon, is not a task he relishes. It makes him sleepy and sets him to wonder about alcohol being problematic, especially in a war zone.

"About those two names you gave us," the adjutant continues, "Pfc McDaniels, the one from Arkansas whose girlfriend says he knocked her up, well, he lost a leg and part of an arm last week and was medevaced to Japan. So he's going home anyway, not our problem." Richard winces at the callousness of the lieutenant.

"The other one, a lance corporal from Echo, as of yesterday he was still with the battalion over at Echo," he continues. "We'll check with his first sergeant, find out where he is, and let you know." Richard thanks Kelly, excuses himself, and leaves for his hooch.

When Richard gets back to his hooch he is again reminded of the reddish clay dirt that is everywhere. Cleaning the dust and dirt off your bed, your clothes, your gear, and your body does no good because within a few minutes another layer will take its place. He picks up his communion kit and lays it on the bed and begins packing. This essential piece of equipment is unique and different for each chaplain, depending upon the denomination to which he belongs. In this case, the kit includes a small brass altar crucifix and cross six inches long, two small votive-type candleholders two inches high, three communion linens with embroidered crosses, twenty-five field interdenominational worship service books, some New Testaments, a few Hebrew psalm books, a can of unleavened breads for communion, a small chalice and paten—a silver plate that holds the consecrated hosts—and an assortment of rosaries and religious medals. It is Chaplain Strom's duty to minister to all his troops, regardless of denomination, in any way he can, respecting each Marine's religious tradition.

He then empties the entire contents of a bottle of navy issue altar wine into a canteen. Since Chaplain Strom will be celebrating Holy Communion each time he holds services, he will need an adequate supply. And last, he packs his small reversible purple-and-white, gold-embroidered stole that he places around his neck when involved in "official business." This will be the only vestment he carries with him into the field. It is a gift given him by his parishioners back in New Orleans.

Richard closes his communion kit and prepares to pack the rest of his gear in his field pack, when a Marine walks up to his door and knocks. He opens the door and invites the young man inside and motions for him to sit down on the footlocker. "I'm packing for my first foray into the bush," he tells the Marine as he snaps the buckles on the kit. "Hope I get everything together."

The chaplain sits down on the edge of his bed and notices he's one of the Marines who rode out to An Hoa with him, so he says, "Aren't you one of the fellows just returning from R&R? Didn't I ride out here with you? What's up?"

"Yes, sir. Ah, the first sergeant said you wanted to see me," he says politely, his eyes betraying the depression they all feel when they return from R&R and will be returning to the bush.

"Oh," he responds, "you must be Joe?"

"Yes, sir, is something wrong?" he questions as he sits up straight with an apprehensive look on his face.

"No big thing, Joe," Richard assures him as he continues, "but your mom says she hasn't heard from you in about two months. That right, Joe?"

A relieved smile breaks across his face, then says, "Yes, sir, I guess I haven't been very good about writing her and the family. We've been out in the field so much, then R&R came, and... well, I just haven't written her, sir. I figured she might do something like writing you or the skipper." He finished his sentence with an embarrassed look on his face.

"Look, Joe," the chaplain responds, "families really need those letters from us to help them through a time in their lives that is difficult for them as well, in a different way of course. It's very hard on them not knowing what's going on with you, not knowing what it's really like over here, especially since you're a grunt. Your mom's letter here is just a way of showing her concern for you. I hope you won't get down on her for what she did."

"No, sir, I understand," he says, looking quite relieved.

"Tell you what, Joe, there's no need for your first sergeant to know about this. When he asks why the chaplain sent for you, just say he had a message for you from a friend of yours stationed at Camp Pendleton. Write your mom and family a letter today before you go out in the bush and we'll call it even, okay?" Richard explains to him.

They continue chatting for a few minutes as Richard finds out he's been wounded once and sent back to the bush, comes from a large family back in Connecticut, has three months left before going back to the States, and has deep reservations about returning to the field.

"Too many of my buddies get hit and die just after coming back from R&R," he broods. "I have a gut feeling that something is gonna happen." Joe looks down at the floor, then continues, "It always seems to happen to everyone who's short... It's scary. I don't want to go back out."

Richard is again conscious of that feeling of inadequacy, that same reaction he had yesterday when visiting Dick Harrigan in ICU. "Must not feel very good to have those kinds of thoughts, that something bad is going to happen," Richard says thoughtfully. "Who does want to go back out there and get shot at all the time?" Chaplain Strom is cognizant of a very simple, profound fact: this young man is speaking from experience, whereas his words come, though sincere, from his head, an embarrassing thought.

Lance Corporal Deeves then stands up and thanks the chaplain for his concerns. As Joe walks out the door, Richard smiles and says while shaking his hand. "I'll see you out there. And don't let your mom down, I'm counting on you to write that letter home."

He smiles back and replies, "Don't worry, sir, I will."

It is now approaching noon. Richard wants to get a hot meal before he leaves. "Like having the Last Supper," he thinks to himself as he walks to the regimental area to get something to eat. The food consists of a classic Marine "brunch" of baloney sandwiches with white bread, some sliced vegetables, coffee and milk, and some kind of raisin-like bread pudding that looks more like three-day-old oatmeal left out in the sun to dry and catch flies.

On the way back to his hooch, Richard encounters the battalion doc again. He apparently has finished reading his "skin" magazine and must be ready for something to eat. He still appears grouchy and irritable. "Hey, Chaplain," he says, passing the chaplain by without slowing down, looking straight ahead. Richard notes that he looks like an unmade bed, smiles to himself, and wonders if Bernie ever considered becoming a neurosurgeon.

Upon reaching his hooch, Strom finishes putting together his field pack—toilet articles, poncho and poncho liner, a light comforter-like blanket, extra socks and shirts, flashlight, Kbar knife, shovel, an air mattress commonly referred to as a "rubber lady," his bush hat, and last, six cans of sardines and smoked oysters along with a jar of dried onions to help compliment the taste of the C-rations. He then fills three canteens with water and into a fourth empties the remaining scotch from the Chivas Regal bottle. That makes five canteens on his belt, including the one filled with altar wine.

It is now close to 1300 and Richard is due at the helipad. He slips on his combat belt and suspenders on which his canteens are secured, puts on his flak jacket, then struggles to get his arms through his backpack straps, finally getting the pack on his back. Lastly, he slings the communion kit strap over his head onto his left shoulder so the kit rests under his right arm, then places his helmet on his head, strap hanging loose. He has no weapons per Geneva Convention rules. He is aware of how heavy and constricting all this gear is and what a struggle it must be to hump miles with all this stuff strapped to one's body, especially with the heat and humidity that is indigenous to Vietnam.

Richard padlocks his hooch and heads for the helipad. A staff sergeant passing by says good-naturedly, "Gonna kick some ass, huh, Marine?"

The chaplain's uniform and most of his equipment is brand-new, so it's easy to spot that he is new in-country. As he turns directly toward him, the sergeant sees the gold cross and silver lieutenant bars on the shirt collars. He almost comes to attention, then says apologetically, "I'm sorry, sir, I didn't realize who you were."

"No problem, Sergeant," the chaplain replies as he adjusts his pack so as to make it more comfortable. "Don't know about kicking ass, but I'm going out to the field for the first time. I'm Chaplain Strom, just got here yesterday."

"Glad to meet you, sir." The sergeant shakes Strom's extended hand. "I'm the supply sergeant with *Two-five*. Come and see me before you go back out in the bush again, Chaplain, and I'll outfit you real good. If I'd known you were going out today, I coulda fixed you up with a better pack than what you got there, sir," he says, "that's the old kind."

Richard thanks him and assures him that the next time he goes to the bush from An Hoa, he'll come and visit him.

In walking to the helipad Richard is already sweating profusely and thinks of the poor grunts who carry mortars and machine guns and radio packs as well as their personal gear.

"God, how do they do it?" he thinks to himself. He then remembers what a sergeant major back at Camp Pendleton once told the chaplain how the term *grunt* came about. Richard is suddenly struck again by the radical change of lifestyle he is now facing—going out in the bush—and the simple life-long innocence he has come from.

IN THE BUSH

It's going on just short of two weeks now in Vietnam and the waiting around that Richard is experiencing is boring him to death. "Get my one-niner out here!" was the curt message the exec received and passed onto the chaplain. So now he's been waiting in the hot sun for a helicopter ride to Hill 52, where his newly assigned battalion is pushing toward a place back in the hills called Thong Duc to relieve some encircled special forces out in the middle of the jungle. Chaplain Strom is thinking to himself that if the random way in which troops are transported in the Marine Corps is any indication of the speed and efficiency with which they expect to relieve the troops at Thong Duc, then those boys out there are in some deep trouble!

Finally, after four hours of waiting in the hot, humid sun, eleven Marines are loaded into a waiting aircraft for the ride to battalion field headquarters. "Finally I'll be out in the bush with the grunts," he absently says to a corpsman seated next to him in the helicopter.

Slowly the helicopter lifts off the matting, does a one-hundred-eighty-degree turn eastward, picks up forward speed, and lifts sharply up in a slow spiral motion, finally bearing west into the late afternoon sun. There is only the loud whine of the two CH46 jet engines of the helicopter, the beautiful, lush green countryside below and Richard's own personal thoughts of what may possibly lay ahead.

At this point, if there is any fear or anxiety at going out in the bush, it must be buried somewhere below the level of his feelings of excitement and desire to get on with it. Richard is feeling a sense of wonder, of even adventure. Yet this is tempered by a feeling, way down deep inside his innards of caution and the desire to remain alive.

As he looks out the window of the helicopter, the sun is beginning to set in back of the mountains that border on next door Laos, casting deep hues of green and brown. The beauty is incredible and he is astonished that in all the news reports, in all the briefings and information that he had access to concerning Vietnam, it's beauty was never talked about.

"I wonder why," he thinks to himself.

The sun is now setting and the helicopter is beginning to lose altitude, commencing a spiral descent into an LZ below. Richard sees a number of artillery pieces and many Marines, perhaps close to one hundred, moving on and about the perimeter of the hill. This hill is strategically located next to Highway 4, the main road that runs back to Thong Duc and the mountain passes beyond. Since the immediate area has a number of artillery pieces, this means there is also large quantities of ammunition, which also means if the VC aim rockets or mortars toward the hill, all that ammo could definitely ruin everyone's evening!

Slowly, softly the pilot brings the chopper down into the LZ located in a flat grassy area next to the actual hill. A Marine is standing in the middle of the LZ with a flashing strobe light as dusk settles as a help to guide in the pilot. Chaplain Strom's immediate reaction in seeing the strobe light is that a light like that would make an easy target. But again, he thinks, "What do I know?"

The passengers get up from their webbed-back seats, grab their gear, and scamper out the aft entrance on the lowered tailgate of the helicopter, breaking into a jog as they run to the base of the hill about thirty meters away. Meeting the new arrivals are eight Marines who are on their way back to An Hoa. They look tired, dirty, and burned out.

It's beginning to get dark as Richard removes his gear, including his helmet and flak jacket, and places it on the ground, then watches the passing Marines board the chopper he exited. At that precise moment, just as Richard is turning to pick up his gear again and put on his helmet and flak jacket and head up the hill, a blinding flash is followed by the sound of a loud explosion, like that which greeted him in An Hoa. The rocket hits just beyond the helicopter in the rice paddy. A second flash is followed immediately by another explosion that takes place further south near an artillery battery at the southern end of the LZ. Shrapnel is flying in all directions when suddenly Richard feels something hit him halfway up his back and adjacent to his spinal column, like someone had just snapped him very hard with the end of a wet towel, like he remembered in the locker rooms in high school. A very painful, burning sensation immediately emanates from that hit on his back.

Chaplain Strom has not moved. He is frozen in his spot, not quite sure what is going on but certain that they are under some kind of attack. The helicopter in which he had arrived makes the quickest take-off he's ever seen. Another helicopter further south near the battery was not so lucky. Shrapnel has ripped into the fuselage and has badly damaged the engine. The chopper is thrashed! This has all taken less than five seconds and Richard is still standing up, watching this incredible scene as if he's at an NFL football game, until someone yells loudly, "Get your ass down!" The new chaplain follows this very timely instruction by jumping into the nearest hole he can find.

Realizing now the enormity of the moment—that he is in the midst, again, of being fired upon—and feeling the increased pain and burning sensation on his back, the chaplain attempts to act cool and offers the sergeant in the hole with him a cigarette. Inside, Richard is terrified. The sergeant doesn't respond and keeps his head buried in his arms. As Richard hugs the deck in his hole, he instantly wonders if the Marines, who have been through this stuff many times, are as frightened as he is.

He now reaches around to his back to find a tear in his shirt and blood oozing from a jagged two inches cut. Suddenly Richard has this terrific pain coming from the base of his spine, so painful he believes that he will be unable to move his legs. The first thing that rushes through his mind is that the piece of shrapnel has entered his spinal column and he will be paralyzed for life!

There is no time at all to dwell on that thought because right at that very instant all hell breaks loose. Every single artillery piece on that hill seems to be going off at once, firing toward a mountain range close by and to the south. The sergeant who is lying next to

Richard suddenly gets up without a word and runs somewhere up the hill and disappears. The chaplain has absolutely no idea what he is supposed to do or where he is supposed to go and knows no one on the hill. He overrides the pain in his lower back, jumps out of the hole, and heads up the hill as well.

The new battalion chaplain is now running up the hill without his gear, in the dark, and hasn't a clue as to what may happen in the next moment. He suddenly trips and falls headlong into a foxhole partially on top of and adjacent to another person lying in a fetal position, holding his helmet tightly with his forearms and hands.

The firing stops just as suddenly as it started, casting a deadly silence. The person next to Richard pushes himself up to a sitting position and says, "That was real close," then he turns to the chaplain and says, "Who the hell are you?"

"I'm Richard Strom, the new battalion chaplain," he says. "Sorry I dropped in on you so suddenly. I didn't know what the hell was going on and where to go. Just came in on the last chopper."

The two of them sit silently for a few moments, then the other fellow introduces himself to Richard. "My name is Chuck and I'm the other surgeon in the battalion. Welcome to the bush. That damn Bernie is always in An Hoa when the shit hits the fan. By the way, Chaplain, I hope you can play bridge."

"Ah, yeah, Chuck, I can play bridge," Strom manages in his confusion. "How in the hell can you think of bridge at a moment like this?"

"Takes the edge off the anxiety," he responds.

Richard slowly stands up, surveys the immediate area, and finds himself adjacent to the battalion aid station, a hole dug in the side of the hill surrounded by sandbags with a tarp pulled over the top. At that moment a gunnery sergeant approaches Chuck and says, "Sir, the colonel wants you and some corpsmen down at the battery south of the LZ. We've got some seriously wounded Marines that need immediate attention. We've already flagged an emergency chopper."

With that the doctor calls on two corpsmen to accompany him, then hurriedly pulls out a field medical kit. He turns to the chaplain and quickly says, "Why don't you come along? If they're injured seriously, maybe they'll need your expertise more than mine. Where's your gear?

"I'm not sure, but I'll find it later," Richard replies.

Upon arriving at the makeshift triage area the doctor and corpsmen go to work immediately. One Marine has lost most of his right hand and has a large gash in his upper thigh. Bleeding and shock are immediate issues of paramount concern with this Marine as well as a second who is in even more critical shape. Shrapnel has ripped a hole on the left side of his chest the size of a softball and most of his armpit is missing as well. As a corpsman works on the first Marine, another corpsman and Chuck work frantically on the latter Marine to staunch the flow of blood. The doctor anxiously directs Richard to help in the procedure. "Chaplain, hold his head up even with his body and make sure he doesn't choke. He might be bleeding internally and choking." Blood is squirting out in massive amounts as they attempt to plug the hold with massive amounts of gauze and pressure.

As the battalion chaplain holds the head of this gravely injured young man, his respirations become rapid and shallow and his eyes roll up and back into this head. Richard recognizes the symptoms of acute, deep shock, feeling helpless as he watches the Marine's life force eroding. In the meantime, the doctor is also attempting to seal off the damaged lung so the Marine can at least breath partially with undamaged right side.

The medevac is now arriving thirty meters away in the LZ, strobe light again flashing. Having stabilized the two Marines as best as possible in the field, they are loaded into the chopper. Richard turns and watches the helicopter take off quickly and climb up in that steep spiral ascent that is the trademark of flight patterns out in the bush. He sees the medevac disappear in some clouds and feels the immediacy and reality of the war—physically and emotionally—and wonders if he can handle the stuff he is experiencing. Will he be strong enough to handle the dead and injured Marines? Or will he buckle under the pressure of incoming or battle? It is just a flash of thought, only momentary. But even now, at this very first hour in the bush with the grunts, he is beginning to wonder what kind of endurance he will have and what combat might do to his head.

With the medevac gone, they turn and walk up the hill toward the BAS and are encountered by the same gunnery sergeant that asked the doctor work on the wounded. "Hey, Doc, the colonel wants to know who was the dumb son of a bitch that was standing down there by the LZ without his helmet and flak jacket? He says he wants to see the stupid bastard immediately!"

Richard winces, turns, and picks up his gear, which he dropped next to the LZ. As he bends over, one of the corpsmen says to him, "Hey, Chaplain, I think you got blood on your back. You okay?"

"Yeah, I think I took a small piece of shrapnel in my back," he responds. "I'm going to have the doctor to look at it. But right now I have more important things to do, like seeing a colonel who is apparently frothing at the mouth because someone saw me after the rockets hit minus my combat gear."

He carefully puts on his helmet and flak jacket, then slowly makes his way to the battalion command post, wondering how to handle the unfolding scene: the new battalion chaplain fresh from Da Nang, meeting the Old Man for the first time, having broken a cardinal rule of the outfit by not wearing proper gear while under and after an attack—then walking around with some shrapnel in his back because of his oversight. "Maybe this is a jinxed outfit for chaplains after all," he mutters to himself as he approaches the CP.

It's almost dark now, so when Richard enters the bunker, he has no trouble making out people in the very dim reddish light. He sees immediately this fellow of average height, slightly bald, in his late forties, yelling over the radio, "I don't give a shit if recon made an insert three days ago in that approximate area. They're supposed to have their asses outta there by now. I want some goddamn artillery on that hillside right now. And if it were feasible, I'd like some air as well. We've got a hillside full of people and ammo, and if Charlie hits us again, we could go up like a goddamn A-bomb! Tell those dumbbells at division I need that hill plowed up right now, goddammit!"

The chaplain is now standing just inside the doorway of the bunker and has a very uncomfortable feeling about the fellow raging on the radio, when an older Marine approaches and asks Richard somewhat ominously, "Sir, are you the new chaplain?"

"Yes, I am," he replies.

"I'm Sergeant Major Gregoer, sir, and the colonel would like to meet you and have a chat with you. Welcome aboard." They shake hands, then he walks to the balding gentleman who had been yelling on the radio and says a few words to him, and they both turn and walk toward Richard.

The colonel stops about a foot in front of the new chaplain, looks him directly in the eyes, and says, "Chaplain, I don't know what in the hell you think you stepped into out here, but when we're in the midst of engaging the enemy, everyone, including sky pilots, wear their damn flak jackets and helmets. Do you understand that, Chaplain? We've had two chaplains seriously wounded in this outfit the past few months, and goddammit, I don't want another one to get hit because of carelessness. Is that clear, Chaplain?"

"Yes, sir," Richard manages as he become conscious of a burning sensation in his back, praying the colonel doesn't know about it—yet!

Still visibly upset but not quite as agitated, he continues, "And I don't want you holding any church services while we're on this hill—it's too damn dangerous. See anyone you want individually but no groups. Are we clear on that, Chaplain? And another thing," he says, his tone more conciliatory, "I want my chaplain out in the field with the men. You can go visit the wounded in Da Nang every couple of weeks, but as long as we are out in the bush on combat operations, you belong out here with us. And you'll be treated like us too, understand? None of this navy crap around here!"

"Yes, sir, thank you, sir," he mumbles, wondering what the colonel meant by "navy crap." With that said, the colonel shakes Richard's hand, turns, and walks away to confer with an officer who has just come into the CP. On the way back to the BAS, he says to himself, "That was worse than the damn rockets!" He makes a mental note that he will never leave his flak jacket and helmet further away than arm's length—ever!

Arriving back at the battalion clinic, Richard is greeted by Wages, the corpsman who also helped the doctor treat the critically wounded Marines a short time ago. He is sitting on an ammo box, eating some rations, looks up at the chaplain, and says with a big grin on his face, "The Old Man jump on your case, Chaplain? Don't worry about it. Everyone who's been with battalion CP has caught hell from him at least once." He then reaches into a big medical bag next to him and hauls out a Coke and drawls, "Y'all like a Coke, Chaplain?"

"I'd like that very much. By the way, you think you could take a look at my back? I think I took some steel back on the LZ. It's not serious but it sure hurts," Richard asks. Chuck has the chaplain lay down on two ammo boxes placed together, and while Wages holds a flashlight, the doctor probes the wound and pulls out a small sliver of metal. After a shot of penicillin and having the wound dressed, the chaplain, fearing the colonel's wrath, turns to Chuck and makes a request. "After the ass chewing I just had from the colonel, I would appreciate you not reporting the wound."

Chuck shrugs his shoulders. "Okay, so you don't want to be a hero and get a Purple Heart." He hands Richard some Darvon and instructs him to take it for pain. "I hope you don't get an infection, I need you as a bridge partner."

Richard spends the next hour fixing his bedding and digging a hole in which to sleep, still paranoid because of the earlier rocket attack and the probability of the VC initiating more incoming during the night. Just as he climbs under his poncho, which he has rigged somewhat like a small tent, and snuggles into his poncho liner, the rain begins. Shortly water is running into the trench because he didn't build a small dike around it, soaking him completely. He exits the hole and just lies under the poncho, awake most of the night—cold, wet, miserable, and anxious. This is Richard's first lesson about water and gravity, a learning curve that will intensify when the monsoons show up shortly.

HILL 52

It is early morning, the rainclouds have disappeared and the sun is just rising over the mountains to the east. Humidity and heat has replaced the rain and mist hangs over the valley adjacent to the hill that runs twenty kilometers to the west and Thong Duc. There has been no more incoming since last evening when the choppers arrived with replacement troops. Most of the hill is now quiet and the majority of the Marines are either sleeping or quietly preparing food.

Suddenly, the ground begins to shake like an earthquake in California, enough to wake up the whole staff at the BAS. The shaking continues, then is followed a few seconds later by the sound of deafening, continuous explosions to the west. As the shaking and thunderous eruptions continue approximately three kilometers away, the Marines on Hill 52 are hearing the awesome, destructive carpet bombing of a suspected supply area along the Ho Chi Minh trail known as an arc light. This is saturation bombing by huge eight-engine B-52 bombers that fly at very high altitudes, creating a silent, deadly surprise for the enemy below!

The whole hillside has now been awakened and most of the Marines have crawled out of their sleeping quarters to watch the awesome destruction taking place on the mountain range adjacent to them. They are seeing firsthand the horrible convulsion of earth and vegetation and can only imagine the terror this must bring to the NVA soldiers in the area as hundreds of two-thousand-pound bombs are dropped on suspected enemy concentrations.

Then suddenly, perhaps after thirty seconds, and just as abruptly as it started, comes the sound of silence, a hushed tranquility culminating in disbelief at what the men on Hill 52 have just experienced.

The Marines on the hill who are now awake—how is it possible not to be awake?—stand or sit in awe, wordlessly observing the huge columns of smoke and debris arising from the hillside beyond, the awesome silence suddenly broken by the roar of two F-4 Phantom jets flying very fast in formation over Hill 52 at five hundred feet, screaming down the river valley toward the huge rising dust column where the bombs have been dropped. Quickly both aircraft pull up into a steep climb, bank left toward the smoldering mountain range and disappear. As this happens, a gunnery sergeant meanders past the BAS, looks toward the mountains, and says in a slow Southern drawl, "They fly up there, take their photo-recon pictures, and are home for late breakfast. Lucky bastards." He then continues toward the battalion CP.

"Son of a bitch," exclaims Wages as he stands and stretches his arms and legs, "the bastards just won't let you get a good night's sleep." Then he strolls over to the chaplain, who is crawling out from under his poncho liners, stiff and cold from sleeping on the wet ground all night. "Hey, Chaplain, how's that wound on your back? Givin' ya any problems?"

Richard stands up, reaches around toward the wound on his back, examines the bandage with his hand, then turns to the corpsman and says, "Bandage still there, I'll have Chuck look at it shortly. Thanks for the good work getting that sliver out of my back." The chaplain is feeling embarrassed at the minor wound he has sustained and doesn't want to dwell on it. He flashes quickly on the previous evening and the gravely injured Marines they medevaced, wondering if they have survived their ordeal and made it to the hospital alive. Right now he just wants to erase those memories and focus instead on the morning and getting something to eat.

Sleep was meager, just like that first night out on Hill 425 with recon. Only there will be no supply chopper to pick him up this morning and deliver him back to the relative comfort and safety of An Hoa or Da Nang. "You're stuck out here, Bucko," he thinks to himself, "and outta choices!"

The battalion surgeon has been up for some time, now walks by Richard, and offers him some hot tea brewed in a drinking cup he has cleverly created from a C-ration can. The chaplain takes a sip, thanks him, then mumbles something to him about wishing he could also fix him some bacon, eggs, and coffee.

"Don't eat bacon. Against my religion," he says with a friendly smile. "But I can fix you some good kosher corned beef hash my mom sent me from Pittsburgh." They both sit down on some ammo boxes, and he continues, "Being a conservative Jew gives me a good excuse not to eat all that crap they call C-rations. They smell terrible and attract flies very fast. The C-rations are okay to eat, you see. It's the flies that aren't kosher, that's why as a Jew I can't eat C-rations."

"Say what?" exclaims the chaplain skeptically, then notices a big grin emanating from the doctor, then continues, "So if the flies were kosher, you could eat them?"

At that moment one of the corpsman brings Richard two rations—the first one is pork, the second ham and eggs, the ration always the last chosen in a case of twenty-four because of the horrible taste and texture of ham and eggs. He apologizes for the choices and says that resupply will come that afternoon with more C-rations. He also hands him a chunk of plastic explosives to be used in heating up the Cs. Plastics can be burned safely when the fumes aren't inhaled and make a good, steady flame for heating up food in a can. The stuff will explode only when a blasting cap is inserted into the plastics and ignited by a detonating device. Although it is against regulations to carry the stuff, all the grunts have a piece stashed in their packs for this purpose. One always makes friends with one of the combat engineers who carry explosives with them.

Strom slowly opens up the box with the wretched ham and eggs, which includes the small can containing the "main meal," four Winston cigarettes, a can of fruit cocktail, some canned bread, and a package of toilet paper and matches. He throws the ham and eggs away and begins eating the fruit and bread. Already the chaplain is beginning to react with disdain to the less-than-gourmet taste of the main meals contained in a box of C-rations. This disdain is an evolutionary process that transpires over the course of a few months spent out in the bush and one which all grunts experience.

This disgust with the main meal finally culminant in just throwing away all main meals, consuming instead the miscellaneous foods in the box such as the canned bread and fruit, peanut butter and jelly, crackers, and a chocolate rice crispy bar called a clutch plate because it is so dry, it sticks to the roof of one's mouth when eaten.

Chuck sits down on an empty, wooden ammo box next to Richard, twists open a can of corned beef, breaks a piece of white plastic from a small rectangular bar he has retrieved from his pack, drops the stuff in a tiny makeshift stove he has fashioned, lights the explosives, and sets his corn beef on top to heat up. He turns to Richard and says matter-of-factly, "If you're gonna throw that disgusting stuff away, you're supposed to punch a hole in the can first so it spoils and the VC don't get it when we leave this place. That is, if we ever get out of here." There was an edge of sarcasm to his last statement.

As Strom absently eats the fruit cocktail and breaks off a piece of the canned bread, Chuck continues, "I hear you're a Lutheran, aren't you guys kind of like the Catholics?"

The battalion chaplain thinks for a few seconds, then responds, "There are some similarities and some differences." The doctor offers him some warm tea, which Richard turns down, then continues, "We're not as Protestant as our Baptist or Methodist brethren but a little more doctrinaire and liturgical, like the Episcopalians and the Catholics. Maybe something like the differences in Judaism where you have the Orthodox, Conservative, and Reformed traditions. As a comparison, I guess we'd be more like the conservative version of Judaism."

Chuck picks up his can of hot food with a hemostat, sets it down to cool, and replies, "Hum, that's an interesting simile."

Dr. Lieberman grew up in an area of Pittsburgh called Squirrel Hill, attended the University of Pennsylvania, and received his medical degree from Columbia University in New York. His family includes a number of prominent physicians, including his father, a highly respected cardiologist. Chuck is still dumbfounded that he ended up in Vietnam with the Marine infantry three months ago, wishing that he had entered a residency instead of entering the Navy

Medical Corps directly out of medical school. He has said on many occasions, both in and out of the military, that going directly into the navy was the single most stupid thing he has ever done in his entire life.

Chuck finishes his corned beef and tea, then leaves to hold sick call at the BAS. Richard goes back to his gear and, remembering the chewing out he got from the Colonel last night, puts on his helmet and flak jacket, then walks up to the crest of Hill 52. As he nears the top, he sees two jets roar overhead and hears the muffled sounds of explosions in the distance. When he reaches the highest point, he gets a panoramic view of their strategic placement. They are located at the confluence of a river, a mountain range, and a valley stretching twenty kilometers back to Thong Duc. He sees the colonel and the sergeant major a few meters away watch the explosions through binoculars. With some apprehension he slowly approaches them, wondering if the Old Man is still upset with him about last night.

The colonel turns toward his battalion chaplain, points to a hill about four hundred meters away in the distance, and says, "See that hill over the, Chaplain, where that smoke is coming from? Well, those fly boys are softening up that hill for us because shortly Golf is going to begin going up that hill and grab it from Charlie. We can't move down that valley to Thong Duc until we have that hill and the one next to it secured."

With a sweeping motion of his arm, he continues, "That arc light we had this morning should take care of that side. Don't think those people up there are going to have much fight left in them after what those bombers did!"

Suddenly the sergeant major interrupts the conversation and exclaims, "Colonel, that last jet that dropped stuff on that hill is trailing smoke badly." He turns and points his arm toward the disabled jet. "I think he's in trouble!"

Gray-white smoke is now trailing the A-4 Skyhawk jet as it makes a slow circle away from the hill it is bombing back toward Hill 52. Then the sergeant major excitedly yells, "He's bailing out, sir!"

A group of fifteen Marines now gather in amazement as they watch the pilot suddenly eject from the aircraft still strapped to his cockpit seat, quickly separate from the seat, and deploy his chute, then drift lazily toward the ground halfway between Hill 52 and the area he was bombing. The colonel turns immediately toward the CP located thirty meters away and yells instructions to Lieutenant Warneke, the assistant operations officer. "Make sure Golf knows about that downed pilot. He may come down right on top of them."

The second jet is now circling around the slowly descending parachute. The colonel races back to the CP to contact Golf Company, and within a minute there is a Huey gunship and a propeller-driven spotter aircraft called an LV-10 circling the downed pilot as well. The Marines watch the pilot disappear behind a tree line. Immediately the helicopter drops down and follows him in, disappearing into the trees.

After one minute elapses, the Huey rises from beyond the same tree line, does its steep upward spiral, gains altitude, then heads east toward Da Nang. Richard trots back to the CP to find out what is going on and hears that the uninjured pilot almost landed on top of the first platoon of Golf Company. He's a lucky pilot!

"I want to know where that fire came from," the chaplain hears the colonel voice with hostility. "I'm going to drop some of our shit right down their throats." With that, the chaplain walks back to the BAS, suddenly realizing that it has been quite a forty-eight hours since he arrived in An Hoa—rocketed twice, wounded slightly by shrapnel, worked alongside of the corpsmen to stabilize badly injured Marines, observed an awesome arc light, witnessed a pilot get shot down and rescued, got an ass-chewing by the Old Man, and viewed the initial stages of a Marine line company attack a well-fortified, entrenched hill of Viet Cong. As Strom reflects on these events, he again ponders those same questions he had just after the wounded Marines were medevaced last night, wondering about his own emotional and spiritual stamina for the next twelve months. As he enters the BAS, he assures himself that he is going to be okay.

Soon the sun is unbearable. For the members of the BAS and Richard, most of them have never experienced this kind of heat. Since no messages have come into the aid station about impending casualties, the chaplain and four corpsmen take off for the river below them and about one hundred meters away. Falling into the cool river water was a big event; it felt so good to cool off—until enemy small arms fire is heard in the distance. Hearing gunfire creates instant paranoia! Within seconds, Wages yells at Strom, "Chaplain, I'm outta here," runs out of the river, grabs his pants and boots, and hauls up the hill with the battalion chaplain right behind him.

Suddenly, the mortars and big guns on the hill start up, followed by concentrated small arms fire in the distant again as Golf is now making heavy contact with the enemy. The explosions are now more concentrated, being initiated by Golf and the fire coming from battalion headquarters—the bazookas, mortars, grenades, recoilless rifles, 105 howitzers, and airstrikes. For Richard Strom, initially watching the battle take place is exciting. The adrenaline kicks in "like the experience one feels just before the initial kickoff of an important football game between cross town rivals," he thinks to himself.

After a few minutes observing the explosions and the battle raging just a few hundred meters away, Chuck Lieberman sits down next to Richard and says, "We're going to be getting lots of casualties soon. Operations said that the less serious will be coming over here by amtrac where we can triage. This is the Marine Corps way of saying to us that there will probably be lots of wounded coming our way because they don't have enough medevac helicopters to take the dead and wounded back to Da Nang like they're supposed to." The doctor stands up and says absently to the chaplain, "Your presence will be needed," then he heads back inside the BAS.

Suddenly, Richard Strom is jolted to a different reality, a reality of the tragic life-death drama taking place a short distance away. Young men on both sides are getting thrashed and killed and he is observing this as if he's at the movies or watching a staged invasion at Camp Pendleton. An uncomfortable feeling begins to percolate up from his innards, thinking about all those kids over there in horrible, miserable conditions, scared to death. "There are no trees on that hill, it's barren, just a chunk of earth," he realizes, then suddenly a childhood memory flashes by. "When we were kids, we threw dirt clods to capture a small hill and drive the other kids off, only now we're using real bullets and real blood is being spilled. Maybe we were already being conditioned for taking hills way back then." Richard is suddenly feeling big time discomfort and for now it is not going to go away.

As the afternoon progresses, the battle ends as quickly as it started. The BAS is not used for triage. Instead this is done close to the hill where the battle takes place and next to three amtracs that are used for cover. The dead and wounded are transported back to the LZ next to Hill 52 by those same amtracs and placed on medevac choppers, which fly the human cargo back to Da Nang. During this battle to take a nameless tiny piece of real estate, fifty-four Marines are wounded and twelve killed in action.

Later that afternoon, two platoons of Golf pull back to Hill 52 to provide security for that night. Richard is sitting on an ammo box writing letters home to next of kin when a gunnery sergeant from Golf walks up to the aid station and asks to see the battalion chaplain. Strom immediately gets up when he hears this, walks to the two sergeants who looked thrashed and dirty, and introduces himself.

"Sir, the skipper would like it if you could have church services for the two platoons that came back from today's fighting. We got chewed up pretty bad this afternoon and would really appreciate your presence."

Richard's first instinct is to say yes, grab his communion kit, and head out to his platoons. But he remembers the colonel's admonition to him last night about getting people together in groups, so he tells him, "Listen, gunny, I'd be happy to have church services right now but last night the colonel said no groups of people on his hill. Let me check with the CO again and see what he has to say. I'll be in touch shortly."

The chaplain takes a couple of minutes to finish his eighth letter, seals it, then observes another airstrike on the hill where so much dying took place earlier. The sun is dropping lower in the sky and a nice breeze begins to cool things down. He puts on his shirt, flak jacket, and helmet, then heads for the battalion CP, pondering what he needs to say to the colonel about Golf's request and how he can work it out without forming groups.

He is met by that same gunnery sergeant from last night who was the bearer of bad news from the CO. He stops and says, "Chaplain, the colonel wants to see you right away, and, sir, he's not very happy."

"Oh God, now what," the chaplain thinks to himself as they silently walk the remaining steps to the CP. Richard walks through the entrance and immediately finds himself face to face with the colonel. The chaplain instantly presumes that a firefight would be safer and more comfortable than this encounter as the Colonel places his hands on his hips and gives Strom that hard look again, then angrily says, "Chaplain, I thought I told you yesterday there would be no church services on this bill!"

"I didn't schedule—" he begins.

"So less than five minutes ago the sergeant major comes back from Golf's first platoon and reports they're going to have church services—soon! Now I don't know who in the hell you think runs things in this battalion, but I'll tell you one thing, it's not your boss! I don't mess with his weather and he doesn't mess with my command decisions, including the decision whether to hold or not to hold church services!" he spits out.

"Yes, sir," the chaplain attempts to talk before being interrupted again.

"There will be no church services on this hill. Period! *Is that understood*, Chaplain?" he says with emphasis on the word *understood*. "You'll have plenty of chances but not now, dammit."

He turns to go back to his task, then spins around toward the bewildered chaplain and says in a softer tone, "I just can't take the chance of having that many people together even though those guys need church right now more than anything else. I can't give that to them, at least not right now. You go down there to first and second platoon and talk to them individually. I would appreciate that very much." With that he turns and walks back to his radio operator and begins talking to the skipper of Golf on his PC25.

The battalion chaplain leaves silently and upset at the misunderstanding. There are no church services scheduled and he is going to walk down to the south base of the hill anyway to talk to the troops. He mutters to himself as he goes back to get his communion kit, "So now I'm setting a new battalion record for getting chewed out by the Old Man. Hell, I've only been here less than twenty-four hours and he's spit me out twice. He must think I'm a real bozo!" Richard spends the next four hours talking to most of the young Marines from Golf. They are tired, scared, overwhelmed, not wanting to be there. He prays with them, comforts them, and listens to their grief and rage at seeing their buddies maimed and killed. In Strom's mind, just being there, hearing them out, is a sacramental act. He also gives out every single Testament, rosary, and religious medal he has brought from An Hoa. It is, in one way, a fulfilling evening for Richard yet very disquieting at the same time. He lies awake late into the evening, remembering the frightened faces and choking voices of all those young Marines.

His prayer that evening as he lies down on his poncho liner was "This is hard work. Keep me strong, Lord." Within seconds he is fast asleep.

No Turning Back

Chaplain Richard Strom awakens to his second morning in the bush with his infantry battalion. It's a beautiful day, the sun is shining, again mist hangs over the valley adjacent to the mountain range that was heavily bombed yesterday morning, and the heat is already notching up. His poncho fell down during the night and he didn't bother to put it back up, choosing instead to sleep in the open under his poncho liner. There was no rain last night to make sleep unpleasant but the armies of mosquitoes and the heavy dew were just as efficient at making sleep miserable. Richard had forgotten to slop repellent on the exposed parts of his body and now has bites all over his arms, hands, and face. It reminds him of those nights during the late summer months back in Minnesota as a little kid when the mosquitoes would fight each other for space on your arm or forehead. "Gotta learn to pay attention to what the 'long-timers' are telling me," he thinks to himself as he scratches the itchy bumps on his arms and face, remembering what Wages told him about the insects before settling down to sleep and the need to slop lots of repellent on your body.

Across the way on Hill 87 where Golf had waged a fierce battle, Alpha Company from the first battalion, Fifth Marines has been temporarily assigned to second battalion and is now picking up where Golf left off yesterday. They began their assault in an area just past the hill early this morning, again encountering fierce resistance. As the Marines on the hill hear the explosions and small arms fire escalate in the distance, Chuck is returning from the CP and the morning briefing. He sees the chaplain hanging out his liner and socks to dry, approaches him, and says ominously, "Hey, Chaplain,

I guess no one told you that you're supposed to attend the morning staff meeting. Major Sulli, the S3, was complaining to the colonel because you didn't show up. He thinks you purposely slept in."

Strom's heart sinks, wondering if this means another chewing out from the colonel. Spike's admonition to him about keeping a low profile and earning the respect of the Old Man is not bearing fruit at all. Each day brings a new goof, another scolding, and leaves the chaplain questioning his own relevance out in the bush and whether the CO will get rid of him and send him back to the division chaplain.

As Richard is about to respond to the battalion doctor, the colonel appears at the BAS, looks slowly in the direction of his chaplain, and says, "Chaplain, where were you this morning during our staff meeting, sleeping in again?" He then turns to Chuck and says, "Well, whatta ya think, Doctor, is he gonna make it with us or should I just fire his ass right now?"

The colonel turns back to Richard with a smile on his face and answers his own question, "Nah, think I'll keep you around for a while, but learn to ask questions about how we do things in this outfit. That will keep you out of trouble and stop the S3 from pissin' and moanin' about you." Then he continues to talk as he walks with Chuck toward the BAS. "I need some of that medicine for that damn ring worm on my ass."

While most of the staff speaks with some deference to the chaplain and usually do not swear or use profanity, Strom is finally aware that the battalion commander interacts at times with irreverence with him just as he does with all his other staff. There is no fluff or smoke with him; he gets to the bottom line very quickly. So Richard isn't sure if he was chewed out, if he was reprimanded, or if the colonel was just having some fun with him. He decides it was probably all three and overhears the CO tell Leiberman that Alpha is taking casualties just past the hill Golf took and that the battalion CP may move later in the day to be closer to the action. As Richard listens to the fighting going on in the distance, he wonders again how many casualties this line company will sustain today. And again, as it did yesterday, a queasy, uneasy feeling begins to percolate up from his insides, as if some kind of insidious process is taking place in his psyche that he has no control over, that will somehow overload him and eventually annihilate his sensitivities.

"Hey, Chaplain," yells Corpsman First Class Savoie, "it's time for sick call. How's that dressing on your back, need to be changed?"

The battalion chaplain is suddenly drawn back to his own reality and away from thoughts about the Marines a few hundred meters away who are engaged in a life-and-death struggle. He again feels that tad of embarrassment, wanting to go away the wound on his back. "It's okay, Savoie, I'll get it looked at later." Then he turns away from the BAS and walks toward the crest of the hill, not wanting to deal with the injury or to even talk about it. The colonel still isn't aware of it because it was never listed on the battalion report as a casualty and Richard wants it that way. "No more goofs, and keep the information to minimal levels. The more he doesn't know about me, the better," he mutters to himself.

Strom is also worried that Savoie, known for his big mouth, might say something to the S3, so he wasn't about to let him work on his back for that and another significant reason. This lifer had been in the navy far too long and had spent too many nights during his lengthy career imbibing in the many forms of ethanol. Some of the younger corpsmen hold this particular staff NCO up to ridicule claiming he suffers from wet brain, a degenerative condition brought about by too much alcohol. A few of them just refuse to obey his orders. The chief and the doctors usually just humor him, hoping he will be transferred out of the outfit soon. Essentially, First Class Savoie is a buffoon that no one takes seriously. So the chaplain isn't about to let this guy poke around in his back!

Morning is the only cool time of the day. By noon the temperature hovers past ninety and is matched by a humidity that is close to eighty percent. The Marines on the hill attempt to stay cool by moving as little as possible and setting up some kind of shade under which they can sit or lay down. The fighting beyond Hill 87 has stopped and Alpha Company is moving strategically closer to Hill 100, the main objective of the battalion for now. Once they capture that hill from the NVA, the rest of the battalion will move down the valley toward Thong Duc to relieve the special forces. The speculation among the Marines is that if they don't get there soon, there are not going to be any special forces to relieve.

After a relatively calm night, with little outgoing artillery to keep everyone awake, the battalion has word from division that they will be moving out shortly. So early that morning battalion headquarters breaks down their equipment and packs up their gear, leaving the artillery behind on the hill with one platoon from Golf remaining as security. The battalion staff gets into column and begins moving off the hill and on the road leading past their old position. What then transpires constitutes an experience common to all Marines serving with the infantry. Just when everything is in readiness, after all the gear is packed, when everyone is psyched up to leave, the order is given to stand down, which means to wait where you are until further instructions come from on high. Sometimes this waiting can last for two to three hours. So having taken down the meager shelters that protected most of them from the hot sun, they now have their helmets and flak jackets on and are fully loaded up, usually with at least sixty pounds of gear, completely exposed to the heat and are told to sit on their behinds frying in the sun, waiting for something to happen.

What usually comes to pass, eventually, after waiting for an hour or two in the sun with nothing happening, is the desire to eat or the need to empty oneself of yesterday's fine gourmet food a la C-rations—which means taking a few minutes to prepare a meal or go hang out in the bushes for five minutes.

The chaplain has been waiting patiently like all the other Marines, assuming they would be there for the rest of the day, when he makes a decision based on biological necessity. This decision becomes problematic because when he is in the bushes, right in the middle of divesting himself, he hears the order being given for the battalion to move out immediately!

Richard isn't about to be caught with his pants down, fearful of incurring the wrath of the Old Man again because he isn't standing in formation. He comes roaring out of the bushes, pulling up his pants running to his gear. As he is doing this, the CO walks by him with his radioman at his side and says, "Chaplain, why are you always doing weird things?" That's all he says as he walks on while Richard is struggling to get his gear together and his pack and communion kit on his back, running at the same time to find his place in the already moving column.

The battalion doctor is following Strom, snickering as he says, "That was right out of a Marx brothers' movie. Way to go, Chaplain!"

The column is slowly heading down Highway 4, which is actually a narrow dirt road, like the type one would drive on in rural America. But here there aren't cornfields and friendly farms, only unfamiliar land and a hostile enemy wanting the Americans dead. Shortly, Richard passes by four Marines and a Vietnamese interpreter interrogating three men on bicycles. They are the meanest-looking Vietnamese he has ever seen, and if looks could kill, especially from the one who disdainfully spit on the ground every few seconds, then all of them would be dead! As Strom passes by the spitter, he can see how powerful he is built, and he has no shoes or sandals on his feet, which look more like bear paws than human appendages. Because of his powerful build and angry look, the chaplain assumes he is Viet Cong and wonders what will happen to him.

After twenty minutes of marching in column, the heat is incredible. The battalion doctor is puking right in front of Richard while he squeezes vomit from his nose with thumb and index finger, pinky sticking straight up in the air. "As if he's drinking a cup of tea," Strom thinks to himself as he experiences dizziness and a headache himself. "God, I hope I don't blow chunks myself," he says absently to no one, perspiration completely soaking his shirt and pants. There are three Marines lying by the side of the road passed out, Corpsmen attending them. Richard's only thought at that moment is how good a glass of his mom's homemade lemonade would taste right now.

The column now stopped. Richard slows turning around and faces a Marine behind him who says, "I'd give my left nut right now for a cold beer," then he realizes he is looking directly at the battalion chaplain. "Ah, I'm sorry, didn't, ah, mean it," he stutters.

"Careful what you give away there. The Lord only gave you two, you know," the chaplain replies with a smile. The young Marine looks at Richard as if he doesn't know whether to laugh or cry.

It is later, midafternoon, and battalion is stopped by a large grove of trees adjacent to the road. The colonel is nervous because S2 reported enemy soldiers have somehow slipped through Alpha's lines and infiltrated the area to which the forward CP is now headed. At this point all battalion headquarters has no security since the two platoons of Golf marching with them had moved on to help out Alpha Company. There is a general aura of uneasiness throughout battalion.

Richard and Chuck are next to each other under a bush, lying down against their packs, attempting to stay as cool as possible, an impossible task given the high temperatures and humidity, but also because the flies have taken over the day shift from the mosquitoes and are buzzing and dive-bombing their faces. Insects are just another one of the discomforting and irritating living experiences grunts face each day: mosquitoes by the millions at night, hoards of flies during the day, and lizards, snakes, centipedes, beetles, and various flying bugs assaulting their bodies minute by minute. It's a zoologist's paradise and an infantryman's nightmare.

"Lousy damn waiting," Strom hisses, impatiently brushing flies away from his face, "this is driving me nuts!"

"Get used to it, Chaplain," Chuck replies, "most of your waking time out here in the bush will be waiting around. Don't let it get you down."

Richard sits up, takes along drink of water from his canteen, turns to the doctor, and says, "Those poor Marines with Golf and Alpha, going up that hill under fire. I don't know how they can handle the heat with all that gear on their bodies."

Chuck turns toward the chaplain with an incredulous look on his face and replies, "You know what, going up that hill under fire, when the shrapnel and bullets are flying all over the place, when you're in deep shit and frightened out of your mind, I don't think anybody is focused on the heat—"

KRUUMP... KRUUMP... KRUUMP... KRUUMP! The loud, horrifying explosions of enemy mortars suddenly go off adjacent to the river one hundred twenty meters away, about the length of a football field, then followed by small arms fire raking the area where battalion is now taking a rest. This isn't measured, aimed rifle fire but rather a fuselage of bullets sprayed toward the general direction of battalion. The explosions and small arms fire lasts fifteen seconds, then stops as suddenly as it started. Dull, endless boredom—immediate, instantaneous terror. The twin elements of life the combat infantryman lives with day after day after day.

"Get special weapons to put some fire on that tree line by the river," yells the S3, "and radio Golf that we need some security right goddamn now!"

Immediately following his directive the Marines open up with their M-16s, bazookas, and grenade launchers, saturating the tree line close to the river, sounding like the Fourth of July celebration in any small town in America. However, this isn't Nebraska or Tennessee celebrating with firecrackers and fireworks but rather this is the deadly sounds of bullets and projectiles being fired for a singular purpose—to maim and kill. There is little organization to the firing and is an immediate, instinctual response to the chaos and confusion brought about when suddenly fired upon.

Chuck and Richard are behind trees, hunkered as close to the ground as possible, paralyzing fear penetrating every thought and emotion in their bodies as the bullets whiz through the trees overhead. When the enemy shooting stops, Richard loudly whispers to the doctor, "Hey, Chuck, what are we supposed to do now?"

"Just shut up and don't move," Leiberman responds in a frightened but irritated voice, "and keep your head down."

Richard feels that throbbing pain in his lower back again, just like the night he arrived on Hill 52 when he was greeted by enemy rocket fire. He can hear his heart beating furiously against his rib cage, his breathing is short and shallow, and he feels a tremendous urge to urinate. He suddenly recalls the conversation he and Chuck were having, then remembers that he had completely forgotten the heat and misery during the recent eternity called a thirty-second firefight, feeling foolish he had made those stupid comments.

"Hey, Chuck," Strom whispers, "know what?"

The doctor responds with irritation again. "Yeah, what?"

"You were right, I completely forgot about the heat and humidity," Richard says with some relief in his voice, "because that scared the living shit out of me."

Chuck says nothing and remains flat on the ground. Beyond them about thirty meters away the chaplain hears the distinct voice of the colonel talking on his radio. Not wanting to be thought of as being timid or panicky, the chaplain stands and sees the CO heading directly toward him with Major Sulli. They stop right in front of Chuck who is now standing himself, and as Colonel Stevens talks on the radio to Golf, he urinates on a tree close by. As he continues his bodily task, he finishes his radio conversation, turns to Richard, and says, "You need to talk to your boss about the progress we're making and let him know we need some help. At this rate we'll never get to our objectives."

Richard wants to respond, but the colonel continues, "That's the kind of hit and, um, stuff the enemy pulls all the time. We were lucky today, no casualties."

He finishes, turns to the chaplain, and continues, "You're supposed to have a chaplain's assistant, huh, Padre? Well, when we secure from this operation and get back to An Hoa, we'll work something out." He looks toward the area when they had just a few minutes ago been fired upon, then turns back toward Richard Strom and says, "Until then, try to stay out of trouble, Chaplain."

Richard can hardly believe what he has just experienced. The enemy had a short time ago fired directly upon the battalion with mortars and small arms, and his assumption is that they may still be in the area. So the colonel shortly after the incident walks over to where he is located and urinates on a tree while he is carrying on a conversation over the radio with Golf and with him. Then calmly walks back to his original position. The chaplain again isn't sure what to think about the Old Man. "Is he fearless? Is he stupid? Why is he always focused on me and giving me a ration of crap?" he ponders.

In the meantime, first platoon from Golf has secured the area next to the river. So the order is given to move out. The battalion column moves slowly down the road, crosses the small river that is knee-deep, and passes through a village just past the stream.

Just as they pass by the village, the column is confronted by one of the odd realities of the war. There are four young children, ages six to ten, standing by the side of the road, selling Coca-Cola by the can to the passing Marines. These kids are standing there with a whole case of sodas, the battalion is miles and miles away from the nearest Marine installation that would even have this item available, and they are practicing the art of capitalism in the midst of a very recent firefight.

Richard shakes his head in disbelief, knowing a case of that stuff costs $2.25 at the PX and also wonders what they do with the military script once they've made a sale. "Numba one Marine, one dolla," says a youngster, who hands a can of Coke to Richard.

The Marines out in the bush usually do not have the luxury of canned soda or beer. So these kids have quite a hustle going for them because the grunts will pay at least that much for a soda or beer, even if it is warm. The chaplain calmly drops his pack to retrieve his wallet, pulls out one dollar in military script, and buys the Coke from the child. As he smiles and gets back in the formation, he is reminded of a hustle kids put on him a few years back when he and some friends went to see the White Sox and parked their car in a lot near Cominsky Park. Three young kids about ten years old suddenly showed up and told them they would "protect" their car for two bucks! Richard paid and nothing happened to his car. His smile came about because he is thinking how universal some of the behaviors kids have. No matter where you find kids in the world, under all kinds of circumstances, they're out there hustling, attempting to stay alive. "Hooray for kids!" he thinks to himself.

That evening the battalion sets up their CP in a large gully-like ravine at the bottom of Hill 87, which was finally secured by Golf that afternoon. So far on this operation the battalion has suffered ninety casualties—eighteen killed and seventy-two wounded, a high percentage since the battalion has a field strength of just over five hundred. Echo is to secure Hill 100 beginning tomorrow, an event that will again stir up the enemy that has been holding onto their territory with tenacity and daring.

The next morning a messenger interrupts the chaplain's break-fast of canned bread, fruit cocktail, and hot chocolate to tell him that Colonel Stevens wants to see him as soon as possible. Richard experiences instant paranoia! "What have I done this time? Did I say something that angered the Old Man again? Does my family have an emergency back home? When am I going to just be left alone to do my job?" he thinks as he hurriedly shoves the food into his mouth.

So that by the time he reaches the CP, he figures he was on his way to another chewing out. Again he didn't keep the initial low pro-file that Spike had so carefully counseled him to keep. "Low profile my ass," he whispers to himself.

The colonel is sitting on an empty ammo box next to the ser-geant major, eating a can of peaches. As Strom approaches him, he can feel his body tense, getting ready for the next onslaught. "Lord," he prays to himself, "have an enemy rocket go off harmlessly out in the rice paddy right now, please?"

"Oh, there you are, Chaplain. We're gonna be stuck in this posi-tion for a few days while Echo secures Hill 100. So I'd like you to catch a ride into Da Nang and see our troopers in the hospitals. I think that's the most important thing you can do for them right now since we can't hold any church services. And what the hell, Padre, it's just as good as church, isn't it?" he says to Richard as he looks up between spoonfuls of peaches.

"Yes, ah, it can, sir, yes." He stumbles through his response, feeling confused, assuming he was in for another ass-chewing.

"Catch a ride back to Da Nang, or wherever they are, and see them all. Get back when you're finished. And no fartin' around in Da Nang," he continues with a smile.

"Yes, sir," Strom replies, then heads back to his sleeping area next to the BAS. Chuck is rotating back to An Hoa today and Bernie will be replacing him. He will be coming out from regiment medical supplies shortly on a medevac he secured in An Hoa. This means the chaplain and doctor will not have to wait for the arrival of the regular supply chopper that could take hours before they would be able to get back to An Hoa.

Within an hour, Chuck and Richard and three wounded Marines are onboard the medevac chopper and head around the mountain range toward Da Nang instead of An Hoa. As they see An Hoa being left far off in the distance, Chuck turns toward Richard with a look of disgust and yells loudly that well-known Marine word that has to do with the act of procreation. He's been here before: stuck in Da Nang with his dirty field gear, more than likely unable to catch a ride back to An Hoa for at least a day, staying overnight in strange quarters.

When they do arrive in Da Nang the wounded are let off at First Medical Battalion, where Chuck chooses to stay. Richard gets a ride up the road to First Recon, getting soaked in the process, where he gets his first shower in a week, some clean clothes to wear and the greatest-tasting cold beer he's ever consumed in his life. Lieutenant Ursini lends the chaplain his jeep and has the top put on so he won't get wet. Soon he's heading across the river, turns right past the Catholic seminary and school, and continues another mile to the Naval Support Hospital.

It continues to rain as the jeep pulls into a large parking lot and helicopter receiving area. The hospital itself is made up of twenty Quonset huts and a number of larger temporary pre-fab buildings. Chaplain Strom immediately heads for the chaplain's office because he will have the most complete and up-to-date list of field casualties. With all the wounded *Two-five* has experienced the past week, Richard will stay busy the rest of the afternoon.

Finding patients from his unit is a hassle and quite frustrating. Every list the Marines give him is at least two days out of date. So he has to check with each individual ward, a very time-consuming job. That afternoon, spread out over five hours, Chaplain Strom sees thirty-eight Marines. Most have non-life-threatening wounds; some are critical and probably will not survive. There are also six malaria cases, two bad cases of dysentery, and one had an emergency appendectomy. Twenty-three have been medevaced out of Vietnam to either Japan or the Philippines. This is done to keep as many beds open as possible should division become engaged in heavy fighting and overwhelmed with wounded.

Initially, Richard feels a level of discomfort talking to the Marines of his battalion because he is new and has not developed a relationship with them. Then he meets a badly injured Marine in ICU—his name is Mateo—who has lost one leg below his hip and his other leg below his knee, while losing one arm below the elbow. He was wounded by an enemy mortar the first day Golf went up Hill 82.

Chaplain Strom is sitting down next to the severely thrashed Marine, holding his one remaining hand as he is telling Richard that someone who speaks Spanish needs to talk to his parents who do not understand any English.

"Father," he says slowly, blurring the normal distinction between Catholics and Protestants, knowing only that Richard is the battalion chaplain, "let them know I'm okay and I'm gonna be home soon." There are tears in his eyes as he exacts a promise from Richard that he will follow through. "Please contact my priest back in Victoria, Texas, he needs to talk to my parents. They will be very upset. Will you do this for me, Father?"

Richard assures the young Marine that he will follow through on his promise that evening. He then prays with him, and as he leaves, again he promises Mateo he will follow through. Strom leaves feeling sad but more relaxed than he did when he arrived four hours earlier. He realizes that when he is relaxed, the Marines are more relaxed as well, creating an environment of openness where they are willing to talk about their feelings, about being in the hospital and the larger issues of life and death. The belief of invincibility is long gone for all of them now that they have experienced the horrifying reality of combat.

Most of the young Marines want to know what is happening to their individual platoons or if they are to be transferred back to the field again. Going back out to the bush from a hospital bed is a very depressing and discouraging event, having survived death and dismemberment. Some of the wounded want to pray with the chaplain; others just wish to chat. Three Marines asked to be left alone. The more seriously they are wounded, however, the greater their need to have their parents reassured they are okay and will be home soon.

Most of them extract a promise from Chaplain Strom that he will write home to their parents as soon as possible. Richard stays up very late, writing letters and sending a radio message to Father John Soto in Victoria, Texas, about the condition of Mateo Ybarra.

As he settles down that night in a bed with clean sheets and a roof over his head, he thinks about how nice it is seeing his friends again at First Recon, at not getting paranoid at the thought of rockets or bullets firing at you. He remembers, just before sleep finally does come, that he is feeling the need to be with his battalion out in the bush. It is the first time he feels a personal need to be with them.

NOAH'S FLOOD, PART II

The monsoons have hit full force! The past two days the rains have virtually stopped vehicles from moving, airplanes from flying, and Marines from fighting. The streets of Da Nang are flooded and the outlying areas surrounding the city are virtually isolated. In between breaks of the deluge, Richard finds himself at First Medical Battalion visiting the remaining twenty-three wounded troops from his outfit, then finally managing to secure a helicopter flight back to his battalion now located adjacent to Hill 87.

At this point he is aware of a desire to be back with his own outfit, but upon exiting the helicopter, he is appalled at the deterioration of living conditions and morale since leaving only four days ago. What really disturbs him is learning that shortly after he left for Da Nang, a supply helicopter and a medevac collided in midair right over the river less than two hundred meters away from battalion. It was raining and the medevac had just taken of while the supply chopper was delivering some needed ammunition and food for the troops. Those not killed by the impact of the collision or by hitting the ground were burned to death after impact. Seven crewmen, four wounded Marines, and three replacement troops were killed in the carnage.

On that fateful day Richard and Chuck had procured a ride back to Da Nang in a medevac chopper that brought in medical supplies and the other battalion surgeon, Bernie Grant. The irony is that Bernie had talked one of the pilots at An Hoa into making a special trip out to battalion to bring him and the supplies. Had he not cajoled the pilot into bringing him out that morning, Richard and

Chuck would have been on the regular morning supply helicopter that was to later crash and burn.

Richard swallows hard as Bernie explains the terrible midair collision, realizing how close he came to dying in a fiery crash—just another cup of coffee, an extra five minutes on the head, a ten-minute talk with a Marine with a problem and he would have been on that chopper. "It's mind-boggling," he finally says to the doctor after hearing about the disaster, "knowing how close I came to getting snuffed." Richard and Bernie now slog toward an amtrac a few meters away, the chaplain still very shaken by the news. "Lives are saved and limbs are lost by seconds and inches," he continues shaking his head. "I guess it's been that way for thousands of years regardless how primitive or sophisticated the weapons."

"Yeah, well, that's just the way stuff happens, can't do anything about it," is Bernie's jaded response.

They approach the amtrac, which is now the battalion aid station, and walk inside. The chaplain dumps his gear and makes preparations to eat, his first meal of the day. The corpsmen are playing cards and have little to do since there have been very few casualties the past few days. With the exception of an occasional rocket, mortar, or small arms fire, things are relatively quiet. Golf and Echo are now located on top of bills 87 and 100 respectively, both under constant fire day and night. It was a very miserable existence with little cover from the elements. Then when night falls, the fear factor goes up to at least a 7 on a scale of 1 to 10. Darkness is the one element the enemy always uses to its advantage since the Marines are in known, fixed positions because they get a bead on their Marine targets in the daytime, sit back until night, then drop their mortars and fire their rockets from a distance.

The next morning, after breakfast, Richard wanders around the area talking to the troops. Most are very discouraged about the rains but also angry that they had been moved off Hill 52, marched only one kilometer, then given the order to set in and stay for a few days.

"At least on the hill we didn't have to worry about drowning," a young corporal angrily mutters as Strom slogs toward the CP to talk to the colonel about his hospital visits.

After spending a few minutes briefing Stevens on the wounded he saw in Da Nang, the chaplain turns away from the colonel and sarcastically suggests to no one in particular that there had been some pretty stupid planning by the "Neanderthals" who had moved the whole battalion off Hill 52 and down into the "valley of mud" the day before "Noah's Flood, part 2 had struck." In doing so, Richard assumes the decision has been made by regiment or division.

Just as Strom is walking out of the CP, the colonel clears his throat and says angrily, "Chaplain, since I made that decision on my own and division concurred, I must be the Neanderthal you are referring to."

Richard cannot believe what he is hearing, then turns red-faced toward the colonel, embarrassed out of his mind. "You know what? I don't appreciate smart-asses, especially chaplain smart-asses," the colonel continues, "so instead of always getting yourself in trouble, why don't you do something useful like going to Golf and Echo and have church for them!"

Dumbfounded, the chaplain is immobile, not sure if he should apologize for his remarks or walk out and follow the Old Man's directive. Stevens stares at the chaplain for a few seconds, a smile slowly forming on his face. The colonel then quickly turns away from Strom and engages Major Sulli, who is obviously enjoying the drama. "Get the sky pilot some security for his hump up to Golf. I want him banished!".

"Yes, sir," is Richard's nervous reply after a long awkward pause.

"Wait here, Chaplain," Sulli then says with derision, "we'll get you three Marines to take you up the hill so you don't get lost."

Shortly the battalion chaplain has three Marines assigned to him as security and told again by Stevens to head up the mountain in the rain and have religious services for Golf and Echo. Richard goes back to the amtrac, packs his communion kit, puts on his helmet and flak jacket, and leaves for the line companies in a pouring rain.

Which is why Strom presently has a special place in his heart for the prophet Jeremiah, who was always getting banished for saying things the king didn't like. As the four of them begin their trek, he prayerfully thinks to himself, "Lord, make me an instrument of your peace, but help me to keep my mouth shut in front of the colonel!"

Although it is raining hard, the climb is slippery and the VC continue to fire intermittently at the Marines on the hill, in one way Richard feels good that he can finally have church services and do something constructive for the battalion. But he also feels somewhat guilty that the three Marines traveling with him are giving up some relative comfort by getting soaked and dirty.

As the group pauses for a rest, Chaplain Strom turns to the Marine in the lead. "Sorry, you have to walk up the hill in this misery for me," he says between some heavy breathing. "Just want you to know how much I appreciate what you guys are doing."

"No problem," responds the sergeant in charge, "this will get us out of going on patrol tonight. This is easy!"

"Maybe they also think it'll get them some brownie points with the Lord as well," Richard muses to himself as they continue their push up the hill.

The four of them struggle for twenty more minutes through swollen creeks, over slippery mud, and through underbrush that is dense and tears at their clothing and gear. The last part is the toughest as they labor over rocks, more mud and brush up a very steep hillside. They finally reach an area close to the top of the hill and emerge into a clearing that is more mud than vegetation where they are greeted by the company commander, apprehensive about their delay. As Richard moves toward the skipper, he now understands why they call him Goofy Golf; he stands over six-five and actually looks like the cartoon character Goofy.

Captain Moore extends a very large wet hand and shakes the chaplain's hand. "Kind of worried about you, sir, still lots of activity with the enemy. You get lost around here and Charlie will most definitely cut your throat," he says in a monotone. Richard is then led toward a thicket of bamboo at the side of the hill where the Golf CP is now located. This is a cluster of sandbags four high surrounding wooden ammo boxes that have been stacked about six feet high to create a makeshift enclosure. Over the top canvas has been stretched to keep out the rain. Primitive but functional as are most battalion, company, and platoon CPs out in the field.

Ed Moore then directs the chaplain inside the CP out of the rain and motions for him to sit down on a box inside the door. After offering him some food, which Richard declines, the skipper then says, "I would like you to have church services for each of my three platoons, Chaplain. Need to do this to avoid a cluster foxtrot. Charlie is still lobbing shit on the hill, so I want to keep the crowd down and leave the other two platoons out there for security. Hope you don't mind having three services this afternoon."

"No problem at all, Skipper," Strom says as he stands and picks up his communion kit from the damp ground. "Let me know where you want me to have services and we'll get on it right now." Shortly, as Richard leaves the CP, anxiety begins to creep up as he ponders the captain's words about the cluster foxtrot, a polite term for having too many troops congregated in one place where taking a direct hit could be disastrous. The word *foxtrot*, in this usage, is mostly used when the chaplain is present instead of that other four-letter word Marines use for the act of copulation.

Captain Moore directs the company staff sergeant to find a suitable place and shortly Richard is standing in a gully-like depression off to the south side of the hill. Were it not raining he would be able to see battalion about a kilometer away down in the valley. He builds an altar out of three empty ammunition boxes and within five minutes there are forty-five Marines with him, all there voluntarily, in the rain, waiting for church services to begin. Most of them came out of their "riggins" where they were relatively dry so they could attend their first church service in a month. Although wet and physically miserable, Richard feels for the first time since arriving in the field that he is in the right place in spite of the Colonel's banishment.'

It rains hard off and on through all three services. If there were Marines who didn't attend, the chaplain can count them all on one hand. It is also spooky on that hillside, wondering if a mortar or rocket will come screaming into the hill during services. Nervous and anxious as he starts the first service, he soon forgets about his misery and fear. Since he is out in the open, the altar the three empty ammo boxes piled on top of each other, he has no way of protecting himself from the rain, especially when he begins to serve Holy Communion. A problem arises because the flat communion breads have a tendency to get sticky and glob together when they get wet. It is at this point that an event transpires that prints an indelible picture in Richard's mind, a happening that alters his normal way of looking at things he usually considers to be either sacred or profane.

Each chaplain is free to utilize whatever tradition he comes from in leading worship services. Strom uses an accepted practice in the Lutheran denomination for serving communion called intinction—a method of dipping the communion host in the wine from a chalice and placing the wafer into the mouth of the communicant. As he begins to serve communion, the rain intensifies, and the paten that contains the hosts is getting wet. Suddenly Richard leans over and says to a young private sitting right in front of the altar, brand-new to the field, "Could you fetch me something to hold over the communion stuff to keep it dry?" The young Marine immediately jumps up and runs off for thirty seconds while Chaplain Strom holds his helmet over the hosts.

When Private Gorman returns, he is clutching a magazine under his arm, opens up the magazine, which he then holds over the hosts, keeping the wafers dry so the chaplain can serve communion. At this point Richard asks the Marines who wish to have communion to now come to the altar, holds the chalice in one hand, picks up a host, and dips it in the wine and places it in the mouth of each communicant. All the while, the young Marine continues to hold the paten with the communion wafers with one hand, while the other hand holds the magazine over the hosts keeping them dry.

It is halfway through serving communion when Richard notices that the magazine the young Marine is holding over the communion hosts is a copy of *Playboy*. Chaplain Strom's immediate thought is, "Oh my God, can you believe this?" He dips another wafer in the wine and says to the young Marine in front of him, "The body and blood of Christ," then another thought comes to him: "A copy of *Playboy* being used as a tabernacle of sorts to protect the consecrated body and blood of Christ, oh boy!"

In an instant Strom is mindful that this action of a young Marine holding a copy of *Playboy* over consecrated sacramental bread and wine is enough to send any liturgical or dogmatic purist into theological apoplexy. Not understanding the conditions and the context in which this magazine is being used, obviously most Christians will think this action by a young Marine, and especially the chaplain who permits this, to be a gross sacrilegious act, or at the very least, extremely tacky. However, Strom gives no credence that this will profane the sacrament. As a matter of fact, after his initial shock, as he continues to commune the rest of the Marines, he is quite moved that this young Marine is willing to sacrifice his magazine to make the distribution of Holy Communion an easier task for him and a meaningful experience for the platoon. Strom realizes this magazine is a very prized possession for a grunt way out here in the field. Aside from whatever entertainment the Marine derived from its reading/looking, he can also trade it for cigarettes, food, beer, and any of the other barter materials that Marines want or need out in the bush. The rain will soon trash the magazine and make it worthless. As Richard turns back to the makeshift altar after communing the last Marine, he thinks to himself, "There's gotta be some kind of lesson here," then places the chalice and paten on top of the empty ammo boxes, covering the paten with his helmet.

Chaplain Strom turns back toward the Marines who are now standing, Gorman by his side, then raises his arm and pronounces the blessing: "The peace of God, which passes all understanding, keep your hearts and minds in the knowledge and love of his Son Jesus Christ our Lord. And the blessings of the Father"—he now makes the sign of the cross—"the Son, and the Holy Spirit be with you and remain with you always. Amen."

Richard immediately turns to the young Marine by his side and says, "Hey, thanks for your help, you did a good job."

"Yes, sir," he responds with a tad of embarrassment, "I hope I didn't do nothin' wrong by using that, ah magazine. It was the only thing I could find in my pack that might work."

Richard slowly retrieves the wet, trashed magazine from the top of the makeshift altar, hands it back to Private Gorman, then places his hand on his shoulder and says softly, "You did just fine, son. In this case, *Playboy* was used very unselfishly and with love. In fact you did so well, I'm hoping you'll help me out with the next two services. How about it?"

The young Marine responds with an enthusiastic smile on his face. "Yes, sir! I would be happy to sir!" With that he runs on to get permission from his platoon sergeant as Richard sets up the next service for second platoon. Within an hour the chaplain has communed the entire company in the most miserable of conditions one can imagine—continuous rain, sporadic small arms fire, and always, the young Marine by his side, now holding a wooden board from an ammo box over the altar and paten. Each service makes Richard Strom aware of a connection he is beginning to establish with these young men, sharing their terrible milieu and lifestyle, experiencing a few moments of peace together, a small, peaceful chunk of time torn out of the ugliness of people killing each other.

Then another of those strange oddities happens. Many of the Marines hang out after the communion service and thank him for coming. For Richard, he is just doing his job. He is doing what he is supposed to do, being where his "congregation" is, going to them instead of them coming to him, sharing in their misery and anxiety and depravation. He is finding out that when he comes to them in the midst of their fighting and dying they are always very grateful and open to him about their feelings, which of course is never the case back at Camp Pendleton or even at regiment back in An Hoa. He never gets that kind of feedback from the troops in the States or in the rear. Out here all the toughness, all the bravado, all the pretenses are pretty much stripped away. It is a pretty basic survival experience. When this happens, the simple priorities of staying alive line up real fast! And that usually means taking care of one's spiritual needs. By the time Richard is ready to leave, he has a long list of wounded Golf Marines that have been medevaced out of the bush and promises to find out their disposition before coming back to see them. He then turns to Private Gorman, still standing at his side. "Listen, son, you did such a great job with me. How'd you like to be my chaplain's assistant, permanently?"

"Yes, sir, I'd like that, sir," he responds enthusiastically.

"Give me your serial number and I'll put in a request through H&S," the chaplain now says calmly to Private Gorman. "It may take a few days, but we're gonna see a lot of each other."

After getting the information down, the ecstatic young private literally runs down the hill to his platoon to share the good news. Richard's thoughts are suddenly interrupted by the skipper, who says Echo is taking too much small arms and mortar fire to go up there. "One-niner return to CP at once," said the message from the colonel.

On the return trip it takes the four of them almost two hours to return to the CP because the two creeks they crossed on the way up are really swollen now and too dangerous to cross. So they walk another path that leads them around the CP instead of directly to it. This again creates paranoia for Strom because by the time they get close to battalion, it is almost dark. Richard is soaked again, muddy, miserable, tired, and hungry. After having slid down the hillside above battalion for over one hundred meters, in thick, gooey mud, the chaplain is reminded of the parable in the New Testament about pigs being driven down a hill into a lake to drown because they are considered unclean and undesirable, wondering if the Old Man is still angry and considers his chaplain to be "unclean and undesirable." Still he is happy to be back in the relative safety of battalion.

Since it's been raining heavily now for the past few days, even the foxholes that were dug earlier for protection are now filled with water. One doesn't attempt to stay dry. One merely tries hard to keep from getting soaked. Earlier in the day before Richard left to go up the hill, he and the doctor had buckled their ponchos together to make a small tent-like covering and are now bunk-mates.

There are a number of noncombat battles in this kind of rain that one must work with simultaneously. For instance, once inside their dwelling, after Richard returned from his sojourn, the two of them are in the dark with their flashlights on, attempting to widen the drip trench around their ponchos with Kbars to keep the water from running underneath their dwelling. If they don't get a deep enough trench, their rubber ladies will float away—literally! As they are doing this, they are also in the midst of trying to wolf down some quick food and fighting off the huge ants that are desperately, by the hundreds, attempting to find high dry ground on their packs, bodies, and bedrolls. If that isn't enough, suddenly they hear small arms fire coming from the platoon just to the south of them fifty meters away. If the firefight gets intense or if any incoming mortars or rockets explode in the area, Bernie and Richard have a choice: stay where they are and continue doing what they are doing or jump into a water-filled foxhole, miss getting shrapnel up their asses, and drown in the process.

After two more hours of heavy precipitation, the downpour finally subsides to a steady rain, most of the ants have been brushed off their packs and bodies, the Mississippi River is no longer winding through their dwelling and the small arms fire has stopped. Bernie is angry since the small arms fire close to them has negated the use of flashlights because it obviously makes a nice target, which means he can't read his latest skin book from Hong Kong. So they just lay on their bed rolls, miserable, wet, bored, wondering how to survive the night. It is the same everywhere with all the Marines and corpsmen, except for the two amtrac crews who sleep in their vehicles dry and comfortable.

"Goddammit, Chaplain, this is miserable and no one should have to live in this shit," Bernie suddenly cries out.

It is right at this miserable moment Richard remembers he still has a mostly full canteen of Chivas Regal. He grabs his canteen belt and lifts out the container with scotch whiskey, hands it to Bernie, and informs the doctor of its contents.

"Bless you, my boy," says Bernie as Richard hands him the canteen in complete darkness. He takes a long, hard hit on the stuff, then hands the canteen back to Richard, and exclaims in a voice feeling the pain of straight whiskey, "Shit, Chaplain, scotch always tasted like puke to me. But tonight, it's the most delicious puke I've ever tasted in my life!"

Within twenty minutes there is a near empty canteen. By thirty minutes they're swacked! They begin singing songs in harmony as they move from good old gospel songs like "Amazing Grace" to pop tunes from Oklahoma to the kind of songs one sings at fraternity beer busts or battalion drinking parties at Camp Pendleton. As the rain again increases in intensity, so does the volume of their melodious sounds. Just as they are getting into a good, loud chorus of "I used to work in Chicago, in a department store, I used to work in Chicago, I did but I don't anymore…," they suddenly hear right outside their tent the very distinct, clipped New England accent of the Sergeant Major yelling at the two of them, assuming they are a couple of young enlisted Marines: "Where the hell were you guys born, in a barn? Knock that damn garbage off—right now!"

Bernie then giggles loudly as the chaplain meekly yells out, "Okay, Sergeant Major," attempting to masquerade his voice so the sergeant won't know he's yelling at his two naval officers.

"We can hear you clear up here at the CP, you dummies! You keep it up and Charlie will unload a rocket right up your ass," he says as the doctor and chaplain are doing everything in their power to keep from laughing out loud.

Richard hears the sergeant major leave, then still laughing, says to Bernie, "That's all we need right now, have the Old Man find out we've knocked off close to a fifth of scotch, the two people in his outfit he needs to count on playing the rules and being straight."

Bernie then whispers loudly to Richard, "Shit, Chaplain, now I can't sing my opera stuff for you. Did you know I can sing a number of operatic arias?"

"Since I'm a somewhat cloddish, uncultured Midwesterner, that's fine with me. I don't believe I can handle opera sung by an Alabama redneck," he responds.

For the next two hours they tell each other their story, Bernie a city boy from Birmingham, Alabama, and Richard the farm boy from south-central Minnesota and sling more bullshit during that two hours than a Bandini salesman could sell in a whole year. And that night Bernie Grant and Richard Strom become the closest of friends in spite of Noah's flood, part 2.

CHANGING REALITIES

Because of the heavy rains, just about everything has shut down except attempting to stay alive. Even the VC and the NVA have withdrawn into their holes and caves up in the hills and have stopped firing their intermittent mortars and rockets. The battalion has long terminated any further search-and-destroy missions within a five-kilometer radius of their perimeter.

The rain is constant, day and night, sometimes heavy. Living out in the open in this kind of a combat situation makes for misery and feelings of doom and helplessness. It sucks the life energy out of the combatant, reducing the living experience to survival only. This in turn creates anger, hostility, and a resignation to depression and hopelessness. There is nothing to look forward to except more rain or getting one's limbs blown away by a sneak rocket or two.

It's been five days since Chaplain Strom returned from Hill 87 and Golf Company. He can't remember feeling as depressed as he does again this morning, waking up once more to the sound of rain pounding against the poncho-tent he and Bernie have constructed over and over again the past few days. Bernie just left to relieve himself in the bushes nearby, Richard is lying on his air mattress ruminating on which important personal chore he is willing to focus on and actually do—eat something cold from his rations, go outside and relieve himself, write a letter home, read a book, or do nothing but stare into space. He decides to go back to sleep.

The noise of the rain on their ponchos has stopped, and just as he rolls over to take another of the hundred snoozes he has taken recently, Bernie sticks his head inside the tent and excitedly says, "Hey, Chaplain, you better get your butt outta bed and see this before it disappears." He then pulls his head back outside and is gone, Richard having no idea what he is talking about.

Strom slowly puts his soggy boots over his soggy socks and steps outside into a new experience: the sun is now shining and the clouds are beginning to break up. Richard feels relief and some mild optimism for the first time in a week. However, the place is a disaster! A tank is stuck in the creek nearby buried over its turret, both amtracs can't move at all because they will bog down in the knee-deep mud, and everything is soaked to the core, including food and ammunition. Slowly the troops are coming out of their riggins and look skyward to the sun breaking through the clouds.

However, the sunshine has its drawbacks as well. Soon the heat will become unbearable again, and Charlie will begin sneaking out of his holes in the hills and start lobbing mortars and rockets and small arms fire not only at Golf and Echo up on the hills but at battalion as well. The humidity is a killer by afternoon, and by evening the mortars are exploding close by and the mosquitoes are again fighting for space on the bodies of the exposed Marines. When it rained, it kept heat down and the temperatures acceptable. However, when the sun does finally come out for a whole day, it creates a hot, muggy night, and the insects will eat right through the clothes and drink up the repellent splashed on any exposed part of the body. This makes sleep very difficult because the usual campaign of nightly terror continues throughout the night, notching up the anxiety. There is no way any kind of normal, comfortable sleep can be maintained.

Richard awakens the next morning to the sounds of loud explosions. He gets up from his soaked bedding, puts on his flak jacket and helmet—he now sleeps with his boots on—and leaves his "living quarters" to check out the situation. He walks one hundred meters to the road heading toward Hill 100 and observes two Phantom F-4 fighter-bombers dropping bombs and napalm. The jets are making passes at an area just past the hill where Echo is located. Strom can distinguish the sound of heavy small arms fire like all hell has broken loose! He sees the colonel off to the side of the road, standing under a tree with four of his staff. Stevens is talking to the skipper of Echo, who has requested the air support and wants the stuff dropped on positions very close to his men and the Echo perimeter. During the night the NVA had crawled up the hill to within twenty meters of the company CP and the Marines woke up this morning eyeball to eyeball with the enemy!

Colonel Stevens is all business again, like he always is when things get heated up. In that sense, it gives the battalion personnel confidence that he knows what he is doing. As soon as one airstrike is done, another sortie takes its place. There is one hell of a battle going on up there. "Break loose first platoon of Golf and get their asses up that hill," Richard hears the colonel yell to his ops officer, "and I want the rest of battalion and support to move up closer." The CO then has the amtracs moved down the road, in spite of the deep mud, so their 106 recoilless rifles can be used as support for first platoon as it moves toward the base of Hill 100.

Chaplain Strom turns quickly and runs back to the CP area, picks up his damp communion kit, and returns to the road with the intention of walking up the road with a second platoon of Marines who are moving in to support Echo. He falls into column and begins walking down the road. Just as he passes the forward CP—the colonel and his immediate staff—he hears this voice yell out, "Where in the hell do you think you're going, Chaplain?" The operations officer is looking at Richard menacingly, like he has committed some kind of egregious act, then continues, "No way are you going up there, Chaplain. Just go back to the CP and stay out of trouble!"

The chaplain slowly walks out of the column toward the colonel and his group twenty meters away. As he approaches them, Stevens finishes a conversation on the radio, turns to Richard, and says, "We're taking lots of casualties, Padre, and the choppers can't get in up there where the fighting is taking place. The amtracs will be bringing back the wounded shortly to the CP back there"—he points back to the battalion CP—"where we'll set up our triage and get our troopers medevaced out of here. I want you back there when those wounded troopers arrive."

Saying that, the CO turns back toward his radio operator and gets back on the radio again as the operations officer, considered a Cro-Magnon throwback by Dr. Lieberman, turns to Strom and says in a tough-guy voice, "You check with me, Chaplain, before you decide to move your ass anywhere in this battalion. Is that clear?" With that he turns and walks away.

As the S3 is saying this to the chaplain, the colonel, who is on the radio but also watching this little show going on between Strom and the major, motions for Richard to walk over and stand by his side. Moving toward Colonel Stevens, Richard is angry about the major's remarks, reminding him of an old Swedish proverb about there being more horse's asses than there are horses in the world. Stevens finishes his radio conversation, turns to Strom, and says, "Chaplain, I sure appreciate your willingness to be with those troopers up there, that's very commendable. But I need you more back here with the wounded. You go back there with old Bernie and take care of my boys."

He winks at his chaplain and turns back to his radio operator. Richard walks back to the CP, where Bernie and his corpsmen are already setting up equipment in anticipation of the expected wounded. Adjacent to this area next to the CP, about fifty meters away, is a flat, elevated area where the medevacs can land and pick up the wounded in a relatively safe spot.

Minutes after reaching the aid station, a message comes from the operations officer that the amtracs are not to move the last one hundred meters back toward the BAS because of the deep mud and the probability of getting stuck in the mud again, which means the wounded are to be carried back to the aid station from the road. Richard immediately gathers up six stray Marines hanging around the area and enlists three corpsmen and they commence running toward the road just as the first of the amtracs pulls up.

Piled on top of the first vehicle are eight wounded Marines. Two corpsmen and Richard climb on top of the amtrac to help the single corpsman working on a critically injured trooper. A piece of shrapnel has pierced his forehead, tearing out the upper right portion of his skull. The dressing is completely soaked with blood and the corpsman is attempting to start an IV, which he has been attempting to do for the past two minutes with no success because the dying Marine is in deep shock. While Richard is lifting off another fellow shot in the leg, the corpsman attempts to do a cut-down on the dying Marine. He takes out a knife and makes a quick incision into a vein near the Marine's ankle and attempts to insert an IV needle. It is quick field medicine. Sometimes this kind of primitive, unsterile surgery will work and buy time until the Marine is medevaced to a hospital. In this case, there is so much damage and blood loss even emergency field medicine will not be enough.

Wages, the corpsman with over four months in the field and fast becoming Strom's good friend, now takes charge of the offloading of the wounded. He's been around so much trauma and fighting, it appears that he is immune to the horror and gore of combat. What has happened in reality is that although scared to death in the midst of combat like everyone else, he has learned to shut down and feel nothing emotionally after the incoming and the chaos of a firefight. Learning to steel himself against any rising feeling is a survival process that is needed to stay alive and somewhat sane. Then in order to stay shut down when out of the bush and back in An Hoa or Da Nang, he gets drunk or slugs down a few Darvon-65, a painkiller used by the troops like, aspirin. This keeps all the horrible images and feelings buried deep inside where hopefully they will never come up again.

"Carter and Swanberg, get your asses up here and help the chaplain and me get the wounded off this vehicle," he says in an agitated voice as the small arms fire kicks up and begins whistling over the amtrac, raising the level of anxiety for those on top. Reluctantly they climb on top and commence lifting down the remaining Marines, the last being the dying trooper with his right frontal lobe missing.

As they slowly help the last two young men to the waiting arms of the Marines below, a second amtrac arrives with another load of wounded as the small arms fire increases in intensity, whistling around the troopers now scurrying for cover. Two rockets explode just down the road, throwing everyone into near panic. The driver then pulls his vehicle around so it's facing the road broadside to act as a protective shield as the group begins to unload the wounded Marines. Most of the injured on this load have relatively minor shrapnel or bullet wounds, with the exception of one fellow who is almost completely disemboweled. A piece of shrapnel has ripped through his abdomen and torn out most of his bowels. When Richard climbs aboard and sees this gravely wounded young man his first instinct is to move quickly away to help another injured Marine off the vehicle. He turns back toward the young Marine, having no idea at all as to what he should do, then places his hand on his neck to see if there's a pulse. The chaplain feels a hand pull his arm away, turns, and sees Wages kneeling next to him, who then says, "Already checked, Chaplain, he was dead before he got here. Let's get the living off here first."

Richard hesitates, wanting to quietly say a prayer but is quickly redirected by Wages, who now pulls him away and says, "Get your priorities straight, Chaplain, 'cause there's more wounded coming, so help me get the living down on the deck."

In the background Richard hears someone yell, "The medevacs are on the way," then he detects the sound of an approaching chopper in the distance. Since the helicopters won't land near their position because of the fire they are taking, the wounded must be carried back past the aid station. The available Marines from the battalion CP are now directed to carry the injured, a very physical, difficult task through the mud one hundred meters back to the LZ.

Chaplain Strom is running hard, carrying a wounded lieutenant from Golf. Instantly, a Marine next to him, who is also struggling hard to transport another wounded trooper from Golf, drops his load like a sack of potatoes and falls flat on his face. Richard, thinking he has tripped, continues on toward the LZ while the lieutenant he is carrying protests, saying, "Oh my God, that guy just got drilled in the head!"

At this point the chaplain pretends he hasn't heard Lieutenant Jeske's exclamation and continues on because of a sense of duty to get his man back to the LZ for evacuation but mainly because he is too frightened to stop.

When Richard arrives at the makeshift triage area next to the LZ, the first helicopter lands in a swirl of yellow smoke. Bernie is checking out the kid with critical head wound and is also attempting to start an IV on another gravely wounded trooper. Eight Marines are quickly loaded onboard the first chopper and suddenly takes off.

It is the doctor's intention to have the young kid he is working on loaded onboard, so when he sees the chopper take off, he stands up, shakes his fist at the airborne helicopter, and yells two sentences of very "blue" epitaphs about the independence of Marine air.

Another yellow smoke grenade pops in front of Richard as he turns back to bring another wounded Marine back to the LZ. Yellow smoke lets the pilot know that fighting is going on in the vicinity and to use caution. It also lets him know the wind direction and the general area in which he is to land. Green means safe, no action. Red means do not land, get out of area immediately!

Bernie is now checking out the IV's started on three Marines, intent on making them functional, as the rest of the personnel at the LZ load the walking wounded, placing three stretchers onboard last. When the doctor walks out of the aft door of the chopper, he yells at Wages to have the less seriously wounded Marines hold IVs on the trip back to Da Nang. This way his corpsmen won't get on the helicopters for this purpose and travel back to the hospital, which is good for at least two days out of the bush before they can possibly return. Bernie will have none of his corpsmen doing this scam today. Too much is happening. "I'll courts-martial any asshole from the BAS who gets on a chopper," he then warns.

After the second helicopter takes off, explosions suddenly erupt near the area of the forward CP where the amtracs are located. It is a very hectic time because the battalion is now spread out on two hills and the area surrounding the road leading to Thong Duc. The NVA seems to be moving in between the line company positions, creating confusion, chaos, and fear. They are also sitting back in the hills, dropping their mortars and rockets at will. So in between loading the helicopters with wounded, the Marines attempt to protect themselves as best as they can, given they haven't had time to dig in and make new foxholes.

By late afternoon the high number of casualties suffered earlier tapers off as does the enemy's engagement. Six medevacs have taken the dead and wounded back to Da Nang, the airstrikes have stopped, the fighting is sporadic and limited, and the colonel and forward CP have returned to the original area from which they started earlier that morning. Richard is sitting on an empty ammo box of eighty-one-millimeter mortars, talking to two injured Marines, neither of whom are seriously wounded.

In front of Richard, sitting on the ground, is this big kid from Lindsborg, Kansas, who witnessed his buddy get disemboweled earlier that day. He has sustained a bad gash on his forehead from a piece of shrapnel and is now shaking and crying as the shock of his head wound is beginning to diminish and the reality of his friend's death sets in again. He shakes his head slowly from side to side and say over and over, "Why, why, why, goddammit?!" Then he cries again. After doing this a few times Richard takes his hand off the young man's shoulder, reaches toward his left side and grabs a canteen off his belt, turns back toward the labile Marine, takes the injured man's chin in his hand, looks him straight in the eyes, and says, "I want you to drink the rest of this."

The big Kansan stops sobbing, looks quizzically at the chaplain, then grabs the canteen in his hand and takes a big swallow, emptying the contents. Richard's directive and the taste of the alcoholic beverage immediately changes his near hysteria to a body shudder as the pain of straight scotch moves down his esophagus.

After swallowing the beverage and shaking his head from the drink, he asks through tear-filled eyes, "What was that, Chaplain?"

"You just relax and take it easy now and wait for the next medevac to take you to the hospital. You're gonna be all right," Richard assures him.

"Thank you, sir," he replies as tears continue to roll down his cheeks. "That was pretty strong stuff." The other fellow sitting next to him has a bullet wound in his arm, now looks up at Strom, and says wistfully, "You got any more, Chaplain? My arm sure hurts."

Richard reaches around to his other side, takes a canteen out of its holder that contains altar wine and says to him, "Nope, but I've got some unconsecrated altar wine. You can take a slug of this, okay?"

Lance Corporal McAully looks at Strom with a quizzical expression on his face and says slowly, "What does, ah, unconsequented mean, Chaplain?"

"It means," Richard says slowly, "that this wine ain't ready for church service yet, so I'm going to use it right now as field medicine. Go ahead and take a hit," he tells him as he is handed the canteen.

The Marine slowly puts the canteen up to his lips, takes a swig, then gives the canteen back to Richard. "I never thought I'd have a chaplain give me church wine for medicine," he says after a short pause. "Can I tell my priest about this when I get back home, Chaplain?"

"Sure, no problem," Richard responds, wondering what his priest might really think.

Just as the chaplain is putting the canteen with the remaining altar wine back into its holder and stands up, the colonel walks up with his radioman, squats down in a half-kneeling position, and says to the two wounded Marines seated on the deck, "How you fellows doing? Sorry about all the shooting and fighting. Seems like we got ourselves into the middle of a big NVA troop movement. You guys all did a real fine job and we're real proud of what you did today. We're gonna get you back to the hospital real soon."

With that he stands up, motions for Richard to walk with him, and continues talking to his chaplain. "Been quite a day, eh, Padre?" They now walk away from the LZ. "What the hell you giving my boys to drink anyway?"

The chaplain begins to mumble an answer, "Ah, well, ah, sir—"

"Sometimes I really second-guess myself," he goes on, "and wonder if I should have done things differently. We took a lot of casualties today. It weighs heavily on me when that happens."

"Yes, sir," Richard manages to say as they reach the battalion CP area.

Stevens then continues, "If we can work it out, I'd like you to take one of the resupply choppers up to Hill 100 so you can spend some time with Echo. They've had their share of trouble and your presence might help out those young troopers. Don't know how much longer we'll be here, so work it out with operations so they can get you up there."

"Will do, Colonel," the chaplain responds as the colonel disappears into the darkness of the command post.

HILL 100

The rains have started up again and it's been five days since that afternoon when Golf took all their casualties, which at last count is well over thirty percent killed and wounded.

Since division intelligence believes the NVA has disengaged from further fighting at this time, the colonel is under the impression his battalion will be going back to An Hoa within twenty-four hours.

The battalion chaplain has been waiting for over three hours in the misty rain to get word on when he will get transportation to Echo Company on top of Hill 100. He is lying down under his poncho, trying to stay somewhat dry and attempting to read a book by Taylor Caldwell entitled "Great & Glorious Physician", a novel about St. Luke, when a messenger arrives to let him know the colonel wants to see him immediately.

Richard places the book in his backpack, emerges from under the poncho into the rain, and walks thirty meters to the battalion CP located under some tall bamboo. Assuming he will meet the colonel, he is instead met by the operations officer, Major Sulli, who glares at him as if he, Richard, is the enemy. "The colonel wants you to get a ride up the hill on the resupply chopper coming in shortly. You better get your shit together, Chaplain, because more than likely you'll leave from there when we secure from this operation," he replies brusquely.

"All right, will do," he says to Major Sulli. "Know where I can find the colonel?"

"It's none of your business to know where the colonel is, you've got your orders, now get to it," he harks back.

As Richard walks back to his gear, he is again puzzled by the major's hostility toward him and mutters to himself, "Somebody ought to put a live frag grenade up his behind." The battalion doctor hears him muttering in disgust, and as Richard picks up his pack and communion kit, Bernie says in mock righteousness, "C'mon, Chaplain, you're supposed to be our moral officer and say only positive things."

Richard explains to Bernie his immediate plans to leave shortly to be with Echo and also recounts his latest interface with Major Sulli. The doctor is definitely not a fan of the operations officer and in a loud, booming voice announces to most of the Marines within sixty meters, "You know what, Chaplain? I'd like to club that son of a bitch over the head with a two-by-four, then do a complete frontal lobotomy on him without any anesthetic—that is, if he has any frontal lobes!"

"You're too much, Bernie," says Richard as he chuckles and shakes his head in disbelief, hoping the major didn't hear the doctor's loud catharsis about the operations officer's mental capacity. "Chaplain," he then says suddenly, "do you know what you get when you cross a Marine operations officer with a gorilla?" Answering himself immediately, he replies, "You get a goddamn retarded gorilla, that's what you get!" Saying that, the doctor shuffles off toward the battalion aid station and afternoon sick call.

Within an hour the chaplain is on a helicopter for the short three-minute ride to the top of Hill 100. As the chopper circles over the hill and descends to a very small LZ close to the top, he can make out dozens of small holes caused by explosions near the summit and observes that the company is heavily dug in and fortified mortar pits with machines guns surrounded by sandbags four feet high. He also sees a number of wounded and the dark green plastic bags of the dead off to the side of the LZ as they slowly set down.

Richard immediately exits the helicopter upon landing, drops his gear nearby, and assists in loading the seven wounded and four dead Marines into the aircraft. Within a minute the aircraft is loaded and airborne, spiraling up into the darkening, raining late afternoon just as two explosions hit the side of the hill about fifty meters away and down the hill. The five Marines who assisted in loading the dead and wounded disappear immediately, like cockroaches in a dark kitchen when the lights come on.

The chaplain is again stunned by the suddenness and the help-lessness one feels when incoming explodes close enough to be lethal. "Over here, Chaplain—hurry up before they start dropping some more stuff," yells a Marine located some twenty meters off to the opposite side of the hill where the incoming hit. He quickly picks up his gear in a panic, half-runs, half-stumbles toward a foxhole, where a Marine grabs Richard by the arm and literally pulls him into a small two-man hole surrounded by a couple of layers of sandbags.

He now finds himself in a foxhole next to the company gunnery sergeant. "Just stay low and wait, Chaplain," he instructs Richard, who is now anxious and scared, wishing he had missed the chop-per ride up to Echo. After thirty seconds, which seems to Richard like an eternity, the sergeant introduces himself: "I'm Staff Sergeant Macintyre, most people just call me Sergeant Mac. Personally I'm glad to have you here, but the skipper is real nervous about you com-ing up here because within the past half hour the NVA has started dropping mortars on the hill again." He then stands up, surveys the area quickly, then squats down and continues. "Since there won't be any more choppers coming in because of the darkness, you're proba-bly gonna be in for a long sleepless night up here. We also got word that tomorrow morning we're gonna secure from this bill and be lifted back to An Hoa. This harassing with mortars at dusk usually means trouble all night long. Hope you brought your prayer beads, Chaplain," says the sergeant with a smile on his face. The sound of his voice, though, betrays the seriousness of the situation.

Shortly, a skinny guy in his late twenties, sporting a scrag-gly-looking mustache, casually walks to Richard's foxhole from the area where the explosions had taken place earlier, sticks out his hand, and shakes the chaplain's hand, then introduces himself. "I'm the skipper, you can call me Wog, Chaplain. Usually I'm happy to have our sky pilot hang out with us, but I'm a little nervous about having you here tonight. I guess the Old Man didn't realize things were heat-ing up again up here."

He takes his helmet off, scratches his head, then continues, "It's just not a good time to have you here. It's dark, it's raining again, we have no air support, artillery has retrograded back to An Hoa... it's hairy enough up here with that stuff supporting us. Without it we are literally on our own. Stay with the sergeant and keep your head down."

"I know you've got a lot on your mind, Skipper, and I don't want to cause you any more concern," Richard says. "I'll be careful, you can count on that!"

"Another thing, Chaplain," he continues, "I can't let you have church services. Too dangerous. And I don't want you going down the hill to the second and third platoons. Hang out here with us, we'll take care of you," he says with a smile. With that he walks back to his CP to talk to his platoon leaders on the radio and give them their night orders.

After the skipper leaves, the sergeant turns to Chaplain Strom and says, "He's a hell of a skipper, Chaplain, he's the best I've seen in fifteen years with the Marine Corps. When the fighting was real bad up here a few days ago, there was no one else I'd rather have as my commanding officer than that man." Richard is glad to hear this but also wonders if the sergeant is just saying this to make him feel better. Either way, it does alleviate some of the tension he is feeling.

It starts to rain again as they walk to the company CP—a sand-bagged hole dug into the hill covered over with wood from ammo boxes to keep out most of the rain. The command posts are glorified foxholes. They are crude and inadequate; they usually stink, are filled with mud, and gives one little relief from the rain. However, it certainly is better than what the poor grunts of the second and third platoons have further down the hill, who have only their ponchos pulled over them for protection. Those who have survived the week-long constant shelling and small arms fire are feeling miserable and tired and just sick to death of it all. And now, just a few hours before going back to the relative comfort of regiment back in An Hoa, the enemy fire and the rains from the skies are beginning all over. It is a gloomy and miserable and anxious prospect because everyone—from the skipper on down to the lowest private—knows that even if they are to be evacuated off this godforsaken hill tomorrow morning they still have the long night ahead of them to contend with the enemy and the elements. The NVA hasn't given Echo a single night off since the company arrived on the hill over a week ago.

The chaplain sits down on an ammo box in the wet, cramped, gloomy CP, opens up a ration of "balls and beans" without heating them, and starts to eat the food absently. He is beginning to dislike all the C-rations, even his two favorites, pork and spicy beef They are all beginning to taste the same. And the fruit cocktail contained in most of the meals, which the Marines commonly refer to as fruit puketail, he now just throws away. As he is eating, Gunny Mac tells Richard that over half of their company has been medevaced on this particular operation. He also tells him that in the six months since he's been Vietnam, the past ten days has been the worst, with all the casualties and the shift from the terrible heat to the cool, rainy weather.

They finish eating their meal in silence, then Gunny Mac says in his soft but penetrating voice, "You're here at a good time, Chaplain, in spite of the skipper's nervousness. I've never seen these guys down lower than they are right now. God, I hope we get off this damn hill tomorrow like we're supposed to. It'll kill our people if regiment or division comes up with their usual crap and tells us to stay. Don't know how much longer we can last up here and do our job. It's been real tough for all of us."

"What would you like from me, Sergeant?" Richard asks as Macintyre puts on his helmet and flak jacket, preparing to leave the CP.

"I'm going to set our evening perimeter, Chaplain, so if you'd like, why don't you come along with me? If you got any testaments or those 'Hail Mary' things I'm sure the some of the Marines would appreciate that from you—even if this is our last night here," he says in his calm, steady voice.

"I'll be right with you," Richard replies as he puts on his combat gear and slips his communion kit over his shoulder.

"By the way, sir, where's your chaplain's assistant?" the Sergeant asks as they walk twenty meters down the slippery hillside toward a small group of combat-ready Marines.

"Don't have one, not yet anyway, but I've got a young fellow picked out from Golf who helped me out the other day during church services. I think he's going to work out fine," Richard replies.

The evening is dark and silent when the gunny stops and says, "If the need comes up later on to recruit a chaplain's assistant, let me know because when we secure from this operation, there's gonna be a hell of a lot of Marines in Echo with two Purple Hearts, and as you know, with two hearts they're not supposed to be assigned to a line company any longer." He turns then to a group of five Marines clustered in a group down the hill and quietly gives them instructions regarding security for the company CP that night.

As they move in a parallel line down the company perimeter, twenty to fifty meters from the crest of the hill and the CP, the chaplain finds the grunts to be dirtier and more tired and burned out than he could possibly imagine, in spite of the fact many are recent replacements. All of them exhibit that quiet anxiety, a low-level gut fear, just wanting to get of that hill and back to An Hoa, where living conditions and their chances for survival are measurably higher. As Richard moves among the young men, many of them are surprised to see the battalion chaplain, not expecting him to be in their midst out here in the middle of nowhere. Little did they know that he is the most surprised of all at being here in the midst of combat. Just a few months ago he was safe in a nice little parish in New Orleans, Louisiana!

It is dark when he gets back to the CP and his assigned foxhole. He arranges his poncho as best as he can to keep the rain out and stay relatively dry, drawing it across the hole opening, Richard underneath wrapped in his poncho liner leaning against his pack with his legs pulled toward him, knees sticking up. It is uncomfortable, crude, but makes for a relatively safe profile, a position that keeps all his body below the ground line of his hole. He wears his helmet and flak jacket, which offers extra warmth as well as safety just in case Charlie decides to come by that evening and say hello! Then because of what the captain had said as well as his own rising paranoia, Richard's belief system now assumes that because he is on the hill and because this is supposed to be their last night there, Charlie will give it one last shot.

The chaplain is certainly not disappointed! It starts just after midnight when things are real quiet, during a light rain, when they begin launching grenades and mortars randomly all over the hill. Then they fire two rockets very close to the CP, close enough to make one feel that horrible panic that grips you minute by minute, day by day, on and on into each month of existence. As Richard hunkers down further into his hole, he suddenly realizes that he prefers small arms fire to mortars, rockets, and grenades. At least with small arms there is a measure of protection when one is dug into a hole. With missiles, there is no escape from a direct hit or near miss no matter how well one is dug in. This is what makes incoming so terrifying!

By 0100, elements of both the second and third platoons are in heavy contact with the enemy. The rain hasn't let up and the mortars continue to fall sporadically over the hill all night long. Since it is overcast and raining, it is impossible to spot the flashes from the enemy mortar tubes, which means the company mortars have no idea where to fire back at the enemy.

In the meantime, Richard can hear the skipper on his radio to battalion and to his platoon leaders, attempting to assess the situation and casualties. What makes it especially bad for the injured is that calling in an emergency medevac for the critically wounded is out of the question on this night. Not in this weather. All casualties will have to wait until the morning or until a clearing of the weather, which is highly unlikely. The weather conditions also preclude any air support as well. And the big guns have long been airlifted back to An Hoa.

It is a long, scary, wet miserable night for everyone, especially for those poor grunts down the hill engaged in close combat. Richard feels very helpless, a noncombatant who has been told to stay in his hole if the enemy shows up. There are numerous casualties, some critical, some resulting in death with the second and third platoons. Adjacent to the CP and on top of the hill, the causalities are lighter from intermittent mortar fire, but the real hard fighting is taking place down the hill three to four hundred meters away.

About four in the morning, an hour and a half before light, a couple of Marines just down the hill from the CP, those whom the battalion chaplain had just talked to the previous evening, take a direct hit from a mortar. "Get a fuckin' corpsman down here," a Marine yells as small arms fire begins to cover the area of the CP. The distinct sound of Russian AK-47 fire—that *pop, pop, pop* sound like a big cork gun—is a familiar sound that brings immediate terror to any combat Marine, especially now since it seems the NVA has probably broken through the perimeter and the CP is in imminent danger.

"Get those goddamn corpsmen down here," Richard hears the Sergeant yell from somewhere down the hill in the direction of the mortar hit, "and tell the chaplain to stay in his hole." And from the CP area itself, just to the right of his hole, he hears the calm voice of the skipper directing someone in mortars to use illumination rounds set very low under-the-cloud cover to lighten up the area, knowing that in doing this he will probably expose some of his company positions.

The firefight and small arms fire continued on and off for the next hour. In the meantime, Chaplain Strom is getting paranoid. Images are popping up in his mind of the enemy breaking through the perimeter, sneaking up to his hole and blowing him away with a satchel charge of explosives or merely aiming an AK-47 into his hole and emptying a clip of ammunition into his body. Richard feels helpless, alone, frightened out of his wits, praying that this awful moment would end soon! "My God," he thinks to himself, "how do you get used to this night after night, week after week, month after month?" At some level, he actually believes that somehow, some way, with enough faith, he will be able to withstand this horrible onslaught to his emotional, spiritual, and physical self. He doesn't accept yet that one does not get acclimated to this living hell. He is incapable of understanding at this point that you don't get used to combat. You merely began to die inside—slowly!

By morning's light the rain has stopped as well as the enemy fire, at least for the moment. Many Marines have been wounded and killed and are now being brought up the hill for immediate evacuation. The chaplain half-slides, half-walks down the hill to the areas where the fierce fighting has taken place, slippery and soaked from the night's rain, to help the Marines bring the wounded and dead back to the company CP before the medevacs arrive. It is difficult, miserable, heart-breaking work bringing those dead and wounded men up that steep hill—slipping, falling down, dropping the make-shift stretchers made from bamboo and ponchos—attempting to keep them as comfortable as possible and minimize their pain and discomfort. It is the hardest, scariest, most sustained physical work that Richard Strom has ever done in his life, helping to carry those dead and wounded Marines up that hill, expecting enemy fire at any time.

He is exhausted, completely soaked, and caked with mud when he drops on the ground next to his foxhole. He has no idea how many he has helped—both dead and wounded—get up the hill. He just knows the last one was the worst because he died quietly, just before they got him to the top. Richard is sapped emotionally and physically from the night, from the lack of sleep, from the terrible anxiety, from the exhausting climb time after time up the hill, the death and destruction—to all of it! He has nothing left but to just lie in the mud next to his hole, wanting just be left alone.

He has no idea how long he has been lying there when he hears small arms fire again, which immediately jolts his body into emotional and physical overdrive! He gets up to his knees, ready to dive into his hole, and sees a Marine, half-bent over, running toward him. He approaches Richard, drops to his knees, and says, "Sir, you're the chaplain, aren't you?"

"That's me," he replies as a mortar round hits down the hill one hundred meters away, causing both of them to flatten out on the ground. There is no thought at all to this behavior. It's completely automatic.

After a few seconds of silence, the young Marine again gets up on his knees. "The captain wants you to go back with the wounded," he says as another explosion hits closer to the top of the hill. "We're supposed to be secured from here by 1200, and it may get kind of rough toward the end when we get down to the last platoon. He'd like you to be ready when the first chopper comes in, which will be very soon." With that said, the Marine is off for someplace else and Richard quickly packs his wet, dirty gear. The wounded and dead are in a small ravine twenty meters away next to the LZ, so he picks up his gear and heads over there, energy level again high because of the incoming and the AK-47 fire. It is an anxious time for everyone, but especially the wounded. They must rely on the resources of the others to get them to safety. The cloud ceiling has lifted, the rain has stopped, and he can hear helicopters off in the distance. Silently Richard is asking the Lord to get everyone off that bill before the enemy concludes that the Marines are leaving and make it real messy for everyone!

HOSPITAL RUN

The aircraft is slowly lifting off the hill, Chaplain Strom's heart is pounding and he is feeling a deep, primal fear that is beyond description. They are taking small arms fire through the fuselage of the upward spiraling helicopter as mortars are exploding on the hill adjacent to the LZ. Richard's expectation at the moment is that either a bullet will come tearing into his skull or the chopper will be damaged critically and they'll all go down and die in a fiery crash! For the first time in his life, he isn't so sure anymore about his invincibility as he gasps for breath and notices that his body is trembling all over, realizing also that the fear is getting worse, not better as he experiences more and more combat.

Instantaneously, he flashes on an incident in his childhood when he was ten years old, scared to death, sitting next to his Uncle Oscar, who became a lunatic behind the wheel of a car, bulldozing his way through Chicago traffic one summer afternoon. As the helicopter lifts higher into the sky and into relative safety, Richard remembers the fear he had at such a young age, riding in that car, and how that incident of riding in traffic in a large city for the first time in his life caused him a bad case of hives. "I wonder what my fear will bring me this time," he thinks to himself as he notices that his hands continue to tremble, then finding it perplexing and odd that this incident that happened twenty years ago would suddenly percolate up from his unconscious at this moment and time.

As the chopper lifts high into the morning clouds, Richard surveys the scene inside the helicopter, aware of the tremendous relief he is feeling getting out of the bush and back, hopefully, to some semblance of civilized existence. The CH-46, the workhorse of the

Marine Corps, has its usual contingent of four members. However, this time there is a corpsman onboard as well.

The eight Marines lying on the deck are all seriously wounded and are from the second platoon, which bore the burn of last night's attack. Richard carefully helped load these men onboard when the incoming started up again and at liftoff is sitting in one of the webbed seats in the aft section of the craft, terrified that he is going to die. As the chopper lifts into the clouds above, the crew chief and corpsman move among the wounded, attempting to make them as comfortable as possible on a noisy, vibrating, chilly ride back to Da Nang and to either First Medical Battalion or the better-equipped, air-conditioned Naval Support Hospital across the river from the city.

When the CH-46 finally levels off, Chaplain Strom stands up, drops his pack and communion kit on the seats next to him, then kneels down on the deck next to a grievously wounded Marine, missing most of his lower right jaw. His neck is bleeding through layers of gauze, and Richard can hear a raspy, gurgling sound coming from his injured throat as he struggles to breath. The hospital corpsmen, seeing the Marine in distress, kneels down beside him, looks at Richard, and notices the cross on his helmet. "I need your help, Chaplain, he's not getting any air and will choke to death," he shouts over the noise of the engines and hands Richard a scissors. "Cut off the gauze around his throat." As Richard cuts off and removes the gauze, the corpsman reaches into the gaping, open wound with his hand, thrusts down into the area of the throat and pulls out a huge blood clot the size of a large egg. Richard feels his body tighten and prays to himself, "Oh God, please help me get through this, please don't let me puke!"

"The fuckers should have done a trach—ah, excuse me, Chaplain. Damn it, this should have been done right away down there on the LZ," the corpsman yells, completely unaware of the incoming and chaos on the LZ prior to their arrival. He instructs the chaplain to place new gauzes over the wound and apply pressure, grabs the scissors from him, then measures approximately two fingers down from the area of the Marine's Adam's apple, then plunges the scissors straight into the young man's throat. He pulls the scissors out, jams his little finger momentarily into the opening, then inserts a two-inch plastic tube the size of a large pencil into the small, bleeding hole. Immediately, the wounded Marine's relief is evident as he begins to breathe more easily and ceases struggling. However, in spite of the continuous pressure by Richard on the wounds, the bleeding continues, sometimes profusely. The corpsman then tells the chaplain, "I've got to check out the rest of these guys. Keep applying pressure, do the best you can," he yells, then stands up and goes to the forward area of the helicopter.

The young Marine lying on the deck of the helicopter is in deep shock, and except for his shallow, arrhythmic breathing, he is still. There is no thrashing about as he did earlier when his breathing was impeded by the huge blood clot in his throat. His eyes alternate between being closed, then suddenly fluttering a bit and then opening. However, there is no focus. It appears as if no one is home. Chaplain Strom continues to apply pressure on the open, gaping wound with his left hand and softly holds the Marine's right hand, attempting to get the young man to make eye contact with him. Richard is praying now in a whisper, "Please, Lord, give him the strength to make it back to the hospital," then out loud to the young life in front of him says, "Hang on, we're gonna get you back to the hospital real soon, you're gonna be okay!"

Richard Strom wants to believe that the Lord will spare this young man's life, but just as he finishes speaking to him, the Marine's eyes slowly close, then takes two short gasps of breath. And just like that he is dead.

Strom's first instinct is to release his pressure hold, pound on the Marine's chest, and yell for the corpsman. In releasing his hold, the chaplain can also see a huge area of blood on the deck underneath the body of the dead Marine. He stops pushing on the now lifeless chest, takes the young man's right hand again, looks at his damaged face, then flashes on a time and place long ago on a prayer that he had said every night as a child when going to bed. It was a prayer that he knew by rote, a ritual that had little connection to real life events or experience for a young boy growing up in a small upper Midwest community.

But now, as he begins to pray this simple childhood prayer to himself, leaning over a dead, badly damaged human being, he is overcome by the power of the words that he has taken for granted so many times before: "Now I lay me down to sleep...," he prays to himself. Softly holding the dead Marine's hand, he continues slowly:

I pray the Lord your soul to keep.
If you should die before you wake,
I pray the Lord your soul to take.

A simple, powerful childhood prayer. However, the solemnity of the moment is short-lived. The exhausted and harried corpsman, who is unable to keep up with all the medical demands thrust on him, approaches Strom, quickly examines the recently expired Marine, shakes his head wearily, then asks Richard to go forward and help him reinsert two IVs that were improperly started on the LZ. The chaplain hesitates, finding it difficult to leave the dead Marine, whereupon the corpsman yells over the sound of the helicopter engines, "There's nothin' else you can do, Chaplain, and I need your help right now."

There is a momentary hesitation, a gut feeling deep inside that he hasn't done everything he can for the dead Marine, as if his staying will somehow make things better or change the course or finality of his dying. In his hesitation he wonders to himself, "Better for whom?" Then he decides it is his own feelings of anxiety, loss, and inadequacy that has created the guilt he is now feeling.

Fifteen minutes later the helicopter is circling First Medical Battalion just to the south of division headquarters and adjacent to First Recon Battalion. Chaplain Strom is perplexed because he was told they were going to the Naval Support Hospital across the river from Da Nang and the hospital where he assumed most of men from his battalion had been medevaced. Instead, as they head in over Highway 1 next to the division hospital, Richard watches below as another helicopter takes off from the landing pad, makes a quick, spiral ascent, then takes off for the southwest in the direction of An Hoa.

Finally, after a twenty-five minute trip from Hill 100, his chopper slowly eases over the landing area of First Medical Battalion, a forty-by-forty-meter metal pad with a large white circle, a red cross painted in the middle. Immediately, the aft ramp of the helicopter is down and ten corpsmen and Marines are there to assist in offloading the dead and wounded, who are then brought into receiving, an area adjacent to pre-op. It is here that they are triaged, the most critical going immediately into pre-op, the less serious moved into one of the medical wards. Today, the casualties are heavy and the room next to surgery is full of badly wounded Marines on Gurnies, IV's, and whole blood flowing into their veins and their grievous wounds being stanched as best as they can. This is the most critical area in the whole life-saving network of the Naval Medical Corps because it is here, many times, where a life is saved or lost sometimes by seconds or a few minutes. The scene can be frantic as well as being devoid of any activity. There is always a direct correlation between the action out in the field and the amount of activity in pre-op.

Right next to pre-op, opening also to the helipad, separated only by a thin sheet of corrugated metal, is a smaller room called the Rose Garden. This is the room where the killed in action are placed—either those who were killed in the field or those who die before they get to surgery. In contrast to pre-op next door, there is never any frantic activity, even when the medevacs are coming in every three to five minutes and the dead are laid from one end of the room to the other. It is always quiet in there in spite of people moving in and out of the place. It is also a place the chaplains know better than anyone else, giving last rites or final prayers to the lifeless Marines because no one else wants or needs to be there.

Sometimes the dead are laid out just as they came in, without being placed in those drab looking, dark green plastic zip-up bags, with hardly a mark on them except for a single bullet hole through their head or chest. Sometimes they come to the Rose Garden in bad shape, gaping holes in their bodies or limbs missing. And sometimes there is just a green zip-up bag lying there on the dirt floor, flies buzzing about, a human being who a short time ago thought about parents or wives or children or pizza but whose remains are now reduced to body parts representing a third of their former physical self.

After assisting the corpsmen in the removal of the wounded to receiving, Chaplain Strom drops his pack and communion kit at the opening and slowly walks into the Rose Garden to find the young Marine that had died en route to Da Nang. As Richard stands over Corporal Cappazinni, feeling sad but also somewhat detached, he softly recites a blessing, again remembering back to his childhood: "May the Lord have dominion over you. May his holy angels take you to his home in heaven. May he bring you eternal peace, through Christ our Lord."

He turns to the other bodies laid end to end in the room and begins checking each tag. With each tag he examines he notices alternate feelings of sadness and detachment, as if there are two competing processes going on simultaneously. There are five more bodies from his battalion, which he carefully notes, since he will be writing back to the families of these dead Marines. As he notes the name and serial number of the last Marine, Richard feels a deep discomfort, almost a sense of revulsion, of not wanting to be in this room any longer.

He quickly stands, turns sharply, and walks past the bodies to exit the room and is puzzled by the name of the place, assuming it has some kind of gallows humor attached to it. He is met at the opening by a young Marine who immediately salutes him, an action that is beginning to irritate Richard. As he returns the salute in a halfhearted way, he thinks to himself sarcastically, "I wonder if they also salute dead officers?"

The chaplain picks up his pack and communion kit, turns right, and walks to the back of the compound toward the chapel where he hopes to find Lieutenant Commander Bernie O'Hearn, a tough little Irish American priest from the streets of Newark, New Jersey, whom he met a few weeks back at the reception for the assistant chief of chaplains. He also hopes to take a shower and secure some clean utilities, normal life functions that are rare for those who spend weeks in the bush with the infantry.

The rankness factor, the look and odor of a grunt coming out of the field, is in direct proportion to the amount of time spent in the field without these normal living amenities. For those living in the rear—all those support personnel from battalion up through division and above who aren't in the rifle companies—rude, harassing comments are commonly directed toward the grunts, often joking about the animals coming out of the bush and the need to be up wind from them. Although the grunts look and smell terrible and the people in the rear complain about their presence, there is a quiet respect and admiration for what they're going through. And for the infantry Marines, without exception, there is an underlying surliness and resentment toward anyone who isn't walking with a line company, who hasn't been hammered by the terrible stress and deprivation they go through day after day. They are especially hostile toward Marine air, specifically the supply helicopters, who the infantry believed operated a schedule that had little to do with the needs of the Marines in the field. It is a commonly held perception by the grunts that Marine air scheduled their resupply of food, water, and ammunition around the three hot meals they eat each day back at their bases in Da Nang and Marble Mountain.

Richard arrives at the chapel, a screened hooch that is larger than most of the buildings surrounding it. There is a small office for the chaplain in the back, while the sanctuary, a plain room that seats about forty people, has an altar in front with a brass cross and two candle holders on top of a white linen cloth. In back of the chapel is a sandbagged bunker about five feet high, with steel revetment on the ceiling and more sandbags on top of the steel.

The chapel is empty, so Richard moves to the back and through the office door marked "Hospital Chaplain." As he walks into the small office, he notices that Bernie has a small refrigerator, two lamps, a couch, two upholstered chairs, and a metal desk. There is a typewriter, a crucifix and a picture of a large family on his desk. "Pretty comfortable," he thinks to himself, then remembers the old adage about the boys in the rear having all the gear while the grunts at the front have to scrounge for their stuff.

"Hey, Chaplain Strom," Richard hears as the door opens and Bernie appears. "I heard you came in a short time ago. Good to see you... my God, you look and smell like the ass end of a water buffalo." Richard shakes his hand, then begins to sit down in one of the chairs.

"Richard, I think you better shower and get into some clean clothes before you lounge around and get everything dirty," he says with a big grin. "I'll get you anything you want—beer, hot chow, movies. What do you wear, mediums?"

"What I need is a place to stay tonight before I go back to An Hoa in the morning. I also need to get a ride across the river to the Naval Support Hospital. Can you help me out?" asks the tired but less depressed chaplain Strom, now that he knows he's facing a shower and some hot chow, the first in two weeks.

"You can stay in my hooch tonight," he replies.

"Can I assume this hooch in which you live is the rectory, and if so, please tell the housekeep that I would like to have pot roast, carrots, potatoes, and gravy. I'd also like some red wine with my meal as well," Richard responds.

Bernie smiles, then says, "Not quite. I live with an anal retentive anesthesiologist and a sloppy surgeon. One loves to party, the other whines and complains all the time. Both are very good physicians. Bob, the anesthesiologist, is in Japan on R&R. You can sleep in his bunk tonight, knowing that his sheets are clean. So, get cleaned up, then we'll allow you into our living quarters. I'll be back in five minutes."

"By the way Bernie," Richard asks, "why do they call that place next to the triage room and Rose Garden?"

The Catholic Chaplain thinks for a moment, then replies: "I guess you've never been in that place on a hot afternoon when they've been too busy to transport the bodies to the morgue over in Da Nang, or when the body bags have been out in the field for a day or two. The aroma of the place arises in direct proportion to the number of bodies in the place and also how long the bodies have been out in the field. So, calling it the Rose Garden I guess is the Marine way of attempting to use dark humor to cover over death." With that said, he walks out of the office and is gone.

Shortly the hospital chaplain has provided for all of Richard's needs: a hot meal, a shower, cold sodas, clean utilities, a jeep for transportation to NSA hospital and a list of the wounded from his battalion. He isn't kidding when he says the place is full of Marines from *two-five*. Bernie figures over eighty casualties from Richard's outfit have come through triage in the past three days. Some of the more severely wounded have been medivaced to the Philippines or Japan, but there are still over fifty Marines from his outfit in this hospital alone and he would find out shortly that another thirty Marines from Echo and Golf companies are in the Naval Hospital across the river.

As Richard visits his troops, he is beginning to see familiar faces among the wounded, faces with whom he has shared coffee or shared some time with on the road next to Hill 52, or faces with eyes closed receiving Holy Communion from his hands. The war is beginning to get very personal because of his direct involvement with these young men at a very basic, human, living and dying level. It is disturbing enough to see the physical and emotional pain these young Marines are experiencing, but the most painful issue facing the chaplain is that many of the wounded he is visiting will be well enough to be recycled back into the field and therefore open again to being wounded or killed. It is enough to make a grown man cry, which is exactly what Chaplain Strom did upon leaving the hospital after visiting ICU.

Richard always saves his visit to ICU last. The experience of going there is beginning to unnerve him, seeing the blown away limbs, the shattered faces, the sickening medicinal/gangrene/antiseptic smell of ICU and always... ALWAYS... that *hiss-thump... hiss-thump... hiss-thump* sound of the respirators that pumps air into the drained-out life force of those young bodies. Then he would remember clearly, each time he goes into ICU, Spike's words about the place and the look of pain on his face. To Richard, that seems like eons ago!

The most poignant moment, however, is later that afternoon when he is in the Naval Support ICU. What really gets to Chaplain Strom is seeing that young man who had helped him out in the rain a few days back when he had visited Golf on Hill 87 and served Holy Communion. "Mr. Heffner," the chaplain had facetiously called him, the young kid who had retrieved his *Playboy* magazine out of his wet backpack to hold over the communion hosts so they wouldn't get wet, is lying motionless on a bed in ICU with half his brains blown away, waiting to die. He is also the Marine that Chaplain Strom has requested to be his chaplain's assistant.

Richard is sitting next to the young Marine, holding his cold, lifeless hand for a few seconds, or maybe a minute, he isn't quite sure. A nurse comes by to check his IV and the respirator. Suddenly, he feels disgust and anger toward her, thinking to himself, "Piss off, lady. Just let him die." She adjusts the IV above his head. The nurse doesn't say a thing and looks at Richard and the young Marine as if they are part of the wall.

"I wonder where her head is at, working with these guys day after day. Is she losing her perspective, her feelings? Is she just doing her job mindlessly, without any thought?" he questions. In an instant Richard personalizes these thoughts and speculates about his own process since coming to Vietnam: "Will this happen to me, am I becoming a mindless robot-tender, steeling myself against my humanity and my feelings?"

On his way out of the hospital and back to the jeep to carry him across the river back to First Medical Battalion, Richard cannot contain his tears and his anger any longer. "Goddamn son of a bitch," he yells through his clenched jaw, tears streaming down his cheeks. By the time he crosses the river and approaches division headquarters, he is feeling empty inside.

Back at First Med that night, in a dry bed after a hot meal and a couple of beers at the officers' club, Richard goes to bed and sleeps miserably. Emergency medevacs are coming in all night long from the field. Bernie is up each time to greet the lines of wounded and dead coming into triage.

Just as it is getting light and another medevac is coming in, Richard gets up, feeling terrible because of the lack of sleep for the past week. He sees Bernie, who is preparing to leave for the sixth time and says, "You look terrible, Bernie, what's going on?"

"The Seventh Marines are taking lots of casualties about fifteen kilometers southwest of Da Nang at a place called Dodge City," Bernie replies brusquely, then heads out the door to meet the incoming helicopter and administer any needed last rites.

Chaplain Strom is feeling nervous and agitated. Just before morning breaks, as he lies awake, completely exhausted, he becomes aware of the desire to be back with his battalion. He wants morning to come so he can just get the hell out of there. At least, for now, he knows where he wants to be.

II

There is… a time to be born and
a time to die.

Ecclesiastes 3:2

HOME IS CALLED AN HOA

An Hoa is a large, sprawling regimental headquarters isolated from Da Nang and the rest of the First Marine Division by many miles of hostile territory. To the west and all the way back to the Laotian border, high mountains create a benign environment for the North Vietnamese Army to hide their equipment and launch their many offensive forays into the flatlands surrounding the coastal cities. The other points of the compass generally give way to the flat coastal area populated by hundreds of small ancestral villages that are generally considered either neutral or outright hostile toward the Americans. At night there is no neutrality—the countryside is owned by the Viet Cong. The Fifth Marine Regiment was placed strategically at the very center of this main infiltration route into the coastal plains to disrupt the flow of men and supplies into South Vietnam. It's also home to Richard Strom and close to five thousand Marines. This is where he has a cot to sleep on, two meals a day of prepared food in the regimental mess, a sometimes working shower, and on occasion a change of clean clothes.

Second battalion is located directly south of the main airstrip and adjacent to a battery of 105 howitzers. Since the rains have started, the dust that previously permeated everything has now transitioned into mud—everywhere. There is little grass or weeds growing anywhere. What does grow is soon trampled and quickly mud emerges. The noise is constant and at times deafening—from the C-124 and C-130 cargo-transport planes landing and taking off from the helicopters that are constantly resupplying the grunts out in the field, and especially from the many artillery pieces, located both east and west of the airstrip, which fire their deadly missiles twenty-four hours a day.

Since arriving at *Two-five*, Chaplain Strom has slept overnight in his hooch once, which was his first night in An Hoa. He has been out twenty-eight days in the field and spent four days staying in Da Nang during his hospital visitations. Since he's spent so little time back in the rear, he is not used to the constant noise, making it difficult to sleep. However, being back "home" seems like luxurious living after having spent so much time out in the bush. The grunts learn to appreciate things they've previously taken for granted—cold reconstituted milk, a screen-in head where the flies don't constantly harass them, a shower (be it cold), no long marches, and time to do the many personal chores that have been placed on hold.

The afternoon Richard arrives back from First Med, he gets off the C130 airplane and walks to the regimental chapel a short distance away to say hello to the regimental chaplain he met the first day after arriving in-country, vaguely remembering what he even looks like let alone recalling his first name.

At the present time, all four chaplains in the regiment are Protestant, an unusual arrangement because usually the division chaplain's office attempts to provide two Roman Catholic and two Protestant chaplains to ensure complete religious coverage for the troops. The first battalion chaplain has had Protestant services at the chapel the past three weeks because Chaplain Jacobson has been hospitalized with amebic dysentery. His battalion provides the security in and around An Hoa and essentially has not been out in the bush for the past month. He shuttles back and forth between Phu Lac 6, a very important bridge over the Song Thu Bon River nine kilometers away and Charlie Strong Point, a security position on high ground just to the south overlooking An Hoa. Should the bridge go the Fifth Marines would not get supplied by the daily convoy that provides most of their logistical support. And were the enemy to take control of the high ground south of regiment, the Marines would be in deep trouble.

The third battalion chaplain has been on operations with his outfit back in the hills toward Laos. Though they haven't taken the casualties from fighting that *Two-five* has the past month, they've had over one hundred medevacs due to malaria and dysentery. It will be another month before Strom meets the chaplain from *Three-five*, by which time the present chaplain will have been replaced by a new one and rotated back home. Personnel, Richard learns, get shuffled in and out all the time, something one just learns to live with. You meet someone and get to know them, suddenly they're gone—killed, wounded, transferred to another unit, or sent back to the States.

Strom enters the office in back of the chapel and finds Lt. Commander Jacobson in the midst of packing some of his gear. The furnishings are sparse—two folding chairs, a very small foldout desk, two lamps, and a tiny bookshelf. There is a small refer in the corner. Jacobson looking tired and gaunt turns toward Richard and says, "Chaplain Strom, welcome back to An Hoa." He motions for Strom to sit down and continues, "I just received my orders back to the States this morning, I'll be going to the naval air station at Miramar, California, just outside San Diego." He sits down weakly in the other chair, smiling. "I can't tell you how happy I am to get away from the Marines, been with them for the last two assignments."

"That's great—ah, I'm sorry, I forgot your first name…"

"George. Please don't give it a thought, Richard, everything is so transitory one tends to forget names and faces," he replies. "By the way, Bernie O'Hearn, the hospital chaplain at First Med, is transferring out here, hopefully in about three days. I personally think he is getting burned out. Don't know if this place out here will be any better for him with all the incoming day and night."

Strom stands up, picks up his dirty gear, and says to Jacobson, "Bernie is a good priest and I'm glad he is going to be here with us. Good luck to you and congratulations on your fantastic new orders back home." He opens the door and begins the walk to his hooch two hundred meters away. And just like that Lt. Commander Jacobson is out of Richard's life, a few minutes of time sandwiched in between some pretty life-shattering experiences.

"Oh well, can't be tuned into everybody," he thinks to himself as he turns the corner and walks briskly away from the chapel.

One of the chaplain's important duties is to keep in constant contact with the company's first sergeants. They are the heart and soul of the company's discipline and administration. Life in a line company without a good, experienced first sergeant would be chaotic and tend to break down both the discipline and moral of the troops, including its officers. So visiting them will not only open up the channels of communication but will make Strom's job easier when he sees a need for transfers out of the field or for questionable emergency leave for the Marines who really need to be home.

In a navy command, chaplains are mostly accepted as part of "the team" and therefore thought of as integral to the well-being of the personnel, which means generally they don't have to prove themselves or their worth. However, with Marines, being a chaplain is not an automatic entrée into their graces. Acceptance is a process that chaplains must accomplish and work at. Since there are lifers—career Marines—that dislike the chaplain Corps as a whole, the Marine combat chaplain must earn his place by establishing relationships. They don't come automatically! In some cases, the lifers will display overt dislike and hostility regardless of any attempt at relevancy, something Strom has already found out from his operations officer. Walking back to his hooch, Richard makes a mental note to visit them all before evening.

Coming back home to An Hoa feels good for all the troops, not only because of the "luxuries" available but also because one has time to just hang out—take snoozes, drink a beer or soda, read again and again that mail from home, write letters, listen to the Armed Forces Radio Network, go to the head without the anxious thought of wondering if a missile would land in the midst of meditating on the throne. In spite of the incoming, being back in An Hoa means the safety factor goes way up for the grunt returning from the bush.

Chaplain Strom makes a concerted effort the next two days getting aquatinted with the other staff officers who are in the rear while he is out in the field. The personnel officer, the S1, he met the first day he arrived in An Hoa. Lieutenant Kelly is always ready to help the chaplain and is never without a beer in his hand or a few choice swearwords. The S2, also known as the intelligence officer, of course an oxymoron, is a quiet fellow who looks more like he belongs behind the desk in a city library. Captain Peter Pearson the assistant S3 officer, a naval academy graduate, is smart, articulate, friendly and an extremely capable Marine. He previously was a line company commander with Hotel and had recently been sent back to the rear because he will shortly be rotating back home. He has received both the Purple Heart and the Silver Star for gallantry. Lieutenant Wegman, the supply officer designated the S4, appears to Richard to be the busiest of all the officers in the rear. His job is to keep the troops supplied in An Hoa and out in the field when on operations.

Two days later, after securing from Operation Maui Peak, Chaplain Strom is asked to hold separate memorial services for Golf, Echo, and H&S (headquarters and support, being the company designation for all the personnel in the battalion who aren't attached to a regular line company). In the three companies there are thirty-eight Marines killed in action.

Each service is marked by a sadness that is seldom acknowledged, especially out in the field or just after battle. Although death surrounds them daily, it is not something that they talk about—at all! However, here at these memorial services, honoring and sometimes grieving for dead friends, for those with whom they've shared jokes or food or misery or family, it can be a very conflicting experience. Because not only do they acknowledge the death of their comrades but also must come to grips with their own invincibility which is crushed the very first time they experience combat. However, should they focus on this very natural process out in the bush after some horrible encounter, grief then becomes another liability. Lurking below the surface of their consciousness, grief can radically pull the combatant away from the pivotal, core issue of staying alive and supporting his fellow Marine. Grieving has no place in the bush!

Memorial services do not last long, mainly because it makes everyone nervous about large groups of people congregating together for any extended period of time, like the skipper's admonition about cluster foxtrots up on Hill 87. Since most of the Marines haven't participated in a memorial service, Richard is asked to create a format for these brief services. Because mortars and rockets are daily realties, the chaplain asks each company commander to gather what is left of his troopers between hooches in formation of two rows. Sandbags are then placed on the deck in front of the formation, an inverted rifle with bayonet stuck into the bag, a helmet then placed on the rifle butt, each dead Marine represented by one rifle and helmet. While the company is at attention, the skipper reads aloud the names of the killed in action in his unit. Chaplain Strom then reads from scripture followed by the Lord's Prayer. After a moment of silence each company first sergeant plays a tape recording of taps.

It is short, sad and leaves Strom feeling empty and alone. The Marines will leave quietly and go back to their hooches, sometimes weeping silently to themselves, lost in their own thoughts. It is also easy to point the newer Marines, the ones who've been in-country only a short time and have just had their first encounter with the death of a friend. It is they who weep silently to themselves. After being in-country three to four months, living through many deaths and many close encounters, these Marines are shut down and closed to their feelings: the survival art of no-think, no-feel, no-thing—the numbing of reality.

The third service is now being held for Echo Company. It is especially moving for the battalion chaplain because he was a part of their living/dying misery up there on that hill the last night and morning before they were extricated back to An Hoa. Twenty-one Marines from Echo were killed in three weeks of action. As the skipper reads the names, Richard flashes on that young trooper, the last brought up, dying right next to the chaplain as he and three Marines struggled up a muddy hill to get him to the LZ for evacuation. Overwhelming sadness envelopes Strom and he has to steel himself to keep from crying openly. Momentarily Strom is frozen, unable to continue, wondering suddenly if he can get through this particular memorial service. He takes three deep breaths and braces himself against further interruption of his process by feelings.

After the captain reads the names, Chaplain Strom continues: "This is a difficult time and place for all of us, especially when so many young men, your friends are taken from us, as if stopped in midsentence. In spite of the terrible misery fighting brings, I know also the bravery, heroic action, and care that also arise in the midst of these terrible experiences the past three weeks. I ask you then to hold onto this scripture from the Gospel of St. John as you remember your fallen comrades and friends: 'This is my commandment; that you love one another as I have loved you.' Greater love has no man than this, that a man lay down his life for his friends."

Richard is facing the company and sees the tears rolling down the faces of a few Marines in the front row. He decides to not use the Lord's Prayer as he did previously with the other two companies, asks the Marines to bow their heads, and continues: "Father in heaven, thank you for our homes where our loved ones dwell and to which our fondest memories now turn. We praise you for family love, peace, and Corps values that follow us and comforts us in strange, distant, and dangerous places. We are grateful for all things we share in common—the worthy lessons we learn, the hardships and grief we many times bear, the tasks and pleasures that bind us closer to each other, and especially your abiding affection and love. Shelter our homes, oh Lord, and all our dear ones there. Make us strong, unselfish, and brave to defend and protect our family and our family of Marines. Send down your grace and love to each one of us, through Jesus Christ, our Lord. Amen."

After the short service, during that quiet solitude that follows after the Marines shuffle away to be with their individual thoughts and feelings, Staff Sergeant Macintyre slowly approaches the chaplain and in his quiet, serious voice says, "Thank you, sir. The men do appreciate what you gave them this morning. They may not say it but I know they do. For most of them it's just hard to talk about it."

"Yeah, I know, Sergeant," the chaplain responds, "and thanks for your acknowledgment." Slowly, silently they both walk toward the Echo Company office, lost in thought. Entering the office together they are greeted by the skipper. "Thanks, Chaplain, for your service, it was short and to the point. You did a good job. Wanna beer?"

"Not right now, Sergeant. But there is something you can do for me, if you will. The company sergeant here says you have some Marines who have two hearts and can't go back into their platoons. Any chance of snagging one of your people as my chaplain's assistant?" he asks. "The one I had lined up from Golf died yesterday from his wounds."

"I'll check with our first sergeant and be back with you this afternoon," he replies. "Ah, by the way, Chaplain, the Sergeant here and I play a mean hand of bridge. When you get some time and can find a decent partner, let's get together."

Richard is now on his way to the BAS to get Bernie to look at the wound on his back that hasn't healed properly and get another shot of antibiotics to stop the continuing infection. Reaching the aid station, he finds out both Chuck and Bernie are gone and the chief on duty tells the chaplain they are attending a battalion staff meeting and aren't due back for another hour. Strom is uncomfortable with this information because he immediately assumes he is supposed to be there since he is one of the staff officers.

"I can't believe it, screwing up again," he mutters to himself as he arrives at the CP bunker where the meeting is taking place. He is met at the doorway by none other than Major Sulli, who immediately gives Strom a menacing look and says, "Since when are chaplains exempt from staff meetings?" As he is saying this, Bernie is walking close behind the major and gives him the finger. What Bernie is not aware of is that the colonel is right behind him watching the battalion doctor give the universal sign for contempt.

"Hey, Doctor," exclaims Stevens with obvious agitation in his voice and a displeasing look on his face, "is that how you do a proctoscopy or are you just showing us your mental age?"

Then the Old Man walks up to Richard and says in a voice dripping with sarcasm, "I thought you navy people had all the etiquette and us Marines were supposed to be your uncouth cousins. Maybe you better say something to your doctor friend over there about manners and straighten him out!" Bernie hurriedly walks around the corner of a hooch and out of sight. "Chaplain," he now says as he walks toward his hooch, "I want you to get a ride into Da Nang right away and see the troops again. We're going to be going out again real soon and you might not get a chance to see them for a while."

"All right, Colonel, I'll check with regiment and see what's going into Da Nang this afternoon," Richard replies as the Old Man walks into his hooch, closing the door.

Immediately he reopens the door, points his index finger at Strom, and says, "Chaplain, you're one of my staff officers. When we're back here and I hold staff meetings, you be there! Understand?"

"Yes, sir," Richard's immediately replies as Stevens closes the door, wondering if he'll ever do anything right to please the old bastard!

When the chaplain gets back to the BAS, Bernie is laughing about the CO catching him give the finger to the S3, then "jumping in the chaplain's shit," letting Chuck and all the corpsmen present in on the latest drama concerning the battalion chaplain. He then turns to Richard, who is listening patiently, and says in a calm voice, "Let's get a look at that wound on your back. We'll give you another shot, and if it doesn't clear up, I'll send you to the hospital to get the infection surgically removed.

After getting a new dressing, Dr. Grant gets a beer and offers one to Richard, then proceeds to tell the chaplain, since they are going out on a new operation shortly, of the lineup. This is a happening that always takes place just prior to any new operation, usually twenty-four to forty-eight hours before the actual embarkation time, when the Marines start lining up at the doctor's or chaplain's office.

Mostly they start out at the BAS, limping, whining, complaining of back, kidney, head, liver, knee, shoulder problems—anything to get them out of going to the field. As Bernie is explaining the lineup to Richard, the chaplain is thinking to himself, "Really can't blame these poor bastards for trying to negate their chances for getting killed!"

The lineup will start at morning sick call with about three times the normal numbers showing up. If they can't get the doctor to sign either a light or no-duty chit—which gets them at least a few days in the rear—they then head over to the chaplain's office. "They will then get down on the doctor and tell the chaplain he's insensitive, he's a quack, just doesn't understand, is a lackey of the command and so forth," Bernie explains to Richard, "so you better be ready for these bastard brains because they'll drive you nuts! Don't let them give you any shit, especially because you're new. They'll try to jerk you around like a feather in the wind!"

As Bernie finishes his diatribe, Richard is thinking that the good doctor has missed his calling: he should have been a company first sergeant.

When Chaplain Strom gets back to his hooch, a Marine is sitting on the steps awaiting his return. He remembers what Bernie said about the lineup and thinks to himself that the word got out real fast about the coming operation. "Here's my first customer."

Strom invites the young Marine inside and offers him a seat and asks, "What's up?" assuming he's going to get a big line laid on him.

"The first sergeant sent me over, sir. He said you need a chaplain's assistant," he replies in a soft voice. "My name is Private First Class Bob Marshall, sir."

The Marine can't be any more than eighteen years old, is skinny as a rail, and has that scruffy-looking mustache that so many young Marines attempt to grow over here with very limited progress. "Oh, right," Richard responds. "Like a cold soda?" He nods as the chaplain continues, "Do you have any reasons, Bob, why you wouldn't want to be a chaplain's assistant?"

"I don't think so, sir," he says with some hesitation, "but I'm not sure what a Chaplain's assistant is supposed to do."

"Well, mainly you do two things," he replies. "First, you kind of be 'my man,' you know, help me get my administrative stuff done, run errands, set up for worship services out in the bush, stuff like that. And second, since I carry no weapon, you're supposed to be my bodyguard. I'm not sure what that's supposed to mean except to stay kind of close to me, especially when the you-know-what hits the fan," he says with a smile.

Bob then tells the chaplain he just got out of the hospital four days ago, has been in-country for three months, and has been wounded twice by shrapnel, the second time on Hill 100 just days before the chaplain's arrival. Richard then asks him the last time he attended church service. "Probably not since I was confirmed in the Lutheran Church when I was thirteen," he answers. The note he brings from his first sergeant says Marshall has consistently high proficiency marks since boot camp and will be promoted to lance corporal soon. Richard's intuition tells him that he should go with this kid and not mess around with any more interviews. He doesn't know it at the time, but this will be the best decision he will make while in Vietnam.

"Listen, Bob," Richard now says to the young Marine in front of him, "if you think you can put up with me, you've got the job. That's a free choice that you must make though, so why don't you think about it for a while, then let your first sergeant know tonight what you've decided, then let me know tomorrow morning."

"Sir," he responds, "if it's all right with you, I'd like to be your chaplain's assistant. It's okay with me right now."

This is how Chaplain Strom acquired his assistant, one of the nicest, brightest, and most responsible enlisted Marine he was privileged to know while serving with the Marine Corps.

THE LEPER

It's afternoon and Chaplain Strom is just back from Da Nang visiting the wounded. The battalion continues to have a high census in the hospitals—sixty-one. As before, most of the severely wounded have been medevaced out of country—to the Philippines, Japan, Guam, or Hawaii. Those remaining in Vietnam more than likely will be "recycled" back into the field again, always a depressing thought for all those young men lying in hospital beds. He stays overnight with his recon buddies and finds it to be the same animal house it always was.

He also attends his first division chaplain's meeting since he left for An Hoa, a ritual that is required of all first division chaplains each Wednesday morning. McConnell does not require attendance by the battalion infantry chaplains in the division—nine in all—because they are usually busy doing more important things, such as ministering to their troops out in the bush and attempting to stay alive. Most of the administrative chores are done by the assistant division chaplain, a nuisance that Spike mostly avoids because he claims that "if given the chance, I'd fowl up a free lunch when it comes to administration." His forte is people—a warm, sensitive, decent human being. Richard decided back at Camp Pendleton that he would take that kind of chaplain any day over the pseudo-administrative-military focused chaplains who placed little emphasis on the ministry part of their jobs and are more interested in keeping their noses up the asses of the command so they can get promoted and secure good assignments.

The battalion left this morning for the bush instead of tomorrow as planned, so the chaplain spends most of the afternoon getting his letter writing done to the families of the dead and wounded. He then requests that First Sergeant Rooney transfer his new assistant from Echo to H&S Company and gets his gear packed for the evening "express" to the field.

Shortly before dusk, Bob and Richard are waiting, along with supplies of ammunition, food, and water, at the helipad. The "express" hauls the daily supplies and shuttles personnel in and out of the field for battalion and each of the line company. First, the Marines are loaded onboard the chopper, then the aircraft takes off and hovers over the supplies that have been stacked inside a cargo net. As the chopper hovers at about six to seven feet off the deck, the nets are attached to a hook underneath the helicopter by reinforced loops that are a part of the netting. Then the chopper slowly lifts up into the air, the net hanging fifteen feet or more below the aircraft, to rendezvous with their assigned unit.

This new operation has been dubbed Henderson Hill, and Strom's battalion has been assigned to an area north of An Hoa called Arizona Territory. This is a section of land about ten by ten kilometers north across the Song Thu Bon River. The area has been declared a free-fire zone, meaning the civilians were cleared out of there a few months ago and directed to stay in one of the resettlement areas closer to Da Nang. Because it is a free-fire zone the area is constantly pounded day and night by airstrikes and artillery. Since the coastal plains continue past Arizona to the mountains a few kilometers away, this particular area became one of the major routes from the Ho Chi Minh trail back in the mountains to the coastal area surrounding Da Nang and Hoi An to the south. There are always plenty of NVA and VC troops engaging the Marines in Arizona.

By the time Richard and his assistant get to battalion, it is almost dark. The large load of supplies are gently lowered to the ground, the loops connected to the helicopter are released, then the chopper quickly swings around and lands in the LZ next to the supply drop. Exiting the aircraft, they make their way in the semidark to the BAS, where Chuck and three corpsmen are sitting around a circle attempting to play cards. They unpack their gear, fix as best they can in the dark their poncho-tent, eat a cold C-ration, and go to sleep. This would be one of the few nights out in the field when Chaplain Strom didn't get soaked overnight from rain or wake up in the middle of incoming mortars or a firefight.

The next morning Chuck and Richard walk toward the CP for the morning staff meeting and briefing, the chaplain again wondering if Stevens is going to rag on him about something. He's standing with the intelligence officer, a Vietnamese interpreter, and a platoon leader from Golf. As the two naval officers stand apart from the conversation, Richard hears the colonel telling them to round up any civilians they find left in the area, check them out for any enemy troop movements, then move them across the river to the refugee camp next to regiment called Phu Duc. As this conversation is going on, the chaplain turns to the doctor and quietly says, "This is a hell of a thing to do to the peasants around here, kick them off their ancestral lands that they have farmed for generations, stick them in refugee camps where there is rampant disease and nothing to do, then tell them we are bombing their lands for their own good."

Chuck stares vacantly ahead as Richard, then says loud enough for the colonel to hear, "Doesn't make much sense to me, and I'm an American! Wonder what kind of 'sense' it makes to them? No wonder we can't get them off their land for their 'own safety.' Maybe that's why the VC seems to move so freely way out here in the boonies."

Colonel Stevens abruptly finishes his conversation, turns toward Richard, and asks him to join him in a cup of coffee. Conditioned to expect anger or disapproval from the Old Man, Richard feels an instant jolt of paranoia come over him.

They sit down on a log together, Stevens gives his chaplain a cup of coffee and says, "Well, Padre, whattya think?"

Strom now believes finally has a clue as to what the colonel's attitude is going to be when he interacts with him. When he uses the title *Padre*, a greeting utilized by many in the Marine Corps whether the chaplain is Protestant or Catholic, he has no beef with his chaplain and things are okay or casual between them. However, mostly when Richard is addressed as *Chaplain*, the Old Man is either tense about some situation or he's perturbed at something his chaplain has done or said.

"How are the troopers doing back there in Da Nang?" he asks while munching on some crackers and slurping his coffee. "You think they're getting adequate care in those navy hospitals?"

"Yeah, I think so," Strom casually replies, "they seem to be doing all right."

Stevens stops his munching, turns toward Richard, and says, "In the Marine Corps, Chaplain, commanding officers, especially colonels and above, are normally referred to as Colonel, General, or sir. You might want to note that little reminder and file it away for future reference."

"Yes, sir," Strom meekly replies.

The colonel then opens a can of his favorite peaches with his John Wayne, a small can opener usually kept on the chain next to one's dog tags, slurps up some fruit, and says, "Padre, we have three line companies strung out along this here road"—he then points with his spoon—"and we're gonna sit tight here for a while. Instead of wasting your time here playing cards or jackin' around with your navy buddies over there, I want you to go hang out for a day with each company, then come back to battalion. That'll keep you outta my hair for a while, and it'll make the major happy as well," he declares with a final slurp from his can of peaches and a broad smile on his face.

By noon Richard and Bob have walked the three hundred meters to the Echo CP and find the skipper, company Sergeant, and two other Marines locked into a bridge game being played on top of ammo boxes. "Welcome aboard," Captain Woggins says without looking up from his game, "let's have church sometime later this afternoon, say 1800."

They unpack their gear close by the company CP. It's hot and muggy but immediately Bob starts digging a hole. "What are you doing?" Richard asks incredulously.

"I think we'll be safer, sir, by digging this right away," he replies.

Richard, feeling somewhat embarrassed, helps his assistant dig their foxhole big enough for both of them to fit into. It is difficult work because of the heat and the hard clay ground. As they are finally finishing their dig, a new replacement Corpsman casually strolls by, laughs at them, and says, "Ain't nothing happening around here, Chaplain. How come you digging that hole?"

"Staying on the safe side," Richard grunts, throwing a shovel of close enough to his feet to get his boots dirty. The corpsman frowns, turns, and walks away, shaking his head.

Later that afternoon, Richard and Bob are setting up for church services. In front of them they watch a Marine with a guard dog walk toward two captured VC suspects, who are now squatting on the ground, blindfolded. The Marine dog handler then lets his snarling, barking German shepherd lunge very close to the suspects, nipping them on their arms. "What the hell is going on over there?" Richard demands from Bob, perturbed at the scene he is seeing thirty meters away from the altar where he will shortly be having worship services.

Bob turns toward the chaplain and replies, "They usually won't talk at all, so using the dogs, that's how they get information from them. They're scared as hell of our dogs."

At that moment Richard sees the dog jump on one of the suspects who is still squatting on the deck, growling viciously, his teeth sinking into the poor fellow's shoulder and neck. Strom flashes on pictures he's seen of German SS troops during World War II turning dogs loose on innocent civilians and Jews. He suddenly feels sick to his stomach as the dog and handler suddenly leave and the two suspects are lead away to another tree line down the road for transportation back to regiment. Richard looks at Bob and he just looks down at the ground as if didn't want to deal with what he saw. Neither did Strom!

Ten minutes later there are seventy Marines in front of Richard on a small hillside protected by a grove of trees surrounding three side of the area. Chaplain Strom cannot get that scene of the dog and the VC suspects out of his mind's eye, particularly when he raises the chalice in his hands and says the words of consecration: "This is the blood of Christ shed for you."

After the service, when he and Bob are packing the communion kit, Richard remembers the conversation with his dad up in the mountains, which seems so long ago, about the conflict he would eventually need to resolve concerning the cross on his left collar and the lieutenant bars on his right. "Maybe he knew what he was talking about—idealists and clergy don't belong here," he ponders to himself, then quickly focuses on the evening ahead of him.

Later, just before dark, after walking the perimeter with the gunny and visiting with both new and familiar faces, the chaplain returns to the CP. Bob is sitting down on an ammo box preparing a meal from his C-rations. At that very instant three mortar explosions take place close to their position, creating that instant terror inside. Corpsman Jacobi, who earlier that day made fun of Bob and Richard while they dug their foxhole, dives headfirst, in front of Strom, into the hole that he and Bob had labored over earlier that day.

Panicked, Strom instantly runs the ten meters to the foxhole, leans over and grabs the corpsman by his belt, lifts him out of his hole, and literally throws his young ass off to the side, then jumps into the hole that he and Bob had spent an hour preparing in the hot sun. In that moment of time, Richard learns quickly the limits of idealism and altruism as it relates to self-preservation.

The company CP is lucky tonight. Only four Marines are injured with minor shrapnel wounds. Bob simply lies down on top of his meal and hopes no more incoming will land close by or on top of us. The corpsman seems to understand where the battalion chaplain is coming from. Because immediately after the attack, in the dark, he begins digging a foxhole of his own.

The next night, one kilometer down the road, right after church services for Hotel Company, just as Bob is packing the communion kit and Richard is turning toward him to ask him if there is any kind of chow available, Charlie begins dropping mortars all around Hotel CP. To add to the confusion, the two resupply choppers are almost on top of the CP bringing in their evening loads of supplies.

One of the helicopters immediately drops its load from about fifty feet out in the middle of the rice paddy. The other chopper beats it for An Hoa. The stuff dropped in the rice paddy is ammo and the aircraft that got outta town has all the rations and water, which means no food or water for the troops tonight.

After a decent interval five Marines run out to retrieve some of the ammo cases scattered about. When they do, small arms fire erupts from a tree line further down the rice paddy. They retreat back to the safety of the company CP. The small arms fire and mortars continue sporadically on and off throughout the night. Miraculously, not one Marine was killed or wounded.

The following afternoon, Bob and Richard walk three kilometers to Golf, which is at the opposite end of the road past Echo and Battalion. The chaplain holds worship services again at 1800 with nearly one hundred percent attendance, including the company commander. Being on the southern flank of the battalion perimeter, Golf finds itself in a very vulnerable area next to the foothills leading up to the high mountains and Laos, which means the troops expect action shortly, always a prerequisite for good church attendance.

After services and upon returning to the Golf CP, Richard is unable to find his assistant and is told that a few minutes ago, a staff sergeant directed Bob to go out to first platoon and stand duty tonight on the lines. As the chaplain is being told this, Staff Sergeant Sualua, a short, tough-looking Samoan with a huge mustache and also the individual who sent Marshall out on the line, strides by Richard.

Strom walks directly toward the sergeant, stops in front of him, and says to him, feeling the anger arise, "Sergeant, you the one who sent my man out on the line?"

"Yes, sir, Chaplain, that's the way we do things here. No one has a free ride," he slowly responds, then turns and walks away.

"Sergeant," Richard shoots back in the nastiest voice he can muster up, "I don't give a shit how you do things around here. You get him back here right now. He's with me. Nobody messes with my man! You hear?" The five Marines standing nearby have a shock look on their face, not believing what they are hearing.

Startled, the sergeant turns and looks at the chaplain for a moment, then responds slowly with a forced, somewhat bemused smile. "Well now, Chaplain, sir, those are orders from the captain. Why don't you talk to him about it… sir!"

Richard immediately turns and walks into the company CP, interrupts the skipper's evening meal, and says in a voice betraying his agitation, "Captain, I just want you to be aware of the fact that my assistant, who has two Purple Hearts and is actually not even supposed to be out in the bush, is to be with me at all times. He is not to pull duty with any of the platoons, nor is he to go out on any patrols. Your sergeant here just sent Marshall out on the line."

Thinking he needs to emphasize his point, he now communicates to the skipper a stretch from the truth: "You have countermanded a direct order from the colonel about my assistant and I know he'd be very unhappy to hear that it's happening again."

The captain stands up, towering over Richard, and replies: "I'm sorry for the mix-up, Chaplain Strom." He turns and looks directly at Sergeant Sualua. "I can assure you this will not happen again. Isn't that right, Sergeant?"

"Yes, sir," the sergeant replies, then looks directly at the chaplain. Richard believes, at that moment, Sualua would probably derive pleasure from putting a bayonet in the battalion chaplain's gut!

From that day on, Captain Moore would allow the chaplain to do pretty much anything he wants to do as long as it conforms to his own orders and command directives. And the nasty sergeant would in the future deal with the battalion chaplain with a cool, steely, indifferent politeness, the kind of behavior that hides deep feelings of dislike and malice.

That night the enemy lobs grenades right into the CP, badly injuring eleven Marines and one corpsman. Bob and Richard are lucky again escaping serious injury. While the first platoon secures the area around the CP, the chaplain and his assistant helped triage the wounded and get them aboard a nighttime emergency medevac. Although no more incoming comes and the rifle fire has stopped, the anxiety and wariness remain throughout the night until morning's light.

Richard and Bob return the next morning to battalion where that evening more mortars are lobbed near the CP. Shortly before morning a large firefight erupts in the area between Echo and the battalion, then stops as abruptly as it started, the VC quietly disappearing into the hills or their villages that are supposed to be uninhabited.

Assuming the enemy has disengaged at least for the time being, Richard and Bob are preparing some quick food. Richard is squatting over his makeshift stove cooking some meatballs and beans for breakfast. He hears the familiar voice of Colonel Stevens approaching him, suddenly panicking because he's left his helmet and flak jacket next to his poncho thirty meters away. Strom stands up, expecting some choice words from the colonel. He turns as the Old Man stops and says, "Chaplain, what's this I hear about you drawing fire all the time? You're supposed to be a spiritual rabbit's foot for us instead of bringing all this enemy fire wherever you go. The S3 suggests we should hang a bell around your neck, like they did with the lepers in the Bible, and send you away from us. Maybe that'll keep Charlie from pestering us!"

Momentarily, Richard is startled by Steven's words, but when the colonel breaks out into a big smile, Strom answers, "I have a solution to that issue, Colonel. I need some religious supplies—communion wine, religious medals, stuff like that. With your permission, I'd like to take a chopper into An Hoa tonight and come back out in the morning. With me at regiment, the VC will fire at An Hoa and leave you guys alone."

As he finishes talking, the S3 is standing next to the colonel, again with that nasty, menacing look. "You sure you're using that communion wine for church only, Chaplain? I sure as hell don't want you and your buddies over there drinking that stuff for recreational purposes," the colonel asks, quickly jerking his head in the direction of Chuck and two corpsmen sitting on the ground nearby. "You wouldn't do that now, would you, Chaplain?"

"I wouldn't think of it, sir," Richard replies instantly, "kind of borders on the sacrilegious to even consider that." The chaplain, of course, is stretching the truth—the wine in his canteen is not consecrated, only that which is poured into the chalice and used for communion during the Eucharist is considered consecrated. At this point he wants them to believe even the canteen wine is "holy," thinking to himself, "What they don't know…"

Krump! Krump! Krump! Krump! Mortars are now walking their way closer and closer to battalion. Just as suddenly, small arms fire rakes the battalion CP area, creating immediate chaos and again, that instant primal fear.

The colonel and his immediate staff instantly retreat into the makeshift bunker nearby, Chuck and the corpsmen are lying flat on the deck at one with the earth while Richard and Bob have jumped into a bamboo thicket nearby. Quickly, first platoon of Echo, which is now security for battalion, rapidly deploys toward two tree lines to the east and initiates small arms fire and launches grenades. The scene is disorganized, not tidy and focused like the Marines learn in his rifle training at Edson Range or infantry school at San Onofre back at Camp Pendleton.

The unfolding scene is now familiar at battalion level. Enemy mortars or rockets are suddenly dropped into the area in which field headquarters is located, followed in quick succession by small arms fire, then withdrawal into the villages or back into the hills to the west. If the enemy is pursued into the next tree line or village, the Marines will usually receive sustained heavy fire as they approached a ville and suffer a number of casualties. However, by the time they sweep through the area, the enemy has disappeared. Next the medevacs swoop into the area to take the dead and wounded back to Da Nang. After the troops search the area, they will then withdraw to their original positions prior to the enemy action.

So that by the time first platoon has searched the area the platoon leader, 1st Lt. Brian Collins, is already calling in emergency medevacs for the casualties. Another morning, another quick search-and-destroy operation resulting in three dead and eight wounded, including three critical Marines who need immediate attention.

The aftermath of this experience creates a tense vigilance that stays with the combatant for a few hours, then the episode slowly fades into the monotonous background of living and staying alive in the bush until the next event transpires. The bipolar, instantaneous transition between total boredom and sheer terror is a repetitious experience as common to the grunt as is going to work for the civilian. It also wears down the emotional and feeling processes and is a disaster as well for the autonomic system of the body that controls so many of the vital functions of the body, including the very important fight-or-flight function. Day after day, night after night, up and down, in and out of rocket attacks, firefights, booby traps, hanging out, nothing to do, waiting for the next event to happen, blocking out any thoughts of the inevitable.

Richard is sent back that afternoon to An Hoa as requested, then catches a ride into Da Nang to visit his troops again in the hospital, a duty he now considers vital to his ministry, yet subtly becoming more upsetting to him with each visit. He stays at First Medical Battalion that evening with the new Catholic chaplain, Jim Reitch, returning to An Hoa the next morning on Sunshine Airlines, a new moniker the chaplain has assigned to the helicopter group now providing services for the Fifth Marines. To his surprise, the battalion is being airlifted out this morning back to An Hoa and will be relocated tomorrow morning in an area thirteen kilometers east, northeast of regiment on the south side of the Son Thu Bon River. At the briefing that afternoon, military intelligence—this is Strom's favorite oxymoron—reports numerous VC in this region who are gathering food and hidden supplies for what may be another major Tet Offensive in a few months. This area, and the island adjacent to it, the infamous Go Noi Island, is a major crop growing and distribution area for both the NVA and VC. Go Noi is infamous because even after the island is blasted with saturation bombing from B-52s, the Marines always take heavy casualties when they enter this domain of the enemy.

By noon the next day, the helicopters have just dropped off battalion field headquarters and two platoons of Echo next to the riverbed. The humidity and temperature are unbearable. Humping in this kind of weather takes a heavy toll on the grunt's endurance causing dizziness, nausea, and weakness, early signs of heat exhaustion and later, if not attended to, the dangerous condition known as heat stroke. Most of the personnel are packing in at least fifty extra pounds of gear plus wearing their helmets and flak jackets making ventilation quite difficult. Adding to this physical discomfort, the area is also notorious for booby traps and hidden mines.

Walking directly in front of Chaplain Strom is Valenta. He's a well-experienced, excellent field corpsman and also one of the crustiest and most profane individuals Richard has ever met. He is humping in, besides his own gear and a twenty-pound medical kit, a whole case of beer. Just before leaving the BAS this morning, he informs Bernie Grant and Richard that since this is his last foray into the bush before getting an assignment back at regiment, he is going to have beer in the field. This is a very risky venture because the Old Man expressly forbid any alcoholic beverages out in the bush—chaplain's wine and doctor's ethanol exceptions—and said he will court-martial anyone who disobeys his directive and gets caught.

Bernie is walking in front of Valenta and the both of them are sharing the burden of carrying the valuable cargo, which they do openly, humping it in on their shoulders. To disguise the beer, they've emptied a Pepsi Cola case and refilled it with beer and glued the case shut.

"Hey, Chaplain," Bernie groans at one point as they slog through ankle-high water across a rice paddy, "how about doing the Lord's work and share the burden here for a while."

Richard is apprehensive about being part of the conspiracy, given the somewhat adversarial relationship he has heretofore developed with the colonel. But since the Old Man is at least one hundred meters away, he relents and carries the case for one kilometer, complaining to Bob about feeling like a Clydesdale horse.

By late afternoon, after three hours of humping, battalion headquarters pulls into Cu Bon, a small village, and digs in for the night, having had no contact with Charlie the whole day. Bob and Richard set up their "quarters" between two big logs, find some water in a well nearby and fill their canteens, then began preparing food.

Valenta has just brought Marshall and Strom a beer, thanking Richard for the help. He's well into a six-pack and Bernie is not far behind. It's quiet and dark. Except for those guarding the perimeter, most of the Marines have set in for the night and appear comfortable. Without any warning, AK-47 fire erupts, spraying the entire battalion CP area. It is the most intense small arms fire that Richard has yet experienced. Bob and Richard are lying between the logs, bullets smashing into the logs and into the supports holding up the thatched roof. Valenta crawls back twenty meters to the small hooch, which serves at the BAS.

"Get your ass over here, Chaplain, there's a bunker where y'all be safe," Strom hears the doctor yell.

Instantly Richard's young assistant spits out, "Sir, stay where you are," as a fuselage of bullets strike the supports and roof over their heads, then says in a voice betraying fear and agitation, "You'll get hit if you go out there."

At that moment, the chaplain's thoughts are not about moving but rather, "If I could just melt into the ground…"

The AK-47 fire stops after five minutes just as suddenly as it started. Bob and Richard then crawl very fast in the darkening evening like two cockroaches on the kitchen floor when the lights have suddenly been turned on. When they reach the enclosed thatched hooch, they scoot into a two-foot-deep depression off to the side. It is a much safer spot than where they had been, just like Bernie had said. Grant and Valenta have also resumed their beer drinking but are soon interrupted in their pastime by a message saying their presence is needed at the battalion CI to give medical attention to the injured Marines. Off they go, half-smashed, to get the wounded in shape for medevac.

"Good luck," Richard thinks to himself, shaking his head in disbelief, feeling guilty because he was part of "the conspiracy" and what could turn out to be a possible medical nightmare! Later that night Valenta, Bernie and Bob finish off the rest of the case. Valenta definitely is drunk, Bernie is falling asleep, Bob is asleep, and Richard is still experiencing the sting of guilt, hoping the doctor and corpsmen didn't mess up medically with the wounded they treated. As he lies on the hard clay deck inside the hooch, attempting to fall asleep, he begins to reflect on the war and how his experiences are getting a little wackier each week he is out in the bush. "What kind of nuttiness is this, getting shot at, then drinking beer like nothing has happened at all? Lord, help me out, carry me through all this craziness, I'm starting to come apart. Please keep me glued together so I can cope," Richard prays silently to himself as tears slowly well up in his eyes and roll down his cheeks.

The next morning Bob and Richard are on their way to Golf located approximately three hundred meters away across a rice paddy.

The skipper has requested the chaplain's presence and has asked that he stay for a couple of days. The S3 said that since it was daylight they would need no security. So they are now walking on a dike that separates two rice paddies. Bob, in the lead, appears nervous and says quietly to Richard as he is walking, "Sir, I don't like being out in the open—"

AK-47 fire erupts ahead and to the left about one hundred meters away. Marshall immediately dives into the water next to the dike while Richard instinctively takes off running across the paddy in the opposite direction away from Golf and toward battalion that is in the process of moving out. Chaplain Strom, a top sprinter in high school, is running as fast as he has ever run in his life, all his gear on, driven by primal fear and a deep, inherent instinct to stay alive. He is vaguely aware of the AK fire and the sounds of rounds hitting the water around him, until he finally throws himself over a dike into a foot of water, finally separating him from the hostile fire. As he lies there panting, frightened again out of his wits, his first thought is, "I think I crapped my pants!"

Then that horrible pain arises again from the base of his spine, just like that first night on Hill 52 when those rockets hit. Only now he understands what this pain is about. It is the body's way of handling the extreme, life-threatening stress. He doesn't understand the physiological process, why so many of the grunts experienced this painful sensation at the base of their spines under horrible duress; he just knows that it happens frequently and is painful and scary!

Richard vaguely hears a helicopter in the distant firing its machine guns, hoping they are hitting targets in the tree line that fired at him. He begins crawling in the water, protected by the dike, back toward battalion less than one hundred meters away. He is extremely anxious and paranoid, fearful the firing will resume, keeping his head well below the level of the dike slowly making his way back to some semblance of safety.

He finally reaches the end of the dike, then jumps over the embankment and runs twenty meters into a tree line and a small ville in which the battalion is now located and also where Bob has recently arrived. Richard is exhausted, soaked, and scared and walks toward a group of six Marines clustered around the colonel, who is busy talking on the radio to Golf. The S3 has a smile on his face as the chaplain approaches and says sarcastically, "That was a hell of a trick you pulled out there, Chaplain."

"What trick was that?" Richard asks perplexed by the major's statement.

"Walking on water, or should I say running on water," he responds. "Learned that from your boss?"

Richard doesn't appreciate the major's humor, especially in light of Sulli's disastrous assessment of enemy positions that had the potential of getting both the chaplain and his assistant killed. "The only trick needed here is to stop putting your personnel at risk," Richard shoots back with anger in his voice, obviously irritated at the major's cavalier attitude and sarcasm.

The S3 appears startled at the chaplain's comment, quickly turns, and walks away. "The stupid bastard doesn't possess the necessary verbal skills to respond in any intelligent way to my affront," Richard then reasons.

Toward evening, the colonel is perturbed at reports that Marines from Golf are setting delayed fires to the hooches of villes they are passing through. Apparently they take a hunk of plastic explosives called C-4, make a small pencil-sized hole, place a newly lighted unfiltered cigarette into the hole, and place the device in a corner ceiling by the thatched roof. When the cigarette burns down to the C-4, it ignites the plastics, which in turn spreads the fire to the roof and burns down the hooch. By the time the fire starts five minutes later, the Marines are gone.

"Tell those boys in Golf," the colonel is yelling at his S2, "that anybody that is chicken shit enough to pull that kind of stunt will get their asses court-martialed. And I goddamn mean it!"

An hour later, as battalion is passing through the ville that Golf earlier passed through, all seven hooches have been burned to the ground. Apparently Golf took unfriendly fire from this ville, wounding five Marines. Since the VC had disappeared by the time Golf finally took the ville, this was their way of venting their frustration and getting even.

Just outside the ville, on the main path leading to a larger village complex about three hundred meters away, Richard sees one of the most startling sights he has seen to date. During the skirmish Golf kills a number of VC. So that later, when battalion passes through the ville they come across the bodies of six Viet Cong that had been hidden under some rice sacks in shallow graves. So Golf digs up the bodies and lines them up in a sitting position, side by side, with their backs resting against a rice paddy dike, lighted cigarettes in their mouth, just like six, relaxed construction workers eating sandwiches on their lunch break.

This infuriates Colonel Stevens. He gets back on the radio and chews ass loud enough to be heard for two hundred meters. "Captain, if this kind of thing happens again—I don't care who does it in your company—I'll haul your tall ass up for court-martial, do you understand me, Captain?" It was the last time any desecration of dead bodies took place in *Two-five*.

That night a badly wounded VC suspect, who has compound fractures of an arm and a leg, is brought into the BAS where Richard is sleeping. Bernie puts on air bags as splints and does what he can to medically help the poor man. Obviously in great pain, the VC suspect never saying a word, not even a groan. He lies next to Richard all night, silent and motionless.

In the morning the chaplain offers him a drink of water, which he drinks slowly. When he finishes, he nods to Richard as if to say thank you. The chaplain looks into his eyes and sees a distressed, fearful human being in extreme pain, not some cutthroat VC. When Richard and two corpsmen later carry him to the waiting helicopter and lay him down on a stretcher inside, Strom reaches out to the captive and gently pats his free hand. For a moment there is pure contact.

The chaplain then walks slowly off the chopper, suddenly aware that the capture of this young native is a death sentence. The South Vietnamese Army will kill him when they get whatever information they can get out of him. Richard believes the young man understands this.

Watching the helicopter lift off, Richard remembers his dad's comments that night up in the solitude and safeness of the Sierra's, when he insinuated that idealism and rules of fairness cannot exist in the midst of warfare.

There is a bottom line rule, however, that is operative in combat, one that has always been true as long as war has been waged. You either kill or be killed!

Richard James Strom is slowly beginning to shut down inside. The crack in his insular worldview has just been widened.

Diary Entry—60 Days In-Country

Waiting is a fierce, debilitating process that wears you down in this war. I suppose it has been no different since that time when Homo sapiens *first organized themselves into raiding parties to hunt food or drive off other marauding groups of animals or hunters. I wonder if they waited around as much as we do? Poor bastards! At least we have* Playboy.

Waiting around drives everyone to distraction because it invades especially the basic necessities of life. You wait in the chow line, you wait to take a shower if one is even available—you wait for your mail, you wait to see the doctor or the chaplain or the first sergeant. You even have to wait many times to go to the head. Waiting just grinds your ass down, that's all!

Once, while sitting under the hot sun waiting for a chopper ride to wherever, it occurred to me that maybe the people who dream up these wars purposely planned all this waiting around. Because lots of waiting around takes the edge of all the frustration and anger generated by the unconsciousness of war. It kind of saps your energy. Waiting round causes the energy of anger to turn into energy of listless boredom, which is why I've always felt the military leaders have a stake in keeping us as bored as possible. Waiting around dulls your mind and body. It's a great sedative to give soldiers in a war zone. It keeps them from the thinking rebellious thoughts.

Waiting around, aside from being very boring and depressing, also leads to some creative endeavors as well. For instance, sitting on a landing pad waiting for a chopper ride back out into the field, Marines sometimes will organize a spitting contest—who can spit the farthest, who can hit a fly in the tarmac at ten feet, who can spit the biggest load, and so forth. Red and black licorice and chewing tobacco make this a real interesting enterprise.

Another favorite the grunts play while waiting is to have a belching contest. First, you drink a warm soda or beer to get the gas reservoir built up in your stomach. Then you release! The belches are judged on a number of factors: resonance, volume, length, and creativity, which usually translate into an attempt at belching a sentence.

Waiting around appears to be the only thing the Marine Corps has an excess, unless it is the sometimes incredibly stupid decisions that come to battalion from on high.

But there is also an ironic, sad side to this business of waiting around as well. Sometimes, young men are waiting to die. Of course, none of us ever see ourselves getting killed, at least not for the first three or four weeks of combat anyway. Injured maybe, but getting snuffed? Never! We are invincible.

However, over here, invincibility is just a concept. Dying is the indisputable reality.

A GRAVE MISTAKE

It is a misty, wet overcast early morning as Richard is preparing to begin church services for two platoons of Echo Company. He is standing in back of a crude altar made out of three sixty-millimeter ammo boxes stacked on top of each other. On top of the makeshift altar are a six-inch brass crucifix, two small votive-type candle holders, a chalice half-filled with altar wine, and a paten filled with communion wafers with embroidered linen over the paten. He is facing about seventy Marines sitting on the ground in a semicircle in a small clearing surrounded by trees on three sides. On the fourth side three Marines stand guard with their rifles. He is wearing his usual "vestments": Marine utility pants, combat boots, a dark green T-shirt, and a small purple-and-white stole draped around his neck and over his shoulders down to his belt buckle. There is an unusual quiet this morning as the chaplain begins his services, a quiet that is void of the sounds of artillery and aircraft and troops on the move. It is an eerie silence that is rarely experienced by any grunt, especially out in the field in contact with the enemy.

"I've been told that shortly Battalion and Echo will be moving out again, this time up that big hill south of us so we can observe Go Noi Island and see what kind of enemy movement is going on over there," he begins. There are audible groans along with a number of disgusted looks as they anticipate their fourth move in as many days. "Since we'll be moving out within the hour, this will be a short service. Give you time to get your gear together. So we'll just have general confession and absolution followed by Holy Communion," he continues.

"I'm aware that there are many denominations and traditions represented here this morning, and how I conduct services may be different than what you are used to back home. I wish there was some way to have each of you represented by your own tradition, a way to bring you closer to those experiences of home that are so important to all of us here."

At this point Richard walks in front of the altar and closer to the men seated in front of him. "As with so many things in the Marine Corps, you rarely get what you want and instead have to take what you get. And for now, for better or for worse, I'm what you've got, you're stuck with me," he says with mock seriousness, shrugging his shoulders, directing his hands upward.

Then in a more serious tone he says, "I'm here to serve all of you in the best way that I can. Let me know what you want from me. With that said, I want you to know that each of you is welcome to receive the sacrament. I will leave that up to you and the dictates of your own conscience. Please make that decision based upon you own personal views and spiritual needs, not upon what you believe you should do, especially out here in the bush. I also want all of you to know that, as far as I'm concerned, with all the living and dying that's happening, denominational differences don't mean jack out here."

The chaplain then moves behind the altar, faces the troops, and begins with the invocation: "In the name of the Father, and of the Son, and of the Holy Spirit." He makes the sign of the cross and commences the short three-minute liturgy before communion. When the liturgy is finished, he hands the paten to Bob, who has been standing next to the altar since the invocation. Richard takes the chalice in his hands and he and Bob walk in front of the makeshift altar to give communion. He has learned that attendance at worship services out in the bush is nearly one hundred percent, and most of the Marines receive Holy Communion as well. It is no different this morning as most of the young men trudge up to receive the sacrament.

The last young man in line walks up to the front of the altar with his hands folded, the chaplain dips a communion wafer in the wine and places it in his mouth, saying, "Body and blood of Christ... Hey, Joe, written home lately?"

Joe crosses himself, opens his eyes, smiles, and says softly, "Yes, sir," then turns and walks back to the group and sits down.

Chaplain Strom puts the chalice and paten back on the altar, turns and says, "The Lord said, 'Don't be anxious for tomorrow...'" Just then there is a burst of machine gun fire from the ville he is facing about two hundred kilometers away. There's that automatic, nonthinking flinch and tightening response from all those present that goes way down deep into their limbic instincts as he continues. "That's kind of hard to get together, especially out here." This is followed by nervous laughter. "But with some luck, using some common sense, and by the Grace of God, we'll see a tomorrow," he says, then makes the sign of the cross and closes the short worship service with the Benediction.

Later, as Bob is packing up the communion gear, he says to the chaplain, "Sir, what was that all about with Joe. You know that stuff about writing home?"

"Oh, ah. His mom hadn't heard from him in quite a while," Richard replies, "so two months ago she sends me a letter wanting to know if something has happened to him." He pauses to scratch the cut healing on his back. "I think she thought he had VD or something and his brain was rotting out." Bob laughs and shakes his head.

"His mom and every other mom, dad, and wife have every right to be worried about their sons and husbands," he continues. "None of them can really grasp just how bad it is over here. I guess it's good the folks back home don't know, for a number of reasons. Hey, Bob, isn't your buddy Joe pretty short?"

"Yes, sir, about twenty days," he says as he slings the communion kit over his shoulder and they walk toward the skipper of Echo about fifty meters away.

"Pretty good attendance today, huh, Bob?" Richard asks.

"Yes, sir," is his reply, "always is out here."

The chaplain turns to Bob and says with a smile. "Listen, Bob, knock off that sir crap all the time. Do it when you have to in front of other officers, but not to me," he tells him.

"Yes, sir," he automatically responds. Richard laughs and shakes his head at the absurdity of his statement, telling a young Marine he doesn't have to address an officer as sir. These young men are so conditioned to respond to authority, they salute anything that wears a hat, including the driver of a bread truck.

The company CP is breaking down its gear and getting ready to move out. Captain Woggins is on the radio to battalion, talking to the colonel, as Richard reaches for his helmet and flak jacket. Suddenly the sound of an approaching jet becomes very loud. He looks up and sees an F-4 Phantom jet roaring over the ville across the rice paddy over two hundred meters away. He also notices that the jet has released two bombs, which shortly hit the village with a tremendous explosion. The Phantom jet roars away and for a few moments there is absolute, shocked silence.

Suddenly the skipper starts screaming, "Jesus, those are my men in there, goddammit!" He is actually yelling at the passing jet, then talks directly into the radio again. "Colonel, our own air just dropped a load on one of my platoons in the ville." Richard drops his backpack and communion kit and immediately runs toward the rice paddies separating the company CP from the ville, yelling at Bob to stay where he is. He still has the same clothing on that he had when conducting services earlier and is not wearing either his helmet or flak jacket. As he continues to run in the rice paddy, he is met by three Marines who are now kneeling in the water, facing the village. Running past them at full speed, he jumps over a dike into the next paddy, trips, and falls headfirst into six inches of muddy water. He struggles to stand up in the slimy brown muddy water, soaked and caked with mud, and commences running again. Just before the chaplain gets to the edge of this rice paddy and the tree line in front of the village, he sees another Phantom coming in on the same trajectory. He dives for the ground next to the trees, holding his head between his forearms, attempting to protect himself from what he assumes will be another shattering explosion. Instead, there is a loud WHHUUPP sound, which is followed immediately by horrible suffocating heat.

A huge fireball and black smoke is arising beyond the tree line. Richard is absolutely terrified as he puts his head again between his forearms and draws his legs up to his stomach in a fetal position, expecting the jets to return momentarily with more explosives, assuming that he was going to die.

Chaplain Strom has absolutely no idea how long he laid in that position by the trees—half a second, half a minute—before he hears someone yelling from beyond the tree line in the village: "We need some corpsmen right now!" And from another direction came, "Corpsmen up, on the double!" He quickly gets up and makes his way through the bamboo tree line into a clearing near the main part of the village. He sees shattered trees, smashed hooches, and smoldering debris everywhere. At that point he breaks into a trot, horrified at what he is seeing, heading in the general direction of some smoking ruins sixty meters away.

He runs by two burning, completely smashed, broken bodies and gags at the stench of burning flesh. Slowly, Chaplain Strom stops and surveys the scene of destruction surrounding him, feeling absolutely helpless. He cannot take in what he is experiencing—the sight of ripped-apart, burning bodies—and says quickly to himself, "This isn't real, this isn't happening." He then turns to his right and sees ahead of him just a few meters away a corpsman leaning over a Marine. The corpsman looks up, sees Richard, and yells, "Chaplain… Chaplain, it's Joe. Oh God, he's bad!"

It takes all of Richard's willpower to walk over to the corpsman and the Marine, whereupon he kneels down, reaches under Joe's back with both arms, and draws him up to rest with his back against his leg and stomach. He is black all over from flash burns, a hole the size of a fifty-cent piece slowly oozing blood and brain matter from his forehead. One leg is missing at the knee, and the other is mangled badly, as are both arms below the elbow. His eyes are open, staring vacantly straight ahead. There is no movement in his body except for an occasional gasping for breath. The corpsman is fumbling through his medical kit in a panic.

"Oh God, Chaplain, oh God, he's hurt so bad," he says as Richard holds Joe's head against his chest as the corpsman continues to rummage through his kit, completely freaked out, desperate at being unable to help his good friend Joe.

For the first time since arriving in the tree line Richard is dimly aware of yelling and confusion in the background. He quietly says to the corpsman, "Let him be... let him be."

"Is he dead, Chaplain?" Holdridge responds, grief written on his face.

Richard slowly nodded, quietly lays Joe back on the ground, stands up, and walks toward a smoldering hooch a few meters away where three Marines are frantically attempting to remove bodies from the debris. In the midst of the debris Richard sees two legs sticking out of a pile of rubble. What is horrifying about this scene is that the legs are not connected to a body. One of the Marines is pulling out another mangled body, saying, "Jesus Christ Almighty, I don't believe this is happening. This ain't real!" It is understandable why the young Marine is responding with so much disbelief—there isn't a complete body in the whole area, just a bunch of body parts grotesquely scattered about the area.

Chaplain Strom is astounded by the destruction around him as he helps the three Marines attempt to locate any survivors in the immediate area. Suddenly, he calmly turns around and faces away from the destroyed area, puts his hands in his pocket, and walks to a tree about twenty meters away, looking down at his feet. When he gets to the tree, he leans against the trunk, hands in pockets, and begins to vomit. When he finishes, he calmly wipes his mouth and blows his nose on his T-shirt. At this point he is aware that he no longer feels fear and revulsion, only numbness. His only thought at this time is that he will get sick again if he goes back to the main area of the village.

However, he believes that because of his position in the battalion he cannot show any signs of weakness, aversion, or fear. So he slowly returns to the area where there formerly was a ville and notices a number of Marine in full battle gear running across the rice paddy that he had crossed just a few minutes earlier.

The first one to arrive in the area is the platoon sergeant, yelling at no one in particular. "Has anyone seen the chaplain?" Richard slowly walks toward him, and as he approaches, Sergeant Mac says,

"You okay, Chaplain? We got some bad feelings when you disappeared in that tree line and thought that maybe the napalm got you."

"I'm all right," the chaplain says to him flatly.

The gunny then turns and points to a large, open space south of the village and says, "We've got at least two medevacs on the way, Chaplain, let's get the wounded over there in that open space, sir."

The entire Echo CP has now arrived and, along with what is left of the second platoon, is carrying the wounded and dead Marines and to the clearing. Confusion, shock, and disbelief permeate everyone as some continue to search for more bodies while others just aimlessly mill about.

By now the skipper has calmed down and is on the radio talking again to the colonel. In the direction of where battalion headed out this morning, Richard can hear the sounds of a fierce firefight going on as Woggins is telling the colonel, "Our count is eight dead and twelve wounded. And one is unaccounted for. We're not sure about that but I'd say they have about the same casualties as us."

Shortly the captain is off the radio and gives instructions to the gunny: "The colonel says send the first platoon up to battalion for security. They've just made contact and the Old Man is nervous. The third platoon and what's left of the second can stay here until we get this mess cleaned up, then we'll join battalion."

The sound of approaching helicopters can be heard in the background. A yellow smoke grenade goes off in the clearing to let the choppers know the area is secure. Two CH-46 helicopters come over the clearing at one hundred meters and circle slowly and land just to the south of the village. The next task is to evacuate the dead and wounded Marines and civilians to the clearing. The chaplain makes five trips and helps carry wounded civilians to the waiting choppers. On the last trip he stops by a demolished hooch and sees this small child, maybe two years old, lying motionless under some partially burned straw mats. There appears to be no marks on the body as he gently picks up the small child in his arms. He has only a white T-shirt like garment covering his body from the shoulders to the knees. Richard is just standing there softly holding this baby in his arms against his chest, flashing on his own young child back in

California, feeling enormous grief for this child, for Joe, for the dead Marines, for these poor people living here—for everyone.

"Hey, Chaplain, we gotta get this kid on the chopper, they're leaving," a corpsman explains as he grabs Richard by the arm.

Richard continues to hold the small child and answers him slowly, "It doesn't matter. He's dead."

The corpsman disregards Chaplain Strom's statement as if nothing at all has been said, grabs the child out of his hands, and runs for the waiting helicopter. At this point Strom turns to see a number of men from Echo Company struggling with those green zip-up body bags with bodies or partial bodies of dead Marines. Shortly they'll be in the Rose Garden back at First Medical Battalion. Within fifteen minutes the last of the body bags are loaded up and the wounded civilians are placed aboard a large CH-46 helicopter bound for Da Nang.

As the battalion chaplain watches the helicopters take off and slowly spiral up and northeast, he feels enormous emptiness, an overwhelming exhaustion, a desire to withdraw and be completely by himself. But he steels himself, turns, and walks back to the area where second platoon—or what's left of it—is located, just inside the tree line next to the smoldering village. A staff sergeant is sitting on an ammo crate, head in hands, looking down at his feet. He is sobbing softly. Richard slowly walks up to him and squats down in front of the sergeant.

"Wiped out," he says as he snaps his fingers, "just like that!" There is grief and sadness in his voice as he continues, "Jackson was real short, so I gave him my family's phone number back in Detroit just this morning." He begins to softly sob again. He then looks at the chaplain and says to him between sobs, "My whole platoon… my whole fucking platoon wiped out." Then he points his index feeling at him and says angrily, "Doesn't make one fucking bit of sense what you say at your damn church services, Chaplain? It's just a bunch of shit, that's all!"

The chaplain says nothing as the sergeant begins sobbing softly again. "And my men were killed by our own air, the dirty flickers! I hate those sons of bitches!" He puts his head back in his hands, looks down at the ground again, and says softly, "Whatta ya do… whatta ya say."

Chaplain Strom is aware that for the first time in his life he has absolutely nothing to say and knows that there is absolutely nothing he can do. He feels completely powerless and helpless and slowly responds, "Yeah, I know… whatta ya say."

Slowly the sergeant takes his hands away from his face, stands up, and wordlessly walks away from the chaplain and disappears into a tree line. Richard has some thoughts that the sergeant's anger isn't really directed toward him, that he is just venting his feelings of loss and rage. However, at this point Richard isn't very certain about anything and quickly speculates that perhaps if he had not had church services earlier this morning, this disaster might never have happened. Then he notices, again, a strong desire to isolate and be completely by himself.

Instead, he responds to his Scandinavian, upper Midwest sense of duty, to his clergy instincts that overrides any need to care for or take time for himself. So he trudges back to the CP area, helps in the cleanup of gear, talks to the some of the remaining members of second platoon, and collects the information needed to write the family members of the dead Marines.

Bob has remained back in the area where the chaplain originally ordered him to stay, where third platoon is now just leaving to hump up the hill behind battalion. Fortunate for him he didn't see the results of his close friends literally being blown away. Richard is now making his way back to that area to get all his gear ready for the move up the hill.

Marshall is sitting down next to his pack and rifle by a tree, looking very dejected. He looks up as the chaplain approaches and says in his soft voice, "They wiped out the whole squad, didn't they? And Joe too?" Richard sits down next to him and nods, placing his hand on his shoulder as big tears well up in Bob's eyes. "I heard you were holding him when he died, sir?" he says as tears roll down his cheeks.

"Yeah, that's right, Bob," he replies, feeling deep sorrow for him. "I don't believe he ever knew what hit him. He went real fast. I'm really sorry, Bob. I'm terribly sorry."

Bob slowly gets up and disappears into the bushes close by. He is silent that whole day on the hump up the hill with second and third platoons. He has lost every single remaining friend left in Vietnam. It is a harsh reality for an eighteen-year-old kid.

He never did recover from that day. Neither did Chaplain Strom. Nor did any of them.

SOME PLAY TIME

"Whatta ya say, Rich?" exclaims Strom's good friend Wallace Treadwell, a chaplain with the Third Marine Division near the DMZ in Quang Tri province, who is vigorously shaking Richard's hand, then patting him on the back.

"Not much, Wallass, sure good to see you again," Richard answers as he pulls out some script to pay for a beer at the bar.

"Strom, you look like a tank just ran over you," Treadwell continues as they turn away from the bar and walk toward a table with three seated Marines. "Anybody ever introduce you to a shower? You look like hell!"

"I feel like hell," Strom responds, whereupon they sit down at a table and Richard introduces Treadwell to his recon friends, Ursini, Vella, and Norquist.

Chaplain Strom has come straight off the hill to Da Nang and the Naval Support Hospital the day after the tragedy at Thon Bon to visit his troops as per the colonel's request, leaving his assistant behind to help with chores at the battalion aid station. While at the hospital, he happens to come across his three friends from recon who are visiting some of their wounded personnel as well. They invite Richard to dinner with them at the Stone Elephant.

"We'll hose you down and delouse you, Strom. You stink like a pig's ass," Ursini had said as they laughed and climbed into his jeep. However, instead of going back to recon as Norquist had promised and get Richard showered and cleaned up, they drove directly to the naval officers' club in downtown Da Nang.

Chaplain Strom hasn't shaved for three days, his combat boots are scuffed yellow and muddy, his utilities stink because he hasn't had a change of clothing in over a week, and his eyes look, as Norquist frequently says, "like two piss holes in a snowbank" from lack of sleep. And Vella is telling Richard to stay downwind from him. It is the chaplain's impression that these friends from recon enjoy "showing him off" in this grungy condition, their grubby chaplain friend from the Fifth Marines.

As they nurse their beers and wine, the battalion S1, 1st Lt. John Kelly, shows up. "Hey, Chaplain, what the hell you doing here? You're supposed to be out in the field," he says as he walks toward their table waving a bottle of wine. "Tell your friends here to come outside to the patio," he continues in a voice that betrays a number of glasses having already been consumed. "We've got a big table out there and we'll get some more Mateus."

They all get up from the table, Wally, Richard, and the three recon officers, filing out the back door into the patio. The patio is surrounded on three sides by an eight-foot brick wall. The courtyard is neatly decorated by a number of covered tables just like a nicely appointed, fancy restaurant back in the States. As they get closer toward the center, Richard spots the Monk sitting at a table with a Marine. They have not seen each other in a month. Strom continues toward the table, the Monk stands up, recognizing his good friend, and says, "Hey, Lutheran, whattcha doing here? You're supposed to be on an operation." Grasping Strom's hand, he says, "Damn, it's good to see you again you dumb Swede."

Richard is even more astounded when he sees that Gerlitis is sitting at the table with both the S1 and adjutant from *Two-five*. "What's going on, Bill? Colonel know his adjutant is in Da Nang raising hell?" Richard asks 1st Lt. William Farley with a laugh.

"No," he shoots back, "and he isn't going to know unless you tell him."

"Oh sure, Bill, one of my jobs as the religious and moral leader is to be the battalion cop and let the Old Man know when people like you are sneaking around, screwing off," Strom responds.

At that moment the Vietnamese waiter brings four more bottles of Portuguese wine. There are now eight of them, three chaplains and five Marine officers seated at a large table. Most of the other patrons are either naval or air force officers with a smattering of American civilians. Soon the crew of chaplains and Marine officers decide to move inside where they can order a meal and also continue their drinking. So that by the time they have eaten an hour later and have consumed numerous bottles of wine, most of them are in various stages of inebriation, especially Lieutenant Kelly. They've also been very boisterous, as Marines tend to be when partying, and have been warned once about the noise and obnoxious behavior emanating from their table.

The Monk has just told a very, very funny joke about the pope—the same one that broke him up two months earlier at the III MAF chaplain's party—and the chaplains and Marines are cracking up. The adjutant, good Catholic that he is, has fallen out of his chair onto the floor he's laughing so hard. Suddenly Kelly jumps up with a wine bottle in his hand, swings it across the table as if to get everyone's attention, and knocks another wine bottle and two glasses to the floor, which break with a loud noise.

The S1 is obviously drunk by now as Wally and Richard stoop down and began to pick up broken pieces of glass. The context in which this is happening is a tradition-laden navy milieu that is supposed to respect the long observance of proper decorum and behavior in the naval club in the same way an officer and a gentleman behaves in the wardroom of a ship.

With a sweeping gesture of his arm, Kelly says loudly, "Piss on it! Let it sit there, Chaplain. I have another toast. Here's to you religious squids that take care of us Marines." He then turns and faces the room. "And to all you navy pukes." He goes back to the table, forgetting what he was going to say in the first place.

By this time the whole dining room is quiet and just about everyone is staring at Kelly and the show that is going on. The Monk is sitting next to Kelly, his hands holding his head, elbows on the table, looking straight down at the table, a very embarrassed smile on his face. He is shaking his head slowly from side to side. The three recon officers are still laughing loudly while the other two chaplains continue picking up broken glass.

At that moment a navy lieutenant commander and the manager, a civilian, approach table. Lieutenant Kelly faces them as the naval officer addresses the S1 and the entire table. John is weaving badly and it is deathly quiet in the club.

"This is the second time that you have been asked to keep the noise down and respect proper decorum. You are bothering the other patrons and creating an objectionable scene," he says with obvious agitation in his voice. "You are therefore to pay your bill and leave immediately." Strom and Treadwell stand up and place more broken glass on the table as he continues, "If you do not leave the premises immediately and comply with this order, your commands will be notified of pending charges."

As the two gentlemen leave, from way across the room comes the sound of the recon trademark—"*Aaarruuuuugghhh!*"

There is scattered laughter throughout the club. Kelly continues to stand weaving, staring blankly at the adjutant. The Monk, still smiling, looks up at the Richard and says deliberately and slowly, "Dear Reverend Abbot: this letter is to notify you that that one of your monks has just been arrested for being drunk and disorderly."

Richard leans over and sarcastically responds, "Don't worry, Monk, I'll get some of my Dominican friends to buy some indulgences to get your ass out of. What do you call that place, Vince? You know that way station you Catholics go to before you can get to heaven? And if that doesn't work, maybe I can get some Protestant ones from my friend Martin Luther." Gerlitis continues to shake his head slowly from side to side.

Richard is now beginning to feeling self-conscious because of how he must look to the other clean and neatly dressed officers in the club, like he's some kind of crusty animal that just crawled out of a hole. As they walk toward the entrance with all the eyes glued on this noisy crew of troublemakers, the Monk is walking next to Richard and says in a voice loud enough for most of the seated officers to hear. "Chaplain Strom, this is the last time we take you anywhere with us. You're always getting us in trouble!"

Chaplain Strom's embarrassment goes up another notch when walking out the door, they are met by two navy captains no less, who look him over as they pass by and say, "Those Marines are disgusting."

"Hey, heretic," says the Monk to Richard when they get outside, "where you guys going now?"

Kelly, still weaving but ready for anything, says, "Hey, let's go party at the gunfighter's club. Let's kick some flyboy ass!"

"No way," says the Monk as they all walk going the parking lot outside the club. "I'm securing from this gig! To First Med and stay with John tonight.'"

"Who's John?" inquires Wally.

"Oh, he's the indulgence salesman at the hospital," says the Monk. "On the side he says mass every Sunday."

And that's how three chaplains got kicked out of the Stone Elephant one night for disorderly conduct unbecoming an officer and a gentleman.

GOOD-BYE, VALPACK

The Monk and Richard are both on their way back to their respective battalion commands. They've just come from the division chaplain's meeting, which both agreed was god-awful boring. Just like they always are! The speaker Spike imported to bestow some words of wisdom on the chaplains is the division lawyer, who rambled on for over an hour on the provocative and exciting subject of the UCMJ. For Strom and Gerlitis, who are now somewhat jaded and refer sarcastically to "the code" as the "holy book," there is an understand that the military, especially Marines, revere the Uniform Code of Military Justice in much the same way that Jews revere the Torah or Christians the New Testament. However, the steaks were good, the beer and sodas cold, and Spike was his usual warm, nurturing self.

Richard suddenly turns to Vince and says in a voice dripping with sarcasm, "Hey, Vince, does that lawyer really think that this legal crap is relevant to us out in the bush getting our ass shot at all day? He gets an F!"

Chaplain Gerlitis grins and says, "You know what, Mr. Tough Guy? The food and drink was good. Let's just give old Spike an A for effort?"

"Yeah, you're right about that," Strom responds with a sigh. "Spike is a good man!"

The jeep is now pulling up to the helipad adjacent to the Eleventh Marine artillery regiment one mile north of headquarters. The Monk and his driver will be heading back to their battalion shortly since they are less than ten kilometers from the First Marine Regiment. Highway 1 from the Monk's battalion into Da Nang is usually secure enough for vehicular travel. For Richard it's a different situation. An Hoa is located fifty kilometers southwest of the city through some of the most dangerous countryside in I Corps. The road past First Regimental headquarters, when open, is traveled only by caravan and gunship escort. Lone vehicles are forbidden.

Richard jumps out of the jeep, slings his pack over his shoulder, then grabs the valpack he filched earlier from the division chaplain's office and places it on the deck with a clank. "What in the hell you got in there, Strom?" Vince asks, somewhat puzzled by the sound.

Richard bends over, zips open the valpack, and says, "A little altar wine, my son." He slowly folds back the valpack, exposing ten glass bottles of various alcoholic beverages that have been carefully pack in paper and towels. Richard grabs a bottle of wine, stands up, and says, "See, Monk, altar wine."

The Monk nods with a smirk on his face and responds, "Yeah, right, and the rest of the stuff?"

"Well, let's see here, got a couple bottles for the first sergeants, for administrative purposes of course. Helps me in my problem solving with the troops. Then there's a couple of bottles for my friends in An Hoa." He stoops over to repack the row of bottles. "A couple bottles of the Lord's sanctified vintage," he continues, waving another bottle of altar wine in front of the Monk, then zips up the suitcase. "And finally a little cheer for the boys in the field who might need a snort to settle them down." He now stands up facing the Monk and says, slapping a canteen on his left side, "One bourbon." Then he slaps a canteen on his right side. "And one scotch. Ready or not, here I come!"

Vince gets out of his vehicle, steps toward Chaplain Strom, then gives him a quick hug and says, "You turkey, I've gotta get back to my outfit before you get me into more trouble. Take care of yourself, Lutheran. God be with you."

"You take care too, my friend," Richard responds. "Let's get together again, I really enjoyed last night."

Vince climbs back into his jeep, turns and says, "And say hello to your crazy friends at *Two-five*. Tell them I enjoyed getting kicked out of the Stone Elephant last night!" He laughs hard as his jeep pulls away.

In twenty minutes, Chaplain Strom is halfway to An Hoa in a large CH-53. He is seated adjacent to the starboard door of the helicopter next to the machine gunner. His eyes are closed, lost in thoughts about home. Suddenly the machine gun next to Richard begins to fire rapidly, literally causing him to jump out of his seat. The helicopter does a steep downward bank to the right while the gunner continues to fire.

Trepidation fills the chaplain as he hears a loud metallic grinding noise coming from above, then realizes quickly that something is wrong with the chopper. He sits back down in his seat and grabs onto the webbing above and holds on tight, aware they are going down much faster than on a normal rate of descent. The chopper straightens out for a few seconds, then drops into a steep spiral turn. He's feeling that primal fear again and notices a horrified look on the faces of the other Marine passengers. Richard suddenly flashes on a conversation he had with a pilot back at Camp Pendleton, telling him about the ability of a helicopter, if not badly damaged, to auto-rotate down at a faster speed than normal but able to land without smashing into the ground. Not having any idea how badly the chopper is damaged, his thoughts immediately go catastrophic, assuming they will smash into the deck and be killed!

He is now repeating over and over "Oh God, oh God, oh my God…" as the helicopter descends even faster toward earth. The blades are still whirling when the chopper lands quite hard in two feet of water in a rice paddy. As this is happening Richard is thinking about his family in a weird, almost frame-by-frame slow motion: "Where are they? What are they doing? Are they aware of my present terror?"

The occupants are all stunned as the chopper slowly tilts to the left, then jerks violently as the rotor blades tear into the earth, the craft coming to rest on its port side, jerking everybody about in their safety belts like shaken ragdolls. There is an enormous shocking silence for a few seconds, then someone yells, "Anybody hurt?"

The machine gunner on the starboard side climbs out of the door and hollers, "We're on fire!"

At that moment the copilot sticks his head of the small window on his side of the cockpit and screams, "Someone help me get the captain out of here. He's been hit!"

The crew and passengers are all struggling out of the starboard door and windows of the craft since the fire in the art sections precludes any exit there. The crew chief and copilot are experiencing difficulty getting the pilot free from his harness, finally managing to get him through the cockpit door. The chaplain and the sergeant crawl out of the doorway and lift the wounded captain out and onto the ground. Just as they get him into a sitting position in the water that very distinct *pop, pop, pop* sound of multiple AK-47 fire is heard. There is no doubt in anyone's mind that the fire is directed toward the Marines and the helicopter.

Simultaneous with the enemy now shooting at the Marines, who are mostly grouped in front of the helicopter, the fire in aircraft is spreading from the aft to the forward section. The fuel may explode and the machine gun rounds may go off at any time. In the background the Marines can hear an approaching helicopter.

The copilot, crew chief, another Marine, and Chaplain Strom now struggle to carry the skipper in the knee-deep water, each step a difficult endeavor because the sticky mud underneath the water makes it very difficult to lift their feet. By now the VC who are firing the AK-47s are getting a line on the Marines because the telltale signs of water spurts are beginning to kick up around them. The helicopter is burning furiously and the machine gun rounds are going on as well, firing random missiles in all directions.

The five other Marines onboard have made it to the tree line another fifty meters away. Suddenly the Marine in front of the chaplain that is part of the group helping the injured skipper falls hard into the water, screaming, "Aahh, shit… my leg… Oh God!"

The three remaining people half-drag the captain through the tree line just as they hear machine gun fire coming from someplace in the distance. The wounded Marine in the rice paddy is immobile, screaming in pain, as Chaplain Strom runs back through the tree line and out into the rice paddy. The trooper is struggling desperately with his injured leg and attempting not to drown in the process. As Richard approaches the young man is totally out of control, thrashing about in the knee-high muddy brown water. The chaplain drops immediately to his knees, unaware of the bullets kicking up in the water around them, grabs the Marine by his shirt, jerks him around to face him directly, then screams at him: "I'm going to help you. Get off your ass right now!"

Richard then struggles to pull him up to a standing position, places one of the Marine's arm around his own shoulder and grabs that hand, then places his other arm around the young man's waist. He half-runs, half-drags the continuously screaming Marine toward the tree line, falling hard on the deck when they reach the trees, at which time two other Marines grab the young man and drag him through the trees on his belly.

There are now two helicopter gunships overhead firing rockets and machine gun fire into the position across the rice paddy from which they took small arms fire. Adjacent to them is a small ville made up of six hooches absent of civilians. The area is surrounded by trees on three sides, the fourth side opening into a large dry clearing.

Two grunts are leaning over the prone and injured Marine, who had been shot out in the rice paddy. The bullet has shattered the bone in his leg and part of his femur is sticking out. They're attempting to keep him still while they wrap a heavy cloth around his thigh. He is in terrible agony, continuing to scream in pain, "Oh God... oh God... help me... someone fuckin' help me!"

After getting inside the tree line, the chaplain runs to the wounded pilot just as a Marine is stripping him to his waist. The crew chief is bandaging the gunshot wound to the captain's left shoulder, attempting to staunch the rapid flow of blood. There is also a nasty four-inch cut on his forehead, which Richard attempts to squeeze shut.

"We've gotta get a medevac here right away," Richard exclaims as he sheds his shirt, then takes off his T-shirt and folds it into a four-by-four-inch compress bandage. "Put your hand under his head," he now tells the crew chief, "and hold this compress while I get a gauze and wrap it around his head to stop the bleeding."

The copilot, followed by one of his machine gunners, runs back from the ville fifty meters away to the wounded skipper, a .45-caliber pistol in hand, kneels down, and says to the chaplain, "How's he doing? Is he going to be okay?"

"We've gotta get him out of here right now, he's bad," Richard says in a loud voice, betraying his agitation.

"I think our people saw us come in here," the copilot gasps. "There's a clearing just beyond the ville and hidden from Charlie's view. I'm hoping they'll spot us."

At that moment a loud explosion goes off just at the spot where they had all entered the tree line. Debris from the trees and shrapnel is dangerously flying throughout the area where the Marines are now located. Another explosion takes place one hundred meters down the line.

"Let's get out of here!" yells a grunt lying on the ground adjacent to the captain. "Those are fuckin' rockets!"

At this point the copilot gets up off the deck, turns to the three Marines lying on the ground close by, and says, "You guys will help the sergeant here carry the captain to the clearing. The rest of you get the other wounded over to the tree line beyond the ville and wait. We'll try to get a bird over there to pick us up."

The gunships are putting heavy fire into the enemy area as the wounded are moved to the clearing. A 46 passes overhead very swiftly at seventy-five feet, does a quick steep starboard bank, and sits down in the clearing just beyond the tree line where they have all been waiting. Another helicopter gunship is circling above the landing craft at about three hundred feet, putting machine gun fire into the tree line on the other side of the rice paddy where the chopper crashed earlier.

It takes less than one minute to get all eleven of the crew and passengers of the crashed helicopter onboard. The two wounded Marines are lying on the deck, covered by blankets while another Marine, who broke his arm in the crash, is sitting in a seat. The chopper lifts off the ground, hovers for a few seconds, then picks up ground speed. As this happens Richard watches through the window as another explosion rips into the ville below. The helicopter continues to pick up speed, trees whizzing by. Then suddenly the aircraft veers up quickly to the left, spiraling up into a steep climb. And just like that they are out of the immediate danger zone, as if what had transpired in the past fifteen minutes was only a bad dream.

Chaplain Strom's pack with all his gear and family pictures, his valpack with his "administrative supplies" and a little bit of his life are back there in that burning helicopter. As their helicopter reaches its normal cruising range, the horrible primal fear of this most recent traumatic event is leaving. Behind that comes the numbness and emptiness. "I don't want to be here anymore, doing what I'm doing," he thinks to himself. "And I still have nine more months to go. Damn!"

BERNIE

Richard is back in An Hoa, sitting on an examination table, Dr. Grant checking out his cut and swollen left elbow. Strom had whacked it hard when he went down yesterday with the helicopter. In all the turmoil of yesterday's trauma, he hadn't paid much attention to his arm until this morning when he awoke with a very sore elbow that is stiff and almost immobile.

"Hell, Rich, there isn't even any shrapnel in your arm," says Bernie as he slowly flexes Richard's arm and rotates his elbow. "What y'all do, jab yourself with a stick, hoping they'd give you a Purple Heart?"

"Oh sure, Bernie," the chaplain responds, "only one more to go, then I get to go home, you nitwit!"

"I'm going to get a corpsman to dress up that cut on your elbow. I think you've just banged it a good one and it'll be all right. Get some ice on it and don't do any lifting, except beer of course," he says casually. "And we'll give you some antibiotics to stop any infection," he continues with a mischievous grin, "which will also help that case of clap you've had for the last year." Bernie laughs loudly and begins walking toward the doorway leading to his quarters.

Strom stands up, flexes his arm for a moment, then says in mock seriousness, "Such a way to talk to a man of the cloth." Bernie turns toward the chaplain, still smiling, as Richard continues, "You know what the Lord did to those who made fun of his prophets, Bernie? He sent pestilence and diseases and caused the brains of some of those kings to melt! So watch out, Bucko. I'll expose you for what you really are, an ex-piano mover mechanic from Rat's Ass, Alabama."

Bernie laughs hard as he disappears through the door way as Richard yells, "Quack." Suddenly Bernie sticks his head around the comer and points his finger at Richard, saying, "I'm going to write your bishop, Chaplain Strom, y'all can count on that! Do they still burn Lutherans at the stake?"

The enigmatic Dr. Bernie Grant is indeed one of the more famous characters know around regiment. Aside from having the best "skinbook" collection in the area, he also is known to be a card shark; has an obsession for guns; is extremely knowledgeable about the fine arts, especially renaissance art and opera; has total recall of faces, events, facts, and situations; and can manifest one of the nastiest and rudest bedside manner in the whole I Corps. Yet those who have seen him at work both in the field and back at the BAS in An Hoa can attest to deep compassion and excellent work on sick or wounded Marines.

The doctor's nasty manners usually begin in the morning, when he's doing sick call, which resembles a Marx brothers' movie rather than a clinic. Sick call starts somewhere between nine and ten in the morning, depending on when Bernie gets up. A number of Marines will have already arrived and are milling around—naturally—in the hallway.

The corpsman in charge of sick call, a navy petty officer first class with over twenty years on active duty—not what one would call rising up fast in the ranks—has spent the past two hours getting everything ready: medical records, sterile trays, towels, pencils, coffee, dressing materials, most of the items one would see in the States. Bernie has just arisen, is drinking coffee, and has splashed water on his face and brushed his teeth. He has only his thongs, pants, and a T-shirt on as clinical attire as he grabs his stethoscope and sits down in a chair.

"Okay, Savoy," he says with some slight irritation in his voice, "bring 'em in."

Savoy has a slight speech impediment and talks slowly, most of the corpsmen feel, from his brain being pickled by too much ethanol the past twenty years. With medical records in hand, he walks out into the hallway and with all the authority and official-ness he can muster up in his voice yells, "Eh, ah… stand by for the, ah, doctor!"

He ushers in each Marine separately and has them sit down in a chair in front of the doctor. Old Bernie leans over, puts his elbow on his knee, chin in hand, gives them a penetrating once-over through his wire-rimmed glasses, then says, "Okay, son, what's wrong?"

If this is their first visit or if this is a genuine ongoing medical condition, Bernie is usually very understanding and takes their complaints at face value. If their ailments persist or their wounds aren't healing fast enough, he will usually refer them up to the regimental doctors or to one of the hospitals in Da Nang for a second opinion. However, if he believes someone is trying to get out of the field by feigning illness or injury by malingering, Dr. Grant gets nasty very rapidly.

Richard is returning from the living quarters of the BAS after having chatted with Wages about the condition of a corpsman badly wounded the previous week. Just as he walks by the doorway where Bernie is holding sick call, he hears him angrily say to a Marine seated in front of him, "You again? Listen, you lazy son of a bitch, I don't want to see you in here again unless your damn arm is missing or your nuts are shot off." The doctor stands up and continues, "Now get your ass outta here!" As the Marine leaves the room, Bernie yells at him, "Actually, I hope it's your goddamn head that's missing! Next!"

At that moment, the chaplain walks in the room, smiling, and says, "I've heard about your fabled bedside manners, Bernie, what did this guy do to pull your chain?"

The battalion doctor explains that about three weeks ago he had given the Marine a no-duty chit to stay out of the bush for a week because he said he was having terrible muscles spasms in his back and was in constant pain. After sick call that same day, as Bernie was going into the mess tent for lunch, he sees this same Marine running and jumping on the makeshift basketball court that happened to be next to the mess tent.

"I had his ass back in the field by four that afternoon," hissed Bernie, still agitated by the chutzpa of the Marine wanting another no-duty chit. As he is saying this, Richard remembers a conversation he had a few days back with the S1 who said *Two-five* has the lowest number of known malingerers in the division. "A couple of sessions with Old Bernie will make anyone well," he said with pride.

As Richard is preparing to leave the room, Bernie places his hand on the chaplain's shoulder and says, "Hey, Rich, did the chief tell you about the party we're having tonight? You and your assistant are invited. We're getting some skin flicks from Hong Kong and just got a whole palette of beer from Da Nang this morning," he says with an excited look in his eyes. "Should be one hell of a party. Now y'all come, Chaplain, that's doctor's orders! It's going to be all navy though, we don't want any of those damn jarheads coming to our party. They'd fuck up a free lunch!"

"That's what I like about our BAS culture," Richard replies sarcastically. "I'll come for some beers but I don't want any part of the skins, Bernie."

"All right," he responds, "the three doctors from regiment are going to be here to play some poker as well. So if you're going to be a damn prude, at least you can come and play some cards."

Finally a corpsman gives the chaplain his shot. He pulls up his pants and puts on his shirt as Bernie continues, "Y'all know that first sergeant from Fox, that self-righteous hard-shell Baptist I told you about who said your sermons aren't really Christian because you don't have altar calls and you don't talk about being born again?"

"Yeah, I just talked to him this morning," Strom replies. "He is kind of overbearing, isn't he?"

"You damn right, Chaplain!" Bernie says. "Well, listen to this, when he heard about the beer and the skin flicks, guess who was the first one to come over here and invite himself to our party?"

"Let me guess, Bernie," the chaplain replies in mock consternation, "First Sergeant John the Baptist from Hotel Company?"

"You got it, Chaplain!" is his reply.

The chaplain brings Marshall that night to the party. There are only two Marines in attendance, Bob and the first sergeant from Hotel, who was never asked but had the audacity to assume that he is welcome. He also sat in the front row and enjoyed some of Hong Kong's finest cinema.

Bob has a good time and makes some friends that night with the corpsmen, something he needs badly since losing all his close friends in the Cu Bon tragedy. Richard plays poker, loses ten bucks to the regimental surgeon, and falls asleep for the night in the spare bed in Bernie's room.

OPERATION MEADE RIVER

It's early morning and the light is just beginning to break in the eastern sky. The entire operational battalion of *Two-five* is adjacent to and just south of the airstrip lined up, waiting to be airlifted in one of the largest I Corps helicopter assaults thus far in this war. Forty tandem blade CH46 helicopters are lined up in a row from one end of the runway to the other. The Marines are attired in full battle gear, awaiting word from the loadmaster to board the helicopters. The sight is awesome as the Marines have never seen so many helicopters in one place.

The briefings that have taken place the past four days were held under very tight security with visits from both the division and corps commanders. Seldom has An Hoa seen so much brass at one time. The operation will attempt to block the retreat of a crack regiment of NVA soldiers and two battalions of local VC by encircling them with a quick-action aerial assault. The First Marine Regiment will block the eastern section along Highway 1 and the Twenty-Sixth Marines will stop any escape north. The Seventh Marines will use the railroad tracks on the west as their initial blocking force while one battalion of the Fifth Marines and a battalion of Korean Marines will form a line to the south.

By pushing the perimeters closer each day and blocking escape from any direction, division hopes to corner the enemy in an ever decreasing circle of entrapment. Surprise will be the main ingredient in making this blocking action work. The Marines will be operating in an area twenty kilometers southwest of Da Nang and familiar to both the First and Seventh Marines, a place where both regiments have suffered many casualties over the past year, at places the Vietnamese call Dong Bang and Dong Tien and Ha Nong Tay. The Americans appropriately call it Dodge City. There's always a shootout going on!

The field Marines of *Two-five*—all seven hundred six of them—wait quietly in the growing light, paradoxically anxious for their individual turn to come so they can get on with whatever is to come yet also wishing this major event would somehow be canceled or wasn't even happening. The wait takes on the quality of "no think" and "no feel," one just kind of exists in an emotionally neutral holding pattern. Too much thinking and wondering cause high anxiety and emotional flooding. There's enough of that in the midst of combat. The grunts learn early, after two or more skirmishes, that in order to keep one's sanity, you learn to shut down. Emotions get in the way of survival because they cripple any long range chance for endurance and stability in the face of constant, horrible life-threatening events. Feelings for the grunt on the line are like a cancer and can eat away at whatever reserve the combat Marine has left just to stay alive.

Chaplain Strom, LCpl Marshal, Dr. Grant, and five corpsmen will be lifted out with elements of the forward CP, which includes the colonel and some of his staff. They are standing in a column as Richard turns to see the stoic faces in back of him, all flat, emotionless, silent—that look of being permanently on hold. Not knowing what to expect, the combatant is ready for anything and nothing simultaneously, incomprehensible to those who have not experienced the ongoing, daily prospect of battle.

At the briefings the staff NCO and officers were told to expect some initial resistance upon getting off the choppers but more than likely would not see any fire after that for two or three days until the enemy finally figures out what has taken place. At that point, they will begin probing the lines in order to break out. Intelligence assumes the enemy will attempt their breakout either west through the Seventh Marines and to the mountains beyond or through the Fifth Marines to the south where they can then escape before encountering elements of the Army's American Division forty kilometers away.

After waiting an hour, two platoons of Echo and the forward CP are the first of the battalion loaded into choppers. As Richard sits down on a web seat in the aft section, he is aware of a sudden anxiety and a surge of discomfort, remembering his last episode in a helicopter. As the engines on his chopper rev up, he can see through the starboard windows a number of helicopters lifting off the tarmac carrying the two platoons of Echo. Lifting off the ground, slowly, his aircraft circles south over the battalion area, then swiftly spirals up and to the northeast toward their planned destination.

After fifteen minutes in the air, the chopper begins to descend in a slow spiral. Bernie is sitting immediately across the aisle from Richard, head back against the webbing, eyes closed. The helicopter then does a very steep port spiral down, which immediately creates paranoia in Richard, remembering last week's semicrash into a rice paddy. He looks across the aisle at Bernie, who is still sitting with his eyes closed, then at Bob, who is seated next to the doctor, who has now grabbed the webbing above him and has a panicked look on his face, sensing what Richard is feeling. The pilot is now coming in at a radical angle, appearing to the observer as being almost perpendicular to the ground. He finally straightens out, slows the chopper by coming in with the aft portion of the aircraft about five degrees lower than the forward section, diminishes forward speed and downward descent, hovers for a few seconds, then lands in a dry field. As the aft door is opened, Richard discovers right at that moment in time that he does not like helicopters any longer. Standing up and placing his communion kit over his shoulder, he quietly vows to himself that if he survives this war and makes it back home he will never set foot in a helicopter again—ever!

The first and second platoons of Echo have already landed and are setting up a safe perimeter within a two-hundred-meter radius of the arriving forward CP. Bernie, Richard, and the entire contingent of passengers now run out of the chopper and follow the H&S Company gunny, Mark Korinsky, to a narrow roadway nearby. They then get into column and march east for one kilometer toward a strange-looking building looming on the horizon. As they get closer to the building, Richard remembers that in the briefings, their initial objective was an old Chinese crematorium dating back about one thousand years. The building is a narrow brick structure about fifty feet high that is still in surprisingly good condition and affords some protection as well as an observation point for the battalion. There are a number of small three-foot-high stone elephants scattered about the area as well as numerous small Buddhist shrines that have incense sticks and flowers placed on small altars.

After one hour, the remaining troops from battalion headquarters have set in, including the members of the BAS. Bernie has set up the medical station adjacent to and north of the crematorium. The brick structure will afford some protection for any injured that will be triaged by the BAS and is close to the road should the need come to call in a medevac.

Two hours after getting settled down, an old Buddhist monk and an elder from the nearby village come into the area of the CP and ask to speak to an officer, requesting their sacred ancestral grounds not be desecrated by the Marine presence in and near the crematorium grounds. The operations officer is brought in with an interpreter to listen to their concerns.

After the Vietnamese men calmly tell the interpreter their concerns about their sacred grounds, the ARVN soldier turns to Major Sulli and explains as delicately as possible their apprehension about the American's presence. The major's response to the interpreter was, "Tell them to get their asses outta here!"

Then to show the two men and the other villagers how much the Americans respected them and wanted them to be their friends, the Marines drove tanks, amtracs, trucks, and jeeps all over the grounds and dug their heads in the middle of their sacred burial spots. Richard is appalled at the arrogance and insensitivity of the operations officer. "Surprise, surprise," the chaplain thinks to himself. Since the colonel is down the road conference with the skipper of Echo, Strom decides to approach the ops officer and complain to him about his and the battalion's cavalier approach to the local Vietnamese.

"Listen, Chaplain, keep your nose out of running the war and keep it where it belongs—reading your Bible and passing out rosaries," is his contemptuous reply. At this moment Chaplain Strom isn't sure if Sulli is more disdainful of him or the indigenous population. The chaplain walks away, shaking his head in disgust, remembering what a sergeant once said to him about a month ago as they watched some peasants cook and wash their dishes in a small ville: "Say what you want, Chaplain, about these Vietnamese. Because as far as I'm concerned, these damn people ain't got no couth and live like animals."

"Who are the real animals here who have no couth?" he ponders, angry and upset at the chicken-shit response by the major but also disturbed at himself as well that he can do nothing to help these people. He makes a mental note to himself to enlist the help of the interpreter within the next two days and go into the village with Bob to engage the villagers in dialogue. The four line companies are now strung out for three kilometers west along the dirt road known as Highway 4. On Golf's west flank, a battalion of Korean Marines is located just south of the Seventh Marines on the north bank of the Song Ky Lam River. For the first three days of the operation there has been little contact in the Fifth Marines area of containment. But fierce fighting has broken out on the western flank with the Seventh Marines as the enemy first begins probing their lines, then initiates a full-scale assault by the second day. By the third day, with the rains starting up again, the attack stops as suddenly as it started. This only means that the enemy will probe another area for a breakout.

The rains again create mud—everywhere! For the past two days the chaplain has had six church services, most of them in the rain. Two were held in small fields surrounded by trees, a third was next to a huge bomb crater, one inside a hooch in a ville, one in the courtyard of a large village, and the last one underneath a tree next to the crematorium. As before, Richard is walking the lines out to the individual platoons. It is miserable and dangerous out there and Bob is nervous and vigilant throughout the worship services and humps to the platoons. Again, the troops flock to the services, even if it means getting out of their relatively dry surroundings, just like it was up on the hill with Golf. "My God, that seems so long ago," Richard thinks to himself as he and Bob finally turn off the road into the battalion CP area.

On the fourth day of the operation, after having searched unsuccessfully in two villages for the Buddhist monk and elder, Chaplain

Strom is asked by the skipper of Echo, Captain Woggins, and two of his platoon leaders to join them in a game of bridge. Little is happening in the eastern sector so his company is generally pretty relaxed, which is good because if a line company ever needs to be cut some slack, Echo does.

Right in the midst of the chaplain bidding a grand slam, artillery starts landing about three hundred meters away. Then they start "walking" the stuff toward the village in which the bridge players are now located, each explosion about twenty-five meters closer than the last one. Soon the impacts are close enough that shrapnel is flying all over the place, all four players are now flat on the deck at one with the ground and Strom has long since given up on making the contract on his slam bid.

The artillery stops as suddenly as it started. The skipper jumps up and yells for his radio operator, then runs out toward his CP area fifty meters away, yelling, "Tell those fuckin' ARVN assholes to learn to shoot straight!" This would not be the first time ARVN artillery will be dropped dangerously close to our troops. But it's the last time Richard will play bridge again for the next two months.

That afternoon, in the rain, Richard and Bob are back with Hotel Company one kilometer down the road from battalion. Division intelligence is right about one thing, Charlie will more than likely attempt to break out first west, then south. Because the Viet Cong is now probing battalion's lines and things are heating up. The chaplain is asked by 1st Lt. Byron Kott., third platoon leader, to have services for his unit out on the line. Richard is eager to go out with them no matter what the conditions, even when he is anxious and fearful about things heating up, understanding that these feelings just come with the territory. He is very mindful that the grunts out on the line have a life expectancy much lower than his because he can always retreat to the relative safety of a line company or battalion CP.

The last two times Strom held church for third platoon, Byron volunteered his services and would help him serve communion. He said it reminded him of his childhood days as an altar boy in the Catholic Church and he also believed it set a good example for his troops to see him participating in religious services. Richard reminded him that he was of the Lutheran denomination and that there might be members of both the Lutheran and Catholic persuasions that might have a difficult time reconciling their ecumenical behavior. "I'm in agreement with your statement, Chaplain, when you say denominational differences don't mean jack out here," he reminded Strom with a smile on his face.

There is an innocence and sincerity about Byron Kott that is very engaging, a breath of fresh air that places him in a class above most other young officers. For some reason he is not caught up in the inflexible tough-guy image that many of the Marine officers project. He is quiet and sensitive and commands the admiration and respect of the troops under his command.

Chaplain Strom is holding services in the rain next to a burned out amtrac in a shallow crater. Having communed the Marines, he now covers the chalice and paten and is turning back toward the troops to give the blessing when small arms fire erupts hitting the amtrac, bullets ricocheting all over the place. The noise sounds like the shooting gallery at a carnival or an amusement park. Bob and the three sentries hit the deck and begin firing across a large rice paddy toward a tree line to the north. The rest of the Marines also lay low while Bryon charges back toward his CP in the trees thirty meters away. Within ten seconds, the firing stops and the shooting is over. Bryon is now on the radio to the company commander to get some sixty mm mortars on the tree line from which they took fire. It is Chaplain Strom's first "interrupted" worship service and, he will come to find out, certainly will not be his last. Fortunately, no one is wounded because the old, damaged amtrac acts as a shield, deflecting the bullets.

That night Richard and Bob stay at the Hotel CP. Sergeant Mertins fixes a tasty stew of six different cans of C-rations, mixed with chopped onions, some hot peppers off a bush nearby, and a half bottle of ketchup, which he shares with Richard and Bob. They settle down next to the skipper for what they hope will be a quiet night but also anticipating more probing by the VC. Marc Dufonte is the new company commander, and Richard discovers to his delight that he was born and raised in the Gentilly section of New Orleans, not far from the area where he served his first congregation.

Echo company 2/5 memorial service November, 1968.

Waiting Fifth Marines start Operations Meade River.
Notice faces: **no think, no feel......... nothing!**

Chaplain Lippert on Medcap with corpsmen
bringing needed food and medicine to villagers.

Shortly after 0200 the Hotel CP and second platoon area are suddenly hit by small arms fire, rockets, and mortars. Sleep and boredom turned instantly into paralyzing fear and chaos. Combat is difficult enough during the day but at night it becomes terrifying not knowing the direction or concentration of fire.

As they lay on the deck, Bob questions out loud their need to be there: "Sir, I think we should fade back toward second platoon in back of us. It'll be safer there." Just as they start scooting on their bellies toward the trees in back of them, a squad of Marines next to them fire their bazookas toward the area of the burned out amtrac two hundred meters away. The firing of these projectiles creates a monstrous noise frightening both of them, assuming now the Viet Cong has finally infiltrated their position. So that by the time they did get back to the trees most everyone believes that not only are they probing Hotel's position but are actually attempting a breakout right in the CP area where they can easily cross the river in back of Hotel and scoot out of sight—which means the battalion chaplain is right smack in the center of the action *again*!

When Richard and his assistant get to the tree line in back of the platoon CP, he experiences another of those strange phenomena of the war. After the word is spread that the chaplain is in the immediate vicinity, promptly a number of Marines start "clustering" around Strom and his assistant, hanging out next to them as if he is a rabbit's foot and take on an assumption that somehow the chaplain will shield them from injury.

"Hey, Chaplain, you all right?" comes a whispered comment from a few feet away in the blackness of the night. "Ah, Padre, you got any more of those rosaries you had earlier today?" he hears from another direction. "I lost the one you gave me today." Richard can hear a number of other Marines scurrying around, as if to get closer.

Abruptly Bob whispers harshly to no one in particular, "You guys get back to your positions. You're gonna get us all killed." Chaplain Strom is thinking that these Marines don't know just how dangerous it is clustering around the chaplain but not for the reasons Bob is giving. Because by this time, after having been in-country for three months, Strom is beginning to believe that instead of being a shield against Charlie, he's more like a magnet. Everywhere he goes he draws fire!

Suddenly the familiar sound of enemy AK-47 fire rakes the area—bullets are smashing into the trees and the CP area, appearing as if the enemy is in reality attempting a breakout right over their position. Lieutenant Kott is on the radio to the company commander, frantically requesting mortars from battalion and some illumination rounds from artillery. Immediately the gruff, angry voice of Staff Sergeant Mears can be heard over the fire and chaos of battle: "You get your asses back on the line right fucking now because I'll shoot the next asshole who leaves his post."

Mears stumbles by Strom on his way to the CP in the midst of fire, drops to his knee, and says to him in an agitated voice, "Sir, get back to one of the—"

At that moment Richard hears a dull, flat sound, like the sound of food thrown against the wall, then immediately feels a warm liquid falling on his face and arms as the sergeant wordlessly crumples on top of the chaplain like a sack of potatoes. The chaplain is horrified, realizing the sergeant is hit and bleeding, maybe fatal. Bob instantly reaches over Mears and pulls him off Strom, exclaiming, "Oh shit, Chaplain. Shit. Let's get him back by those sandbags." They both pull the sergeant, completely still and motionless, back down the hill and away from the CP area where the bullets will not hit them for now.

When they arrive at a small depression in the ground three by three meters, the chaplain cries out, "Get a corpsman here on the double!" He and Bob discover, to their horror, that the sergeant has been shot clean through his head, the bullet entering just below his left eye. Richard is quickly attempting to find a pulse, and to his dismay finds a gaping exit wound below the sergeant's right ear, realizing Mears was probably dead before he fell on top of the chaplain.

Illumination rounds suddenly explode high above the rice paddies in front of Hotel and the second platoon, exposing enemy troops one hundred meters in front of them and strung out along a line one kilometer long. At that moment all the available rifles, company and battalion mortars, machine guns, and special weapons are now directed to the enemy troops in front of Hotel as the Marines open up with as much fire power as they are able to muster. It is now obvious that the NVA is attempting a full-scale break out right over Hotel's position. However, the quick action of battalion's mortars and Captain Dufonte immediate response to a very critical situation has at least temporarily stopped the enemy from completely overrunning their positions.

When the illumination mortars initially go off exposing NVA positions, the AK-47 fire and enemy rockets taper off so that within an hour the North Vietnamese have swiftly vanished north leaving small pockets of local VC to harass and fire at the Americans.

The battalion continues to fire illumination rounds out in front of Hotel all night long and small arms fire and mortars continued until the light of early morning. By the time the sun arises in the east, the Marines are warily climbing out of their foxholes and protected areas to discover the enemy dead sometimes only twenty meters in front of them. Further west with first and third platoons, the enemy has actually penetrated their positions, causing havoc and multiple casualties.

The chaplain and his assistant stay in the immediate area where they brought Sergeant Mears body, helping triage the wounded throughout the night, ever mindful of the fierce battle taking place in front of them. Aside from Mears, three other Marines from the platoon die and eleven sustain wounds. Since battalion is four hundred meters away, the dead and wounded will have to wait until morning's flight to have them transported back to Da Nang by helicopter.

Richard's focus is to keep the wounded as comfortable as possible, praying with them and just being near them as support during the long, chaotic, and fear-filled night. Especially for the wounded, during combat, it is a very vulnerable, helpless time for them that can exacerbate their shock and bring about death. Focusing on the wounded and sometimes dying Marines helps the chaplain to deflect his own feelings of helplessness, vulnerability, and fear, which would dissipate immediately when the next batch of rifle fire or rockets would come slamming into the area, bringing instant terror to all.

"I can hear the chopper coming," Richard says softly just before dawn to Pvt. Markus Jordan, hit by a bullet that has shattered his mouth and right jaw. "I'll see you soon in the hospital where they will take good care of you," he continues as he holds the young Marine's hand, mindful of the fear he is seeing in Jordan's eyes and the pain wracking his face. It is a look that is beginning to stamp an indelible imprint on Richard's mind, an experiential process that he wants to shunt aside, feeling more and more a helplessness of spirit, a pathos he himself is beginning to experience that is almost too much to bear any more, seeing these young men killed and maimed over and over again.

After the second medevac chopper leaves, Richard walks back toward the platoon CP. 1st Lt. Kott approaches the chaplain with his radio operator next to him and says in his calm, quiet voice, "Sorry you got into all this stuff, Chaplain Strom. I sure want to thank you for your presence and working with my men." They turn now and walk toward the road leading back to battalion. "Whether you know it or not, the troops always feel good when their chaplain is here."

"Ah, sure, thanks," is Richard's unenthusiastic response, again feeling inadequate and not wanting to experience the sadness and despair that is beginning to come up. "Listen, Byron, think it's okay to go back to battalion now, looks like Charlie is gone, at least for now?" Strom is aware of his personal need to be back with battalion, a need that stems more from a preference for greater safety than it does for any humanitarian need.

"The colonel has already called and asked that you get back as soon as possible. The road is as safe as its going to be so you can leave when ready," replies the platoon leader. Bob has already packed Richard's gear. They sling on their gear and walk the four hundred meters back to battalion, arriving at the BAS in time to see Bernie just getting up from his rubber lady. He yawns, puts on his glasses, laughs softly, and says to the chaplain and his assistant, "Hey, Chaplain, sounded like a hell of a firefight you got into last night?"

Richard sits down on a box nearby, dumps his gear on the deck next to him, and says somewhat caustically, "Don't give me any of your shit, Bernie, just give us something to eat."

The doctor, taken aback by the biting statement of the chaplain and now aware of the chaplain's fatigue and irritability, responds softly, "Kind of rough out there last night, huh?" Then he turns to a corpsman and says, "Fetch the chaplain and his assistant some rations." Strom removes his boots and socks and begins massaging his toes and feet. Bernie then says in a gentle and sympathetic way, "Y'all be safer here with us, Rich."

Strom looks up at Bernie and absently says, "I hope so, Bernie. I really hope so." Battalion becomes no safe spot either. Small arms fire, enemy mortars, and rockets are fired into the compound sporadically over the next four days. Because of this the BAS is moved away from the crematorium and into the middle of battalion headquarters for safety reasons, which is a very timely move in that twenty-four hours after the BAS relocates a rocket slams into the exact area where the doctor and chaplain slept and killed two Marines in their sleep.

Five days after the operation started and the day before Thanksgiving, the entire battalion is on the move, past the burned out amtrac where Strom held church services and was the focal

234

point of the enemy breakout. They hump four kilometers to the Son Binh Long River northwest of the tower, pushing the south flank of the perimeter north and making the enemy area even smaller and more compact. During the march at one point the battalion wades through waist high water infested with large, ugly leeches sticking to the skin on their legs, arms, and bodies. This can create health problems because the leeches leave sores, which can become easily infected by water infested with human and water buffalo feces. Sometimes Marines sink up to their armpits and find leeches moving up their arms underneath their shirts, having them sometimes end up on their necks. This is one of the more disgusting problems faced by the grunts, especially during the rainy season. By the time the line companies have moved into position along the river and the battalion headquarters has set in between them, the troops are wet and exhausted and look forward to tomorrow and Thanksgiving—helicopters will be flying in warm food, the first time this has happened for any of the troops in the battalion.

The next afternoon, two hours before sunset, a lone chopper lands in the field next to the battalion CP bringing them hot turkey, mashed potatoes, vegetables, and cold milk, the line companies having already been served their hot meal earlier in the day without incident. Since the Marine Corps has a tradition that officers eat only after the enlisted men have been served, Richard, two gunnery sergeants and the assistant ops officer, Captain Peter Pearson, the naval academy graduate whose instincts and intelligence far surpasses his boss's innate ability, serve the battalion headquarters their hot turkey dinner.

After serving the remaining Marines huge portions of turkey and potatoes, there is just enough left over for the servers, who now fill their plates. Richard is carrying his full plate back to the BAS where he can sit down and enjoy this feast when AK fire erupts from the direction of Hotel two hundred meters away. He immediately and instinctively falls on his belly, his hot turkey dinner flying in all directions in the dirt and mud. As he fearfully lies on the deck away from his foxhole, bullets whizzing right over his head, his Thanksgiving dinner in ruins, an odd, very strange phenomena again percolates up from his though process. Richard is suddenly remembering the words and music to a hymn that was always sung at thanksgiving services when he was a kid: "We gather together to ask the Lord's blessing..."

"Hey, Chaplain, how'd your turkey taste?" comes a question from the area of the battalion CP, a voice that is very familiar to Richard from past encounters. Strom doesn't respond, being preoccupied with the fire they are taking. However, he does entertain the thought of telling the ops officer where he can put his dumped dinner!

The next four days are a collage of airstrikes across the river, firefights, rockets, and mortars. Day and night, especially around the area that Hotel is holding, some very fierce fighting is taking place. There are also reports that the Seventh Marines to the north are in heavy contact as well.

Chaplain Strom has just held services in a secluded tree line for two platoons of Hotel. He and Bob are moving further up the river to hold services for the second platoon, the outfit that had clustered around him last week like he was St. Christopher. The area affords little protection and both he and Bob are quite nervous about having church. However, the platoon leader insists, so the chaplain and his assistant set up an altar on a three-foot-high mound of dirt. Richard doesn't even hand out the field service books because he wants to make this service very brief. The area is very unstable and Strom asks Bob to have at least six Marines stand around the area as sentries.

Chaplain Strom then raises his arm above him to make the sign of the cross and says, "In the name of... hit the deck!" A bullet has just creamed one of the candle holders and knocked it twenty feet off the makeshift altar. The sentries immediately open fire, and the worshipers, including the chaplain, take positions on the deck similar to that a monk would take when offering obedience to his superior during ordination. Only there is no abbot and the smell of incense has been replaced by the smell of exploding gunpowder.

Two Marines standing guard are cut down by the withering fire while Bob jumps behind the dirt mound with the chaplain. Immediately a familiar cry goes up: "Get a corpsman up on the double!" Then the firing stops as suddenly as it started, replaced by three incoming mortar explosions one hundred meters away near Hotel's CP. The two wounded Marines who are shot standing guard for church are helped back to a depression next to the altar and given immediate first aid by a corpsman arriving from another platoon. Both have flesh wounds, one in the leg, the other in the arm, and will be medevaced as soon as the area is somewhat secure. Although all incoming has stopped, the troops are still huddled around and in back of the altar area, not wanting to move, fearful of another fuselage of bullets.

Richard is leaning over Pfc Kramer, the young trooper who had asked for a rosary in the dark earlier in the week, helping the corpsman dress the bullet hole in his upper thigh. He was the first Marine to volunteer his services and stand guard and the first to get hit when the firing started. "I'm really sorry you took a shot, Kramer," Strom says to him, seeing the pained look on the young man's face and simultaneously aware of his own guilt. That remorse is there because he had not been assertive and allowed the platoon leader to talk him into holding services in spite of his intuitive sense that something bad was going to happen.

Kramer forces a smile through the pain and responds, "It's okay, Chaplain. Maybe I got lucky." Then he screams in pain as his leg is lifted to apply a compress to his bleeding leg. "Ah, shit. Ahhhh, shit!" Richard winces as they wrap the compress tighter, then watches sadly as Carter gives him a shot of morphine in his other leg.

Within five minutes a helicopter is landing close by as both the young troopers are loaded aboard. With a smile on his face, Kramer's last words to the chaplain are "It ain't so bad, Chaplain, this will get me home alive." As the chopper lifts up and heads southeast, Strom walks toward Hotel CP, mulling over a perplexing question that is now bothering him: "Because of my enthusiasm to please, do I bear responsibility for these two guys being shot? Or am I off the hook since they're both going to survive and be home shortly? Ah, hell with it," he finally mutters to himself, then shuts the images and the thoughts out of his mind, a process he is beginning to get quite good at.

Marshall has stayed behind to get the communion gear together and to talk to a friend he knows from boot camp and is unaware that Chaplain Strom is now walking away from Hotel and toward an area that is not part of the company perimeter. Richard assumes that his assistant has already left for battalion. The chaplain suddenly hears AK-47 fire coming from just across the river and instantly breaks into a run toward the nearest tree line fifty meters away, again driven by primal fear. He sees a small depression ahead of him and dives into it for cover on top of a horrified Marine who thinks the battalion chaplain is the enemy.

"Ah shit, you scared the hell out of me. Oh jeez, Chaplain, what are you doing here?" the young trooper manages to blurt out upon discovering who his new roommate is. "I'm really sorry, sir, I thought you was the VC!"

"We'll just keep our heads down and pray Charlie picks another hole," Strom jokes, mindful of the frightening image of an angry Viet Cong guerilla showing up above their hole and blowing them both away!

The firing stops again as suddenly as it started. Both of them, believing it is safer anywhere else in the world than in the middle of a field raked with enemy rifle fire, simultaneously bolt from their hole and run from tree line to tree line, waiting for a few seconds within the trees, then continuing their frightening trip back to battalion three hundred meters away.

Upon reaching the tree line next to battalion, they both drop to the deck, exhausted and distressed from the experience of being separated from other Marines. Richard turns to the adolescent he has joined in this race back to battalion and asks him quietly, "So you going back to battalion headquarters then? Don't remember seeing you around."

The young private meekly answers, "I don't know where I'm going, sir, I'm just following you. I'm with Hotel, second platoon."

The chaplain's thoughts at that moment are the words about the blind leading the blind, then motions for the Marine to follow him the remaining thirty meters to the relative safety of battalion headquarters, assuming someone there will let his outfit know he's okay.

As they approach the CP, Bob Marshall walks out to meet them, a look of consternation on his face. "I'm sorry I got separated from you, sir. I thought you had gone on ahead, so I made my way back here as soon as I got the gear packed." Richard can see that the young Marine is upset with himself because he believes he had badly compromised the chaplain's safety.

"Don't worry about it," Strom assures his assistant. "I took off before checking out the situation. It's my fault." Marshall shakes his head sadly, still believing he was at fault. Unless they were logistically separated, it will be the only time the chaplain's assistant isn't by Strom's side when things get nasty. Later, when the chaplain would describe this incident to his friends and acquaintances, he would laugh and say, "From that day on, once Marshall and I would arrive in the bush, he would consistently hover over me like flies on you know what!" It was a statement that also conveyed the care and respect Strom has for his assistant.

Arriving at the BAS, Richard feels like a walking casualty, drained of energy, anxious, constantly pushing down those nagging, distressing thoughts about the demise of his own mortality. He sees an empty cot, flops down on it, closes his eyes, and immediately falls asleep. Within five minutes Strom is awakened by a corpsman shaking him softly. "Sir, sorry to do this to you, but the Old Man wants to see you right away."

Startled, the chaplain sits straight up as if he is expecting incoming, grabs his helmet and flak jacket by his feet, stands, and feebly says, "What... ah... what?"

"Sir, the colonel wants to see you as soon as possible," repeats the young corpsman, aware of the chaplain's exhaustion and feeling badly that he had to awaken him. But rank has its privileges and he isn't about to disregard the colonel's request.

Strom slowly puts on his helmet and flak jacket and walks the thirty meters to the battalion CP. Upon entering the sandbagged CP, Richard again expects some sort of chewing out from the Old Man but is now aware that he could care less what Stevens has to say to him. This is a far cry from two months ago when he would be filled with trepidation when summoned by the colonel.

"Yes, sir, you wish to see me about something, Colonel?" Strom says in a dull, flat voice betraying his exhaustion.

"Yeah, Padre, I'm glad you're here," he says in a calm, soothing voice. "You've been getting out there to see all my boys on the line. I want you to know how much I appreciate the good job you've been doing." He turns to the S3 at his side and continues, "The major here tells me that you and your assistant have had services for every single one of our platoons the past couple of days. You've done well and I want to commend you on your devotion to duty." As he is saying this Major Sulli stares at Richard without expression, as if he didn't want to be included in the affirmations going to the chaplain.

Richard mumbles a quick thanks, turns, and walks away as the colonel gets on the radio to division. Major Sulli quickly walks next to the chaplain and says in a quiet but definitely hostile voice that can't be heard by Stevens: "You check with me before you go out to the line companies. You're going to get your ass blown away and get other people killed by going into unsecured areas. It's just damn stupid, Chaplain!"

The battalion chaplain slowly turns directly to the S3, looks him straight in the eyes, and says slowly and deliberately, "Sir, if you don't like the way I'm doing my job, then you just go ahead and get my ass fired, the sooner the better!" With that Richard turns and walks away, too mentally worn down to give a rip about his response to the S3. Meanwhile, the major is standing still, staring at Strom as he walks away from him back to the BAS, dumbfounded at the chaplain's response.

Bernie is watching the verbal exchange going on with Sulli and Strom and asks Richard what Stevens wanted. Strom goes over the encounter with the doctor, then lies down on the cot again, wanting to go asleep.

"Chaplain," Bernie intones, "while you were gone, Charlie dropped a mortar nearby and the major got a tiny, tiny piece of shrapnel in his arm." With rising agitation in his voice, Grant continues, "And the bastard is going to get a Purple Heart for it. Too bad the thug didn't get hammered with a piece of shrapnel up his ass!"

Richard rolls over in the cot so he's facing Bernie and replies, "Thank you Bernie, I really needed to hear that." He giggles, then within fifteen seconds is sound asleep.

After four more days of mopping up, Operation Meade River is declared a success. I Corps has reported to all the regimental commands that most of the enemy have been killed or captured with very few escaping. Most of the Marines know better. Somehow, the core of the enemy troops has managed to escape as they always seemed to do. It is either that or intelligence has grossly overestimated the number of NVA troops they had encircled.

On December 1, the battalion packs its gear and humps the twelve kilometers to Phu Lac 6, the bridge crossing over the Son Thu Bong River. The troops are told that regiment will provide transportation for the remaining twelve kilometers back to An Hoa once they reach the bridge. The transportation statement is greeted with skepticism by most of the Marines. Because being in the infantry means that in spite of readily available motorized conveyance, getting trucks together for exhausted troops is far too complicated for the Marine Corps. In essence, they save all their energy, equipment, and supplies for more important things like having division or regimental change of commands and the like.

Exhausted mentally and physically, the grunts are hopeful that maybe the S4 will really come through for them and transport them back to An Hoa. Instead, arriving just before dusk, they are told to set in for the night at Phu Lac 6, then continue doing search-and-destroy operations all the way back to An Hoa. *Two-five* will be cut no slack today. Were they ever?

*

Diary Entry—105 Days In-Country

In the Corps, the F-word doesn't mean copulation—necessarily. For most marines it is a whole new type of word in the English language, an adjective/adverb/noun/verb/interrogative that means that biggest, most complete encompassing there is about something, an emphasis about or on an object action.

For instance, here we are coming off a tough three week operation. We've had lots of casualties again and we are hungry and thrashed to the max! Instead of picking us up with trucks as regiment promised, we are left to walk the remaining twelve kilometers back to An Hoa through rice paddies and tree lines and villages and hot dusty roads on a very smoggy day. We are exhausted beyond words from the heat, from the walking, from the fighting, from being here—to all of it!

Just as we finally round the corner by Charlie Strong Point, right outside the An Hoa perimeter, a young Marine walking in front of me trips, and as he does, his rifle slips off his shoulder down his arm and lands in a puddle of muddy water in front of him.

For a grunt in the Marine infantry, everything else about him and on him can be dirty, broken down, ripped apart, and destroyed. But his riffle is clean and spotless and he takes care of it like it's a brand-new Porsche Spider. A clean, spotless rifle is a ready rifle and can be the difference between life and death in a firefight!

So this grunt who has survived this terrible three-week ordeal and is nearly back home to regiment and relative safely, bends over, picks up his M-16 out of the puddle, and quickly examines the wet, muddy rifle. Then in total frustrations, in a fit of rage, he raises his M-16 over his head and throws it as hard as he can back into the puddle of muddy water, exclaiming loudly: "Fuck that fuckin' fucker!"

This is essentially what the F-word means in the Marine Corps.

THE SILVER STALLION

Chaplain Strom is back in Da Nang visiting his troops in the hospital. Just prior to his leaving An Hoa, he spoke with Chuck Leiberman about his health since he hasn't felt well for the past ten days—stomach cramps when he ate, some bloody stools, fever on and off. So after seeing his troops at First Med, Richard checks into the clinic at NSA Hospital across the river for a checkup.

The chaplain has lost fifteen pounds the past three weeks, and the doctor, after having done a number of tests, explains that he has all the symptoms of shigella dysentery and feels it best that he be hospitalized at least overnight and check the stool and blood tests in the morning.

Feeling even worse the next day in spite of not finding shigella bacteria, Richard's blood count is still high and is told he will need further tests since they are now considering amebic dysentery, an even more insidious parasitic disease. This necessitates at least another three or four days in the hospital. This creates a conflict because when told of the timeframe, he soon feels guilty that he is not out in the field with his outfit.

The medical ward Richard finds himself in is full of Marines with similar complaints and most are being treated for parasites and dysentery. There are the daily rituals of bathing, clinical tests, eating, and sleeping that are a part of the normal routine of any hospital, whether civilian or military. However, there is a daily happening on this particular ward that is not routine anyplace else in any kind of a hospital, including civilian, an event the Marines call "riding the stallion." This is a daily crisis for every Marine on the ward because each grunt is put through this infamous and uncomfortable medical procedure of having the doctor examine the inside of your colon with a proctoscope, looking for the critters causing all the disruption and eruptions in the GI tract. The consensus of opinion among the examinees is that the docs doing this examination must gleefully place the tube on ice prior to the procedure.

By the third day, after three rides on the stallion, the doctors still aren't sure what is ailing the chaplain since his stomach cramps persevere and the GI eruptions continue on the average of about fifteen a day, which is pretty much the story of the other Marines on the unit. So with their usual flair for mocking situations they despise or for which they have no control over, the grunts will inevitably invent some crazy process to dispel the tension and discomfort.

The poor lieutenant in the bed next to Richard went to the head twenty-six times the past day, a unit record. Because he sets the record for the most numerous eruptions in a twenty-four-hour period, 1st Lt. Marion Parker is propelled into a high state of discomfort but goes on to win a seventeen-dollar pool for being the most prolific and egregious of all the stallion riders in pursuit of the diarrhea championship. When the condition of the GI tract is tenuous to say the least, one gages the distance from the head very carefully, which is why at one point earlier in the day, instead of going back to his bed, he simply sits in a chair next to the head for three hours awaiting his expedition to infamy!

By the fourth day Strom does feel better after taking medications that he believes makes him sicker than the illness. The doctor treating most of the Marines on the unit approaches Richard's bed with chart in hand and says casually, "Well, Chaplain, we believe you have shigella, just as we had thought. So we'll keep you here for a few days until you're stronger and then send you back to your outfit."

Sitting up in his bed, the chaplain quietly asks, "I thought you said it wasn't shigella, so how come it's suddenly shigella again?"

The doctor shrugs his shoulder, then says sarcastically, "I have to put something down for a diagnosis. You know damn well, Chaplain, the navy will never allow for a blank space on a military form, so I put down shigella. Doesn't make any difference what I put down as long as there isn't a blank in the form. The navy could give a shit."

The chaplain winces at the doctor's jaded reply, wondering how much time in-country he has. Wanting to change the subject, Strom stands up in front of the doctor and says, "Since you say I do have shigella but I really don't, how about getting me discharged from this place? I'm starting to get stir crazy."

"You gotta be shittin' me, Chaplain, pardon my pun, but people don't ask to be discharged before their really ready so they can go out in the bush and get their asses shot at again. You're either very dedicated or you're a couple cards short of a full deck," he shoots back.

Richard laughs, then sits back down on the bed and replies, "I'm neither, at least I know I'm not the former, I just want out of this place. It is driving me a little nuts. I'm doing better and I want to be back with my battalion. It's a simple as that."

1ˢᵗ Lt. Parker is listening to this conversation in the bed next to Richard and interrupts the conversation. "Hey, Chaplain, you know you're right about getting out of here. Because if you stay here any longer, you'll turn into an asshole and shit yourself to death!"

The doctor laughs, then says, "Well, Chaplain, with that kind of Marine medical wisdom as a guide, what can I say? So if you can keep down solids and your diarrhea has stopped by tomorrow, I'll consider discharging you. But for the life of me, I can't figure out why anyone in their right mind would want to go back to An Hoa. You've really got to be mentally disturbed, Chaplain!"

"I resemble that remark," the chaplain jokes, then in a more serious tone says, "My mood is really dropping and I'm getting more depressed each day. Getting back to my outfit will really help, so I'm counting on you to get me discharged." While saying this, the doctor is slowly shaking his head as if he can't believe what he is hearing. His experience has been just the opposite—most of the Marines will feign relapse or do anything short of shooting themselves just to extend their stay in the hospital and delay the appalling reality of returning to the bush.

That evening Richard, Marion Parker, and two sergeants are playing cards just after evening chow. The chaplain is feeling better and his GI tract has settled down with no more eruptions. Suddenly they are startled by three loud explosions close by. This is followed by a siren going off and continuous machine gun fire. Aside from the instant and spontaneous panic and fear that arises anytime incoming occurs, Richard and the rest of the grunts on the unit are faced with a new dilemma they have yet to experience. Their experience and training has taught them what is expected of them out in the bush and have some savvy about knowing how to stay alive. However, lying around on beds in a hospital ward is a brand-new, confusing experience leaving them bereft of any understanding as to what to do or where to go.

At that instant two doctors run through the ward, waving loaded .45 pistols, yelling at everyone to take cover by crawling under their beds, a timely instruction that all the patients follow immediately. Both Chaplain Strom and Lieutenant Parker grab their pillows and slide under their respective beds.

As the firing continues outside, Marion Parker loudly says to no one in particular from under his bed, "Damn, I'm not sure what is more dangerous at the moment, Charlie's rockets or those lunatic doctors who've probably never fire a gun before, running through the wards with loaded .45s in their hands!"

Two more explosions are heard nearby as Richard responds with agitation in his voice and his pillow over his head, "Marion, this is exactly why I'm getting out of this joint *stat*! Those doctors will kill us before Charlie gets a chance."

Within five minutes the enemy rockets and machine gun fire from the Marine security has stopped. "Just like out in the bush, hit and run," Richard thinks to himself as he gets out from under his bed, again feeling that shakiness from too much adrenaline rushing through his system. This incident creates the absolute resolve in his mind that whatever it takes, he will get of this place and be back in An Hoa without sleeping another night in the hospital.

By late afternoon of the next day, after Strom has placed a call to First Recon Battalion, Al Ursini, and Tim Norquist arrive to bring him back to division. However, before they go back to their outfit, they tell Richard they are first going to stop by the hospital officers' club so they can have a cold beer, unaware that the two of them have a little gig planned for their chaplain friend.

Al knows the bartender on duty—a young Vietnamese woman—and proceeds to introduce Richard to her as "that mean chaplain with the grunts I told you about." Strom laughs this off as she gives him a blank stare, then orders seven up for himself and asks her to bring them whatever they want. "The drinks are on me," he says to her with a smile.

Richard turns and asks Norquist how things are going, and while he is chatting with him, Al places a small box that he and his friend have rigged on top of the bar. On the side it says, "Poor Box." It has a slit on the top and a hinged door, just like what one would see in a church. As the bartender places the drinks in front of the three officers, Al, making a big deal out of the box in front of him so as to attract her attention to it, opens up the top of the box. He then pulls out a handful of MPC, lays it on the table, and says, "Hey, thanks for the drinks, Chaplain. I hope those starving kids at the orphanage get that food they need." He then hands her two dollars.

The Vietnamese bartender looks at the money, then at the box, then at Chaplain Strom, and says angrily, "You numba ten, Chaplain! Take money from poor. I no take your money." With that she throws the money on the bar and hustles off to serve another customer as Al and Tim howl with laughter.

That night back at recon where Chaplain Strom stays overnight before returning to An Hoa in the morning, Al and Tim tell the bartender story over and over again to anyone who will listen, then laugh hard each time the tale is told. Richard wonders if that poor lady really thinks he and other chaplains rip off poor boxes to buy drinks. Ursini never did tell the chaplain if he ever set her straight.

LZ PIKE

The new operation is called Taylor Common and it started the day that *Two-five* humped back to An Hoa from Phu Lac 6. Richard has been in the hospital for the past six days, so by the time he returns to regiment, his outfit has already been lifted by helicopters to Hill 214 in the mountains west of An Hoa. It is also known as LZ Pike. The battalion has joined elements of the Third Marine Infantry Regiment from the third division, which has been airlifted south from the area around the DMZ. This will be another major operation that has as its goal the ferreting out of major NVA troop and supply, concentrations located in the mountains between An Hoa and the Laotian border. Intelligence reports have assumed that this big buildup of troops and supplies is a precursor to another Tet Offensive in late January, less than forty days away.

Two-five will be operating in an area of Vietnam that is completely new to them. Up to this time they've done all their fighting on the coastal plains with some intrusions into the foothills, such as the fighting they did around Hill 52. However, now the topography is triple canopy jungle and small type hit and run combat operations will proceed out of major landing zones and staging areas such as Pike.

Arriving at his hooch after waiting four hours for a ride back to regiment from division, Chaplain Strom wearily opens his door, walks inside, and drops his pack on the floor next to his cot. He then slowly shuffles to his field desk, sits down heavily on the chair, and notices a written note to him from the new executive officer, Major Ed Cahill. The note states that upon arriving back from Da Nang, he wants to see the chaplain immediately. At this point all Richard wants to do is to lie down, sleep, and just forget about everything. He is exhausted beyond words and simply lays his head down and immediately falls fast asleep.

He is awakened by a knock on the door. Weary and numb, he lifts his head to see Bob Marshall entering the hooch and also notices it is almost dark outside. "I'm sorry to disturb you, sir," his young assistant says quietly.

Strom rubs his eyes, slowly stretches his arms and upper torso, yawning, and says to Bob, "It's okay. Ah, what time is it? Have a seat. Does the XO know I'm back?"

"Yes, sir," he replies, sitting down on the only chair available. "He wants to see you right away. I think the colonel wants to know where you are and when you're gonna be back in the field."

"Tell Major Cahill I'll send a message out to the Old Man right away that I'll be out in the morning," Strom responds slowly as he lays his head back down on the desk, "and let the XO know I'll be over to see him shortly."

"Yes, sir," Bob replies as he stands up to leave. "Lots of people been asking about you. Glad you're back, Chaplain."

"Thanks, Bob," Strom responds, not lifting his head. "Can't say that I'm happy to be back, just glad to be out of that asylum I was in."

An hour later Richard walks into the battalion combat center hoping to find Major Cahill and also to find out if there is any response to the earlier message he sent. He is met by the XO, who smiles, extends his hand to the chaplain, and says, "Welcome back from the dead, Chaplain Strom. Hope you are doing better."

Richard slowly shrugs, implying that he's neither good nor bad, then asks, "Did the colonel get my message?"

Cahill smiles and says, "He sure did, Chaplain. I like your creativity and sense of humor." Holding both notes in his hand, he begins reading Strom's message: "To six, from one-niner—have new bowels. Will travel. Returning ASAP to your position."

Looking up at Strom, he continues, obviously amused, "Now here's the colonel's reply, and I'm not sure if he's pissed or just playing with you: 'To one-niner, from six—you're fired!'"

"Don't I wish!" is the chaplain's immediate reply.

Major Cahill again laughs, then motions for Richard to sit down as he sits casually on top of the only desk in the operation center. "Chaplain Strom," he continues, "you look like you need some more rest before you go back out in the bush but that won't be possible. Our esteemed operations officer thinks you get too much time off and he's been complaining about your lack of presence. So I think it best that you get on a chopper tomorrow morning so we can keep the major happy." He winks and smiles as he is saying this.

Cahill then stands up and says, "Chaplain, I talked to some of the men both in the rear and those who have been in the field. You have a good reputation and mingle well with the troops. Keep up the good work."

Richard stands up, shakes his hand but wanting to deflect the executive officer's comments because he doesn't really believe he's been doing a good job. Although the chaplain has no respect for the ops officer, his comments create feelings of guilt and resentment.

"Don't take Major Sulli that seriously, Chaplain," Cahill continues. "He's got a one-dimensional view that is seen through only one process, and that's the Marine manual. Just keep doing what you've been doing and keep your command informed. And as far as the colonel is concerned, I know he likes you, and he'll probably never tell you that. So keep at it Chaplain Strom, you're doing a great job."

Richard turns and walks outside into the fresh air, wondering if he looks that burned out and therefore needed that pep talk. "Thought I was supposed to be the moral officer," he mutters to himself, questioning how Cahill would know whether he was a good chaplain or not.

Richard and his assistant are on the helicopter and it is late afternoon of the next day, having sat around the helipad for five hours, waiting for a ride out to battalion. Bob comments to the chaplain just before their ride comes: "Marine air just plain sucks, that's all." He shakes his head in disgust. It is a malediction that every single grunt in every single outfit will utter each time they wait for a ride or for resupply.

They are passing over jungle now and the mountains ahead of them are very high and steep, covered with thick, lush green growth.

As they continue in a westerly direction away from An Hoa the chopper begins to descend toward a hill below them that is brown on top, where the thick green undergrowth and trees have been removed. There are a number of Marines, artillery pieces, and equipment scattered about on the top of the large hill. The aircraft does a starboard bank, circles the hill once, then slowly comes in for a landing on a small flat area next to an artillery battery.

The engineers have blown all the trees and brush away and cleared an area two hundred by fifty meters wide on top of the hill. Included in this area is the battalion CP, the BAS with a small field hospital of six beds, a battery of 105s and a battery of 155s, three eighty-two-millimeter mortar pits, two separate ammo dumps, an observation post next to two of the batteries, a supply dump for food and water and equipment, an LZ for the helicopters bringing in supplies, and a line company ringing the hill for security. The earth is stripped bare one hundred meters down the hill on all sides by using explosives and a defoliant called agent orange. Three different strands of razor-sharp barbed wire surround the entire perimeter. Just outside the barbed wire, claymore mines and various kinds of explosives are located every ten to fifteen meters. It is next to impossible to break through these fortifications. But if they do, Golf has fortified positions all around and near the top of the hill every twenty meters manned by three Marines.

It's been raining again the past three days, so getting off the chopper they walk in ankle-deep mud slipping and sliding in the gooey clay. With so much equipment and men in a relatively small area it doesn't take long to turn the place into a quagmire. Richard is directed to the BAS, a completely fortified, roofed, sandbagged bunker measuring six by ten meters inside. It contains, besides the beds, equipment for emergency surgery, including a small generator for electricity should the need arise. Bernie is in charge of this operation because Chuck went back to Pittsburgh on emergency leave. Battalion has only one surgeon now and it is unlikely they'll get another replacement for Chuck for some time. And old Bernie has been in an extra-sour mood lately at the prospect of staying out in the bush for a month without rotation time back in An Hoa. He is definitely not a happy camper!

Two days later, after heavy rains, it is Christmas Eve. The battalion has had no contact with the enemy, no casualties, and suddenly it is very quiet. Both sides have worked out a truce up and down all of Vietnam from noon the twenty-fourth through noon the twenty-fifth. No killing!

Richard and Bob have just finished having Protestant church services for the Twelfth Marines, the artillery outfit located on the hill with *Two-five*. They have their own chaplain, a priest from Brooklyn, who will be saying mass tomorrow morning for both his and Richard's outfits. Then Richard and Bud Douly plan to hump down the hill to Hotel Company on Christmas Day and have services for them. That will be Bud's first real foray into the boonies with a line company.

It's almost dark as Richard is walking toward the BAS and sees two big CH53 helicopters circling the hill. As one continues to circle, the other chopper lands on the LZ. Inside are bags and bags of packages and mail from home. The battalion hasn't had any mail for the past eight days. As Richard rushes toward the helicopter, he thinks to himself, "What a Christmas present, flying in mail and packages on Christmas Eve, just like Santa Claus."

Suddenly, dozens of Marines show up, like little kids at park, laughing and joking, unloading all the packages of gifts and mail. As soon as the first chopper is unloaded and takes off, the second aircraft lands and the spectacle is repeated. The bags of mail could fill a twenty-by-twenty-foot room eight feet high. Lots of stuff for lots of very delighted Marines. It is an incredible scene, these tough, battle-hardened Marines acting like little kids, forgetting for a few hours the terrible life-threatening milieu they live in each day, as if they are suddenly transported back to a time and place where their reality is school vacation, the smell of gingerbread and turkey permeating home, when love and life are realities instead of bullets and death.

It takes close to one hour to get all the mail and packages sorted. Many receive more than one package—from friends, family, even from people with no names or faces who have sent gifts to Vietnam so nameless Marines will have something to open on Christmas. Inside the BAS, the four corpsmen, Bernie, Richard, and Bob have opened their many boxes and mail, receiving gifts from family and friends. It is an abundance of food, pictures, mail, and small "stocking stuffer" gifts.

"Hey, Marshall," exclaims Frenchie Arseneaux, half in the bag from drinking contraband vodka smuggled in the day before in the medical supplies, "whatcha gonna do wit all dat stuff you got in doze packages? You musta been good boy for Santa."

Bob looks up from the abundance of packages spread before him, smiles, and replies, "Nah, the chaplain and I are going to give these out to anybody who comes up short and didn't have their mail come through for them. He must have at least twenty packages from his friends and families, plus some gifts from people he doesn't even know."

At that moment Chaplain Strom leaves the BAS and heads out into the night to deliver two packages to the CP, one of which was addressed to Major Sulli. He walks into the CP, a small three-by-three-meter enclosure dug out of the hillside and sandbagged on three sides, encountering the ops officer. Remembering Major Cahill's appeal to work with his nemesis, Richard offers Sulli the package and says in a cheerful voice, "Somehow your package got shuffled into our stuff at the BAS, so I wanted to get this to you right away. Merry Christmas, Major."

Sulli examines the package for a few seconds, looks up at Richard with a bland, neutral look on his face, and simply says, "Thanks," then turns away to talk to Colonel Stevens.

"Must be Christmas, no menacing looks," Strom thinks as he turns and walks out of the CP having made his delivery. Just before getting back to the BAS, he sees a Marine sitting on a rock next to the door, by himself in the semidark, looking quite dejected. He stops, puts his hand on the young man's shoulder, and says, "What are you doing out here by yourself?"

The Marine says nothing, continuing to look down at the ground. Richard sits down next to him, sees that he is empty-handed—probably received no packages, no mail, no Christmas cards—and attempts to comfort him: "Looks like you're mail got fouled up somewhere along the line."

The young Marine continues looking down at his boots as happy, loud noises emanate from inside the BAS. He then shrugs his shoulders and replies, "Nah, I don't get no mail from home anyway. Don't expect none."

The fact is that he didn't get any mail from home or from anywhere else as well. However, Richard saw the look in his eyes earlier that evening as he helped unload the helicopters of unending bags of mail and packages. He saw the wistful expectation that was there, the deep human need written on his face that someone, somewhere cared, that somewhere in all those letters and packages that care would be manifested in something for him. But right now the chaplain is seeing the pain and hurt and loneliness that he is attempting to shrug off amid the joy and laughter around him.

At that moment Bernie walks out with a pint of Southern Comfort that a medical school friend had sent him, offers Strom a hit off the bottle, and says, "Hey, Rich, how come y'all not inside having a good time with the rest of us?"

Richard excuses himself from the young Marine, takes Bernie off to the side, and explains to him why he isn't inside and the situation with the young man sitting on the rock. In less than five minutes Bernie has Pfc Leroy Adrian inside the BAS, has given him two of his own packages as well as one of the chaplain's, and has directed the corpsmen to share their loot of cake, cookies, and other goodies with Adrian. As the young man is opening up a package of cookies and candy, Bernie leans over and says, "Look, son, ain't no difference where the gift came from, back in the States or right here, it's still a gift."

"Right on, Bernie," Richard thinks to himself.

Chaplain Strom moves around the hill that night for the next three hours to all the positions, making sure everyone has a gift of some kind. Both he and Bob have carried the many anonymous gifts sent by the folks back home and have distributed them to the thankful Marines.

When Richard gets back to the BAS, he sits down in the corner by himself on one of the cots and opens the package from his wife. In it are all the goodies he had asked for—sardines, dried onions, steak sauce, canned tuna, relish, and loads of fudge and chocolate chip cookies. And packed way down on the bottom is the most precious gift of all, twenty colored pictures of his son, Timothy, now seven months old, a beautiful baby that was only two months old when he left for Vietnam.

He carefully, mindfully looks at each picture, taking care not to smudge them. Then he slowly wraps them in the cellophane wrappers, places them in his pocket, and goes outside to be by himself—and begins to cry. "Oh God," he whispers to himself, half in prayer and half as a statement of the pain he is feeling. "I miss the little guy so much. Will I ever see him again?" He attempts to stop the tears that won't stop flowing?

Ten minutes later, having sat alone and the tears finally stanched, the chaplain goes back inside the BAS and sits down in the comer. Bernie approaches Richard and softly says, "Chaplain Strom, why so glum and quiet?"

"I really miss my family right now and I don't want to be here anymore," he replies, "but who do I tell that to, Bernie?" The doctor sits down on the cot next to the chaplain. "Since that's what I hear all the time from everyone else, who in the hell do I go to? Ah hell, Bernie, I'm just feeling sorry for myself right now, and I'm real homesick, that's all."

The doctor puts his arm around Richard's shoulder and says, "Yeah, I know, Rich, we're all feeling that way right now. Y'all just sit here and relax. Let old Bernie take care of you. How 'bout two fingers of Southern Comfort, my boy?"

Richard smiles, feeling a little better. "Good old Bernie," he thinks to himself, "underneath that sometimes rough and tough exterior he's a good, warm person. I guess that's why he is my good friend." Soon he is asleep on his cot inside the BAS, the constant noise from the artillery and the mortars suddenly noiseless, bringing a significant and truly silent night for all the combatants up and down the war-ravished countryside.

On Christmas morning the hillside next to the LZ is filled with Marines from the battalion CP and Golf next to piles of concertina wire that will shortly be strung out along the already fortified perimeter. Chaplain Strom has them sing Christmas carols, followed by a service of Holy Communion. Richard has never heard Marines sing so well, so free of self-consciousness as they raise their voices in praise this Christmas morning, free for just a few more hours before the guns and the shooting and the killing will begin all over. As he closes the service with the benediction, "May the peace of God which passes all understand, keep you in his love and abide with you always," an intrusive thought rushes through his consciousness: "Is this twenty-four-hour 'piece of peace' just a refresher for us so we can battle more efficiently?" He is surprised by these automatic, sometimes cynical, quite negative thoughts that are now popping into his head with more frequency the longer he is in-country, quickly recalling the Monk's cryptic remark months ago about how subtle emotional changes begin to take place inside our psyche the longer we are in-country.

Bob and Richard gather up the small Christmas songbooks, repack the communion kit, and head up the hill toward the BAS where he is met by Bud Douly who has just returned by helicopter from two other LZ's where he had Christmas mass for two of his artillery batteries.

"Hey, Rich, let's get down the hill and get back here before the truce is over this afternoon. I don't want to get my ass in a fix and have to stay down there overnight with those damn grunts, there're all a little crazy," he says in his Brooklyn accent, with a look of consternation on his face.

"No problem, Bud," Strom replies. "The colonel says we have the bird for the afternoon. I'm just delighted you can say mass for Hotel. The Catholic boys haven't seen a priest for about two months. They'll be very happy to see you."

Shortly they take off and arrive in three minutes at the bottom of the hill. Douly is not too keen on the thought of walking back up the hill and wants the chopper to return in two hours exactly. The crew chief, after hearing the request, simply shrugs his shoulders and yells to the chaplain over the sound of the helicopter that it all depends upon priority. Bud turns to Richard and says, after the helicopter takes off, "What in the hell does that mean?"

Strom shrugs his shoulders. The company skipper is heading their way so Richard quickly says, "When you're with the grunts, you get emotionally and physically conditioned to accept the fact that you probably will end up walking anyway, no matter what plans are made."

The Catholic chaplain scowls noticeably, shakes his head, shifts his communion kit, then turns as Richard introduces him to Captain Dufonte. The skipper then tells the chaplains he will split the services, having mass first followed by Protestant services. Richard directs Bob to help Douly set up, then leaves to hang out with his good friend Gunny Carter, who also taught the chaplain the culinary skills of gourmet grunt stew. Byron Kott, the young lieutenant that impresses Chaplain Strom so much, he will not see today because he is set in with his platoon further up the hill a kilometer away. The chaplain will see him again when he returns three or four days later.

When Chaplain Douly is done saying mass, Bob sets up for Strom while the captain takes Bud to his CP to lunch on some of the goodies received by helicopter last night. During the Christmas worship service for Hotel, Richard is feeling Brian's absence today. He would have gone to mass instead of coming to Richard's services, but there is something incomplete about his nonpresence that he can't put his finger on.

With Christmas services over, Bud is anxious to leave and lets his wishes be known to Captain Dufonte, who directs his radioman to get a chopper down to their CP quickly. The two chaplains and Bob wait for two hours and still their transportation hasn't come. Actually, the helicopter never shows up at all. Bud is fuming, the skipper is nervous, and by late afternoon they must make a decision—give up on getting a chopper flight back up the hill and do one of two things: stay overnight or hump back up the hill with a squad of Marines for security. Richard gets on the radio to the Old Man.

"This is six, over," says Stevens.

"Sir, one-niner here. The bird didn't show. We can stay here overnight or hump back now. The skipper can send security with us, over."

"Best you hump back. Don't want two of you sky pilots down there overnight. The truce is officially over and we're expecting trouble, out," he responds.

Bud is visibly upset by the news. "Hey, Strom, do I get extra combat pay for this ordeal you're putting me through? In artillery we don't walk," he says half-joking, half-serious.

As the three Marines assigned to them walk toward the chaplains, Richard picks up his gear, slings it over his shoulder, and says with a smile on his face, "In the infantry, everyone walks, and until you get back on top of the hill with your outfit, you're in the infantry!"

As the group starts—a sergeant leading the way, next the two chaplains followed by Bob and two privates—the sun has gone down and it's getting dark. The squad is moving fast because the skipper wants them back before dark as they move up a very narrow path in triple canapé. It is hard work because the path leading up the hill is very steep, which necessitates rest stops about every five minutes.

After fifteen minutes of humping, about two-thirds of the way up the hill, when it is getting dark, dark enough so one's sight begins to play visual tricks and one sees things, the paranoia starts percolating in the thought process. The group has stopped and Bud is leaning against a tree, exhausted, turns to Richard, and says, again half-joking, half-seriously, "You bastard, Strom." He pants furiously. "Why did I let you"—*pant, pant*—"talk me into this!"

Richard doesn't reply but prevails upon the sergeant, who is getting antsy and wants to move on immediately, to wait a few more minutes and allow Bud some more time. Wanting to comfort the weary chaplain, he then turns to Father Douly and says, "The sergeant says the path gets a little wider and is not as steep. Apparently it's been used quite a bit over the past few months."

"By whom?" Bud grunts, shaking his head. "The Marines have only been here about two weeks. You telling me this is a VC path?" He continues shaking his head, attempting to catch his breath, then says with resignation, "See, I told you that you guys are nuts! Nobody in their right mind would walk up this path in the dark. The damn VC has probably had their eye on us the whole time." Chaplain Douly takes a big breath and says directly to the sergeant, "Let's get the hell out of here!"

Ten minutes later, exhausted and wringing wet from perspiration, the group gets to the top of the hill and makes their way through Golf's security in the dark. They wind their way past the CP where the colonel has been waiting outside for them to pass. "Hey, Chaplain," he says to Douly as they silently walk by, "now you've got something to tell your buddies back there in arty. Welcome to the grunts!"

Bud doesn't respond and heads straight toward his sleeping quarters under the observation tower, so exhausted he's fearful he may stumble and fall, unable to mobilize the strength to get back up. Without turning around to face Richard, who is immediately behind him, he says loudly, "I'll never listen to you again, Strom. Short hump up the hill my ass!"

The three Marines from Hotel stay overnight at the BAS because that darkness that comes from nighttime in triple canopy preempts any trip back before daylight. The corpsmen provide food, blankets, holiday cheer, and some "squid hospitality," which for them is a break from the austerity of existence that permeates infantry life in the field.

The next morning things begin to heat up again. Echo and Hotel are making contact and three rockets hit halfway down the hill. It will just be a matter of time before the enemy rockets, wherever they're coming from, gets a bead on the distance they need to drop their stuff right on top of the hill.

Chaplain Strom walks into the CP per the colonel's request where he sees Stevens and Sulli consuming a breakfast of cookies and hot chocolate. The colonel looks up and says casually to Richard, "Padre, Fox skipper just gave us a call and is requesting your presence down there. As you know, they've been assigned to first battalion the past three months, so this will be your first opportunity to be with them. Frag a bird and get down there ASAP so you can get back before dark, all right?" He slurps a big hit of his hot chocolate, smiles, then continues, "Think your buddy over there in artillery would like to go with you? Why don't you invite him along." He then breaks into a laugh.

Major Sulli watching the discourse then says sarcastically, "Yeah, Chaplain, see if you can talk him into another foray into the jungle. Because if you do get him to go with you, I definitely will reconsider a belief in miracles!" The two officers guffaw loudly as Richard turns and leaves the CP.

Within twenty minutes a helicopter has dropped off supplies and troop replacements on the hill. Bob and Richard board the chopper and give the crew chief a "guesstimate" as to where Fox is located. They take off and drop down into the valley southeast of Hill 214 and begins circling around and around the area where the pilot assumes the company is dug in. This makes the chaplain nervous because if Charlie is around he is certainly aware of the circling chopper. Finally, the pilot sees a clearing in the jungle, hovers over the area, slowly dropping in between the trees.

The two passengers run out of the chopper and watch as it slowly lifts off, does a half circle, then banks off sharply to the east and disappears. They simultaneously do a complete full-circle sweep of the area and suddenly discover there is absolutely no one in sight. They haven't the slightest idea where they are let alone where Fox is now located.

"Jesus, Foxtrot, where in the hell are you?" Bob exclaims in an agitated voice.

Richard's plan is to get back to battalion in the afternoon, then leave for Echo and stay with them overnight six kilometers up the mountain range from LZ Pike. So they come with only their basic gear—communion kit, helmet and flak jacket, and a sack of cookies and goodies, Bob with his M-16 but with limited ammunition. "Bob," he says with understatement, "I think we're in trouble."

"I think so, sir," he responds, doing another sweep of the area around them, "what should we do?"

"I don't have the slightest idea," is Richard's reply as he begins to warily walk toward the protection of the trees, "but I'm sure as hell not going to stand out here in the open!"

They then collectively decided to walk toward the direction of Hill 214 having no compass to give them a specific hearing. The trees are too high to see anything except that which is right in front of them. It is difficult attempting to push through the thick underbrush. But they can hear the big guns going off in the distance on top of the hill and know that at the very least they are heading in the general direction of Pike. Within ten minutes they both hear voices up ahead—American voices. Sweet music to their ears!

"We'd better be careful, sir," Bob cautions. "They might blow our heads off if we surprise them."

So Strom starts yelling, "Hey, Marines, we can't find you. This is the chaplain. We can't find you. Can you hear us?"

After fifteen seconds of this, they hear voices and the sound of movement in front of them. Suddenly, three Marines, M-16s pointed directly at the two lost Americans, emerge from the underbrush. Bob has instinctively dropped to one knee, safety off his rifle, ready to blast the intruders as Richard is frozen in place.

"Wow, am I glad to see you guys," is the chaplain's immediate response. "Didn't know if that noise was VC or American." Bob stands up, looking less tense as the three Marines walk up to Strom.

"There are three patrols out looking for you, sir. We're just as happy to see you," a very relieved sergeant explains to the chaplain.

Within five minutes the group of five is at the Fox CP and a worried company commander is on the radio to battalion: "Yes, sir, they were dropped in an old abandoned position One of our patrols found them about half a click away." There is a pause as he listens to the voice on the other end, suddenly smiles, then says, "Yes, sir. I'll tell him, sir. Out."

Captain Ron Holdridge has been in the Marine Corps for twenty years. He began as an enlisted Marine but was promoted as a "mustang" in the early sixties, having seen action as a grunt during the Korean War. Although he has been exclusively with the infantry throughout his career, this is his first command as a captain and was transferred into Fox at the beginning of the operation two weeks ago.

"I'm Ron Holdridge, Chaplain. Glad you're here with us today," he says, shaking the chaplain's hand. "Major Sulli says," he hesitates to say, then continues, "well, I won't say what he said, glad you're safe with us. Sorry for the inconvenience."

Shortly Richard is having Christmas church services again, three in all. They sing Christmas carols followed by a short communion service. Bob then distributes the goodies they brought from the BAS. He spends the next three hours talking to the troops. Aside from their normal crankiness, homesickness, and administrative problems Richard generally hears from the troops, a number of Marines are complaining about getting sick with flulike symptoms and high fever and not being taken out of the field. He tells them he will take this up with Dr. Grant when he gets back to battalion.

Late that afternoon a chopper brings in supplies and takes Richard and Bob back to the hill. There will be no Echo Company tonight. They've been in heavy contact with the NVA and they are now on the move to a new position. So after they dump their gear at the BAS and Richard speaks to Bernie about the illnesses that are suddenly cropping up with Fox, he goes outside in the dark and sits down on the sandbags ringing one of the mortar pits adjacent to the BAS. He is shooting the breeze with the "fearsome threesome" who work together in mortars and come from as diverse a background as is possible.

Johnny Parkhill is a self-described redneck from east Texas; Lynell Woods grew up in a tough black inner city neighborhood in East St. Louis; the third member of this tight group is a Mescalero Apache from New Mexico who calls himself Chief Running Mortars.

Chaplain Strom turns to Billy, the young Marine from New Mexico, and says, "So what's going on with—"

Krump! Krump! Krump! Three rockets scream into the hill on the south end adjacent to the 105 batteries, two landing just below the crest of the hill. The third is a direct hit on one of the berms containing increments for the 105s. Immediately a huge fire ball boils up from the berm as the increments—the powder bags put inside the artillery piece to propel the projectile—explode. If a direct hit slams into the actual projectiles, the whole hill will flatten out like a giant volcanic eruption and everything will be blown away including most of the Marines on the hill. Immediately, Marines are running in two directions: those who are running away to safety and those who are running toward the explosion to help with casualties and to put out the fire before it becomes any worse.

After falling into the pit of sandbags, Richard's first reaction is to run for cover around the small hill that separates the battalion CP from the rest of the area. He immediately senses that if another berm goes off that small hill might offer some protection. As he initially starts out in that direction, he hears the familiar "Corpsmen up" and stops dead in his tracks, feeling a tremendous, immediate conflict brought on by that primitive instinct to stay alive on the one hand and also responding to another part of him that believes it is his duty to assist with casualties. Frenchie and Carter run out of the BAS toward the fire with their first aid kits. Chaplain Strom reluctantly follows them. When they reach the impact area, the corpsmen head toward the battery while Richard stumbles ten meters down the hill to one of the small outposts that is a shambles and contains two badly injured, unconscious Marines. There is burning debris lying about and he is aware of noise and confusion and a fierce fire burning above him. One of the Marines has a shattered arm and his shirt still smoldering and on fire. The chaplain digs him out of the debris and lays him on the ground as he feels the intense heat from the fires above and rips off injured trooper's shirt. He next pulls out the other poor fellow from the dirt and debris. He is burned all over his body, his clothing blackened and in shreds. As he is doing this, the chaplain is yelling, "Someone get down here and help me with these wounded!"

Instantly a corpsman and two Marines appear over the crest of the hill to help the distraught chaplain pull the two badly burned and wounded young men away from the fire, onto stretchers and up to the BAS. Both remain unconscious and in critical condition as Bernie and two corpsmen start IVs and work to staunch the flow of blood and clean up the burns.

"Get a goddamn emergency medevac up here stat," he advises to no one in particular as four additional wounded Marines are brought into the BAS. "And, Chaplain, please stay here and help me get these guys ready for evacuation."

Richard walks toward Bernie, who is examining the last Marine brought in and hears his friend say in a somewhat irritated tone: "Ah shit, he's dead. Put him outside by door, we don't have any room for him in here. Hey, Rich, help Frenchie bath the burns and stop any bleeding." He then turns back to insert another IV.

Within thirty minutes all the casualties are gone, the fires are out, there are no more explosions, and Charlie isn't throwing anymore stuff on the hill. When Richard lies down on one of the empty hospital cots that night, after the BAS is cleaned up from the mess initiated by the casualties, he is more fully aware of how sick he is of the war, of the suffering, of the dying, to all of it. Lying in the dark, his mind ruminating on and on about events past and present—a collage of childhood, family, school, friends, the military—the indelible memory of his father's comments about idealism and war suddenly hits him, like a shot in the dark: "Idealism can't exist simultaneously where people are killing people in the name of peace or in the name of anything else. Killing is killing, war is war, peace is peace."

"No wonder I feel so fragmented, like two parts of me are being pulled in different directions, as if the soldier part and the minister parts are competing so strongly for my soul, my essence that I can't hold onto myself anymore," he silently, sadly concludes. However, at this point, Richard Strom is so weary and burned out by the day's events and his own inner struggle that he is able to push down any thoughts about what is going on inside him quite effectively now, a process of nonawareness that began his first day in-country.

"When are those stupid bastards at division going to send us another surgeon? I'm sick of all this shit out here all the time. I need some relief," the chaplain wearily hears from Bernie the next morning as he slowly sits up to another day in Nam, aware for the first time of some blistering on his hands that came from yesterday's fire. He also notices that all the hair on both arms is gone as well.

"Let me see those hands, Rich," the doctor grumpily says, then asks Frenchie to find some burn medication. "Wash your arms and hands real good, then put this antibiotic salve on any burn spots. Since we're all sitting on our asses around here and I can't leave, can y'all run into regiment and get us some medical supplies? Marshall is busy with the corpsmen helping to reinforce the BAS with more sandbags, I hope that's all right with you. Besides, we also need some beer, which of course is more important than the Ringer's and saline you'll be bringing back."

"Sure, Bernie, anything you say," replies the amused chaplain. "It'll be so quick, the Old Man won't even know I'm gone."

When Richard arrives in An Hoa, he can see the changes that are taking place. The airstrip and regiment is being rocketed daily, especially when the resupply airplanes land. There is a siege mentality, which means everyone has close access to some kind of bunker and protection. Daily casualties are mounting and a constant, underlying tension permeates the place. However, to Richard and those grunts being rotated back to An Hoa, this place is a step down in the hierarchy of danger and peril.

The oppressiveness of being in the field lifting somewhat, Strom gets some clean clothes from his hooch, takes a warm shower, then heads for the BAS, where he will pick up a case of beer and have the chief pack up the medical supplies for the ride back to Hill 214.

"You look burned out, Chaplain," says Chief Cooper as he shifts the jeep into gear and heads out for the airstrip. "Malaria is starting to show up with Fox. Take care of yourself out there, sir."

"No more burned out than anyone else," the chaplain replies absently. "Besides I've got it easy compared to those poor grunts that live in misery twenty-four hours a day. So what's this stuff about malaria? How do you know that it's not just the flu?"

The jeep turns onto the frontage road adjacent to the airstrip, then continues the two hundred yards toward the south end where one of the helicopter pads is located. "It's like having the flu in spades," drawls the chief in his thick Georgia accent, "but y'all need a blood test to confirm that you have the little buggers in your blood." As he finishes, they pull up to a waiting helicopter.

The battalion chaplain jumps out, exclaiming, "This should set a new record of efficiency for Marine air—back in An Hoa for only two hours, returning to the hill before noon!"

The old skipper of Fox is waiting for the helicopter along with eight other Marines to take them to Hill 214. Richard walks to Major

Farley, shakes his hands, and says, "What are you doing out here, Major, thought you were on your way back to the States?"

"Just a quick trip out to see the colonel, then I'll return tonight," he says wearily. "Also want to get this 106 recoilless rifle back up the hill." At that point he turns and directs the Marines to load the 106 onto the chopper just as the pilot begins to start the engines. The chief has already ordered three of the troopers to load the medical supplies. Richard is going to hand-carry the twenty-four cans of Budweiser encased in a root beer box.

Within fifteen minutes the chopper is circling LZ Pike coming in from the northeast, turns left, then does a quick starboard bank. Strom is watching them come into the LZ, and just as the pilot straightens out to hover and then land, to his dismay he is aware that they are coming too fast and are in all likelihood going to miss the LZ completely. The helicopter comes in hard fifteen meters below the LZ at an awkward angle. The wheels hit the slanting hillside and it stops dead, then slowly rolls over on its starboard side.

The passengers are all thrown upside down while the heavy 106 is tossed about like a matchstick. There is a deadly silence for a few seconds, then the sound of a loud groan comes from the Marine immediately to Strom's left. The 106 is lying across his chest and head. Since they are upside down, fuel is now spilling on the aircraft and engines.

The heat from the forward engine immediately ignites the fuel and within seconds the area around the engine is burning. The Marines who are not seriously injured exited the aft section of the craft. Although stunned and bleeding from the nose and mouth, Major Farley, Strom, and two Marines struggle with the difficult task of lifting the heavy recoilless rifle off the mortally injured Marine. The gun fell across his body and has crushed his skull.

The dying Marine is pulled out the back door and laid next to the craft. "Corpsmen up... Corpsmen up," yells Farley as a group of Marines run down from the LZ and began carrying or helping the injured Marines up the hill. Shortly the helicopter is burning furiously and the machine gun ammunition is beginning to go off sending projectiles whizzing about. The heat is getting worse necessitating a move further away from the burning craft. Suddenly the skipper from Golf shows up.

"Anybody left inside?" he yells over the noise of the fire and exploding rounds.

"No, they're all out," is Strom's quick reply.

He and Richard quickly drag four injured troopers lying next to the chopper forty meters away behind two large logs. The fire is burning furiously now and the ammunition is exploding in all directions, making it a very precarious environment. They remain in this position while the fire and exploding rounds burn themselves out.

Major Farley and seven of the eight Marines are injured. The young trooper with the crushed skull lasts only a few minutes before he is declared dead. After spending an hour with the injured Marines, the chaplain has nothing to show for the crash except the absolute, hard resolve that when he gets back to the States he will never, ever ride in a helicopter again!

The next morning Bernie asks Richard if he will go back into An Hoa again. "No way in hell Bernie!" is his reply.

Bob is listening to the two naval officers, then makes the observation: "Chaplain, I think you need a new rabbit's foot."

Strom turns to his assistant and says in a voice dripping with sarcasm, "No, Bob, I don't need a new rabbit's foot. I need a damn discharge immediately from the navy. You go to An Hoa, Marshall, and get whatever Dr. Grant needs. I'm going down the hill and visit Hotel. If I can't get a ride back up, then I'll just stay there. It's safer with them anyway."

At midafternoon, Strom has bummed a ride from a Huey gunship that had stopped by the LZ. As they spiral up from the hill, the crew chief leans over to the chaplain close to his ear, then speaks loudly over the sound of the engines, "Sir, we've got to drop you off immediately at Hotel CP, one of the platoons is heavily engaged and we've gotta request to help them out!"

Richard groans, shakes his head, and says to himself, "Damn!"

The Huey does a quick drop into Hotel's position and hovers over a flat area at three feet as Richard jumps out of the craft and runs immediately to three kneeling Marines thirty meters away. The chopper quickly rises straight up, turns southward, picks up speed, and heads toward the embattled platoon one kilometer away.

The three Marines stand up and motion for Richard to follow them. When he reaches the tree line, he sees Captain Dufonte on the phone and can also hear small arms fire a few hundred meters away. "Get the lieutenant down here as fast as you can. We can't get a medevac up there. I'll have the mortars firing into those coordinates when you give me the word your troops have pulled back. Out."

He turns to the chaplain and says, "We've got a lot of casualties coming, Chaplain. Maybe you can give the troops a hand." As he is saying this, some of the casualties are already arriving.

Richard runs twenty meters to an enclosure protected by bushes and high trees, which will be the holding area for the evacuation. There are four wounded and one dead as he scans the area ahead of him.

"Oh shit, Chaplain," says a wounded Marine as Richard bends over him. "Ah, God, it hurts so bad. They got the lieutenant. We couldn't get to him," he says as he agonizes over the bullet hole just above his knee, a terrified, powerless look frozen on his face.

"It's okay, son, he's being cared for. We're gonna make sure you're doing okay and get you back to the hospital," Strom reassures him. "The medevac will be here shortly."

The chaplain turns away from Corporal Swank, noticing a corpsman working on a Marine a short distance away. This poor fellow has been shot in the face, tearing out his low jaw and chin and was just lying wordless in shock while being patched up and given morphine. Just as he moves quickly toward the gravely injured young man, Richard sees three Marines half-carrying, half-dragging another trooper into the clearing, then hears a second corpsman say, "Put the lieutenant over here."

When the chaplain reaches 1st Lt. Byron Knott, the corpsman is already attempting to seal the bullet wound in his chest. Richard kneels beside his injured friend as Chrestman finishes his medical procedure as best as he can. "He's lost lots of blood, Chaplain, so can you help me roll him over on his side?" The sound of a helicopter can now be heard coming into the small LZ thirty meters away.

Byron is chewing gum slowly and reaches up for the chaplain's hand. Suddenly the small arms fire starts up again this time much closer to the CP. The chopper, which has almost landed, immediately lifts up and speeds out of sight beyond the trees not to return.

Byron tracks the helicopter moving out of sight as Richard holds him in his arms, ready to roll him on his wounded side, thereby keeping his good lung from being flooded with blood. The young lieutenant wordlessly motions with his hand not to roll him over, removes the gum from his mouth, takes a deep breath, then his body goes limp and he dies. Just like that.

"Bryon... Bryon," Richard repeats as he slowly shakes his young friend, still holding him in his arms, then turn and looks upward. "Come back here, you bastards," he screams at the nonexistent helicopter. He looks back at his dead friend lying limp in his arms. At that moment he feels his body go limp as well, like both of them had died, each of them in a different way.

"Come on, Chaplain, let's get these Marines outta here," the chaplain hears a familiar voice yell as others began moving the dead and injured away from the area of fire. Richard looks up and sees the face of Gunny Carter, who leans over, softly disengages the chaplain's arms from his dead friend, and says firmly, "Sir, we've gotta get everyone outta here before we get overrun."

Thirty minutes later the enemy has withdrawn back into the jungle and the dead and wounded have been medevaced out of the area. Richard climbs aboard the last helicopter, and within fifteen minutes is back in An Hoa at the regimental aid station adjacent to the airstrip.

Down for the Count

It is early morning in An Hoa. The big guns have been firing throughout the night and a pall of smoke and mist hangs over the countryside like a blanket. The sun has been absent for the past four weeks and the constant rains have permeated everything producing the unpleasant smell of mildew everywhere. The weather and environment this creates adds another layer of despondency and depravation to the already harsh and crushing experience of being in the infantry.

After hours of twilighting—that quasiconsciousness that brings neither sleep nor wakefulness—Richard wearily sits up on his cot, feet on the deck, elbows on his thighs and head in his hands. He is feeling depressed this morning and is absolutely devoid of any kind of enthusiasm or focus. His thought is to just lie down on his cot, withdraw from the world, and just go back to sleep. He considers this momentarily. However, being well conditioned to respond to his Midwest middle-class work ethic, he is shortly onboard a helicopter on his way back to Hill 214, the thought of which creates even more despondency for him.

Since there has been close to two hundred people consistently on this hill for almost a month now a number of ecological changes are beginning to take place. First, the rats—big, fat, ugly suckers—have decided to share the neighborhood with the Marines by living alongside of them, sharing both their garbage and their essentials. They like the nighttime best as they can be heard scurrying about by the garbage pits or near the food and water storage areas. The braver rats will casually walk over sleeping Marines and are known to assume that the poncho liners are also heads!

Then there are the heads, scattered about every sixty meters. These creations, of course, are examples of Marine ingenuity and quality engineering. A three foot deep hole, one foot by two feet, is dug over which a two-foot-high empty ammo box is placed after cutting a hole in it. And bingo, you have a Marine field head that smells appalling and shortly becomes a paradise for an entomologist studying the effects of multiple insect saturation. This kind of impromptu bathroom facility can also promote the spread of such exotic things as ringworm, crabs, and dysentery.

Being isolated on a hill also changes the nature of how one eats. Since the grunts aren't down in the flatlands where they can utilize the rice and peppers found in the villages, they must rely almost exclusively on C-rations for their daily food sustenance. After four straight weeks of Cs, one has a tendency to generalize and say that one, they all taste the same; two, they all taste like shit; and three, even the rats leave them alone.

One of the most omnipresent ecological changes is the gooey mud, which challenges the motor coordination of every Marine on the hill. For instance, even walking on a flat area is a hazard, and if one chooses to saunter along safely without slipping, it is done with legs spread apart, like a conductor walking on a fast moving passenger train or a three-year-old kid ambling along with a load in his britches. The real adventure is walking down a hill, which resembles somewhat the experience of a brand-new skier attempting their first journey down the mountainside.

The Marines have only two issues of utilities and boots, which means their clothing takes on the quality, both in smell and texture, of used sweat socks at the end of football season. After three weeks no one seems to mind either their own or someone else's vintage smell. This of course makes it difficult for new replacements coming into the battalion, who generally find the odors offensive for a few days until they too become acclimated to their own body aroma. After a few weeks in-country, it doesn't matter anyway because the major focus always, out in the bush, is to stay alive and concurrently be as comfortable as possible. Smelling good isn't a priority.

It is now New Year's Eve on Hill 214. The colonel has just finished giving out his directives at the daily staff meeting and is ready to dismiss his officers and staff NCOs. Suddenly he turns toward Bernie and Richard, who are sitting side by side and says in a voice resonating with sarcasm, "We're expecting trouble tonight. So if any of you boys over there in the BAS or anywhere else have any thoughts of boozing tonight on this hill, and I find out about it, I can tell you with certainty that I'll have their young asses drawn and quartered!"

As the two naval officers leave the CP and walk slowly back to the BAS, Bernie turns toward Richard and says, "All Colonel Stevens said was no booze. Isn't that right, Chaplain?"

Richard whispers back, "You can't use my altar wine, Bernie, I only have half a canteen and I'm going to take off soon for the line companies."

"Heaven forbid that we would use the sanctified squeezings of the Lord's vintage," he responds with a smile on his face as they enter the BAS, "because old Bernie has something else in mind."

The doctor turns toward Arseneaux, who is repacking a field hospital kit, and says in a voice betraying no guilt or fear whatsoever, "Frenchie, I want you to get out a pint of the navy's vintage one hundred eighty proof ethanol that we have locked in that cabinet over yonder with the morphine." He turns back toward Richard with a grin on his face and continues, "We are going to celebrate tonight. I'll just write the shit off as being lost in transit."

Chaplain Strom shakes his head in disbelief as Bernie turns toward Marshall and says, "Bob, get me a couple cans of grapefruit juice over at supply by the observation tower." Marshall leaves the BAS as Bernie now laughs and says to everyone present, "The Colonel said no booze. This, gentlemen of the navy, is not booze. It is medicinal ethanol and since one of the pints somehow got open, it is our duty and also our responsibility to see that it does not go to waste and is put to good use."

A skeptical Richard shakes his head again, throws his hands up in the air in mock consternation, and says to the battalion doctor, "That's the most sociopathic, outlandish explanation for ripping off medicinal alcohol that I've ever heard in my life. What ja have in mind, Bernie?"

Within three hours the doctor, chaplain, Arseneaux, Carter, and Marshall are drinking "salty ethanol dogs" and toasting the New Year in spite of what the Old Man threatens to do. Frenchie is feeling brave, so he actually drinks a straight shot of the stuff. He turns red, grabs his throat, and hollers for a chaser of water. Within five minutes he is passed out—both from the effects of that straight hooker and some previously drunk alcoholic beverages he scored earlier. The ethanol is so strong that it is absorbed directed into the body when it hits the stomach. Bernie just laughs and says, "Ah hell, he'll be all right. Put him to bed."

Just as they are laying Frenchie down on his bed, Bud Douly shows up. "What kind of mischief are you guys up to now?" he says as he smells the aroma of alcohol.

Bernie then offers him a slug of the mixture. Bud takes a hit, his body shakes in a mild convulsion, then turns back to the doctor and says in a voice filled with pain, "Jesus, Bernie, that's nasty. I'd better get back and take some Maalox before the stuff eats through my entire GI tract. Damn, you grunts are suicidal. It's not healthy being around you guys.

And that is how this selected group got toasted drinking salty ethanol dogs on New Year's Eve, an event that Richard believes will eventually get back to the Old Man, or Major Neanderthal as he is now commonly called. And in spite of his protestations and disparaging comments about infantry Marines, Chaplain Douly actually spends more time hanging out with grunts than he does with his own troops.

Within three days the rain stops and Marine air is back in the sky, dropping bombs and napalm on suspected enemy concentrations about four kilometers away from Hill 214. The ordinance is being guided into selected targets by feeding calculations into a little black box by the forward air controller on the ground. He then radios the results of those calculations to the A-6 medium bombers flying overhead. This gadget is so accurate, the error factor is less than fifty meters from ten thousand feet. In this case the bombers are dropping explosives on suspected NVA hospitals in the jungle.

The next morning, after numerous bombing runs the previous afternoon, both Echo and Fox move into the area. Aside from numerous firearms captured, the line companies come across huge stores of medical supplies and equipment. There is also evidence of a hasty retreat by a large contingent of people. When Richard hears about this recent attack on the NVA, he wonders what they do with all their seriously wounded. It doesn't seem right to him that the Americans are bombing hospitals, regardless of who owns them.

Upon leaving the staff meeting on their way back to the BAS, Richard turns to Bernie and says, "You know what, Bernie? I'm left with a bad feeling about what we did out there yesterday to those NVA hospitals. First we drop bombs on them, then when they're crawling out of their holes we send in the F-4s and drop napalm on them. If we can't blow 'em away, we'll fry their asses!"

Walking inside the makeshift field hospital, Bernie just shrugs his shoulders and says, "Yeah, well, that just the way it is, Rich. War is war. It's just a bunch of jackin' off to think wars can be fought morally. You put war and morality together and you have one big fuckin' oxymoron!"

Strom really doesn't want to hear this, especially coming from Bernie. He would expect it coming from one of the Marines, say like the ops officer or the menacing staff sergeant from Golf. He still has in his mind—*yet*—after all that has gone down thus far that war can be fought with rules, perhaps even with a tad of compassion.

Richard had previously brought up issues like this with Bernie. Grant just shake his head when the chaplain talks like this and say, "Look, Chaplain, why don't you have a beer or do something more useful, like taking a shit." Then he would walk off.

By the next morning the Marines on the hill are in full preparation for a big event. Colonel Stevens has just received word that the commandant of the Marine Corps, the head man, is going to visit LZ Pike. Their hill has been selected as the lucky choice of all the forward bases in all the I Corps area. He and his staff want to find out what a typical fire support base looks like and how it functions.

The irony of this visit is obvious to everyone from the colonel down to the lowest private. For the past three weeks, the Marines have had reduced water rations, no clean clothes, and limitations of the type of supplies that make life on a fire support base at the very least somewhat tolerable—like fresh fruit, cold milk, canned bacon, and a new pair of boots or utilities. Now that the commandant is coming to the hill within forty-eight hours, the Marines get clean supplies of utilities and new boots, enough water is being brought in to shower all the men on the whole hillside, a bulldozer is lifted in and the mud is literally scrapped off the hill, fresh food supplies are brought in and everyone is ordered to ready themselves for inspection, like at Camp Pendleton, when the general arrives—a fitting reminder that the politics of war isn't confined to Congress, the White House, and the Pentagon but invades even the lowly existence of a private.

That evening, after the staff meeting, the bulk of which is devoted to the discussion of the commandant's visit, the battalion chaplain approaches Stevens and says, "Colonel, I think it's time I hit the road again and visit the troops."

"You're just trying to get out of here because the commandant is coming," he responds with a smile.

"Yes, sir, that and also because I need to make the rounds again," Strom says casually. "Haven't seen Echo for some time and the skipper wants to finish the bridge game we started a few months back."

"Okay, Padre, if that's what you feel you need to do, take off tomorrow morning," he responds. "Bernie tells me you've been sick again, you sure you should go up there? Forecast says more damn rain, maybe tomorrow. Don't want you to get stranded up there."

"Just a cold I'm getting over," he responds.

A subtle change has come about between Stevens and Strom. Their communication is more relaxed and open, and the chaplain doesn't feel so intimated by the colonel's sometimes brusque mannerisms. At this point the colonel allows Strom to develop his own plan of ministry to his troops free from any interference from the staff, including Major Sulli. As Richard turns to leave, he thinks to himself, "I'm beginning to like and appreciate the old fart."

Walking out the entrance he is once again confronted by Major Neanderthal. He glares at Richard with that menacing look of his and says in a voice dripping with malice, "Hey, Chaplain, in the Marine Corps you don't tell your commanding officer what you're going to do. You ask permission! Who in the hell do you think you are anyway?"

Richard Strom has already figured out that this guy isn't capable of speaking in or understanding most polysyllable words, so he replies in a somewhat insolent voice: "I am attempting to do my job and stay alive while surrounded by a depressed evolution of cortex-limited quadrupeds called the United States Marine Corps. That's who I think I am."

"I don't know what the hell that's supposed to mean, Chaplain, but in my estimation you're nothing more than a pain in the ass," he says contemptuously out of hearing range of the Old Man.

"It means, Major, that I'm just trying to make the best out of a very limiting situation," is the chaplain's reply. He then simply turns around and walks away, wondering what profundities of information he might be passing on about him to the colonel and staff behind his back. "Who cares," he thinks to himself, "he a pleasure to get fired and sent back to some easy duty in Da Nang." It is at this moment, walking a short distance down the hill to one of the rifle squad emplacements that it dawns on him that it really is more desirable to be out with the line companies in spite of the quantum leap in discomfort and danger.

It is now midmorning and Richard and Bob, packed and ready to go, are standing on the LZ next to a Huey that landed ten minutes ago. The regimental commander from the Third Marines, Colonel Smith, has dropped by to pay a visit to Stevens and to discuss the upcoming visit of the commandant. The regimental sergeant major, Bob Crum, has just returned from the meeting and is talking to the pilot. When he disengages from the conversation, Richard approaches him, drops his pack and communion kit on the deck, immediately thrusts his arm forward to shake his hand, and says quickly, "I'm Chaplain Strom."

This confuses Crum, who has automatically begins his salute to the chaplain. He hesitates for a moment, then smiles and reaches out to shake Strom's extended hand. This is a little trick the chaplain has devised, which gives him some indication as to the type of Marine he is facing. If they are the real hardcore Marines, they will hold the salute, grim-faced, and stiff-necked, until Richard returns the salute—sometimes. If they are more relaxed, like his executive officer Major Cahill, they generally respond by extending their hand.

"I'm glad to meet you, sir," he says, smiling. "I'm Sergeant Major Crum. Looks like you're traveling somewhere, so if you and your partner here need a lift, maybe we can help you out? I'll check with the colonel. He should be here shortly."

"That's exactly what I was going to do, bum a ride from you," is Richard's instant reply.

"I've got the coordinates so you can drop us off at one of our line companies up in the hills above us."

Shortly Richard meets Colonel Smith, a soft-spoken and highly respected officer. He and Strom spend a few minutes chatting about the conditions of the troops and also about the life of a battalion infantry chaplain before taking off in the helicopter. What is surprising to Smith is the amount of time battalion-level chaplains spent with individual line companies generally quite a distance away from battalion.

"Comes with the territory, Colonel," is Richard's reply as they step into helicopter for the ride up the mountain.

Echo is located six kilometers above Hill 214 at just over five kilometers. The LZ is very small and narrow and drops off precariously on three sides. The chopper pilot does a slow, cautious descent, drops Strom and Marshall off, then lifts slowly and heads up and over the mountain pass above them.

Within five minutes they have met with the skipper and have found a place to bed down for the night. However, the chaplain is again feeling shaky and sick to his stomach. The corpsman gives Richard three aspirins. "Chaplain," he says in a southern drawl, "y'all might have malaria. We've had to medevac four people out this week."

"Nah, I don't have malaria, just the flu," Strom replies, as if he should know what malaria feels like. His temperature is taken and reads 101.5.

Within an hour Richard is feeling better, Bob is off visiting two of the remaining acquaintances he has left in his old platoon, and the skipper, staff sergeant, second platoon leader, and battalion chaplain are heavily into a hot game of bridge. Richard's partner, 1st Lt. Martinez, is in the midst of bidding a slam when the group is interrupted by the skipper's radioman saying that a helicopter is shortly coming into the LZ with a naval officer onboard.

Strom is wondering whether it's a chaplain or a doctor as Woggins gets up from the game and complains, "Shit. Why didn't the colonel notify me about this arrival and why a naval officer?" As he is saying this, the helicopter slowly, cautiously drops into the LZ.

Out steps a chief corpsman and a navy commander, equivalent in rank to a lieutenant colonel in the Marine Corps. Wog greets the commander, then invites him back to the CP area and instructs his radioman to get the colonel on the radio and find out what this is all about.

The skipper and commander, a career medical corps officer, sit down next to the radioman and Woggins offers him some coffee, cheese, and crackers, which he declines. Commander Peters then begins to lecture Captain Woggins. "I am up here because of the unusually high rate of malaria we are experiencing from your battalion, especially with your company and Fox. I've been asked to investigate this phenomenon by the division medical officer, who believes the battalion may not be following standing operating procedures in malaria containment."

Corporal Beavins has the colonel on the radio now and has the speaker on so the commander can hear the conversation. "Yes, sir, they just arrived here," says the skipper while the two navy people listen to the conversation.

"You tell that naval officer that it is standard operating procedure and common courtesy to notify the commanding officer when a ranking officer wishes to visit a command, over," replies the CO.

"Yes, sir, ah the, ah, colonel here says we have far too many malaria," Wog mistakenly calls the commander.

"Whattya mean, Colonel, that damn navy commander wouldn't make a pimple on a colonel's ass?" exclaims Stevens.

There is this very long awkward pause, then Wog responds by saying, "Ah, yes, sir, ah… the commander wants to check out our living conditions. Thinks we're not doing enough to help in mosquito control. He also wants to know if we have a regular schedule for taking our chloroquine-primaquine every week, over."

"You tell that damn commander we're doing everything we can to get at this malaria problem contained and continue fighting Charlie. Remind him, goddammit, that this is the infantry out here and not some pussy navy supply depot," he says in an agitated voice. "And when he's done up there pissin' up a rope, I want him to stop by the hill here because he and I are going to have a little chat, out!"

The conversation is now over. The commander is visibly upset because the colonel's monologue was heard by everyone in the CP area. The bridge game is halted and the skipper is walking around with the commander. The company sergeant leans over to Richard, and with a touch of anger in his voices, says, "Sir, that short, sawed-off, stiff-necked little runt of a commander is going to try to get our asses in trouble."

"Put a hat on the bastard and he'd look like Napoleon," Strom replies sarcastically, shaking his head in disbelief.

As Wog and the two navy people walk off toward the garbage and head areas, Richard hears Commander Peters say in a voice that betrays an elevated self-importance, "I'm going to get to the bottom of this malaria epidemic." Of course, the fact two NVA hospitals filled mainly with malaria-sick soldiers have been overrun by Fox and Echo and the jungle is infested with disease carrying *Anopheles* mosquitoes seems moot and inappropriate to this little caesar. It appeared he is intent on focusing the blame for the malaria on Colonel Stevens, especially after hearing the less than complimentary comments coming from the commanding officer.

The aliens, as Richard now calls them, stay for most of the afternoon interviewing troops and examining tin cans, puddles, and the heads and garbage area for mosquito larvae. Finally, the two are picked up by helicopter and leave, not bothering to stop by the hill to see the Colonel as he had requested. When word comes back to the skipper that Peters has beat it back to Da Nang, Staff Sergeant Mac angrily says to Woggins, "Skipper, that chicken shit little wimp is going to get his ass back to division before the colonel chews him a new asshole!"

The captain gets on the radio and reports back to Colonel Stevens what the navy people have done. Stevens is livid and tells Woggins, "If that cowardly son of a bitch shows up again, you evacuate your CP immediately and I'll drop some goddamn 155s right up his self-righteous asshole!"

Later that night the chaplain is feeling ill again—bad headache, nausea, shaking, high fever—and sleeps fitfully in a hammock the sergeant has rigged for him. By morning after another six aspirins he feels better, the high temperature is gone, and Richard believes the fever is busted and his flulike symptoms will not come back again. Captain Woggins approaches Richard who is drinking some hot chocolate and requests that he hold church services this morning. His voice gets quiet and somewhat awkwardly says, "Ah, Chaplain, got some bad news for you. We just got word that the helicopter that brought you in yesterday with that colonel was shot down just after they left here. Everyone aboard was killed."

Richard looks up, experiences the initial shock of hearing this horrible news, then feels himself going numb. "I'm sorry to hear that, Wog, that colonel and sergeant major were good people, something." Then he stops abruptly.

"Something that's a rarity, Chaplain?" the skipper responds with a smile.

Strom shakes his head sadly. "Nah, there are some real good people in the Marines. We both know that. It's just, ah, well, it just seems like, well, in the Bible it talks about the wheat and the chaff, the good and the bad. It seems like the good are taken and we are left with a lot of the chaff. That's what it seems to me."

"Yeah, I know what you mean, Chaplain," Wog says softly as he turns to leave.

The chaplain schedules church services to be held in the woods just down from the CP. Most of the Marines from the company attend, including Sergeant Mac and Captain Woggins, first for him. The worship service goes along fine until Richard is to serve communion. His hands shake so bad he can hardly put the communion hosts in the mouths of the Marines. After the services end, as he and Bob are packing up the communion kit, a corpsmen walks up to Richard and says in a voice filled with concern, "Chaplain Strom, I think you better get back to An Hoa and have a blood test along with the six other Marines that I believe may have malaria. Sir, I saw your hands shake and you've been running a fever as well."

Richard thanks him for his concern, turns to Bob, and says, "Well, let's get a bird fragged and see about getting back."

"Yes, sir," Bob replies, "I think that's a real good idea. You don't look so good." However, when the skipper requests a routine evacuation for the sick personnel on his hill, he is told this isn't possible today because all available "birds" are to be used for security and logistics for the commandant, who will be shortly visiting the troops on Hill 214. This means the sick are going to be preempted because of the commandant's arrival and forced to wait for a later medevac.

Some of the Marines in the CP and the chaplain watched his arrival and all the pomp and circumstances through binoculars—can't see that much from six kilometers away—as the four-star general comes and stays for thirty minutes. Watching the group load back up in helicopters, Woggins suddenly says with glee in his voice, "Too bad Charlie didn't give him a little welcome, maybe just a rocket or two down the hill where it would hurt no one but scare the shit out of those weekend warriors."

The routine evacuation never comes and the chaplain is again running a fever. There are now eight people in the CP area who are sick and in need of more medical attention than can be offered by the company corpsman. To make matters worse, it begins to rain and they are now socked in by heavy cloud cover. There is no way a helicopter can get in to evacuate the sick even if one was available.

The next two days are a blur for the sick Marines, their fevers going up and down each day, being placed in the small stream close by to cool down. Through it all Richard has this dream, day and night, of a helicopter overhead, hovering but never quite able to land in the LZ. Each time his temperature spikes up, he would hallucinate, actually believing he was someplace other than Vietnam. The second night his headache is so bad and his shaking so great he actually believes he is going to die. He finally realizes that he is very sick and his flulike symptoms are not going to go away just by wishful thinking. So by the third morning after the commandant's visit, when there is a break in the weather, they are finally able to get two helicopters into Echo's LZ. For two of the Marines it will be too late as the malaria has caused renal failure, referred to as black water fever, and their body functions have begun to shut down—a direct result of the tardiness of proper medical attention. A medevac on the afternoon of the general's visit could have meant the difference between life and death for these two Marines.

When the evacuations do come, instead taking the sick into An Hoa or Da Nang, they are dropped off instead on Hill 214. As they are unloaded and brought into the BAS, Bernie groans as Frenchie arranges to make them as comfortable as possible, then hurries to the CP to talk to Stevens.

Rushing inside, out of breath, he confronts instead Major Sulli and says angrily, "I don't know what bastard brain decided these malaria patients should come here. I can't treat them because they're too ill and need to go to Da Nang immediately!"

"Just settle down, Bernie," replies the major. "We've got a number of resupply choppers on their way right now. We'll give you top priority, so don't get into a navy snit about it."

The doctor turns to leave and says in a voice dripping with sarcasm and venom, "I'll get into a snit about it if I want." Then pointing his finger at him he continues, "This commandant bullshit is the reason two of our people are going to die. So don't give me any crap about critically ill people being given top priority. It's just a bunch of shit, that's all it is, Major!" With that he stomps out leaving the dumbstruck major to finish the task of using the supply choppers for medevacs.

Six of the Marines who are critically ill are flown by emergency medevac directly into An Hoa. Richard and two Marines who aren't as critically ill are loaded aboard a Huey. The chaplain is so weak he is literally lifted up and shoved onboard because he is unable to climb onboard the helicopter by himself. The three are offloaded at An Hoa, the two Marines left at the regimental aid station while Richard is driven to his BAS south of the runway. He is placed on an exam table where blood is drawn, then he is stripped of his clothes and bathed in a solution of water and alcohol.

That evening his temperature shoots up again, this time between 104 and 105 degrees. Two corpsmen take Strom outside butt-naked and stand him under a cold shower for ten minutes to cool him down. Through it all Richard continually begs them to let him go back inside and lay down on a bed. Once inside again, after hooking up an IV of Ringer's solution, he is made to lay naked on a cart in front of a giant fan where the same two corpsmen sponge him down with a water and alcohol mixture every fifteen minutes.

In the meantime, in the room adjacent to the exam room, a hot poker game is in progress. Every few minutes either a corpsman or one of the regimental doctors—two of them have been invited to the poker game—walk in to check the chaplain's temperature, then return to their poker game. Over the next few hours, Richard's experience is a hazy collage of voices raising bets, the sound of chips being thrown into the pot, laughter and swearing, and the steady hum of the giant fan blowing air across his overheated body. And through it all, into the wee hours of the morning, good old Savoy, the corpsman they all make fun of, is right there making sure everything is okay with Chaplain Strom, staying with him until the sun comes up.

By 0900 the chaplain's temperature has dropped to 100 and he is evacuated to First Hospital Company, which is located next to First Medical Battalion in Da Nang. This organization was set up exclusively to house and care for all the malaria patients coming in from the field.

Each ward is a self-contained, big balloon-like structure that has a shape and size similar to a Quonset hut. The uniqueness of these structures lies in their ability to stay at a temperature of sixty-five degrees by having very cool, continuous air blown into them. And should the air stop blowing, the structure would collapse like a deflated balloon.

That evening more troops with malaria arrive, mostly from the Fifth Marines. Soon the ward is full of troops whose temperatures are all spiking up between 104 and 106 degrees. All of them are losing critical body fluids faster than they can be replaced because most of them are unable to keep anything down. So the patients who are most critical, whose temperature has been elevated for the longest period of time are placed on the "green monster"—this is a machine that pumps a liquid through rubber sheets at a temperature of about sixty degrees. The sick patient, who feels he is freezing to death any-way because of the elevated temperatures, is placed between these sheets on his bed having only his shorts on. It is a very, very miserable existence for very, very sick grunts just out of the field.

Early the next morning Chaplain Strom's temperature shoots up to 105.4 and he is immediately put on the monster. The only time any of them are allowed out of bed is when they must go to the head. Into his second hour lying between the cold sheets, the strange though of sitting naked in a two-holer outhouse in the middle of a Minnesota winter comes to mind—strange how the unconscious works in times of stress.

That evening, when Richard's temperature is at its highest, when he is feeling absolutely the most miserable he has ever felt in his life, when he is moving back and forth between semiconsciousness and hallucinations, his good friend the Monk walks into the ward and slowly makes his way to Richard's left bedside. The very ill chaplain is lying between the green rubber sheets staring at the ceiling. Vince bends over and says in a slow, deliberate voice, "Hey, Lutheran, this is your last chance. Convert!"

Then he laughs that funny laugh of his and continues, "Strom, you'd do anything to get out of the bush, wouldn't you? I brought you some reading material"—which he places next to his bed—"and I'd bring you some Chivas Regal but with all these Marines around here they might steal it." Richard is too sick to say much, thanks the Monk, and slips off to sleep.

The next morning, just after getting back into bed and in between the sheets, the division chaplain walks in for a visit. He has next to him an older, grandfatherly gentleman who looks like he would be more comfortable in bishop's robes rather than the starched utilities of the Marine Corps. "Rich, this is Father McGinty. He's the new division chaplain."

The new incoming chaplain shakes Strom's hand, then murmurs some comments about how sorry he is that Richard is so sick. "We can't stay long, Rich," Spike continues, "but I wanted to see you before I left. Sorry it has to be like this. I'm gonna miss you, Rich. You take care of yourself and get back home safely. You will be my prayers of intention tonight." As he is saying this, Strom is shaking uncontrollably between the sheets.

After they leave, Richard vaguely remembers their visit and also of pleading with the corpsman on duty to get him off the monster. He is very miserable. Things are really blurred for him now—events, time, thoughts all run together—going to the head, taking his temperature, lying between the sheets hour after hour, shaking uncontrollably, hallucinating, the time moving ever so slowly.

"Get me off this goddamn son of a bitch," Strom hears a Marine yell in the bed across the aisle from him. This poor bastard has been on the monster for thirty-six hours, his temperature still hasn't broke and now it is driving him nuts. His endurance has reached rock-bottom! So two corpsmen and a doctor run over to the bed with straps and restrain the poor devil.

By late evening Richard's temperature has dropped dramatically—to 100—which is sufficient to get him off the monster. As the corpsman is removing the sheets, he says, "The worst is over, you're over the hump, Chaplain. Besides, we have so many new cases we need to use the monster for another patient."

However, the chaplain is unable to keep anything down because of the nausea, so just after being "set free," he is given a shot of Compazine to settle his stomach and diminish the sick feeling in his stomach. Within an hour his body begins tightening up, his legs start to draw up against his chest as if some uncontrollable force is drawing them in. Then his breathing becomes shallow and shortly, he finds it difficult to even breathe at all, as if his diaphragm is paralyzed. Even his speech becomes tight and constricted. Within fifteen minutes the chaplain is freaking out and believes he is dying!

The corpsman who is watching the progression of the chaplain's constriction runs out of the ward to get the doctor out of bed. Within three minutes he's back with the doctor, who takes one look at the chaplain and orders seventy-five milligrams of Benadryl IV stat! Within seconds Richard's body is totally relaxed and the trauma is over. Chaplain Strom is the first case of dramatic extrapyramidal reaction on the ward. Soon a number of Marines will also have the same reaction until they finally stop giving the malaria patients Compazine for nausea.

Richard Strom stays at the hospital for eight more days. He and all the other Marines on the ward are diagnosed with falciparum malaria, a less common but far more deadly type of malaria than the more common vivax, which was the type epidemic in the south pacific during World War II. Strom receives quinine and Daraprim to combat the malaria parasites and Gantrisin for his kidneys because the process of black water fever had started when he was brought in and folic acid for his anemia. The quinine is the worst of the medications because it causes terrible ringing in his ears and messes up his hearing for weeks.

Two days before Richard is to be released, he is eating in the mess hall, his first meal outside the ward since his arrival. His appetite is negligible and he is still feeling weak and dizzy. Just as he is ready to get up, none other than the sawed-off runt of a commander he met out with Echo a few days back arrives at his table.

"Well, well, what do we have here," Commander Peters questions as he sets his tray down across from the chaplain. Richard is more shocked than annoyed by his sudden presence. "Listen, Chaplain," he begins, "we have reason to believe that people in your outfit are not taking their chloroquine-primaquine tablets."

Right now Chaplain Strom just wants to be left alone and to eat in peace and this mindless bureaucrat shows up bugging him with baited statements. Richard feels his anger going up a notch, then says, "Hey, look, Commander, I take my pills regularly, I also got malaria. You calling me a liar?"

"No, I'm not," he says with an edge to his voice, "but there are lots of people here at division, me included, who are asking lots of questions, and I'll tell you this"—he waves his fork in Richard's face—"your colonel is in some deep trouble. There's no excuse for all that malaria in *Two-five*. He's the commanding officer and he is ultimately responsible. What do you have to say to that, Chaplain?"

Richard is feeling really pissed—"Hooray for feelings," he thinks quickly to himself—then picks up his tray and says to him, "Here's what I have to say to that. Why don't you take a jar of *Anopheles* mosquitoes and stick them up your ass, Commander!"

The little shrimp immediately jumps up from his seat, walks in front of Strom, his eyes almost bugging right out of his head, and replies, "Do you know you're talking to a commander in the United States Navy, a field-grade officer?" he sputters as the chaplain continues walking to the refuse cans and dumps his food and stacks his dirty dishes. "I'm going to nail your ass, mister. You can't talk like that to a superior officer!"

Richard turns and faces him, hands on hips, and says, "You just do what you gotta do, Commander. And while you're at it, why don't you see if you can get me fired from the navy and sent back home." With that Chaplain Strom turns and walks back to his ward to catch some sleep.

In the evening Richard and two other officers venture out of their hospital beds to the officers' club to watch a move. They are all blown away by the selection. They see, of all things, *Green Beret*, starring John Wayne, a movie about the special forces in Vietnam. Every single one of the officers who watch the movie that night are incredulous at what they are seeing. The audience hoots, laughs, and hisses throughout the whole movie.

Strom wonders how the folks back home experience this movie. "Are they gullible enough to believe the kind of crap portrayed in this movie?" he thinks. "No wonder many Americans think this is a winnable war when Hollywood puts out this kind of hackneyed junk."

Two days later, after being dewormed for hook and round worm, Richard is discharged from the hospital and sent back to his unit in An Hoa. His discharge weight is 126 pounds, down from his weight of 165 when he left Camp Pendleton. Boarding the chopper ride back to his unit, Richard is feeling weak, tired, and more dispirited than he has ever felt in his life.

R&R TIME

Chaplain Strom is weak and still feels loaded from the worm medicine taken earlier in the day as he slowly ambles off the helicopter. An Hoa looks and feels the same—muddy, dirty, stinky, and noisy. He crosses the helipad and walks the three hundred meters to his battalion area. He notices that there are many more bunkers now than when he arrived a few months ago. When he gets to his hooch, he immediately falls asleep on his cot, awakened two hours later by the loud sounds of incoming rockets landing close to the battery north of the airstrip. Although feeling weak, Richard's instincts are still intact. He grabs his helmet and flak jacket and takes off running for the bunker in back of his hooch.

Inside the bunker he sees most of the rear staff including the executive officer. He is also aware that there are a new faces that he's never seen before. He is beginning to feel like an old-timer in the battalion. In the dim light Major Cahill sees the chaplain, turns toward him, and says with a smile on his face, "Well, whattya know, the chaplain's back from his brush with malaria and the US Navy." He shakes Strom's hand. "Glad to have you back with us. We've missed you." Just then four more incoming explosions are heard, then Marine artillery begins their answer by firing twenty rounds in quick succession.

"Boy, did you stir up some shit, Chaplain," Cahill continues. "What in the hell did you say to that navy commander? Apparently the general is involved in this skirmish. Hell, maybe we're gonna lose both you and the colonel." He continues to smile and shake his head as if he can't believe the audacity of his battalion chaplain.

"Look, Major, the guy is a self-righteous, sawed-off little jerk and he really ticked me off when he accused the Old Man of being neglectful," Richard responds. "I mean, being a neglectful commander of troops is the exact opposite of what the colonel is really about."

"Well, Chaplain, from what I hear, you didn't handle the situation in the most diplomatic way," responds Cahill in a kind but firm voice, then smiles and continues, "You 'sky pilots' are supposed to be gracious, but I can understand why you got pissed. I'm going to let the colonel know what happened with you and the commander. It should get you some points with Stevens and the rest of the staff when they hear about it. Hopefully the whole damn thing will just blow over. You know, Chaplain, they could really jump in your shit if that bird brain of a commander wants to make a case out of your insubordination."

"Oh yeah," Strom replies as they now leave the bunker and walk back toward their hooches, "what do you suppose they'd make me do, punish me by making me go back with the navy?"

The major laughs and states quickly, "A couple more months with us and you'll be too far gone to make it any longer as naval officer and a gentleman!"

When they walk by the chaplain's hooch and Richard is just ready to open the door, the major stops and turns toward Richard. "I understand you'll be going on R&R shortly," he says in that all-business-like voice of his, "so you better let the Old Man know about it. He's been asking about you and when you'd be back."

Within twenty minutes of the all clear signal, there are five Marines waiting at the chaplain's doorstep. It doesn't take long for the word to get around when the chaplain is back in An Hoa.

The first Marine wants emergency leave back to the States because he claims his wife just had a miscarriage. Since a miscarriage doesn't qualify for emergency leave, Richard explains to the worried husband that he will work out an early R&R for him so he can meet his wife in Hawaii. The second fellow, a known malingerer in the battalion, the same Marine Bernie banished to the field, has been court-martialed twice for theft, fighting, and disrespect to an officer. Richard tells him that because he is so good with his hands at fighting, he more than likely will be rejected for CO status. "Sorry, Private, but don't see how I can recommend you for conscientious objector status," Richard states flatly.

"So you're gonna do nothing for me, which means I can't get home?" he angrily asks.

"Conscientious objectors don't start fights, Sheldon," is the chaplain's reply.

The Marine stands up, points his index finger at the battalion chaplain, and says loudly, "You're like all the rest of the jerks around here." He turns to the door, kicks it open, and walks out, saying, "Fuck you!"

The chaplain says nothing, stands up, and motions to the next Marine to step inside.

The third young man is facing court-martial for refusing to go back to the field. He has been wounded and has seen too many of his buddies killed and maimed the past eleven months. In speaking to him Richard feels he has reached his limit and is very serious about disobeying an order directing him back out in the bush. "Corporal Baker, here's what I'm going to do. I will get in touch with your first sergeant and talk to him about getting you orders to stay in the rear with us or regiment. You may lose a stripe but I believe I can get it done for you. However, there is something you need to know. If you tell anyone that I am responsible for getting you stationed back here, and suddenly I have twenty-five Marines coming to me with the same request, I'll have your butt shipped back out in the bush that same afternoon. Do you understand me?"

"Yes, sir," replies the relieved Marine.

The two Marines want to know the procedure for getting married to a foreign national. Both of them have just returned from R&R—one from Bangkok and the other from Kuala Lumpur. Neither will probably end up getting married. The paperwork and waiting is enough to do in any good midlevel bureaucrat, let alone these unsophisticated young Marines. Richard listens to them, to their reasons for wanting to marry these nationals, which is all he can do right now.

Most of the women these guys want to marry in Singapore, Hong Kong, Bangkok, and Kuala Lumpur are professional hookers. Their job is to put themselves up for hire when these young men come off the planes from Vietnam. They make their money by providing pleasure and companionship for the five days they are on R&R.

Consider that for the past year or two these young men have faced sadistic drill instructors, relentless pressures from their commands through all their training, and they find themselves deprived of just about every conceivable human need, getting their asses shot at day and night, being treated as a replaceable statistic if they are blown away, yelled at all the time and always told what to do. Suddenly they are turned loose in a large oriental city with a few hundred bucks in their pockets and are treated as a human being, as someone who is special, for five straight days.

Chaplain Strom has an understanding about these young men who have faced the horrors of combat, that some of these returning Marines do feel as if they are actually in love and want to marry one of these women. More than likely these ladies are the only people in a long, long time that have treated them with dignity and respect. So instead of reprimanding them or going critical on them, Richard just listens to them and their stories of falling in love. Then he explains to them all the necessary paperwork and calmly lets them know the average waiting period to get the paperwork done is six months. Usually within a month, most of them drop their requests—either because they see the situation more clearly down the line or because they are dead.

It is at times like these—getting a Marine out of the field or scoring an early R&R for a grunt—that those quarts of Old Grand-Dad or Chivas Regal come in handy. Grandpa and Uncle Chivas, as Richard calls them, get him lots of mileage in his business dealings with the first sergeants, especially with his buddy, First Sergeant Francis Xavier Rooney. On one of his last runs, Strom had procured a quart and a fifth of Old Grand-Dad for him—the quart was for his personal use while Richard was out in the field; the fifth he and Rooney would sip in the evenings when Strom was in An Hoa.

Rooney is a short, tough old-time Marine who dreads the day when he will be forced to retire and become a civilian. His history with the Corps goes back to Guadalcanal, the Marine Raiders, Okinawa, and the old days of "piss and punk," a term used to describe the shit-kicking that went on with prisoners in the brig. He said that in the old days of the Corps, you could get sent to the brig for a weekend just by looking at an officer in the wrong way.

Richard is visiting Rooney the evening before leaving for R&R, which the first sergeant had personally arranged while the chaplain was in the hospital. As they are sipping some one-hundred-proof Old Grand-Dad, Rooney explains to the chaplain why the Marine Corps isn't what it used to be.

"The problem, Chaplain, is that we've lost the authority to discipline our troops. There's too damn much coddling," the first sergeant says tersely. "Ass kicking makes for good morale, keeps the troops in line, and builds character." Rooney suddenly smiles, takes a sip of his drink, then continues, "I guess you and I are at opposite poles about this discipline stuff, huh, Chaplain? I poke 'em and you stroke 'em." He laughs hard and takes another sip of his Old Grand-Dad.

"That's probably a very accurate way of looking at our jobs," Richard replies, "never thought of it that way."

Rooney then sits back in his chair and says thoughtfully, "You know, Chaplain, never in my twenty-eight years in the Marine Corps have I had any kind of relationship with a chaplain before except for doing official business, like disciplinary stuff. Most of them just pissed me off. So my way of dealing with them was to keep them from screwing around in my business and by staying away from them. Only been in the chapel twice: once for a wedding and another time for a funeral. Chaplains don't fit into my way of doing things." Chaplain Strom is listening intently as Rooney continues, "If someone would have told me that I'd be sitting down with a chaplain, sippin' whiskey, shootin' the breeze, and doing favors for each other—"

There is a knock at the door. Rooney stops his monologue and turns toward the door. "Yeah, whattya want, Marine?" he asks, visibly irritated by the interruption.

The Marine walks into the office and immediately starts complaining about how his request for transfer is being handled. First Sergeant Rooney scowls, gets up from his chair, and says to Strom, "Will you excuse me for a moment, Chaplain? I have some business to take care of." With that he turns to the Marine and says tersely, "You, Marine, come outside with me."

They both walk outside and go in back of the hooch where the chaplain hears some terse, angry talk, then scuffling and banging around for a few seconds. Shortly Rooney appears and sits down, takes a hit from his drink, and says, "You know, Chaplain, I don't like it when these administrative chores interrupt my social hour."

Richard smiles and shakes his head, wondering how in the world the two of them became friends and why they enjoy each other's company. Their relationship certainly is a paradox to say the least.

The next morning, shortly before Richard Strom is to leave for Da Nang and R&R, he is in the mess tent eating breakfast. A Marine sits down at the table next to his and the chaplain sees it is the same trooper that came in to see Sergeant Rooney last night. He also notices the young man has a bandage on his nose and a huge black eye. This is Rooney's way, many times, of handling administrative problems. Richard winces at seeing the Marine with his injuries. It is a result of the raw autocratic milieu of the Marine Corps, which allows this kind of "discipline." But he also knows this same kind of discipline is responsible for keeping many Marines alive and functioning out in the bush, where staying alive is a direct result of an absolute hierarchical structure.

He gets up from the table, walks to the garbage can and places his dirty dishes on the table next to the kitchen area, and remembers again his dad's cautionary remarks about idealists and war. "Rooney's the realist and I'm the idealist. Wonder which one of us is going to get ground up first," Strom thinks to himself as he leaves the mess tent.

As Chaplain Strom walks back to his hooch, he realizes just how burned out and weak he is from the effects of the malaria. Doesn't seem very exciting right now that shortly he will be meeting with his wife and nine-month-old son in Hawaii. He realizes that for some reasons yet unknown, something has been lost inside, that spark of life which keeps his energy level high, that flow of feeling from within that keeps his hopes and dreams a living reality. It is really hard for Richard to imagine, intellectually and emotionally, that within forty-eight hours he will be in Honolulu with his wife and son. It just didn't seem real at all to him!

MELANCHOLY

The helicopter has just taken off from the airstrip at An Hoa and is heading for Hill 547, near the Laotian border. Richard is feeling depressed and scattered. Less than twenty-four hours ago he said good-bye to his wife and son at the R&R center at Fort DeRussey in downtown Honolulu. If there was ever a time in his life when he didn't want to follow through with a commitment, it was then. It was god-awful, getting that one last look/kiss/hold/touch before getting on the bus that would take them back to the airport and eventually Vietnam. There were lots of very hard swallows and tears. The deadness of heart and the crushing of spirit on that bus ride out to the airport was overwhelming!

"It was a maze, a rush of time and space and living and feeling again that ended far too soon. Did it even happen?" he thinks to himself as he watches the jungle pass far below, climbing higher and higher over the mountains of interior Vietnam.

That experience of no-feeling has come back again. He felt it coming on when he stepped of the plane in Da Nang and rode out to the helipad. Each step—the 707 stop at Anderson Air Force Base in Guam, the CH-53 helicopter from Da Nang, the CH-46 from An Hoa and soon Hill 547—brought him closer to the reality of war and further away from the reality of hamburgers and dirty diapers and smiling faces. Chaplain Strom feels no more deep sadness, only deadness as he looks out the window of the helicopter and lapses into a rush of thoughts and memories. "Wonder what Bob's doing... Timmy's cutting teeth... My new combat boots already have mud on them... Been close to twenty days now since I've been in the bush... Clean-smelling fresh sheets... This is really in the boonies... The little guy will be over a year old when I see him again, probably be walking by then… C-rations make good fly shit… Evening sail and dinner at the Waikiki… Colonel is probably pissed at me again… Hope my family gets back to San Clemente okay… Wonder how many friends will be gone when I get out there… Should have a new doc by now, hope he isn't as screwy as Bernie… Ho Chi Minh and Richard Nixon deserve each other… Is it really possible I was in Hawaii with my family?… God, I feel lousy… Is that why so many grunts get killed right after R&R, they're so down they don't give a damn anymore?… Wish I could crawl into a hole and disconnect— from everything!"

Strom's reverie is interrupted by the smiling crew chief, who is tapping him on the shoulder, pointing out the LZ below, as if he could care less. The chaplain is aware that many times he is selected out for conversation because he's the chaplain. Right now he is irritated by the blocking of his thought process. "Why don't they just leave me alone?" he thinks to himself. "I don't want their good humor, their special favors, their well-meaning religious jokes, their attention. Just let me be, dammit," he says quietly to himself as they come in for a landing.

The LZ sits atop a mountain. Standing on top one can look across a big valley ten kilometers across to another mountain range, which is next door to Laos. There are eight artillery pieces on the hill and two line companies within the area. There has been very little contact with the enemy since being airlifted ten days ago and no incoming on the hill.

The battalion chaplain finds his way to the CP to let the colonel know he is back. "I was just about ready to fire you and get some- body new," he says with a smile and a handshake. "Glad to have you back. Thought maybe I'd have to get the major here to have church services for you." He then points to the ops officer next to him.

"I've got more important things to do," he says politely to Stevens, then walks out of the CP area, giving Strom a cold, blank stare.

Richard picks up his gear again and walks the forty meters to the BAS, which is an area dug into the hillside and covered with sandbags and a wooden top made out of old discarded ammo boxes. The area is completely shaded because it is located underneath two different levels of trees, the underbrush having been cleared away upon arrival. It looks cool and comfortable. Marshall sees Richard, gets up from his makeshift chair, and greets the chaplain with a handshake.

"Jeez, Bob, you're improving," Richard says with a smile. "No more saluting. Must be because you've been hanging out with all these navy squids. Does that mean you're turning into one of them?"

"No, sir," Bob replies, returning a smile. "I like hanging out with these guys but I'm still a Marine." Marshall is reiterating a truism about the Corps. You can coexist with or without folks from other branches of the service. However, the hardcore rule of anyone who becomes a Marine is "Once a Marine, always a Marine!" It is a reminder to Strom that even though Marine and navy personnel live, fight, and die together, there is always that line of separation and distinctiveness that comes from being a Marine within the naval service.

The chaplain wearily drops his gear on the deck. A bespectacled, young-looking officer walks up to Richard, extends his hand, and says, "I'm Dennis Jonsen, the new battalion surgeon, Chaplain. I've hear a lot about you."

"Oh yeah," Strom replies while shaking his hand, still feeling depressed and not really wanting to talk to him or anyone else. "What kind of baloney have they been feeding you?" Richard sits down on the deck, leaning against a tree.

The doctor looks at him confused, as if he doesn't know how to respond to Strom's flippant remark, then musters up the courage to offer him something to drink. "Would you like a beer, Chaplain?"

The chaplain remains seated, not moving except to grasp the beer the young navy lieutenant is offering him, "Thanks, Dennis, I see your boys here have already taught you how to get the beer ration out to the field."

As they both lift their beers to take a sip, Marshall whispers loudly, "The colonel's headed this way, sir!"

The four other members of the BAS who are drinking a cold one quickly stash their beers. Stevens is looking around as he walks into the area and toward the doctor, turns to the chaplain, and says,

"Well, Doctor, how are you liking your first few days in the bush?" He shifts his gaze onto Jonsen,.

"Okay, I guess," he replies.

"Got everything you need?" he continues.

"Uh-huh," is Dennis's reply.

The colonel does a noticeable scowl and says, "You sure about that, Doc?"

Jonsen smiles and says, "Yup, I'm sure."

"Listen, Doctor," the Colonel responds in an agitated voice, "I'm gonna set you straight just like I did with your navy compatriot over there," he said, pointing a finger at the chaplain, "You don't go around saying *yup* and *uh-huh* to your commanding officer. This is not medical school or the hallway of a hospital where everybody is kissing your ass. This is the Marine Corps and you answer me by saying "Yes, sir," "No, sir," not "Yup" and "Uh-huh" and "Nope." Is that understood, doctor?"

"Yeah, okay, Colonel," is the battalion surgeon's startled reply, completely unconscious of what he is saying.

Stevens stares at the doctor for a few seconds, looks at Richard shaking his head, turns, and walks off, muttering to himself about why he has to put up with the people the navy sends him. And this is how Chaplain Strom meets the new doctor out in the middle of a rain forest.

Jonsen is a graduate of the University of Minnesota medical school. Dennis is small and appears delicate and scholarly, the exact opposite of Bernie. He looks to Richard as if he'd be much more comfortable taking care of cardiac patients in ICU at a hospital back home than attempting to survive and stay alive with a bunch of cut-throat Marines in the middle of a war zone.

The battalion chaplain leaves the group to be by himself. He is feeling a real void, very discouraged about being in Vietnam for four more months. This is a prospect that brings instant depression, which, combined with the daily boredom of being isolated on a hill far from regiment, creates an underlying sense of despair. However, at least for now, no one is dying. Not yet anyway.

After spending four days on this mountaintop doing little except to sleep, eat, and play cards, the colonel receives word that the battalion will be going back to regiment shortly. An Hoa is taking lots of incoming and the airstrip has been hit so many times they have to close it down to fixed wing airplanes. The only supplies now getting through are the daily truck convoys and that brought in by helicopter. Things are really heating up again in and around An Hoa.

The single search-and-destroy operation *Two-five* has engaged in up through Christmas has now become more complex and they are now a part of a brigade-sized operational command run out of An Hoa. A brigadier general is now in command of the combined forces of the Fifth, Third, and Twenty-Seventh Marines. This means Stevens has another command to go through, which he claims slows everything down, from decision making to logistical supplies.

"All it did was to give some goddamn paper-pushing one-star general an opportunity to screw up out here in the field rather than at his desk playing with paper," says the colonel at the afternoon staff meeting, disgusted with the conflicting intelligence and operational scenarios being put forth and then withdrawn on a daily basis. Stevens has let his hostilities be known before to both regiment and battalion about Task Force Yankee, the brigade under which all three regiments have been laboring the past few weeks. Richard tells the colonel that when he came through An Hoa from R&R, he heard that General Crowley was furious because someone had crawled up the observation tower in An Hoa and had placed a sign on it saying "Yankee Go Home!" in obvious reference to the general and his staff. The Old Man laughs hard and says, "If I had my way, I'd give that damn Marine who climbed up there with that sign the Silver Star!"

The next morning, his sixth on the hill, Chaplain Strom tells Bob to get the word out he will hold church for both battalion headquarters and Hotel. It is the only worship service he will hold while on Hill 547. Just as he is to begin, he remarks to Bob that the boredom must be terrible with so many Marines attending church; in this case over one hundred fifty are in attendance. As he begins services, Strom recognizes two significant changes. First, he notices all the new faces in front of him, which means that both casualties and malaria as well as normal rotation has taken their toll. "My God," he thinks to himself, "it seems like only yesterday when I strapped my gear together for my first trip out to the bush with the grunts, a real rookie! Now here I am, one of the more senior officers in the battalion on the 'down' side of my tour."

The second unusual observation is seeing the colonel at church for only the second time, seated on the deck in the front row. Richard smiles as he recalls Steven's remarks last Christmas that he was a Presbyterian by birth who practiced the doctrine of frugality when it came to going to church. Their relationship has changed dramatically since that first encounter on Hill 52 when the new chaplain, as Dr. Grant described it, was "reamed a new asshole." At this point it is an open relationship and the colonel allows his chaplain to pretty much dictate his own schedule. Strom isn't asking questions anymore about permission regarding his ministry and his "travels." He is making statements to Stevens about what he wants in spite of the S3, who of course thinks Strom impertinent.

Just as Richard is finishing Holy Communion and is beginning the final prayers, gunfire erupts in the valley far below. Golf has made contact for the first time in a week. The colonel quickly gets up in the middle of the prayer and walks to the CP a few meters away. The chaplain simply says, "Keep the faith and pray we get outta here soon. Amen."

The gunfire in the valley below produces more disappointment than anxiety. Because all the Marines are now prepared emotionally, physically, and psychologically to get off that hill and back home to An Hoa. Now, the last day before they are to leave, Golf makes contact with the enemy and everyone is feeling very discouraged that some reactive idiot in An Hoa or Da Nang is going to change plans again and keep them out on the hill for an extended period of time. Some of the Marines on that hill have been out in the field without a break for sixty-four days and are looking forward to going back to the relative comfort of An Hoa in spite of the daily incoming there.

At the afternoon briefing the colonel is livid. Brigade is now thinking about keeping the battalion on the hill and maybe even moving them further north to another hill like the one they are presently on. He is furious because it is common knowledge that the enemy has already made their way inland to An Hoa and places like Hoi An and Go Noi Island. Staying here, in his estimation, is a waste of time and resources when the battalion could be engaging at the enemy down on the plains where they all seem to be presently located. Rockets and mortars are slamming into An Hoa daily, both the First and Seventh Marines are in heavy contact near Da Nang almost every day, while *Two-five* just sits up in the mountain, rotting away with boredom and malaria.

By evening battalion receives an intelligence report that says their hill is going to "ignite" and become a hot spot. Since Golf's contact has broken off, Stevens isn't sure what this means for the battalion. It makes everyone nervous on the one hand and very skeptical on the other because in reality intelligence reports are issued daily that have critical and many times completely contrasting information. The dire predictions seldom pan out.

During the staff meeting, in the midst of getting this latest "intelligence," Richard leans toward the new battalion surgeon and says quietly, "Sounds to me like they're covering their asses again as usual."

The S3 overhears the chaplain's remarks and says back, "Since when did you go to intelligence school, Chaplain?"

"Didn't have to, Major," is Strom's instant reply, "I was already born with some."

The doctor laughs out loud, the major stares at Strom like he's the antichrist, and the colonel says angrily, "We have more important things to do then sit here making smart-ass remarks, Chaplain. Now, how in the hell do we comply with an order that says get your shit together to leave and also prepare to stay? Now you tell me what the hell we're supposed to do about that one!" he says obviously perplexed and angry.

Two hours after the staff meeting breaks up battalion finally gets word they are to leave for An Hoa in the morning. So the next morning all the gear is packed up. The big guns go first, carried off by the large C-53 helicopters, then they retrograde the ammunition, water, and food supplies. Finally Golf is picked up down in the valley and brought back to An Hoa At this point there are fifty Marines left on the hill to take back to regiment. However, good old Sunshine Airlines comes through again. The choppers are called off for another assignment and the remaining personnel are left at this godforsaken place to sit on their asses without any kind of support.

The NVA would have to be blind to not have noticed the airlift taking place. This kind of a situation has a tendency to raise the level of paranoia real fast for those who are left behind. It is almost a certainty that during times of resupply or retrograde the enemy will zero in on the Marine position with rockets or mortars.

This kind of situation also raises one's consciousness about the Marine Corps in particular and the military in general and allows one to see where their priorities really are when it comes to material or men. Their biggest concern is to get the guns and supplies off the hill. That kind of says what is expendable and what isn't. Same way with aircraft—it is much easier to ship over a plane load of Marines than a couple of aircraft. There is an endless supply of human beings, especially blacks, browns, and poor whites. It is the machines of war that are costly and keep the taxes high.

Richard is lying on the hillside next to the LZ, attempting to stay cool, waiting to eventually be picked up by the choppers. Bob, Dr. Jonsen, and all the corpsmen except one left earlier to get the medical equipment back to the BAS from the helipad. It's been four hours waiting now, their brains fried from the heat and their minds getting acclimated to the paranoia of being out on this hillside all alone, when the first rocket hits. A Marine is casually strolling on the west end of the LZ, waiting to get back to An Hoa after sixty days in the field, when he takes a direct hit from the projectile and literally disintegrates.

The reflex that comes is primal instinct, completely no-think! Goes back way beyond that time so long ago when the saber-toothed tiger showed up at the Neanderthal's cave. Richard is looking up at the LZ when he sees this Marine vanish. Shrapnel is flying in all directions from this rocket and another explosion as they all scramble back into the woods on their bellies or dive for cover. The familiar cry for help "Corpsmen up" is screamed.

Firing rockets with that kind of accuracy means they are close by. It also means they know where the remaining Marines are, but the grunts don't know where the enemy is. This kind of perceptive process, a few seconds after an attack begins, allows the level of paranoia to arise to new levels of intensity, especially if the remaining Marines are radio operators, battalion clerks, and such who haven't been on the line. Being isolated and under attack without a weapon and without his assistant raises Richard's anxiety to a belief, distorted or real, that he definitely is going to die. Soon!

Two more rounds hit the LZ. The battalion chaplain is frightened out of his mind but again, as in times past when under attack, thoughts began to percolate up through the horrible fear he is feeling, thoughts of some fat general or regimental colonel who has requested the helicopters they need to get them off the hill, who are now riding up and down the Da Nang / Chu Lai corridor showing some VIPs around, explaining to them how the war is being won.

"You assholes… you assholes," Richard suddenly hears himself say loudly to no one in particular as he awaits more rounds.

No more rockets hit. Nor did any NVA show up on the hill to overrun the personnel left. By dark all the remaining people left on the hill have finally been lifted back to An Hoa. Nothing lost, nothing gained.

Diary Entry—210 Days In-Country

It didn't cost anybody that much, staying on that hill for a few more hours so Marines air could do whatever it needed to do or respond to whomever it was that ordered the evacuation of the hill stopped for a few hours. After all, it didn't make that much difference—maybe added few gray hairs to some of the personnel let behind, scaring the hell out of all of them, causing three Marines to be medevaced because of wounds. What the hell, not that much was lost, was it? Tell that to the mother and father of the Marine who became collage of blood and pieces of flesh on the LZ:

> *Dear parents of Marine:*
>
> *Please accept the heel and shoes and sole of your son's combat boot as a token of our esteem. He died a good Marine.*
>
> *Yours truly,*
> *The UNITED STATES MARINE CORPS*
>
> *PS: They were the only two things we could find large enough to identify.*

BACK TO THE ROUTINE

Strom stays overnight in An Hoa and doesn't get much sleep because the place is under siege, constantly being rocketed day and night. He makes six runs to the bunker last night. Anymore, he doesn't think in terms of how much sleep he gets but rather if he sleeps at all.

He gets a chopper ride into Da Nang from the regimental aid station. They'll be landing at First Med, where he can visit his troops who are hospitalized there. Then he'll get a ride to recon to see who he still knows there, after that bum a ride to NSA Hospital across the river. Richard will hopefully make one of his rare appearances to see the division chaplain. He hasn't attended a division chaplain's meeting in four months.

The helicopter is coming in at one hundred feet around the mountain by the hospital, following the road that leads to division. Chaplain Strom flashes on that time, now eight months ago, when he was riding in a jeep on his way from the airport to the division chaplain's office. Paradoxically, that experience of meeting Spike and his first encounter with incoming seems like yesterday and years ago simultaneously. He sees the familiar red cross on the helipad next to receiving and triage as the aircraft slowly circles the compound, then drops softly on the steel matting.

Shortly Richard is making his way through the wards, getting the names of personnel in his battalion from each of the ward clerks because the records at admissions are always a disaster and never up to date. Many of the injured from *Two-five* have been wounded from shrapnel in the constant rocket attacks out at An Hoa.

Richard visits each ward, talking to his troops as well as personnel from the Twenty-Seventh Marines. He spends over two hours chatting with the young Marines, praying with them, promising to write letters home to their parents or wives. As he finishes visiting the last ward, he again feels a sense of dread creeping up because shortly he must face both ICU and the Rose Garden. He is aware of having some Marines in both places. The dead have not been removed from last night's casualties brought in from both An Hoa and Dodge City where the Twenty-Seventh Marines are in constant contact. He is also mindful that he is not his usual efficient self anymore when making his rounds, little notebook in hand, writing down any details the sick or wounded would like him to handle such as lost mail, those letters back home, present whereabouts of their personal effects. There is definitely an erosion of zeal that was once there.

When he finally gets to the Rose Garden, after finding all kinds of excuses not to stop by, he counts ten dead Marines lined up in various stages of dismemberment. What really gets to him is the smell, that sickening stench of overly ripe bodies that have been too long without refrigeration. He leans over each body and checks each tag for a name and unit, gagging on the stench and ugliness and inhumanity and insanity of it all.

"Well, lucky me," he says out loud, "only two of these fellows are from my outfit." He stands up straight, pauses, then continues, "Must be cracking up—now I'm talking to dead bodies."

"Did you want to have last rites, Chaplain?" says a huge Marine who has walked into the Rose Garden without Richard's knowledge. "I've come to take the bodies to the morgue."

The chaplain jumps noticeably at the intrusion, then turns and says, "Ah, no thanks, I'm just leaving." As he gingerly walks out, he notices the "bloat coach" parked next to the helipad offloading green bags from the parked helicopter. "Don't believe I could handle that work," he thinks to himself, "but maybe those guys on the morgue detail are thinking that about us in the infantry, especially walking point for a squad. Good God, talk about expendable humanity!"

Chaplain Strom walks into the air-conditioned ICU. Just being in ICU means one is in critical shape. In this case, both of his Marines

are beyond critical, Sergeant Anthony Gallo, the always high-spir-
ited Hotel weapons leader from Fresno, California, was mortally
wounded yesterday from a gunshot wound to the head. Much of his
left frontal lobe is damaged and he is breathing only with the help of
a respirator. Richard approaches the bed and softly places his hand
on the dying Marine's left shoulder, remembering those times in the
past when he came to visit Hotel, when Gallo would fuss over the
chaplain to make sure Richard had something to eat and a good place
to sleep. Over the steady *hiss-thump… hiss-thump* intonation of the
machine keeping him alive, tears well up in the chaplain's eyes as he
softly whispers a prayer: "Mercifully take him now, Lord, past his
suffering, away from all this craziness that surrounds us. Bring him
the peace he deserves. In Jesus's name, amen."

Richard lingers for a few seconds, slowly wipes away his tears,
turns, and walks directly across the aisle to his other Marine—he
notices now that he thinks and talks about them as "his Marines." Pfc
Charlie Whitehorse, a young Lakota native from Spearfish, South
Dakota, has been in-country only eight days. Two days ago while
walking point for his squad he tripped a booby trap, which killed
two of his buddies and gravely injured Charlie. He is missing three
of his limbs and has only a hole now where his nose used to be. His
jaw is wired shut and he is being fed intravenously. As Richard looks
compassionately at the destruction wrought on this unconscious
young man—he is one of the worst the chaplain has yet seen and
still living—he begins to feel agitation and anger. Remembering the
corpsman's words at the front desk—"He's still alive"—his hostility
about the insanity that surrounds him again generates acerbic, cutting thoughts: "*Living*. Is that what we call it with most of his face
gone and three-quarters of his limbs missing? Still living, hell!"

He suddenly turns away from the bed, walks down the aisle,
brushes past the doctor, almost knocking him down, kicks the door
open, and rushes outside. Walking down the road to Highway 1,
Richard says out loud to himself, "This vegetable of a human being,
who is missing twenty-five percent of his body and most of his mind,
we're gonna patch him up and send him back so his family can be
real proud of him. Mr. & Mrs. Whitehorse, your son has done so

well and has been such a credit to his country and the United States Marine Corps. He did it all in the name of freedom. Bullshit, bullshit, bullshit!"

Chaplain Strom now reaches the main road, turns right, and walks toward division about a kilometer away. He is pissed out of his mind right now, tears streaming down his cheeks, feeling rage and sorrow and hurt and guilt. "My God, am I feeling guilty because I feel so hopeless or is it because I'm still alive?"

When he walks past recon, his tears have stopped. When he gets past the division surgeon's office, his anger is gone. By the time he arrives at the division chapel, he feels nothing. His motor of feeling has shut down again like an internal combustion engine out of gas. As he walks slowly up the drive from the highway, he thinks to himself again, "Maybe somewhere along the way I cracked up? So what, who cares? Who'd know anyway?"

"Well, well, Chaplain Strom," says the assistant division chaplain as Richard walks through the door, "we were just talking about you today at our weekly chaplain's meeting and we're all wondering how you are doing." He shakes the young chaplain's hand and they walk into his office and sit down as he continues, "You look worn-out, Rich, any truth to that?"

"Nah, I'm okay," Richard lies to him in a matter-of-fact voice. "Same old crap, you know, lack of sleep and so forth. How are things going around here?" he continues as he motions with his head toward the direction of the division chaplain's office.

George smiles and replies, "Oh, you know, things have a way of just working out if you leave them alone. We're doing fine here." He's lying and they both know it and continues on with the charade. "He'll want to see you, so don't take off please."

Commander George Williams, the assistant division chaplain, is a well-liked, sensitive, spiritual person who is also intelligent enough to understand the terrific stress under which the infantry chaplains labor and their sometimes flippant attitudes. He is also a good administrator and knows how to apply pressure when needed. George is a perfect complement to the division chaplain, who is considered flaky, wrings his hands all the time about administrative matters, and generally is intolerant toward the ecumenical spirit and participation among some of the Catholic and Protestant chaplains. The Monk, given at times to hyperbole, once said to Richard that the new division chaplain is a throwback to the days of Torquemada and the Spanish Inquisition.

"Rich," George continues, "I know you and Spike had a special relationship when he was here. He always talked about his 'boys' out in the bush, especially you. He just didn't like to see you guys get chewed up emotionally and physically. Anyway, I'm asking you to give this guy a chance." He looks toward McGinty office. "He's trying very hard to find his way over here. And because he hasn't had much Marine duty, he's working on a learning curve and just trying to get his feet wet."

Richard knows that George is trying to soften him up for the guy because he's heard stories about how McGinty will get all hung up in detail work, like reports and so forth. A clerk suddenly shows up in George's office and says, "Sir, Father McGinty will see Chaplain Strom now."

They get up and walk into the division chaplain's office, where Richard is greeted warmly and seated. "How are things going for you... ah, Dick, is that right? Dick or Richard?" he asks.

"Either one," Strom replies, "my friends at recon call me Dirty Dick!"

Father McGinty scowls noticeably while George shifts his weight in the chair and clears his throat. "Ah, I saw you last in the hospital when you had malaria and I was making the rounds with Father McConnell. That's been quite some time... You, ah, don't seem to make it in to our chaplain's meetings very often. I understand you were here this morning at division. How come you didn't make it to our meeting?" he questions with a polite smile on his face.

George quickly looks at Richard as if to signal him to temper his reply. "Well, Father McGinty, I just felt it is a lot more important spending my time at the hospital with my wounded troopers than coming over here and shootin' the shit with the boys."

The division chaplain gets a startled look on his face as George quickly says, "You've had lots of casualties lately, haven't you, Chaplain Strom?"

"No more than what we usually have," Richard replies as McGinty shuffles some papers on his desk in front of him.

"Ah, yes, ah… Listen, Rich, you're doing a fine job out there with all those young where are you located?" he mumbles.

"An Hoa," he replies, "*Two-five.*"

"Oh yes, *Two-five.* And you're doing a great job with them," he says as the battalion chaplain wonders how he knows if he's doing a great job when he can't even remember what outfit he's in.

"I've told Father here, Chaplain Strom, that An Hoa is a real hellhole most of the time," says Williams.

He is quickly interrupted by McGinty. "We'd like to go out there sometime and see the place and visit the regimental chapel."

"Why not frag a bird this afternoon," Richard quickly replies. "You're a full-on navy captain? That should get you lots of pull with Marine air. That way I can go with you and not have to fry my brains waiting four hours in the hot sun for a ride with Sunshine Airlines." George is shaking his head in the negative as Strom continues with a smile on his face, "All you need is your helmet and flak jacket, a couple boxes of Cs and lots of toilet paper, just in case we get rocketed." Commander Williams just gives up and closes his eyes.

"Well, ah, not today. I certainly would have to schedule that at some later date," he replies. "Oh by the way, in checking our files I see you've only turned in one report and you've been here over eight months. You know how important it is that we have those weekly reports so we can get our statistics to division and on to the chief of chaplains in Washington. Those reports are very important," he drones on, "as they give us all an indication of our religious coverage and commitment. You're going to have to get all those back reports in very soon."

"No problem," is Richard's reply. He turns to Williams. "Hey, George, give me one of those empty sheets, I'll fill it out, then have it Xeroxed thirty times." He laughs, then continues, "Then everybody from here to Washington will be happy."

For the next ten minutes Strom and Williams are treated to a monologue on why the reports are important, why there must be full and complete Protestant and Catholic coverage as well as providing Jewish services if we can get enough Jewish personnel together to pull it off, why it is important that we get together weekly, why oh why, oh why ad nauseam.

Suddenly for Chaplain Strom, the whole scenario of the morning flashes before him—the ride from An Hoa, the hospital encounters, and now this—and becomes a flash point, one of those very crystal-clear moments when one sees clearly beyond the bullshit to the absurdity of it all. He realizes this guy hasn't a clue as to why most of the battalion chaplains refuse to come to these absurd chaplains' meeting anymore to listen to him talk about paperwork, as if nothing is happening out there in the field.

During the monologue, Richard is running through a picture montage of his own: "I've been here for eight months now, had my ass shot at daily, struck by shrapnel, almost died from malaria, had two helicopters go out from underneath me, seen my friends and acquaintances killed, maimed, destroyed, and taken away in green bags, watched helplessly as I see Marines dying in my arms—and this unconscious son of a bitch is ragging on me because I haven't seen fit to come to the weekly chaplains' meeting or get my reports into him so some mindless bureaucrat can compile statistics about meaningless dribble: how many worship services, how many Marines had Holy Communion, how many baptisms, how many counseling sessions.

"Hey, listen, Father, this conversation is getting absurd, dammit." George visibly tenses as Richard continues, "You want those damn reports in, then you tell me where, on that piss-ant form I put down the number of dying Marines I've held in my arms, or the yards I've run chasing down a wounded Marine, or the quarts of blood I've wiped off my body, or the tears I've spilled over my own inadequacies, or the pounds of dismembered body parts I've helped to pick up, or the hours spent writing letters home to a wife or parent, attempting to explain why their son or husband won't be coming home. Where in the hell do I put that down, Chaplain McGinty?

You find me a form that allows for that kind of information and I'll get those damn forms to you every week, I'll guarantee that!"

Right now Chaplain Strom is feeling rage and thinks to himself, "If I don't get out of here right now, I think I might choke the unconscious son of a bitch!" So he simply gets up, wordlessly puts on his helmet and flak jacket, and walks out the door, back down the driveway and onto the road back to division. He has no idea where he is going; he just knows he has to get the hell out of that loony bin.

Hot and fatigued, he eventually ends up at First Med, not bothering to stop at First Recon to borrow Al Ursini's jeep. So he walks back to the chapel and meets his good friend John Reitch, the Catholic chaplain who is also being chewed up by the death and destruction and wackiness of being a field hospital chaplain.

"Jeez, Rich, you kinda dropped a grenade in McGinty lap," says John after hearing about Strom's encounter with the division chaplain. "Hopefully he can get a clue about those damn meetings and change his attitude about you guys out in the bush."

He then offers Richard a cold soda, some cookies sent from home, and his jeep so he can visit his troops across the river at NSA Hospital. Chaplain Strom is feeling calm again after the walk and less fatigued. Just before he walks out the door he turns to Reitch and says quietly, "John, do you think I'm coming apart, ready for a section 8?"

The Catholic chaplain puts his hand on Richard shoulder and said softly, "No, Rich, not at all. I think because you blew like you did you're gonna be okay." He smiles and continues, "When you get back this afternoon, we'll create some R&R." Chaplain Strom leaves feeling like he's going to be okay.

Three hours later, after returning from visiting a twenty-seven Marines from his battalion, he has shut down again. In An Hoa and out in the field one doesn't have time to dwell much on the luxuries of feelings and insight. Part of the survival mechanism in staying alive is the shutting down of one's feelings so one can focus on preventative adaptations in the field that sometimes can significantly reduce combat injuries or death, which is why so many Marines are wounded or killed when they get a "Dear John" letter or discordant news about their families. Their concentration falls dramatically and the "zap factor" jumps dramatically! It also makes sense why there is so much drinking and drug use with personnel in the rear. They have too much time on their hands. And time is what Richard finds he has an abundance of when he is in Da Nang. It is a very disquieting place for him. Shortly John and Richard will be joined by two surgeons and take off for the Stone Elephant. As they are waiting for the two doctors, Strom explains to John his last encounter with the officers' club downtown, how he was kicked out because of rowdiness and his reticence about going back.

"That's okay," replies John. "Dave Johns, one of the docs going with us tonight, was kicked out of there last week for starting a fight. He was sent a letter of reprimand, but what does he care? He's the best surgeon we have here and they aren't going to do anything to him."

Richard smiles, shakes his head, then says to his friend, "Well, what the heck. Like my colonel says, a letter of reprimand is better than no letter at all."

Within an hour, after finishing two sixers, they head out for downtown Da Nang. John and Richard are in the backseat, Dave is driving and another surgeon, Phil Nordstrom, is in the passenger seat. They are feeling the effects of two six-packs and are singing songs loudly as they weave through the traffic and finally get to the checkpoint where the main highway meets the road running adjacent to the river and downtown Da Nang. It is also right next to some of the city's worst slums.

Two Marine MPs salute the men in the jeep as it comes to a stop. Fearful that the MPs are going to hassle them by asking them for their trip ticket, which they do not have, Dave immediately starts talking: "Listen, Sergeant, we can't be detained at all. We have orders to get to the club at once." He turns around to the two chaplains in back and with a sweep of his hand says, "We're doctors and chaplains, as you can see." He turns back toward the sergeant on the driver's side and says with alarm in his voice, "We are on an emergency call!" With that said, he shoves the jeep into first gear and roars off for the Stone Elephant just five blocks away, the MPs yelling at the driver to stop at once.

Upon arriving at the club, the four officers park the jeep and race inside, not wanting to be confronted by the MPs should they show up. Two hours later, after wine, dinner, and the traditional smashing of wine bottles against the back patio wall, expecting but not getting the traditional lecture on proper decorum, the group leaves, all four being in various stages of inebriation.

Dave is too wasted to drive, Richard has no military license to drive, Phil is passed out in the backseat, so John becomes the designated driver. He has lost his glasses somewhere during the evening, and because of all the correction in his lenses, he is blind as a bat without them. Not only that, but the group must drive back to division on back streets and avoid being busted at the checkpoint they came through earlier. John is feeling pretty good himself and is having trouble making out the road ahead of him as the jeep alternately lurches and speeds through the darkened back streets of Da Nang.

At one point they speed through a Vietnamese Army checkpoint—Richard remembers the stories about them shooting first and asking questions later—with Dave yelling in the backseat, "Vive la Ho Chi Minh." John is yelling at Dave to shut up as they roar through the checkpoint with both Vietnamese MPs pointing their rifles at the jeep.

"Stop the damn jeep before they blow our heads off," Richard yells to no avail. About one-half block down the street past the checkpoint, the MPs start firing their rifles. Not knowing if they are firing in the air or at the jeep, John yells "Holy shit!" and turns a hard left out of the line of fire onto a side street almost rolling the vehicle. The four naval officers are now careening around the streets of Da Nang, lost, Dave continuing to sing loudly, Bill passed out, John blind as a bat attempting to drive the vehicle as best as he can under the circumstances, and Richard yelling at no one in particular: "It's safer in An Hoa, it's safer out in the bush!"

Twenty minutes later they find the main road out of town and make their way back to the hospital. Passing through the gate into the compound, John, Richard, and Dave are singing loudly the cho-

315

rus to an old beer bust song: "Let's sing another one, just like the other one, that was a very fine verse."

Nordstrom is poured into his bed and Chaplain Reitch goes to bed because he has the duty starting at 0600. So Strom and Johns go to the officers' club to party some more, getting even louder and more obnoxious. Richard has just told Dave that he is too tired to go on and that he is going back to the hooch. It is at that moment the commanding officer of First Medical Battalion, Captain Harvey Hatch enters the club and approaches the two of them standing by the bar.

"Dr. Johns and Chaplain Whoever-You-Are," Dr. Hatch says with a bite of anger to his voice, "this loud and obnoxious behavior will not be tolerated here."

Standing in front of Johns, he says, "You have duty tomorrow morning. I am ordering you to go to your quarters immediately." He then turns to Strom and says disdainfully, "I don't know who you are, but you are a guest at First Medical Battalion and your conduct is unbecoming of a navy chaplain and a gentleman."

Dave laughs when he hears this. Then he stands at attention, salutes Captain Hatch, and says, "Yes, sir, anything you say, sir."

He then turns to Richard and says, "Chaplain, atteeennshun!" They both turn, as if in close order drill, walk toward the door and out, Dave yelling cadence, "Helup… helup… helup, hup, hup hor," all the way to the hooch where John is asleep and where the two of them will soon be joining him in slumber.

When Chaplain Reitch returns to the hooch at 0900 after having breakfast, both Strom and Johns are awake. John laughs out loud at them, sits down in a chair next to Richard's bed, then proceeds to tell them about the latest developments. "So you guys carried on our little horror show over at the club, huh? Captain Hatch is really pissed at you guys."

John continues to smile and shakes his head. "And guess what, Strom, who do you think his best friend is?"

"Let me see now," Richard responds as he slips into his utilities. "Do you suppose it's his eminence, the archbishop of the First Division?"

"You got it, Strom," he responds, "and you can bet he'll know about the little show you and Dave put on last night when he sees him at the division staff meeting this morning." He shakes his head again, almost in disbelief, and continues, "Both those guys are little old ladies. They must get their asses chewed up by some of those tough old Marines up at division."

Within an hour Chaplain Strom is back on a flight to An Hoa. He knows this is where he is really grounded, where he can still find some semblance of reality left. Da Nang and division and all that crap back there is another world. He feels like he doesn't belong there at all.

Diary Entry—223 Days In-Country

Something has happened to me this past eight months that I can't put my finger on. I'm lying in my hootch in the dark. Been here by myself since I came back from the helipad after returning from Da Nang. Don't want to see anybody!

A wall has come down. I recognized an eternity ago when Bryon died in my arms after he was shot in the chest. It isn't just Bryon, it's been all the stuff—the misery, the anxiety, the hardship and depravation, the dying, the unconsciousness of it all—an insidious dwindling away of my human energy, my optimism that things always have a way of working out. It even feels as if I'm experiencing God's grace slowly fade. "Amazing Grace, how sweet the sound…" Does grace abound when bodies are blown apart?

Tonight as I lay here, I can't feel as damn thin. I don't care if I stay here in An Hoa, don't care if I go back to the bush, don't care if I were to go back to the States tonight; I'm feeling so flat inside, I don't even care that I don't care. Someone stuck a spigot into my gut, opened the valve, and drained my life force.

It isn't that I can't do anything, because if I choose I can. I just don't have feelings anymore, I'm not connected to what I'm doing, as if I'm operating on what I think I should feel. Have I become like that nurse back at ICU who whistled while she changed the IV on that Marine with his brains blown away, oblivious to his deadness? Is that what is happening to me? Hell, I'm not a quart low on feelings. The damn oil pan blew away some place and my engine has seized up. I think I'm frozen shut.

Maybe I'll scoot over to the BAS and have a couple of beers with the chief or Savoy, they're always good for a few laughs. Think I'll tell the ops officer that he proves the old adage that there are more horses asses than there are horses in the world. Politicians are like flies, they eat shit and bother people. This sucks. Will sleep every come tonight? The hell with all of it.

Zzzzzzzzzzzzzzzz…

III

You can't go home again.

Thomas Wolfe

FORTRESS AN HOA

An Hoa is now a fortress. Reinforced bunkers are springing up near all the sleeping quarters and Marines are now living inside of them. The airstrip is badly damaged by daily rocket attacks, and fixed-wing aircraft have ceased landing because the instant a C-130 lands, the NVA launches their ordinance in hopes of destroying a landed airplane. Some days the convoy from Da Nang can't make it because the roads have been blown up the night before and cannot be repaired in time. Food, water, and ammunition are getting scarce. No more showers, only two meals a day, and strict enforcement prevails in the use of ammunition. An Hoa has become an encampment under siege.

It is noon by the time Strom arrives by chopper from division, having waited in the hot sun for three hours. Richard runs to the regimental chapel because anytime a chopper comes into to deliver troops or supplies, the enemy fires rockets into the compound. He finds the regimental chaplain, Bernie O'Hearn, next door in his hooch busy writing letters. Seeing the battalion chaplain, he immediately gets up and greets him warmly.

"Hey, Rich, good to see you again." He shakes Strom's hand, walks to the small refer in the comer, retrieves a cold beer, and continues, "Sorry I missed you last week when you came in from wherever in the hell they had your battalion."

The weary chaplain sits down in a chair next to Bernie's desk, opens the beer and takes a long draught, smiles a sigh of relief as the regimental chaplain sits back down, and says, "You better enjoy that beer while you can. There isn't much left of that or anything else out here because nothing is getting through anymore. So tell me what's going on at the hospital. John Reitch doing okay?"

"He's like the rest of us, Bernie, doing a good job and burning out in the process," Strom replies as he slouches in his chair.

O'Hearn shakes his head slowly and replies wistfully, "Didn't take him long, did it?" There is a sudden quiet, the two of them lost in their own thoughts, then Richard smiles and continues, "Bernie, you're not going to believe this!" He sits forward in his chair and continues, "Reitch and I raised a little hell with two docs from the hospital. I believe you already know Dave Johns, his reputation was already legendary when you lived with him. The other fellow is also a surgeon by the name of Phil Nordstrom, just new in-country."

Bernie is now listening intently as the battalion chaplain continues, "As you know, Dave loves to have a good time and this escapade was no exception. So first we managed to knock off two sixers of beer, after which we ended up at the Stone Elephant. There we got even more whacked, almost got kicked out of the place because Johns starts a fight. We then proceed to drive back to First Med, Reitch driving, blind as a bat without his glasses, got lost, ran through a Vietnamese checkpoint, and got shot at by their MPs, finally getting back to the hospital an hour after leaving the club."

Bernie is now laughing, finally stops, and says, "Good God, Chaplain Strom, you're supposed to be a moderating influence on those wayward surgeon souls, not join in with them!" He puts his head back and laughs again.

"Just a minute, Bernie," Richard replies, "you ain't heard the worst of it." Then he proceeds to describe in detail the encounter he and Johns had later on at the officers' club with the commanding officer of the hospital.

O'Hearn sits in shocked silence, his mouth wide open in astonishment, as Richard finishes his story, saying, "No doubt McGinty has already heard about this little escapade from Captain Hatch."

Bernie puts his hand on Richard's shoulder and begins to offer him words of encouragement. "Don't worry about that worry-wart of a division chaplain, Rich. Your colonel appreciates you. That's all that counts with the Marines."

The catholic chaplain continues, "Did you finally get to talk to the division chaplain? He keeps asking me about you. Did you know that he wants me to order you in to see him and attend those dreary division chaplain's meeting? Can you believe that? Who does he think I am, your bishop?" Bernie puts his head back and laughs hard.

"There's more," Strom continues ominously.

"Oh yeah, whatta ya mean, Rich?" O'Hearn asks, sitting up in his chair, a serious look on his face. Chaplain Strom then tells him about the blowup he recently had at McGinty office. Bernie listens quietly, incredulous at what he is hearing. When Richard finishes, O'Hearn shakes his head, smiles slightly, then says emphatically, "Jeez, Rich, you're a walking San Andreas fault! Let's see now, you've managed to jump into the face of two navy captains and one navy commander the past month. I hope you aren't thinking about making a career out the military."

"Bernie, I keep trying my damnedest to get fired and sent back to the States," he replies. "Unfortunately the Old Man and the Executive Officer like me."

"I'd say you're lucky, Rich, that they do like you," Bernie says quietly. "I've been around long enough to know you could get your ass court-martialed for what you've said." O'Hearn suddenly gets a big smile on his face, declaring, "So who do you think you are, bucko, Martin Luther?" They both laugh hard. Strom finishes his beer and picks up his helmet and flak jacket to walk back to his battalion area one-half a kilometer away.

"Hold on Mr. In-Your-Face, I'll walk with you," Bernie continues. "We can both attend the regimental change of command that is to take place on your way."

Richard scowls at Bernie's remarks, puts on his gear, and says flatly, "Won't all the big shots have to come out of their holes for this?"

The regimental chaplain grabs his gear, walks past Strom, grabbing his arm, and pulls him gently out the door. Continuing their walk toward regimental headquarters, Bernie says, "Do you some good Rich to see some clean, squared away Marines instead of those grungy grunts you hang out with all the time."

Shortly they are standing outside headquarters fifty meters south of the chapel. The change of command takes place in a very small area, thirty by thirty meters, bunkers on three sides, attended by division and regimental staff officers and staff NCOs dressed in starched utilities, milling around, looking nervous. It is a quick, no-frills ceremony, lasting less than five minutes, quite a contrast to the change of command two weeks after Richard's arrival in An Hoa. Eight months ago the Fifth Marines had an elaborate parade and ceremony that lasted one-half hour on the helipad adjacent to the airstrip. They weren't worried about rockets then.

With the ceremony over, Chaplain Strom says good-bye to O'Hearn and continues on to his battalion area. Walking along the mud-filled road, Richard is bothered by developments in An Hoa. He's been out here for eight months now, and the situation is far worse than when he first arrived. They have gone from a time when incoming seldom hit the area to constant, daily bombardment by rockets and mortars. When he first came, the Marines moved about freely, giving little thought to danger while inside the regimental parameter. Now most everyone in An Hoa is living inside their bunkers, afraid to venture out anymore. If the war is being won—as the generals and politicians claim—then how come things are so heated up all the time?

Turning south toward the *Two-five* compound, he is joined by the new battalion sergeant major, who is also walking back from the ceremony. Richard had briefly met him on the return from Hill 547. In contrast to the previous sergeant major, a stiff-necked, hard-nosed ass-kicker who did everything by the book, this veteran of thirty years is a rather soft-spoken, reflective, and engaging Marine who actually seems to enjoy people.

"So, Chaplain Strom, how the Marines treating you?" Rivers says as they sidestep a huge puddle of water and mud in the road.

"There's ups and downs, Sergeant Major," Strom responds indifferently, looking down at his feet, "but then what do I know... only been with the Marine infantry since I've been on active duty, so

I have nothing to compare it with. Don't know if I'm in good or bad company. All I know is that I'm feeling pretty worn down."

The veteran Marine smiles softly and continues, "You know, Chaplain, I fought in some of the biggest Pacific battles of World War II—Tarawa, Saipan, and Iwo Jima. There were good people and bad people everywhere. I was treated well some places and badly at others. And there was some pretty horrible stuff that we all went through during the fighting, which generally lasted two, three, or four weeks."

Continuing on the road, Richard looks up and says quietly, "Must have been awful what you guys went through. Jeez, Sergeant Major, those were three of the worst battles the Marines faced, weren't they?"

Sergeant Major Rivers looks straight ahead for a few moments, a faraway look in his eyes, then turns toward Richard and continues, "Chaplain, as terrible as those battles were for those three or four weeks, once the battle was over, we had a good two to four months of 'refitting' back in a safe area, usually Australia or New Zealand or some secure island somewhere in the South Pacific. We rested and lived like human beings again, we were restored and refreshed."

Turning left into the actual *Two-five* compound, Richard is now fully engrossed as Rivers says, "I believe the emotional pressure and anxiety for you guys out in the bush are sometimes worse than it was during World War II because the fighting and incoming is constantly ready to erupt, twenty-four hours a day, seven days a week, month after month, for a whole thirteen-month tour. I think being under that kind of pressure can sometimes wear you down more than what we faced in the old days." He pauses for a moment, then continues, "I get lots of disagreement from most of my old buddies about that."

Chaplain Strom is silent, thoughtfully engrossed and surprised at the Sergeant Major's words. He always assumed that the big battles of World War II were much worse for the Marines than anything experienced in Vietnam and were therefore more destructive physically and emotionally.

"Where you from, Chaplain?" Rivers suddenly asks as they pass the BAS.

Lost in thought, Richard is slow to respond. "Ah, I'm a Midwest boy, but I live in California now."

"Somehow I figured you were from the Midwest," he says with a smile. There is a long pause as he continues to smile, then says to Strom, "Well, Chaplain, I'm from Montana, where the men are men and the sheep are nervous." Then he breaks out in a laugh.

Richard laughs with him as they walk toward the CP, somewhat astonished at his off-color remark so early in their relationship. "If there's any way I can make your job easier, Chaplain," Rivers continues, "let me know. It's not easy being a chaplain with the Marines, especially with grunts."

The young battalion chaplain smiles broadly and nods in understanding. The sergeant major turns toward the chaplain and shakes his hand, then says to him, "Chaplain, my dad is a full-blooded Crow Indian and my mom is a Mexican. That makes me a cross between a Roman Catholic and a Crow medicine man. If you ever need any help in making your altar wine more powerful, let me know."

Richard stands in bemused silence, smiles, then asks, "What in the heck does that mean?" The sergeant major laughs, shakes his head, then turns and walks into the CP without responding to the chaplain's question.

As Strom turns and walks to his hooch, he is aware that Rivers is another old-time Marine that appears to have a good grasp of the emotional and physical demands placed upon the field grunts. He apparently hasn't lost the experience yet of what it is like to be a private walking point, seeing all the wackiness around you, knowing how it wears you down physically and mentally day after day. There is none of the hardcore Marine about him, yet from what Richard has heard from others in the battalion, he commands the admiration and respect of all those who know him. He quietly goes about his business without having to resort to power or force.

That evening at the staff meeting, the colonel shares the latest directive for *Two-five*, that they will be moving out again in the morning, this time back to the area between An Hoa and Da Nang called Phu Lac 6 and Go Noi Island. This is not a pleasant prospect, having just come in again from the field with only three days' rest.

The battalion is exhausted and feeling debilitated from months in the bush, having no real rest for the past eight months. The entire staff is upset that second battalion again will be thrown into a dangerous assignment and believes that either the first or third battalion should have drawn this assignment. "Not ours to question," says Colonel Stevens, "but goddammit, we don't have to like it!"

Phu Lac 6, the sector surrounding the bridge crossing the large Son Thu Bon River is one of the most heavily booby-trapped areas in all of I Corps. Each time the Marines go into that area they suffer as many casualties from tripped booby traps as they do from enemy fire. It is also the locale where Richard's predecessor was critically wounded when he tripped a hidden mortar over eight months ago.

Adjacent to the bridge running east for fifteen kilometers is the notorious Go Noi Island—always a nasty area. There are enormous stores of produce and hidden caches of rice scattered around island, which the enemy always defends fanatically. It is the last place any Marine in their right mind wants to go!

After the staff meeting, in the dark, the battalion chaplain walks back toward his hooch in hopes of catching his assistant so they can ready themselves for their next encounter in the bush. He is right in back of his hooch, rounding the corner, when he inadvertently bumps into two Marines coming from the opposite direction. Richard staggers backward—as one of them falls on his back, the standing trooper yells, "Hey, man, what the fuck you doing?" Then he comes at Strom like he's going to tear his head off!

The Marine takes a swing at the chaplain. Richard ducks, then falls and rolls through the Marine's legs, knocking the wildly swinging assailant down. While Strom is doing this, the second Marine stands up, suddenly recognizing who he is seeing on the ground, and yells, "Oh shit, it's the chaplain!"

Richard now jumps up just as the other Marine lying on the deck gets up and yells "Fuck you!" takes another swing at the chaplain while his buddy makes a halfhearted attempt at restraining him. Strom again ducks, the blow striking him on the top of his head, whereupon he turns and hits the Marine as hard as he can directly in the belly with his fist, then drives his forearm into the face of the angry young man, who instinctively bends over to grasp his stomach.

The Marine goes down on his knees and falls over in a fetal position, gasping for air, blood flowing from his nose. His buddy just stands there looking at the chaplain, then at his buddy on the deck, then back at the chaplain. Feeling very shaky, Richard manages to say to the standing Marine, "Take your buddy here back to your quarters."

As he is saying this, the chaplain notices the strong odor of alcohol and continues, "You can tell your first sergeant what happened here or you can come to see me tomorrow morning before we leave on operations. I really don't give a damn what you choose to do. But you need to know this right now, anybody that takes a swing at me will get decked. You understand that?"

"Yes, sir," replies the passive Marine as he helps his bleeding friend off the deck, in shock for what has quickly transpired but also by the harsh and uncompromising words coming from their chaplain. Thereupon the troopers shuffle off to their quarters, dazed and chastised by this surprising turn of events.

Richard enters his hooch, still shaking from the encounter and, finding Bob gone, takes out a cold soda to sip on while he ponders the consequences of the past few moments. He is aware that although the drunk Marine threw two separate punches at him, his response can be considered justification for convening a court-martial. Officers cannot strike enlisted personnel under any circumstances.

Quickly his focus changes because he has more important things to think about—packing for the next operation and preparing himself emotionally for the lineup he will face beginning tomorrow morning when word of the impending operation gets out.

Early the next morning, after only a single run to the bunker the previous night, Richard walks outside to a clear sky, the first in days, and meets the Aardvark on his way to the head to divest himself of yesterday's fine residue of An Hoa gourmet food. The Aardvark, a massive staff sergeant with twenty-five years in the Marine Corps, is a lumbering paranoid who sneers at most anyone and everything that crosses his path. Unless there is a batch of incoming rockets that sends him screaming into a fetal position at the bottom of his personal handmade bunker close to his hooch, he can be counted on being at the head every morning promptly at 0650. It is said by those who have spent some time with battalion that one can set their watch by the Aardvark's first moan of constipation—0651 every morning!

In the few times Strom has crossed paths with him he is greeted by the sergeant in exactly the same way he greets everyone else. It will be no different this morning as Richard sees him walking toward him. The time is 0650.

The chaplain smiles and says, "How's it going, Sergeant?"

"Yes, sir, it's a sombitch, sir," he responds, shaking his head back and forth like it is his last day on earth before going to the electric chair, thereupon meandering off to his morning chore. Strom continues on in the direction of the mess tent.

An hour later, coming back from breakfast, he is stopped by First Sergeant Rooney, who salutes, then with a smile on his face says, "Good morning, sir. How's the chaplain feeling this morning?"

"Not bad for eight months with the grunts," he replies, wondering why this nice formality is coming from Rooney when their relationship is much more casual. "Why do you ask?"

"Oh, I was just wondering," he responds as they walk toward the chaplain's hooch. "Understand the Chaplain is pretty good with his hands?"

Strom stops quickly. Feeling some apprehension, he looks at Rooney, wondering just where this conversation is going, then says tersely, "Ah… whattya talking about, First Sergeant?"

Rooney laughs and answers, "Well, sir, it isn't every day I get a Marine coming into my office complaining about being kicked in the ass by a sky pilot. Usually it's the other way around. The chaplain comes to the Old Man complaining about the first sergeant or platoon sergeant kicking a Marine around." He laughs again, shakes his head, and continues, "You know, sir, I've been around a long time and this is the first time ever that I've heard about a chaplain decking somebody. I was surprised, Chaplain."

"So was I, First Sergeant, so was I," Richard replies. "Haven't done anything like that since college."

"I told the two prizefighters to visit you this morning first thing, Chaplain," Rooney responds quickly with a big smile on his face. "That ought to be a real interesting conversation. Boy, would I like to listen in on that counseling session!"

Strom disregards the indirect request as they walk a few more steps. Suddenly the chaplain stops. "Sergeant," he says abruptly and harshly as Rooney stops and looks at the officer like he'd said something wrong. "That wasn't fighting. That was non-apostolic laying on of the hands! See you around." Richard smiles, then turns and walks in the direction of his hooch, leaving the first sergeant, shaking his head in confusion.

Approaching his living quarters, the chaplain walks through the lineup of eight Marines milling about in front of his hooch. He walks inside to see Bob, sitting at his desk in front of the typewriter. His assistant immediately stands and says, "Sir, I read your note and was typing those letters for you to the next of kin."

"Thanks, Bob," Richard replies, "but right now the letters can wait. I had a special meeting with a couple of Marines last night and they apparently have an appointment to see me first thing this morning."

Marshall picks up his rifle and helmet, a big smile spreading across his face, then says knowingly, "Yes, sir, I heard about your meeting, sir. Oh, by the way, Lieutenant Kelly came by and said the battalion won't be leaving until tomorrow morning."

Richard shakes his head in acknowledgment as he arranges seating for the upcoming storming of his office by the troopers wishing to get out of going on the next operation, then sits down at his desk. "The whole damn battalion probably knows about my little dance last night," he muses to himself as his assistant walks out the door. "Jeez, wonder if the Old Man knows about it. So what, who cares? No doubt Bernie and his corpsmen are going to give me a ration of—"

There is a knock on his door that interrupts his thoughts. "Come in," he states flatly. Two Marines make their way into his hooch, walk in front of the desk, and salute the standing chaplain as Richard motions for them to sit down. "You don't salute me in here.

Once you're in here you're talking to my left collar and you disregard the lieutenant bars on my right collar," he says calmly with a smile, then sits down. "Understand?"

The two young men sit down, then Pfc Bobby Martinez, the Marine who threw the punches and has a Band-Aid over his nose is the first to speak. "Sir, I was drunk last night and I apologize for my behavior. I'm sorry, sir. Didn't know it was the chaplain, sir."

Richard can see that this young Marine is scared and upset and responds softly, "I appreciate hearing that from you. How long you been with Echo?"

"Nine months," he replies, swallowing hard.

"And how about you, ah, your name?" Strom continues.

"Sir, Corporal Marcel Washington," the young man responds.

"And how long have you been in-country, Corporal?" the chaplain asks casually.

"Same as Martinez, sir, we arrived here the same week, sir," he replies.

"So both of you have been with the battalion for quite some time then," Strom says softly and kindly. "Which means that you been through a meat grinder and both of you are stressed to the max, considering what we've all been through. Being in the bush for any length of time gets us feeling real crazy, so when we get back here, it is important we do some things that help relieve that tension, including drinking beer. So that's not a problem with me."

They look relieved as Richard continues, "Which means I feel crazy too when I get back here. But getting drunk and reacting to a perceived affront by throwing punches doesn't help relieve tension, it just makes us feel crazier and gets us in trouble. All of us are badly stressed but that gives no one the right to start throwing punches."

Richard stands up, motions for them to do likewise, walks around his desk to them, extends his hand, and says, "I'm sorry as well for my part and I want to apologize to both of you for my actions."

They smile and shake his hand as the chaplain continues, "You and I, Martinez, could both be court-martialed for this—you hitting an officer, me slugging an enlisted man. I don't want this incident to go there, okay?"

The young Marine smiles broadly and replies, "Yes, sir. Thank you, sir."

"Go back to your commands," the chaplain responds, "and get some rest. We hit the road again tomorrow."

They both turn and leave the hooch, but within twenty seconds, Corporal Washington returns, opens the door, and asks to speak further to the chaplain.

"Sir," he says hesitantly, "there is something I need to talk to you about that is still bothering me."

"Sure," Richard replies, "what's up?"

Washington is standing at attention, so the chaplain says quietly, "Relax, Corporal, what's up?"

The young man then stands at parade rest, hands behind his back, and continues, "Sir, I feel that it's wrong for a chaplain and man of God to get out of control and throw punches. I don't think that's right. Jesus never did anything like that. I believe that it says in the Bible you're supposed to imitate Jesus by example?"

Chaplain Strom pauses for a few seconds, then asks a question of the young man: "It sounds like you know the Bible, that right?"

"Yes, sir," he nervously replies, "haven't read it for a while, but yes, sir, I used to read it."

"Well, tell me something then, Corporal Washington," the chaplain continues, "whattya suppose old Jesus was up to when he made a whip and stomped hell out of the money changers in the temple in Jerusalem?"

There is a long dramatic pause as the Marine blinks a couple of times, says, "Yes, sir," turns and walks out of the hooch. Chaplain Strom never heard another thing about the incident except from the executive officer who addressed him as "Rocky" that evening at staff meeting.

Richard spends all of the morning and some of the afternoon listening to the endless reasons why all the Marines lining up in front of his hooch want out of the bush—kidneys are swollen, brain is damaged, youngest brother is dying, uncle has gone crazy, rains have cause the sinuses to clog and affect seeing, allergic reaction to C-rations, girlfriend is pregnant, conscientious objector, parents are divorcing, ad infinitum. Few have any evidence or documentation to back up their dubious claims.

Listening to all of this, Richard is aware that the life expectancy of a grunt, especially with the Fifth Marines, isn't very long. "I'd try to get off the field too, if I could," he thinks sadly to himself as the parade comes and goes.

That evening, after the final staff meeting before they hit the field again in the morning, Richard is sitting in his hooch with three other officers playing cards. Suddenly they hear a commotion coming from the area one hundred meters away and across the road where a battalion from the Twenty-Seventh Marines is located. When they walk outside they are greeted by a cloud of CS gas, which immediately causes burning on the exposed parts of their bodies, especially their eyes and nose. Their collective thought is that Charlie has blown off a grenade of CS gas and they are under attack by the VC!

Strom runs down the hill away from the gas cloud, choking, eyes burning badly, feeling pain and anxiety, assuming this is an act by the enemy to confuse and throw the Marines into disarray. However, within ten minutes the gas is cleared, the mucus membranes are beginning to stop their painful burning and Colonel Stevens is in a rage! The chaplain can hear him yelling at someone in his hooch, "You get me those sons of bitches who popped that grenade. I want those assholes here within five minutes. Do you understand me!"

Everyone had the same immediate reaction that Charlie had popped the grenades and had breached the perimeter. It was a very scary time until the true reality of the situation came to light. Apparently a battalion from the Twenty-Seventh Marines had smuggled a palette of beer by convoy just today—illegal of course because beer is not a commodity urgently needed for survival. When four Marines from *Two-five* approached one of their platoon sergeants and offered to purchase some of their beer before going out in the bush the next morning, they were rebuffed and told to "go fuck off!" They then posted sentries by the tent in which the beer was stored so they won't be ripped off.

So four Marines from Hotel put on gas mask just after dark, popped a CS grenade by the guarded tent, ran inside, and liberated eight cases of beer while the sentries ran off in terror and pain. By the time the battalion realized what was happening, the four Marines had made off with the beer and a case of cigarettes.

The colonel, having been appraised of the situation and why the raid took place, was ready for the four Marines and their platoon leader, who the colonel suspected was in on the conspiracy. Stevens is not a man who minces his words. He climbs all over the five Marines and tells them that every beer and every cigarette is to be returned at once. All of them are placed on report and told they will be dealt with at a later day during "office hours," the Marine Corps term for nonjudicial punishment meted out by the command for infractions.

Just before turning in for the evening, the chaplain gets a message from the S1 that Colonel Stevens wants to see him at once. He walks the short distance to the Old Man's hooch, knocks, and walks inside. The colonel is sitting on his cot, taking off his boots. He looks up at his chaplain and says in a neutral voice, "Well, Padre, what would you have done were you me? Some jackasses throw a CS grenade near our compound and all of us think Charlie is storming the place. Then I find out it's our boys attempting to throw confusion into the ranks of that battalion over there because they want to steal some beer." He points across the road toward the Twenty-Seventh Marines. "Now I have to answer to a battalion commanding officer who is screaming for blood. Tell me, Chaplain, what in the hell would you do in this situation?"

Richard pauses for a few seconds, then says slowly, "Well, sir, we already have the beer. May as well drink it."

The colonel scowls and replies, "I figured you'd say something like that, Chaplain. You've been with the Marines too long." He stands up and walks in front of the chaplain, points his finger at Strom, and continues, "Let me tell you something, if it was feasible, I'd give those young troopers who pulled off that caper a goddamn metal for creativity and gall! But if I did, then I'd have the commander of that tightwad outfit and regiment and just about every other senior officer down on my back. So I had to make 'em give the stuff back and put them on report for office hours. Now if I wait long enough and the incident blows over, I can let the office hours slide. But they've gotta get all that stuff back and think that I'm pissed."

"Yes, sir," Richard replies smiling.

"And I am still pissed, Padre, because my eyes still burn," he says. "Let's get some sleep. We hit the road again tomorrow morning." With that he turns and walks back to his bed. Richard leaves and walks back to his hooch.

"The Old Man is right on," he says to himself. His respect for him climbs another notch that night.

GO NOI ISLAND

Two-five is now spread out around the bridge at Phu Lac 6 for the evening before leaving for Go Noi the next morning. First Battalion has been guarding this bridge and the access on both sides of the river for the past four months. They have a dry place in which to sleep, pallets of cold beer and sodas, a hot meal once a day, and lots of time on their hands. At the staff briefing prior to arriving at the bridge, the S2 had discussed the liabilities facing First Battalion. Because they have too much time on their hands discipline has broken down. An excess of drinking, drug use, and fighting has emerged among the troops. Then three days ago a platoon leader and a gunnery sergeant were killed by a grenade thrown at them by Marines from their own platoon. This was shocking news to the troops of second battalion.

Stories about "fraggings" of officers and staff NCOs by disgruntled grunts have surfaced on occasion in An Hoa of all places, especially with the batteries of artillery surrounding the airstrip. However, it certainly hasn't happened with *Two-five*, not yet anyway. They have been too busy attempting to stay alive out in the field. The fact they have spent so much time out in the bush and on the move is good in that at least they aren't at each other's throats. Since one has a tendency to see the world only through the eyes of one's experience, most of the Marines from the battalion don't give "fraggings" much credibility because they are too busy, too tired, too burned out, too stressed out to even think about this kind of stuff going on around them. After all, this is the Marine Corps. Chaos and anarchism are anathema. Discipline and order will always prevail!

The rains are now over and the weather has turned super hot. Heat, not the heavy torrential rains, has become the second enemy. It is midmorning and the battalion is humping through head-high elephant grass next to the river. During the rainy season this area would be underwater. Now they are walking in ankle-deep sand, making it even more difficult to move. The heat adds another dimension to the stress the grunts are already experiencing.

The battalion chaplain and his assistant are humping with Golf, first platoon. The area they find themselves in alternates between high elephant grass and open sandy ground. The closer they get to Go Noi itself and the farther away from Phu Lac 6, the greater the tension because they have no illusions about what may lay ahead. This is a nasty place and the Marines have always taken casualties the instant they step foot on the island. Richard, like every other Marine on this operation, is hot and stressed from the heat as they wade across the shallow stream that takes them directly onto the island. Simultaneously he is aware of an uneasy, queasy feeling in his stomach. Instantly he remembers it is the same kind of feeling he experienced an eternity ago when he was on the phone with a terrified parishioner who had just witnessed the hideous aftermath of a suicide.

The first platoon has just moved into an open area, past the small ville called Le Bac 1, and Strom is walking right in back of the platoon leader when the first shots are fired. The sand is kicking up all around them from the bullets. The familiar but frightening *pop, pop, pop* sound of AK fire is coming from an area just south of them. The column immediately dives for cover in the grass a few meters away. Richard is gasping for breath as he flops into the sand next to Bob, his heart beating so loudly, the VC less than fifty meters away can surely hear the pounding. Ahead of the pinned down platoon the battalion is nine hundred meters away, negating any immediate assistance from them or the two other platoons from Golf.

The enemy fire is intense; bullets are snapping through the elephant grass, kicking up sand throughout the area. The lieutenant hasn't moved and is standing in the open with his radioman talking to the skipper, his .45 drawn and ready. Strom lifts his head slightly to see the young officer standing in the open, instantly thinking this is probably one of the reasons first lieutenants don't last long on the line. "That is stupidity, not bravery," he suddenly reasons as the small arms fire continues to whistle around him.

At that instant, just as the chaplain is thinking the lieutenant needs to get down and not be such an obvious target, he hears a loud grunt and simultaneously watches the officer jerk backward, arms flopping back, palms up, then fall flat on his back. His legs convulse quickly, then within seconds there is no movement at all. His radioman is now lying on the deck next to the fallen officer, face in the sand, frozen in place, as the Marines quickly and automatically position themselves to return the fire.

In an instant that is simultaneously frozen in time and also experienced as being endless the firefight is over and the familiar "Corpsman up" is heard. Ongoing boredom, then instantaneous terror followed by a very intensified focus on enemy positions and the need to get medical assistance to the wounded. This is a process that repeats itself over and over and over for the grunt on operations in the bush. There is no getting used to this. The fear is primal and arises quite spontaneously deep from within the limbic instincts. However, for the survivors, for those not killed or horribly maimed, there is a human cost. Because in order to get through that kind of experience, all process has to shut down and be buried as far down in the psyche as possible. And there it stays, pushed deeper and deeper after each terrifying encounter.

"Chaplain, you okay?" comes the tense and strained voice of Marshall five meters away in the grass.

Strom says nothing but instead crawls toward the fallen lieutenant, removes his own pack and communion kit, reaches over the still body, and grabs his wrist to feel for a pulse. "Corporal," he yells at the radioman, who is still lying prone, "get a corpsman over here right now!" The radioman gets to his feet and runs off as Richard gets up on one knee, turns the young man's body toward him and sees that a bullet has entered his throat at centerline just below his jaw and had exited right through his brain stem, knocking his helmet clean off his head. Blood is running profusely out of the large exit hole in the back of his upper neck. He was dead before he hit the deck.

"Ah, shit," Richard mumbles to himself in frustration as he lets the still body of Jeremy Browne roll on its back, shaking his head, "this shoulda never happened." A corpsman at that moment arrives as the chaplain stands up and waves him off. "He's dead. Nothing you can do, go save the living."

Chaplain Strom slowly picks up his communion kit and slings it over his shoulder. Instead of praying and lingering over the dead, as he previously did the first few times he was involved in a firefight, he now seeks out the wounded. He isn't sure why he does this, not wanting to deal with dead Marines but rather focuses instead on the wounded. Anymore he does it without thought, like he is on automatic pilot.

Staff Sergeant Baker is returning with Browne's radioman and is on the radio with Golf's skipper. "Yes, sir, he's dead, sir," Richard can hear him say as he quickly walks toward a group of Marines thirty meters away. He observes a number of prone bodies on the sand being attended by corpsmen and slowly walks up to a Marine who is on his knees, throwing up while a sergeant stands next to him. The chaplain drops his communion kit and sees a dead Marine close by with a large hole in his head oozing brain matter and blood. A call is being made for an emergency medevac and another message is being sent to battalion to get the doctor here immediately. However, since battalion is now over a kilometer away and the chopper can get to the wounded quicker, that decision is quickly overruled.

The young kid who is puking his guts out is on his very first foray into the bush. His buddy, whom he met while in Okinawa and was also out in the bush for one week, has his brains and blood spattered all over his side and leg because he was walking right next to him when the bullet went through his head.

Richard walks up to the young Marine and kneels in front of him as he is wiping vomit from his ash-gray face. His hands are shaking badly as Strom looks him in the eye and says softly, "I'm the chaplain, son. You're gonna be all right."

Pfc Walker slowly looks up at the Chaplain. There is a recognition as to who he is, what the words mean, but he does not believe he is going to be all right. He spreads his hands open, palms up, looks at them for a few seconds, then attempts to wipe the coagulating blood and matter from his pants, looks back at the chaplain, then goes through the whole ritual again, saying softly, like some modern day Macbeth, "Oh God... oh God."

Placing his hand on the young man's shoulder, Richard states softly but emphatically, "Tell me what your name is. I want to know your name."

The Marine is sobbing softly as he looks up, shakes his head back and forth two times, then responds tearfully, "It's, ah... my... I'm, I'm..." Then he drops his head back on his chest and begins to cry again. Strom gently places his hand under his chin, lifts his head so he can see the chaplain directly, and reiterates his question: "I want to know your name."

The chaplain is feeling discomfort—again—at this troubling process called reality check by the Marines. The hideousness of these kinds of incidents and the shock and grief that it generates needs time and understanding. Not so in the bush. Shortly the platoon will be on the move and everyone will need to be focused. So the luxury of processing this stuff isn't a reality.

The eighteen-year-old looks at Strom with tears running down his cheeks and replies, "Private Ben Walker, sir."

"Okay, Ben," the chaplain replies, "this is a real difficult time for you having your buddy die right next to you." The young man nods in acknowledgment as Richard continues, "The medevac will be here shortly and we're going to be moving out real soon." Richard now stands and says with his arm outstretched to the seated Marine to help him get up. "Stand up and find out what you're supposed to do from your platoon sergeant over there." He motions with his head toward the sergeant twenty meters away who is talking on the radio. "I'm really sorry about your friend and I know how tough this is for you." Private Walker is now standing, listening closely to the chaplain who now puts his arm around his shoulder and continues, "but right now you need to get your gear together so we can all get out of here. I'll see you later on in the day when we set in. Do you understand, Ben?"

Walker acknowledges the chaplain's directive, picks up his gear scattered about, and says still sobbing softly, "Yes, sir. I will, sir." He turns and walks toward Sergeant Baker. Just a few feet away two corpsmen are working frantically on a Marine who is in great agony with a bullet wound in his abdomen. Richard approaches him and kneels by his side. A blood-soaked dressing covers his abdomen and a corpsman has just given a shot of morphine. The critically wounded Marine sees the chaplain by his side, grabs Richard's hand, and groans loudly, that terrified, pleading look in his eyes that Strom has seen so many times before, that look of "Am I going to be all right?... Am I dying?... Help me, Chaplain!... Someone, please tell me what's happening!"

Many times in situations just like this, Chaplain Strom has also heard that plaintive cry, a cry that tells him they've gone back to another time and place where they've fallen and hurt their little arm or skinned their stubby little knee or had their feelings hurt, when that "little boy" part emerges and they simply reach out with their hands and cry, "Momma... Momma."

Sometimes when he holds them he feels like a momma. Sometimes he feels deep compassion and care as they lay bleeding— sometimes dying—in his arms or against his kneeling body. And sometimes, when the pain deep inside Richard is just too intense, too much to carry, he simply feels nothing at all. It sure is a tough place to be without Momma!

Within thirty minutes the wounded and dead are on their way to Da Nang and the situation is back to routine. The dull boredom of humping toward a destination on a map with a six-number coordinate quickly becomes the new reality. Nothing has changed, except that a few more Marines have been ground up in the process. Any feelings or memories about the previous encounter are abruptly pushed below any level of consciousness and becomes no thought, no think, no thing.

Over the next two days Go Noi lives up to its reputation as being a snake pit—sniper fire all the time, booby traps everywhere, bad insect problems, including sand fleas. And to add to the misery, Marine air hasn't resupplied anyone in the battalion for two days. There is no water to spare and everyone is on two canteens a day when they should be drinking eight, the C-rations are gone so the Marines are resorting to gathering any fresh produce they can find—potatoes, cabbage, lettuce, and rice. The temperature has hit one hundred degrees for the past three days.

Then another tragedy occurs with the battalion. An A-6 bomber drops some bombs on third platoon of Fox, killing seven Marines and injuring thirteen. That makes the third incident in the past five months of mistakes by Marine air, totaling twenty-six killed and over forty wounded. With these kind of casualties—not counting the killed and injured from artillery mistakes—Charlie can stay home and the Marines of *Two-five* will eventually be blown away. When he hears about the latest blunder, Richard wonders if the other battalions have the same kind of figures for "friendly mistakes" that his outfit has. If so these mistakes are blowing away a lot of troops. "What are they telling the folks back home about how these Marines are killed and wounded?" Strom wonders to himself.

Richard is lying down on the ground underneath some brush just a few feet away from the CO, exhausted by the hump, when the skipper of Fox, Captain Ron Kettner, walks into the CP to talk to Colonel Stevens. He is very shaken by the tragedy. After conferring with the Old Man for five minutes, they both turn and look directly at Richard. Stevens points his finger at Strom and says quietly, "He's yours, Captain. Keep him as long as you want him."

Within ten minutes the chaplain and his assistant are humping with the skipper and a squad of Marines to the Fox CP one kilometer away. When they arrive, Kettner has a message awaiting him from Da Nang. After conferring with his XO, the skipper walks toward the small tree under which Strom is lying on his pack, attempting to get cool. He is shaking his head, looking at the message he has in his hand.

"Padre," he begins in a very agitated voice, an incredulous look on his face, "you know what those stupid bastards—excuse me, Padre, but I'm really pissed out of my mind—do you know that I have to send a platoon of my men back into that impact area to look for more body parts because some asshole back there at III MAF needs more parts to make positive identification?"

As he gets up off the deck, Chaplain Strom cannot believe what he is hearing. "What the hell difference does it make if they do find more parts?" Richard responds, dusting off the dirt collected on his utilities. "It's not going to change the outcome of their individual dying. Don't we already know whose dead from the platoon? Seems to me we don't need any more body parts to give us any new information. That is really lame!"

Captain Kettner is now livid with anger. "Listen to this," he spits out as he now reads off the paper containing the message: "Enough parts for four positive identifications. Please forward remains after search of area per routine medevac." There is a pause, then he continues sarcastically, "Please forward remains my ass. Let's cut up one of those water buffaloes and send 'em the asshole!"

The skipper is a mustang—came up from the enlisted ranks and now finds himself the commanding officer of an infantry line company. Since he's been both—enlisted and officer—he has a good feel for both places. The roughness of his speech, however, conveys many years in the Marine Corps as a staff NCO.

Kettner hands the message to the chaplain, then turns and gives his company gunny instructions to send a platoon into yesterday's impact area. Turning back to Strom, he shakes his head and says angrily, "Now I have to tie up a whole platoon for this stupidity. Assholes!"

Richard is looking at the message, then back at Kettner, then says quietly and deliberately, "Skipper, with your permission, I'd like to accompany the troops back into that area. It's not going to be easy for them. Maybe I can be of some help."

Kettner turns and looks at Strom as if he's nuts, then says in that very forthright style of his, "Okay, Chaplain, you go in there with them. If you feel that's what you should be doing, go for it! I just hope you're not going sideways on us." He smiles, then shakes Richard's hand and continues, "All kidding aside, we're glad you're here with us, Padre. Be careful out there, don't want a sky pilot to get whacked on my watch." He smiles and places his hand on Richard's shoulder and continues, "When you get back, we'll have a memorial service out here for those guys who were killed. Okay?"

Chaplain Strom is trudging through tall grass adjacent to the river. Shortly they enter a large village complex called Bao Kay and Bao Dong, turn left, and encounter a tree line just outside the village where the airstrike took place. They pull out those green zip-up bags and begin their grim, macabre chore of hunting for body parts. "So they can satisfy some mindless idiot back at the III MAF morgue in Da Nang who probably didn't sleep last night in his air conditioned hooch because he had to leave an empty blank on some damn navy form," Richard angrily thinks to himself.

The smell of death surrounds the Marines because the villagers were hit as well by the bombs. It takes about twenty-four hours out in the humid heat for flesh to begin its decomposition process and take on that sickening stench. Only here the smell isn't a dead coyote by the side of the road or a poisoned rat underneath the garage. The smell is that of human remains, some of which are to be shipped back to the States shortly, as if this makes any difference to those poor grieving families back in the States. There just isn't that much left of the remains anyway to be shipped back to III MAF, or for the under-taker back home and especially for their loved ones who hopefully won't peek inside the casket when it arrives in Iowa or New Jersey or Texas or wherever those bodies are headed.

Another of the ironies of war comes home to the Marines after picking up pieces of bodies, gagging and getting sick from the smell and horror of it all, zipping up the parts in the bags, then dragging the stuff back to the Fox CP. The Marines haven't been resupplied for over two days because they've been told the helicopters are at a pre-mium right now and they'll get resupplied as soon as they can. They are without food and precious water—the troopers are dehydrating and getting sick from the heat and the lack of these basic elements of survival. Then, right on time, this helicopter comes down near the Fox CP to pick up the cargo of the dead, disregarding the needs of the living.

As the helicopter takes off with its expired freight, Captain Kettner turns toward the chaplain and says out of disgust, "Those bastards in division are going to disregard the needs of the living because some unconscious ghoul back at Da Nang has the clout to get a helicopter out here to pick up rotting body parts so he can fill in the blank space on his report and sleep better tonight." He shakes his head and continues, "Isn't that just the most goddamn disgusting thing you can imagine!"

He turns away and walks toward the CP and says to no one in particular: "Meanwhile our asses are frying and men are dying because this is a greater priority than feeding the living. What a bunch of horseshit!"

There is a theory, highly touted in the Marine Corps, which says everything—air, artillery support systems, supplies—exist only for the benefit of supporting the infantry, which does the fighting. That is their raison d'être. However, when it comes down to the practical application of that principle, it doesn't work. That's why the grunts are always short on critical infantry items such as boots, utilities, food, equipment, poncho liners, and ammunition. However, the boys in the rear always have plenty. But that's nothing new. Generals in all the wars have always relied on the big lie that says, "My boys on the line always have what they need!" It's always been that way, probably way back to Xerxes and the Persians.

After a short memorial service for the men killed two days ago, Richard and Bob hump back to battalion with a squad from Fox. The S3 has ordered the chaplain back because *Two-five* has been ordered to leave Go Noi Island in the morning and head back for An Hoa via Hill 42. The ammo dump at regiment was hit the night before killing twenty and wounding over one hundred Marines. Things are in a bad way there. Colonel Stevens is angry—again—because the battalion has not been resupplied and he wonders how they are going to hump the ten kilometers to Hill 42, then the remaining twelve kilometers to An Hoa without fresh water and ammunition.

HILL 42

Doop... doop... doop... The hollow sounds of battalion's outgoing mortars awakens Strom. He and Bob sit up quickly in the early morning light, the autonomic system instantly jammed into fight or flight from a restless sleep. Marshall jumps up abruptly, grabs his rifle and flak jacket, then squats down next to the chaplain. "Sir, you better get your gear on. Charlie must be out there close by—"

Marshall doesn't finish his sentence because two rockets slam into a small meadow just outside their perimeter but close to the Fox company CP one hundred meters away. In quick succession five incoming mortar rounds explode in the immediate area around the BAS sending shrapnel screaming in all directions. This is followed shortly by heavy AK-47 fire, which rakes the area of the battalion perimeter.

At this point the chaplain is now resigned to being consistently in the middle of combat. During one of the breaks in their hump last night as he and the doctor sat quietly awaiting the order to move on, he had cryptically verbalized a question grunts ask themselves after being in combat for a few months, a question that creeps up from a very uncomfortable, cynical place in the psyche: "Wonder when my luck is going to run out."

Like all the other encounters with the enemy, this strike creates instant terror. However, because of the fierce, arduous, and at times brutal experience the Marines are put through in boot camp and at infantry school, that dread is overridden by their harsh, uncompromising Corps training. They respond automatically and deploy quickly to return the enemy fire. It has been said that if a Marine is properly trained, he will be more frightened of displeasing his platoon sergeant that he is of enemy bullets. Arriving hungry and exhausted late last night from their ten kilometer hump to Hill 42, most of the battalion CP didn't have the energy to dig any kind of hole and those not on duty fell asleep the instant they laid down on the damp ground. *Two-five* again had not been picked up by trucks as they had been promised and their move was delayed until late afternoon. Then to add to the delays, confusing intelligence reports and lack of food and supplies, Lt. Col. Stevens receives a radio message from division that he will shortly be promoted to the rank of full colonel, be replaced by a new CO, and be going to III MAF operations within seven days to finish his tour of duty in an office job. He is happy about the promotion but displeased with leaving the battalion at this time.

The AK fire intensifies and the incoming mortars continue. The CO and S3 are positioned with their staff in a depression adjacent to an abandoned hooch. Stevens is on the radio to Fox Company ordering them to deploy immediately to the small hills just south of their position where the Marines have pinpointed the NVA rocket and mortar launching sites. Simultaneously, Captain Kevin Davis, the battalion forward air control officer, has just fragged two gunships on their way to An Hoa, which are now flying over *Two-five's* position from the northeast. They immediately commence firing their rockets and machine guns over the heads of Fox Company into an area one kilometer south of Hill 42, an awesome display of firepower that can concurrently be inspiring and frightening to the grunt. The "friendly fire" tragedy of last week is fresh in the minds of Fox, especially third platoon, which has been assigned point in the assault on the enemy concentration. Pinpoint accuracy is imperative in any kind of close air support where sometimes friendly ordinance can land within fifty meters of a platoon or company of Marines. It is difficult enough to be hit by enemy fire and booby traps day in and day out. But "friendly fire" mistakes are very, very demoralizing to the combat Marine.

The gunships continue to pour fire into the hills. Fox is fully involved in a fierce firefight, engaging the enemy as they now attempt to flee south into the safety of thicker vegetation and forest.

Quickly Strom and Marshall scurry on their bellies into a bamboo thicket a short distance away, Richard dragging his helmet and flak jacket behind him. More disoriented and confused than panicked, they both wedge themselves in between the large bamboo shoots, hopeful this will deflect the shrapnel and bullets flying about them. Suddenly Richard begins to turn and crawl out of the bamboo, yelling at Bob that he is going to retrieve his communion kit. It is one of those incomprehensible, impulsive behaviors that have their genesis in irrationality and stupidity.

The small arms fire and mortar rounds have not let up. Marshall quickly grabs Strom's foot and yells, "No, sir, you can't go out there." A mortar blast the earth a short distance away. "You're gonna get killed, sir!"

"Marshall, let go of my leg, dammit," Richard replies instantly as he struggles to free his foot from his assistant's iron-tight grip. "I am going to get that communion kit."

The young Marine now grabs the chaplain with both arms and hold onto both legs more determined than ever to stop the chaplain from doing something that he believes will get him killed. Just as determined, Strom now kicks himself free, stands in a crouched position, and runs the twenty meters to his pack and communion kit.

"Jeez, Chaplain, that's stupid," Bob replies, angry and frustrated, as he now scurries out of the bamboo toward Strom, who is now on his knees struggling to get his communion kit over his helmet and flak jacket.

Marines are now returning fire toward the village they came through the previous evening. In the midst of the small arms fire from both sides and the intermittent explosions from enemy rockets, the frightened, disheartened voices of Marines in distress can be heard: "Corpsmen up on the double," and from another direction, "Get a fuckin' corpsmen here now, goddammit!"

The mortars and small arms fire stops as suddenly as it had started. Continuous boredom, instant terror, an ongoing continuum in the life of a grunt; up and down, in and out, shooting and sleeping, living and dying—the collage of infantry existence.

Marshall and Strom are now within fifty meters to the BAS where a chaotic scene is unfolding. Bodies of dead and wounded are littering the ground. Two of the corpsmen are critically wounded and a third has been shot through the shoulder. The battalion surgeon, Dennis Jonsen, is frantically attempting to stanch the bleeding from the multiple wounds of his senior corpsman and good friend, Cory Gleason, while two Marines are dragging the battalion medical bag from a hooch nearby.

Jonsen looks up as Richard and his assistant approach and says apprehensively, "Dammit, Chaplain, we've got casualties all over the place." He quickly reaches over Gleason to tie a compress around Gleason's horribly mangled leg. "I have only two corpsmen left, I need you guys to help triage some of the casualties," he demands.

Quickly Strom directs Marshall to bring the medical bag and the two Marines to the battalion doctor. "I don't care who those Marines belong to, right now they're mine and we're gonna make them corpsmen," he says with authority, "and get me a couple more grunts to help with the wounded as litter bearers!"

Marshall runs off, the chaplain turns toward the doctor, who is now on his knees, holding his head in his hands. He slowly looks up, thrusting his arms and hands in the air, a sad, hopeless look on his face. Instantly Richard knows Gleason is dead.

"I've got some Marines coming who will help us," the chaplain responds quietly. "I'll have them bring the wounded. You and Smitty can organize your triage here. I will grab a medical kit and take Marshall with me and hunt down any troopers out toward the meadow. I'll set up a second triage there."

The doctor nods in agreement, still in shock over the death of his right hand man. Richard quickly picks up Gleason's blood-spattered kit, slips it over his shoulder, turns to see Bob directing four Marines to stay with the doctor, then motions to Bob to join him. Heading toward the meadow, they hear the requests for corpsmen coming from at least three other areas. Just before entering the meadow, next to a large bamboo grove, they come upon five Marines strewn about on the ground, a sixth sitting next to his gear, bleeding profusely from a wound to the forehead, weaving back and forth, dazed and disorganized, mumbling to himself, "Oh shit… oh God… what happened?"

The battalion chaplain kneels next to the young man and states quietly but firmly, "I'm the chaplain and I want you to lay down here next to your gear." The Marine complies as Richard turns to Marshall and says quickly, "Stop the bleeding, get him settled down, then go tell the Old Man we have multiple casualties and that most of our battalion corpsmen have been hit or are dead!"

Strom picks up the medical kit and turns toward the five Marines lying about, moves to the closest casualty, yelling, "Get a corpsman here right now." He hopes that Hotel Company is now close enough to battalion's position to snag a couple of their corpsmen. He is feeling very helpless and anxious because of the carnage and his lack of medical skills.

Close by the ground is torn up, having taken a direct hit by an enemy mortar. Adjacent to the hole, the chaplain comes upon a Marine. Richard can instantly see he is dead, his body is horribly mangled, and he is missing most of his limbs. In shock, horrified by the sight, Strom turns away, feeling nauseated and sick. However, as he has done so many times in the past nine months, he steels himself and quickly walks toward the next body. Although not torn up as badly, this Marine is also obviously dead. Shrapnel has pierced his face and ripped off the top of his head. "That's the way to die, instantly," he thinks to himself as he slowly steps over the lifeless body of a young man whose hopes and dreams have been terminated instantly by a shattering explosion.

Now moving quickly to the next Marine thirty meters away, Richard cups his hands around his mouth and yells as loud as he can, "I need a corpsman here, now!" Just ahead he sees a young private thrashing about, moaning loudly. He has multiple shrapnel wounds on his face, arms, and legs. Strom drops to his knees. With his left hand he grabs the bloody, shaking hand of the wounded grunt, with his right hand he quickly pulls some bandages out of the kit, all the while offering him words of encouragement: "Help is coming. We're gonna get you outta here to a hospital right away. You're gonna be okay. What's your name?"

Gasping for breath because he is hyperventilating, the young man says, "Ah... oh God, what happened?"

The chaplain repeats his question, "What's your name, son?"

"Lemoyne... Ahh, God it hurts... Lemoyne Jackson," he replies, struggling to get the words out.

Wrapping gauze around his head, Richard softly replies, "A mortar round exploded close by and you caught some shrapnel." Then he lays the wounded man's head down, rips his pant leg apart, applies some anesthetic to a gaping wound that has torn open his left thigh, and applies a compress and gauze to his leg. The Marine stares at Strom, noticing the gold cross and lieutenant bars on his collar. "You ain't the corpsman, are you?" he says in an agitated voice. "Where's Doc Gleason?"

"I'm the chaplain and I'm just helping out," Richard replies. "We've had lots of casualties and a corpsman will be here shortly." He has stretched the truth because he has no idea when a corpsman will show up, or for that matter when the emergency medevacs will materialize. He is feeling again the inadequacy of his work, also wondering if he should take the liberty of giving the badly wounded Marine a shot of morphine.

Jackson then grabs the chaplain's hand and says tearfully, "Sir, don't leave me. Please don't leave me. Am I going to die?"

The chaplain is feeling tremendous pressure, his anxiety ratcheting up even more, wanting to linger with this badly injured Marine but also needing to check the other casualties scattered about forty meters away.

"Son, I'll be right back," he replies as he disengages the frightened grasp of the young man lying on the ground in front of him, then reaches into his chest pocket and pulls out his personal New Testament, which he always carries with him when out in the bush. "You take this Testament and hold onto it," the chaplain says calmly. "It's yours to keep. I will be right back, do you understand, Lemoyne?"

Still shaking badly, the young man nods. "I want you to say these words over and over as a prayer to the Lord," Strom continues. "'Heal me, oh Lord, and I shall be healed.' I want you to pray that over and over until I get back to see you. Do you understand, Lemoyne?"

The young man nods again. "Heal me, Lord, I will be healed… Heal me, Lord, I will be healed."

Richard pats him on the arm, stands, and says, "Remember, I'll be back."

The surrogate corpsman picks up the medical kit, turns toward the meadow, and sees the forward element of Hotel Company. Feeling immediate relief, he yells loudly, "Send me your corpsmen on the double, we've got a bunch of casualties." Then he begins to run toward the column about one hundred meters away. Within a minute two company corpsmen are working on the remaining wounded in the immediate area while Richard is directing a corpsman from first platoon back to help the doctor.

Richard James Strom looks at his watch and notices that only ten minutes have elapsed since the time the attack began until now. It has seemed like an eternity, so much life and death, and humanity has passed by in milliseconds and split seconds and minutes that seem like years. The time warp created out this devastation is a fabric of death and destruction. It lays to waste the human spirit and drains the life force of the dying as well as those who live. There are no survivors.

Within five minutes of Hotel's arrival, a yellow smoke grenade goes off in the northern end of the meadow nearest the CP. The first of three emergency medevacs is arriving to transfer the badly wounded troopers back to the Naval Support Hospital in Da Nang. Then the priority helicopter will arrive soon after that to transport the seven less serious casualties to the regimental aid station in An Hoa. Finally, the designated routine chopper will bring back the eight young men killed in that five-minute piece of time to either the Rose Garden at First Medical Battalion or the mortuary at III MAF. Among the casualties are four navy Corpsmen—two killed and two seriously wounded. Never in the history of *Two-five* since landing in Chu Lai three years ago have so many corpsmen been taken out in one single piece of action in one day. Also included in the killed in action is Lcpl. Lemoyne Jackson. He died from his wounds just seconds before the chaplain's promised return.

The chaplain and doctor have been summoned by the colonel and are walking toward the CP, both depressed and numb because of the high casualties but also because of the loss of their two friends, Gleason and Johnson. Smitty is the only BAS corpsman who escaped death or injury. Strom is also feeling terrible about not getting back to Jackson in time. Hopelessness is beginning to set in, fueled by guilt, anxiety, stress, and lack of sleep. Wordless, they enter the make-shift CP inside of a sandbagged hooch.

The CO looks tense and tired. Standing by his side the S3 is on the radio to division. "Yes, sir, we've moved off the hill and are resetting our perimeter." Stevens motions for them to step outside.

"I'm sorry about what happened to your corpsmen, Doc," he begins in a flat, dull voice, "but we've gotta do better to protect ourselves when we set into a new position and maintain the integrity of our perimeter. This can't happen again, to have a couple of mortars wipe out our BAS. You guys are too valuable." He points toward the opening into the CP and continues, "Major Sulli's found a dug-out tank barrier down the road. We're gonna be here for a while, so the battalion aid station will be located there. Order whatever supplies you need and I'll make sure they get here."

Stevens then begins to walk back toward the hooch and continues his monologue: "Right now An Hoa is taking a pounding so you'll be safer here than at regiment. Apparently we ran into an NVA regiment located just south of us. The S2 says they were poised to hit An Hoa in a couple of days. Guess we ruined their day and put a stop to that shit, huh."

He stops and turns directly to his chaplain and says softly, "Heard you turned into a corpsman this morning. Good work, Padre." He then faces the doctor and says, "You too, Doc." Stevens then breaks out into a smile and says good-naturedly, "I don't care what they say about the navy, you guys are all right in my book!" He quickly turns and disappears into the CP.

The two naval officers stand still for a few seconds, then Dennis says quietly, "Guess that's as good as it gets from that old bastard!

That was a compliment, wasn't it?" Richard shrugs his shoulders slowly, turns, and walks off toward the meadow to be by himself. At this moment he truly believes he will never be able to laugh or shed a tear again, ever.

Diary Entry—272 Days In-Country

Something's happened—again?—I never made it back from that bout with malaria, or was it the leeches? Maybe on our way to Thong Duc. Could it have been yesterday's rations? Maybe it's the stinking weather. Never quite recovered each time or quite made it through a day hiding from the bullets or pushing down the images of friends or civilians blown away. So now I'm:

Staring when I walk
Empty when I talk
Full of concrete blocks
Sun frying thoughts
Carrying on as if indefinite
Will it ever end?
This walking
This walking in the heat
In the sweltering, humidity, dust
Of dying far too soon
From bullets...
Or just plain emptiness

CHANGING TIMES

The helicopter slowly comes into the small clearing next to Hill 42, yellow smoke drawn up into the blades and then dispersed into a cloud of dust. The dry season has displaced the wet, rainy overcast of monsoon weather and the land is now arid and dusty. Replacing the rotting, cracked toes, ongoing ringworm, and open lesions from constant rain and moisture, the infantryman now has a new second enemy—heat exhaustion and sunstroke. The weather never gets better, just different. Stifling heat, humidity, and mosquitoes replace oppressive rain, humidity, and mosquitoes.

Strom and his assistant are returning from two days in Da Nang, attending a one day chaplain's retreat at China Beach, then visiting the two hospitals in Da Nang. Strom now finds the hospital visitation a distasteful chore and doesn't like it at all. It is one of the few places that can still get things going for him inside, opening him up to his feelings. The protection of "shut down" doesn't work once he steps inside the ward of the hospitals. He and Bob counted only forty-six wounded Marines listed in both places, the lowest hospital census since Strom was assigned to An Hoa. Statistically, this means that instead of eighty wounded and twenty dead, there are only forty wounded and ten dead, which means the Marines have only ten widows or parents from battalion to see this week when they contact the next of kin back in the States. Ten is better than twenty any day, especially when America is dealing in "peace with honor."

There is no honor in that duty, however—a duty Richard had done a number of times when stationed at Camp Pendleton—when you ring the bell and say to the face behind the door: "Are you Mr. or Mrs. Smith, Balbinni, Chavez, Greenberg, Chan, Waszkowski? On

behalf of the United States Government and a very grateful nation…"
There is no getting used to or honor in that distressing and depressing act of bringing horrifying news to loved ones—watching that process of shock, then deep grief and anguish unfold—whether one does that one or ten or a hundred times.

Strom and Marshall quickly exit the chopper and walk the one hundred meters to the BAS. Bob is carrying a duffel bag filled with a new supply of small hymnals, New Testaments, rosaries, and an assortment of religious metals and communion supplies. Richard has two cases of "sodas," which he liberated from his recon friends. The liberated supplies always bring pleasure and relief to the grunts in the field. He once remarked to the Monk that as far as he was concerned, the beer and sodas are just as consecrated and holy as the bread and wine. Vince nodded in agreement.

The two of them approach an amtrac located next to the six-foot-deep, thirty-foot-long trench housing the BAS. The S3 suddenly shows up and walks directly to Strom. "Whatcha got there, Chaplain?" he says with a smirky, shit-eating grin on his face. "I better have a look."

Strom places the two cases on the ground, mindful of the colonel's orders that there will be absolutely no beer brought to the field. He bends over and rips open the top of the first case exposing the twenty-four Pepsis. The second case, previously full of root beer, had been opened partially on the side and emptied of its contents, then refilled with twenty beers and four root beers placed strategically next to the small side opening. Continuing the ruse, Richard reopens the side, pulls out a can of root beer, and tosses it at Sulli, saying, "See, Major, a case of Pepsi and a case of root beer, or would you rather have a Pepsi?"

Major Sulli examines the can, then looks at Strom, casually tossing the root beer back, and says, "Nope, don't want any." He turns and walks back toward the CP. As this little sleight of hand is going on by the chaplain, Bernie is watching the show intently, freaking out lest the Budweiser Express gets busted and they all get into trouble.

The network of the Budweiser Express goes far beyond the chaplain or someone in the BAS bringing beer to the field. Orders are placed by routine radio traffic to the regimental or battalion rear BAS through coded messages by the corpsmen attached to battalion staff. Or when Richard can't get out of the field and he wants a case of beer sent out, he will send a message to Bernie O'Hearn requesting "special communion supplies." The regimental chaplain will have it in the next day's supply via helicopter, always in soda cases marked "Religious supplies—Chaplain's eyes only!"

After the S3 leaves, Bernie approaches the chaplain, a wild look in his eyes. "Shit, Rich, I thought old Bastard Brain was going to bust your ass and we'd all be in trouble."

"That's why we pack the beer like we do, for emergencies just like this," Strom replies, smiling.

Marshall looks relieved and takes the duffel bag to the amtrac. Bernie grabs both cases, motions for Richard to follow him down into the pit, then into a small darkened sandbagged enclosure, directing Strom to sit down.

"Here, Rich, have a beer," he says quietly, "I got some important things to tell you."

"What can possibly be of any importance around here?" Richard questions as he reaches for a root beer instead.

"While you were gone," the doctor continues, "Colonel Stevens was sent back to Da Nang for his new assignment at III MAF." There is a quiet pause as Bernie takes a long draught on the recently opened beer and continues, "Do you know what that means, Rich?"

Strom smiles and replies, "It means Stevens won't have his chaplain to get pissed off at any more?"

"No, goddammit," the doctor continues, "it means that Major Neanderthal is acting CO until we get a new replacement. You know as well as I do Rich that he couldn't piss a hole in a snowbank!"

"Ah, come on now, Bernie," the chaplain replies, "he's mellowed a little. When do we get our new CO?"

"Not soon enough," Bernie grouses.

At that moment Smitty sticks his head inside the BAS and says, "Hey, doctor, a helicopter is coming in shortly with the new CO.

The gunny says he knows him from Camp Pendleton and says he's top-notch."

"Anything is better than we all got now," Bernie mumbles.

The young corpsman walks inside and continues, "Another thing, sir, we aren't going back to regiment. The new orders say that since all three battalions are out in the field we're to stay out here and harass the NVA so they can't get to An Hoa and create havoc."

Richard stands, throws his hands up in the air, and says with resignation, "See, Bernie, that's why we get paid those big bucks. Gotta keep harassing the enemy!"

The chaplain now hears a helicopter approaching. He walks outside and up out of the tank pit to see a Huey slowing descending into the grassy meadow seventy-five meters away. The helicopter lands and three Marines exit the aircraft. Richard walks back down into the pit and into the sandbagged enclosure, grabs his helmet and flak jacket, and runs to exit the enclosure.

"Now what y'all dressing up for Chaplain," Bernie drawls in his best Alabama accent. "Church, incoming, or you gonna go out there and be on the brownnose committee welcoming the new colonel?"

Strom puts on his gear, turns toward his good friend, and replies, "I'm ready for all three, Bernie. Finish your beer, get your shirt on, grab a rifle and my communion kit, and I'll let you to be my bodyguard and acolyte and we'll baptize the new colonel into the brotherhood of *Two-five* while you hum 'Anchors Aweigh'!"

Dr. Grant laughs and says quickly, "I've got more important things to do, like take—"

"Don't even go there, Bernie," Richard retorts immediately, "you're worse than the Marines with all this scatological talk!"

"What the hell is 'scratilogical,' or whatever that damn word is?" Bernie questions.

Chaplain Strom just shakes his head and walks out of the BAS area and heads toward the battalion CP as the helicopter shuts down, something unusual out in the bush. Three Marines have exited the aircraft and are being greeted by Major Sulli. Richard slowly strolls toward the abandoned village hooch containing the CP and watches Sergeant Major Rivers and the executive officer, Major Cahill, accompany the new CO to the forward battalion headquarters. Strom stands casually off to the side as the S3 walks past him as if he is a lamppost. The new CO suddenly stops directly in front of his battalion chaplain, smiles, thrusts his hand forward for a handshake, and says as Strom reciprocates.

"Chaplain Strom, we meet again."

Richard is dumbfounded. He is looking at his old commanding officer from the Twenty-Eighth Marines. "Yes, sir," he replies, "I'm surprised and very happy to have you here with us."

Major Sulli is standing inside the hooch stone-faced. Lt. Col. Huggins invites Richard inside. Cahill faces Strom and says, "I told the colonel that aside from Major Sulli and Dr. Grant, you are the most senior officer we now have in our battalion." The S3 turns toward some sandbags that have two maps on top and states emphatically, "Ah, Colonel, here are the position maps you were asking about."

Facing the S3 he responds, "Sure, Major, we'll get to that in a moment." He then turns back toward the sergeant major and chaplain and continues, "When I'm through with my briefing with Major Sulli, I want to sit down with you and have a chat about our troopers and see how they're doing."

"Chaplain, I told the colonel that you are definitely a good field chaplain and know what's up with our Marines," Sergeant Major Rivers continues with a smile, "and I said that I didn't think there was any navy left in you anymore—too much time with the Marines!"

The Chaplain smiles back at Rivers and says to Huggins, "Yes, sir, no problem with the chat." He turns to walk back to the BAS, the S3 finally getting to secure his place with the colonel. Although Richard is aware that his relationship with the new colonel is well established and positive, there is no change inside; his mood is the same—flat and unenthusiastic. The only time the juices can get going anymore is when there is incoming, when in the midst of a firefight, or when a booby trap goes off. A very unfortunate but true commentary for anyone with too much time in the bush.

Within two days the battalion is tramping around the foothills and rice paddies between Phu Lac 6 and An Hoa. Lots of coming here and going there. A Marine shot here, another one blown up there. No heavy engagement, just the little stuff that wears you down. Each day brings that quiet rage that arises from encounters with hidden booby traps. How does one get even or destroy the enemy that placed a device a week or month ago in the ground to kill? A very effective weapon. It is so sudden so unexpected. Here today, gone tomorrow in a millisecond!

Two-five is now going through the same old places, doing the same things, treating the villagers the same way as they did seven months ago—with disrespect and like they are the enemy, which in some cases is true. Only a lot of Marines have been ground up getting to this place, doing everything all over. If the enemy is in his place—as the generals and the news reports say—then how come the troops must build fortresses each night to keep the enemy out of the cities and villages and regimental and division CPs?

Richard now has vehicular transportation up and down the road between Phu Lac 6 and An Hoa and he can get what he wants out to the line companies. So daily he rides up and down the road between line companies and the battalion CP, dropping off a case of sodas here or a "mixed" case there, a few pounds of fresh food or some sandwiches "lifted" from the regimental mess. In between time he has worship services every day for one of the platoons.

"Hey, Chaplain," says Richard's whacky buddy Wager, a corpsman with too much time on the line, "see you brought some medical supplies." He helps the chaplain carry a duffel bag full of "supplies" to the BAS inside a dark, smelly, insect- and dust-infested building just south of An Hoa at a place called Charlie Strong Point. Inside the chaplain finds out his good friend Bernie just received new orders to Chu Lai—the Riviera of I Corps—as the battalion surgeon for the Ninth Engineers. For Bernie this means getting out of the bush, an assignment close to the beach and the South China Sea, clean sheets, and three hot meals every day. What a change after being with the Fifth Marines! Bernie of course is deliriously happy.

So the chaplain and his driver (Marshall), the two battalion doctors, and five corpsmen drink the four cases of beer the chaplain "liberated" from the regimental aid station and cook the five pounds of canned Danish bacon Richard was going to pass out to Hotel Company that remains way out in the boonies. There goes all the special stash the chaplain had scrounged for the past week. Another day, another four pounds of bacon and four cases of beer. There'll be more. If not, so what?

Diary Entry—291 Days In-Country

Settled into a routine now—is there anything else left alone any-more? Up and down the road, from Phu Lac 6 to Charlie Strong Point. A night here, a day there. It all seems the same.

> *Bright sun*
> *Humid earth*
> *Hot flash*
> *Of gun*
> *And death*
> *Quickly*
> *Come/goes*
> *And then*
> *The boredom*
> *Sets in…*
> *Again*

BACK TO ARIZONA

It is evening in An Hoa, the setting sun is now a collage of amber, magenta, and rose in the western sky. The cadence and consistency of the ongoing twenty-four-hour sounds of helicopters and C-130s and artillery and machine gun fire has suddenly stopped. This sound of silence quickly creates a low level apprehension, an anxiety that feels like having stepped into a surreal, otherworld experience. The unusual quiet sets off an alarm way inside, a conditioned response to the silence that has preceded the storm so many times before, jacking up the adrenaline and preparing the body and mind for flight or fight. It isn't supposed to be this way—quiet is supposed to create peace, serenity, and sleep. Not out here! Quiet brings vigilance, a projection of catastrophic thinking and diminishes any semblance of repose for the combat Marine.

Lest there be inadvertent friendly fire, the silence of the heavy guns on this evening is a calculated, coordinated scenario to move all three battalions back again into the bush quickly under cover of darkness. *One-five* will head south past Charlie Strong Point into the hills surrounding the Dap Tich reservoir believed to be a major staging area for the NVA. *Three-five* will move east into the hostile and heavily booby-trapped Phu Nhan and to the bridge and major river crossing at Phu Lac 6, an area well-known to all the Fifth Marines. *Two-five* will hump north into Arizona Territory, a major infiltration route from the Ho Chi Minh trail in the mountains west to the coastal plains and Da Nang. Division believes an all-out thrust outward from An Hoa will push the enemy back far enough to stop the constant shelling of regimental headquarters and hopefully reopen the airstrip again to normal, daily flights. *Two-five* will be without two line companies—Echo has been attached to *Three-five* while Golf will remain behind as security for regiment. Hotel, then battalion staff followed by Fox left An Hoa in the late afternoon, humping two kilometers through the villages of Phu Da to the banks of the Song Thu Bon River. It is normally too deep to cross during the rainy season; the Marines now wait in the growing darkness ready to ford the river. Lt. Col. Huggins is on the radio to regiment awaiting the word to move across the huge, open two-hundred-meter sandbar, then ford the waist-high river. The new ops officer, Major Dan Copeland, is briefing the staff and company commanders on objectives and placement once they reach the other side.

"This is a free-fire zone over there, gentlemen, so anything that moves, shoot it," Copeland says with authority. "There are not supposed to be any civilians over there, so anybody not shot and found in the villages are to be detained and assumed to be VC."

Chaplain Strom is sitting on the ground next to Dr. Jonsen and the intelligence officer, First Lt. Rick Brunner, hardly able to make out faces anymore because of the darkness. "That's pretty damn brutal," replies the doctor under his breath but loud enough to hear. "Let's see now. Assume everyone, including women and children over there, is VC so we can blow their asses—"

"Doctor," the S3 replies tersely, "just keep your goddamn mouth shut and hand out pills." The chaplain stares vacantly ahead. The doctor shakes his head in disgust as Copeland continues, "They've been warned. If they get shot or bombed, it's their damn fault, not ours."

Huggins then appears and whispers loudly while slinging on his gear, "Time to hit the road folks, we've got some humping to do. Most of Hotel has reached the other side and is securing the far bank for us." The CO then turns to Strom who is struggling in the dark to get his communion kit over his head and shoulder and says, "Bet they never taught you in the seminary how to survive with a bunch of cutthroat Marines crossing a river in the dark, huh, Padre?"

"No, sir," the chaplain replies flatly, then turns and walks toward Gunny Buckner, unhappy the battalion will be going back into Arizona again, aware of that low-level anxiety grinding at his

insides again like it always did when kicking off on a new operation. Whispering in a hushed tone, he turns to the sergeant and says,
"Marshall is on R&R, Gunny, so if you don't mind, I'm gonna stick
close to you."

"You do that, Padre," the gunny replies as he slips his pack
through his arm and onto his back. "Stay close to me and we'll be
each other's rabbit foot."

"Don't count on me being a rabbit's foot," the chaplain responds
quietly, "hasn't worked so far."

They fall into a column, Huggins and the forward CP following
the last remnants of second platoon of Hotel, then the BAS personnel and special weapons. Fox will be following battalion ten minutes
after they cross to the other side.

Slowly, spread out in a single file column, battalion personnel
first crosses the open seventy-five meters of the large sandbar on the
south side of the river. Deliberately, as noiselessly as possible, they
begin to cross the river itself in waist high water, careful to keep
their weapons above the waterline. The complete blackness makes
it even more anxiety-producing than during daylight because the
milieu of darkness, wading through water and anticipation of enemy
ambush creates visual paranoia as the mind begins to invent objects
and movement.

As Chaplain Strom wades into the river, first ankle-high, then
the dark water slowing moving up to his waist, he lifts his communion
kit over his head, mindful that his pack with his poncho liner and
food supplies will probably get soaked. He continues to walk carefully, the current tugging lightly at his body as the cool water moves
slowly east toward the South China Sea, getting more paranoid as he
progresses further into the moving water and away from the river's
edge. As the high anxiety grips him, he wonders if the Marines ahead
of him are feeling the same intensity of distress and apprehension he
is experiencing. He is barely able to make out Buckner six feet ahead
of him; it is so dark and he has no idea how much distance there is
to the far bank. "This is definitely not fun," Strom thinks to himself,
then begins to pray: "Give me the strength I need to do my best. This
is scary, Lord, keep me in your hands—"

At that moment Richard trips over a rock under foot, stumbles, and almost falls headfirst into the river, thrusting the communion kit high over his head so it won't get soaked. Simultaneously AK-47 fire erupts from somewhere across the river directed right at the column. A round slams into his kit and noisily ricochets off a piece of metal inside as he struggles to regain his balance. The firing continues for an eternity—which in this case is just a few seconds—then stops just as suddenly. Struggling to get to the far shore as quickly as possible and not drowned in the process, Richard and the Marines around him suspend any notion of silence and surprise and quickly make it to the river bank. As in all firefights or sudden ambushes, confusion reigns supreme!

"Gunny Buckner up, on the double," comes the harsh, whispered cry from Major Copeland. Then again he said, "Anybody seen the gunny?"

Strom, Jonsen, and the two corpsmen following them are lying on the ground next to some bamboo a few yards from the water. "Hey, Chaplain," Smitty whispers, "where's the gunny? He was right in front of you."

For the first time Richard can focus on something other than his own safety and the terror he is feeling. "I don't know," he whispers back. "In the confusion I thought he was ahead of me and made it here."

About thirty yards away from the riverbank Huggins is on the radio with Hotel. Copeland is requesting the mortars be set up immediately and fired into an area called Phu An a kilometer away, a known VC enclave. Hotel is deploying in the villages along the river called Phu Nam in an attempt to find the VC that fired at battalion, an impossibility in this darkness.

There is a rustling in the bushes in front of Richard, Smitty, Wages, and Jonsen. Strom tenses as he hears, "Where's the corpsmen and the chaplain? The colonel wants them up front on the double!"

Soaking wet, including his pack, Richard slowly arises and picks up his communion kit as the doctor and two corpsmen stand and grab their medical gear. "Hey, Marines, we're over here," the chaplain responds, still feeling shaky from the latest encounter with near death. Quickly two Marines make their way to the mobile battalion aid station. "We've got wounded Marines up front. Colonel wants the doc and chaplain up there to get them patched up."

Chaplain Strom taps the closest Marine on the shoulder and says, "Let's go, we'll follow you." They then walk and stumble their way about one hundred meters inland to a temporary CP set up next to some bushes and an old burned-out hooch. Huggins is still on the radio with Hotel's skipper. The S3, upon seeing the doctor and chaplain, immediately approaches Richard and asks in a voice filled with apprehension: "You was walking next to the gunny, Chaplain, have you seen him, has anyone seen him? We can't find him." Turning to Jonsen, he points toward a bamboo thicket and says, "Doc, we've got our wounded over there. Go help them out. I've already fragged an emergency medevac."

Suddenly Richard has a sickening feeling inside, a terrible sense of dread that the gunny probably got hit with the same fuselage that creamed his communion kit. But in the commotion and panic to get to the riverbank, his awareness of the gunny's or anyone else's presence at that time was zero. He is silent but there is a raging committee meeting going on in his head. "Oh my God," the chaplain thinks to himself, "what if he got hit and went under and I could have done something to save him." Immediately waves of guilt began to engulf the chaplain as he silently stares at Major Copeland.

The CO is off the phone and now approaches the guilt-ridden chaplain. "We've got some wounded over there that are going to need more than medical intervention, Chaplain Strom, so I'd sure appreciate some prayers for my boys."

Richard nods absently wet and cold, picks up his kit, and is guided to the triage area by the colonel himself. "God knows you know your job, Chaplain, so I hope I'm not sticking my nose into yours," he says gently as they approach the wounded. "I'm what you consider a pretty devout Catholic and I do believe in prayer."

The chaplain can feel tears welling up in his eyes and hopes the colonel doesn't see them, apprehensive he might actually break down and cry. "Thanks for your support, Colonel," Strom replies softly, quickly walking the remaining steps to the four Marines lying prone on the ground.

A Marine is holding a flashlight over two wounded troopers. One has a hole clean through his face and out the back of his head and was dragged dead from the water. The second grunt is groaning loudly from a bullet wound in the upper arm, shattering his humerus bone. Jonsen is leaning over the groaning Marine. "Smitty, let's get this arm splinted right away and give him an injection of morphine stat!"

The chaplain has already moved beyond to the two other wounded lying nearby. Three Marines are kneeling next to them as Richard quickly pulls out his flashlight and kneels between them. The young man on his right has been shot through the hand lying open the fleshy part under his little finger. Turning to the Marine on his left, he is horrified by what he sees. The young trooper is lying quietly on the deck in deep shock, bleeding profusely, a bullet having smashed through his left cheek and exiting through his right mandible underneath his ear, completely ripping open his cheek and lower right jaw. The chaplain quickly reaches into his kit still slung around his shoulder, grabs the four communion linens he always carries, then stuffs them into the huge hole as he tenderly holds the young man's gravely injured head in his free arm.

"Dennis, get over here right away," Richard says in a commanding voice, simultaneously keeping pressure on the bloody linens. "We've got a serious facial wound." The Marine makes no sound and just stares vacantly at the chaplain.

"I'll be right there, Rich," Strom hears, "gotta get this splint set."

Continuing to hold the makeshift compress in place, Chaplain Strom leans over the badly wounded Marine and says softly, "You're gonna be all right, you're gonna be okay. The helicopter is on the way. Dr. Jonsen will be here real soon."

The combat weary chaplain flashes on that time eons ago, in that helicopter taking off from Hill 100, when he had a Marine die in his arms with a similar wound. Richard quickly looks up at the three Marines who are now standing off to the side and says, "Anybody know this Marine's name?"

"I think his name is Merrill or somethin' like that," is a quick reply. "He's new in-country, Chaplain."

"Merrill… Merrill," the chaplain begins, then hears a guttural groan, which he interprets as an affirmation of his name. "We are here to protect and help you, just as God will now protect you and get you back to the hospital and your loved ones." The young man slowly lifts his right arm and places his hand softly on Richard's forearm. "We commend Merrill to your holy keeping," Strom continues, "relieve his suffering and pain, take away his anxiety and suspense, and we ask you to bring him home safely to his loved ones, through Christ, our Lord." As he finishes the short prayer, he is relieved to see Dr. Jonsen arrive with a corpsman ready to take charge.

Twenty-five minutes later an emergency medevac arrives. It is a very anxious producing time for both the helicopter crew and the Marines in and around the LZ. Strobe lights are used as markers for the pilots, which also can be seen for miles and usually alerts the enemy. Second, the air controller has to direct and "talk in" the pilot so he can land in the dark and miss trees, hooches, and other obstacles that are unseen from above. Once landing, the severely wounded are put onboard, then the chopper must exit, usually straight up to again miss any obstructions, hoping the enemy hasn't the presence or the skill to zero in on the LZ before he can take off. The bravery and the skill of these helicopter crews save the lives of many seriously wounded Marines. Tonight everyone is fortunate—no rockets or mortars fired at the chopper or the grunts left behind.

Within twenty minutes of the chopper leaving, battalion and Fox pack up and head southwest and march for the next four hours in the dark, leaving Hotel to secure the area by the river. They finally reach their destination at 0300 six kilometers northwest of An Hoa at a hill region called Phu Bac. Gunnery Sergeant Buckner is still missing and is presumed killed in action. Chaplain Strom does not sleep and watches the sun rise in the east, exhausted and filled with guilt about the death of his new acquaintance, Gunny Buckner.

"Hey, Chaplain, how's it going?" says his good friend Wages who has less than one month left in Vietnam. "Got some hot chocolate brewing, would ya like some?"

"Nah, don't think so," Richard responds, "got kind of a gut ache right now, but thanks anyway." He is kneeling over his open communion kit with the contents spread out on the deck. Slowly, deliberately with his left hand he picks up the six-inch cross, which is badly dented in the middle and missing the silver crucifix attached to it. In his right hand he is hold the shattered crucifix, having taken a direct hit from the AK-47 fire while crossing the river.

"Jeez, Chaplain," says Wages incredulously, "how the hell did that happen?"

Strom continues to stare at the broken crucifix, then answers softly, thoughtfully, without taking his eyes off the shattered metal, "It got whacked last night when we got ambushed crossing the river."

Wages is quiet for a few seconds, then responds slowly, his voice and eyes betraying astonishment, "Wow, Chaplain, that's heavy, and I ain't talking about the metal, sir!"

The battalion chaplain says nothing but is aware—again—that after each devastating encounter, one never quite recovers from the terror of the incoming or the terrible, hideous, debilitating experience of seeing your dead, dying, or wounded friends and comrades. One never recovers back to the level you were at before the last combat. Each time, if there is any time to recover, the mending brings you back a notch below the last time, dropping the combatant a little deeper into numbness. There is a terrible consequence to this process called normalization. The combatant hardly knows that after each encounter he is slowly slipping deeper into the abyss of depression.

Diary Entry—302 Days In-Country

Sniper fire, mortars, and occasional rockets are hitting our area each night starting at sundown. Not a lot you understand but enough so you never really are asleep. And the next day is exactly the same thing—yesterday becomes tomorrow's today, the insidious numbing of the combatant.

> Not knowing
> Not remembering
> Not seeing
> Not feeling
> Not waking up
> To a day that's different
> Than the rest
> When that happens
> Clarity
> Is lost
> Sometimes it seems
> Like forever!

MORE INSANITY

It has been seven days since the river crossing. Seventy-Eighth Marines are sitting in a semicircle next to a grove of bamboo outside a group of small villes called Nam An in the late afternoon. The villages are adjacent to a mountainous finger jutting into the flat farm land of rice paddies. Six sentries rim the group facing away, watching for any movement or sounds that might indicate the presence of enemy troops. It is very quiet—no mortars or helicopters or gunfire or jets overhead. Only the soft voice of the solitary person standing in front of the group of men can be heard.

"One of our great American writers, his name was Emerson, once said that a person is a hero not because he is braver than anyone else but because he is braver for ten minutes longer. That bravery, we all know, is widespread and common every day among our Marines. It is the spirit of perseverance, the last spark of energy you draw upon, that sometimes marks the difference between success and failure, victory or defeat, even life and death. I have seen that perseverance and determination from all of you as you labor and toil through each difficult day, especially out here in the bush."

The battalion chaplain pauses for a few seconds, takes a few steps closer to the Marines assembled in front of him, and continues, "For many of us we have struggled hard over the past few months, made it through some very tough and difficult times, especially losing our close friends and fellow Marines. This is not easy to do, especially out here where we haven't the time or energy to grieve like we need to do. It is therefore important we come together to remember and pray for our fallen comrades."

At this point Richard turns to his left nods to four Marines standing to the side who are holding their M-16 rifles, each with a fixed bayonet. They slowly walk in single file until they are standing adjacent to the chaplain. Facing the seventy Marines, the chaplain asks them all to stand, then continues, "Lord of heaven and earth, we commend the souls of our fallen comrades to your keeping."

Chaplain Strom takes three steps back, then says solemnly, "Private Jimmy Johnson." As he says this, the closest Marine to Richard inverts his rifle and jams it into the ground, then places his helmet over the rifle butt. "Private First Class Jake Schlichman," he continues as a second Marine repeats the ritual. "Lance Corporal Kendrick Adams." A third rifle is placed into the ground. "Gunnery Sergeant Jack Buckner." The last rifle is placed in the ground as the chaplain lifts up both of his arm.

"Merciful Lord, our Father, when the tragedies of life surround us and anger grips us and we feel helpless, bring us some moments of peace and comfort. Grant us the courage to accept what cannot be changed and the strength to face bravely what is to come." Making the sign of the cross, he continues, "In the name of the Father, Son, and Holy Spirit. Amen." He bows his head, folds his hands, and remains silent. After a pause of fifteen seconds, he looks over the Marines standing in front of him and says solemnly, "Please take care of yourselves, and each other, out there. That's what it's going to take to make it through all this terrible stuff!"

The standing Marines at first do not move, frozen in place by the solemnity of the moment, each lost in their own thoughts about the living and dying reality of existence in the bush. Slowly the group begins to disperse and walk back to their respective areas. The chaplain has turned toward the four Marines who participated in the short memorial service and is thanking them as Lt. Col. Huggins slowly walks toward Richard. Strom turns toward his CO and says in a flat, emotionless voice, "Yes, sir?"

Huggins places his hand on his chaplain's shoulder and says quietly, "Chaplain Strom, I need to have a talk with you. Can we have a few minutes together?"

"No problem, Colonel, what's up?" he responds.

They walk away from a number of Marines milling about and head toward an abandoned hooch forty meters away. The colonel sits down on a large smooth log adjacent to the small hut, motioning for Chaplain Strom to have a seat.

"Chaplain," he begins, looking out toward the area they just came from, "I have some information that I need to talk to you about."

Richard gets an apprehensive look on his face as Huggins quickly continues, "No bad news, Chaplain. Or maybe it's kind of bad news. It's about your assignment to a rear battalion."

Richard is now staring at the colonel and says flatly, "And?"

"Some background," he continues, "I knew Father McGinty back in the States when we were both assigned to the pentagon a few years ago. So when I came here three weeks ago I looked him up and had dinner with him the night before I came out to An Hoa."

Strom now visibly tenses, expecting some harsh criticism about the blowup he had in McGinty office eons ago.

"Aside from talking about old times, we also talked about the chaplains in the division, especially the one's assigned to infantry battalions," he states quietly, "and how important their role can be, especially out in the bush. These young kids are stressed out to capacity and you guys can he really pivotal in helping some of them keep their sanity. I sometimes wonder how they are able to stay with it day after day."

"Training," Richard responds rather absently but also wondering just where this conversation is going.

"You're right about that," he states quickly, "but that's not what I want to talk to you about."

Richard is looking straight ahead as Huggins continues, "Since Dr. Grant and Major Sulli have left, that makes you the officer with the most time in-country in our battalion—going on ten months now, isn't it?" Without waiting for an answer, he continues, "What is really important to me is that the officers and enlisted Marines know you and trust you." He kicks some mud off his boots in an attempt to gather his thoughts. "So yesterday, I sent a message back to the division chaplain's office—to Chaplain McGinty—to request that you not be given orders to another outfit but remain here with us for a few more weeks."

There is a deadly silence as Richard stares straight ahead. The colonel turns toward his chaplain, pulls a piece of paper out of his pocket and says calmly, "I know you're about three months over you time with the grunts. They must have had a good reason for keeping you here with us past the normal six-month rotation." He unfolds the piece of paper and says slowly, deliberately, "So just before the memorial service, I received a message from division one-niner. I'd like to read it to you."

The chaplain turns toward his CO, shrugs, and says flatly, "You're the boss." Colonel Huggins begins reading the message: "Short on chaplains right now. Infantry comes first. Chaplain Strom can stay. D. McGinty."

There is a long silence. Richard is staring at the ground in front of him while Huggins continues looking at the piece of paper he is holding. "Do you think you can make it through a few more weeks with us, Padre?" the colonel questions earnestly.

Richard says nothing for close to one-half a minute, then turns toward his CO finally responding, "Hard to answer that question— about being able to make it a few more weeks with the battalion. Three months ago I didn't think I could take another ninety days with *Two-five* but I made it. So I don't know what to tell you, Colonel Huggins." His voice now trailing off into silence. However, concurrently the chaplain is aware that way down deep inside he hardly could give a rip one way or the other!

The reverie is broken by the sound of rifle fire off in the distance and the beginning of a fierce firefight. Huggins stands immediately, thrusts the message in his pocket, and says quickly, "Chaplain, I won't force you to stay but I'd like to keep you as a part of my staff. You do a good job with our troopers. Let me know tonight what you're gonna do, okay?"

Chaplain Strom nods, then watches the colonel hurry off to the CP one hundred meters away to find out what Fox has run into. He has mostly forgotten about the normal procedure of sending chaplains back to the rear after six or seven months in the bush. It just isn't something that comes up in his mind anymore. His focus now is on staying alive and garnering whatever energy that is left in him to just face each morning. He is also keenly aware that each day he remains in Vietnam, it takes more and more energy and personal resolve just to make it through the collage of terror, boredom, and repetition that marks the living experience out in the bush.

Strom remains seated on the log for many minutes, staring down at the ground, listening to the sounds of the heavy firefight and mortars going off in the distance, as if that living and dying experience two kilometers away might just as well be six thousand kilometers away or on another planet.

He slowly takes his Kbar out of its sheath, leans over his feet, and begins scraping the dirt off his boots, then digs at the mud stuck on the bottom of the soles, aware that he is essentially withdrawing from whatever is going on now with Fox or battalion. Six or eight months ago he would have been proactive the instant he heard any sounds of battle, immediately rushing to the CP to find out what he could do or where he could go to be near the wounded or dying. Such a long time ago! But now it's almost like he cannot hear, see, feel anymore—as if he can just disconnect from the whole scene and clean his boots or pick his nose or just sit and stare.

The dissociative, blank non-thought is suddenly broken as Richard is startled by the sound of the doctor's voice: "Hey, Chaplain, whatcha doing over here, having a nervous breakdown?"

Richard slowly grabs the knife by the blade and throws it into the ground between his feet and the doctor. He looks up and says flatly, "Nah, it's much more complicated than that. What's up?"

Chaplain Strom stands up as the battalion surgeon continues, "Colonel says we've gotta get our shit together right now. As soon as it's dark, which will be in about a half hour, we are going to have another night move."

Although the chaplain is staring right at Jonsen's face, he is looking right through him, images of the past two night moves flashing in his mind. Both of them have been marred by destruction and the death of the few remaining friends and acquaintances he has left in battalion.

He blinks his eyes a few times, slowly shakes his head, turns, and walks toward the BAS, resigned to his fate whatever that might be, not caring whether he stays with battalion or be sent back to a rear assignment in Da Nang. As he approaches the corpsmen who are presently packing their gear for the night march, a kneeling Smitty looks up at Strom and says with a grin on his face, "Hey, Chaplain, heard you're gonna stay with us till it's time for your freedom bird?"

Richard stops to observe the young corpsman who still hasn't seen enough to be jaded and jagged, then kneels down next to him, and replies, "Don't know where you heard that. Nothing has been decided." Smitty zips up the remaining medical bag, then turns toward the chaplain, still kneeling, and responds, "Chaplain, you know that I'm really glad you're out here with us in the bush. We all are. But with all due respect, sir, why are you staying out here when you can get a life back in the rear? It's much healthier in Da Nang!"

Still kneeling, Richard is quiet for fifteen seconds, stands, and slowly surveys the village fifty meters away, then turns toward the young man who had grown up in the black ghetto of south central Los Angeles, aware of the care and admiration he has for him.

"I don't know how to answer that, Smitty," Strom answers slowly, deliberately, "if I had to do it all over again I would have taken that assignment three months ago when the division chaplain offered me a position over at the Eleventh Marines near Da Nang. But at the time I just couldn't see myself with an artillery outfit—playing cards all day, sitting around every night, bored out of my mind. I guess, well, maybe I just felt like I was needed out here." The chaplain shrugs his shoulders and continues, "Then again, like everything else over here, we are all expendable commodities. There's always someone to take our place. Kind of vain, isn't it, to think we can make a difference. Anyway, ahh, don't know, maybe I'll get early orders back to the States if I stay out here."

"Don't sell yourself short, Chaplain," responds the young corpsman, "you are making a difference."

Richard Strom smiles, recognizing the irony of the moment, replies quickly, "You know what Smitty? I'm the one who's supposed to be spreading morale and listening to people. Thanks for the pep talk."

"No problem, sir," Smitty replies as he stands up, a big smile on his face. "Just leave a donation in my poor box. Help defray the cost of that '65 Mustang I'm gonna buy when I get back home."

The battalion chaplain returns the smile and turns away to go back to his equipment, feeling a tinge of nostalgia and sadness as he quickly flashes on the many friends and acquaintances that have passed through his life the past ten months. Lost in thought he nearly bumps into Major Copeland, who has his full gear on and is ready for the night hump.

"Whoops, sorry, Major," the startled chaplain quickly blurts out, then steps back to observe the fully combat-ready ops officer, who is holding a message in his hand. "Chaplain, I think you better read this," Copeland responds ominously.

He hands the slip of paper to Strom who quickly reads the message. Wordlessly he looks up at the silent ops officer, then reads the message again. "Chaplain," the major begins softly, "the colonel hasn't seen the message yet so you'll need to get to him right away. Better get your gear together first because we're scheduled to leave within ten minutes." With that said he softly places his hand on Strom's shoulder and continues, "If you need me for anything, let me know." Then he turns and walks away.

Richard slowly walks toward his gear a few meters away, reading again the message given him by the major. He quickly throws his loose gear into his pack, puts on his helmet and flak jacket, and slings his pack onto his back and communion kit over his neck and left shoulder, then makes his way in the growing darkness toward the area where he assumes he'll find the colonel. Within seconds he sees Huggins ahead on the radio talking to one of his company commanders and walks slowly toward him as he finishes giving instructions.

Colonel Huggins turns toward his chaplain and says quietly, "Ready to roll, Chaplain?"

"I guess so, sir," Richard responds nervously. "Don't know if I'm ever ready for a night move. Ah, Colonel, if I could just have a few private moments with you, sir?"

"Sure, Chaplain," he says immediately, always cordial and accommodating toward his chaplain, "but we've gotta get a move on shortly."

Richard walks with his commanding officer away from the six Marines clustered around the colonel, then stops with him thirty meters away. He is holding the message in his hand as he turns toward Huggins.

"Colonel," Strom begins, "we've just received some bad news about your father. Sir, he passed away yesterday from a heart attack."

The silence is stunning as the colonel continues to stare at Chaplain Strom as if the words he had just heard were uttered in error or he was experiencing some kind of surreal dream state.

"Can I see the message," he responds softly, slowly reaching for the piece of paper in Richard's hand. For an eternity, perhaps twenty seconds, he reads and rereads the brief message: "Father died yesterday heart attack. Plans incomplete. *Can you come home?* Love, Marian." Huggins takes off his helmet, turns, and slowly walks away from Chaplain Strom and sits down on an empty ammo box twenty meters away, continuing to stare at the piece of paper containing the shocking news of his father.

Strom is immobile, not sure if he should intrude on the colonel's solitude. He waits for perhaps thirty seconds, then slowly makes his way toward his shocked commanding officer. He stands in front of him for another thirty seconds, then Huggins looks up at him as Richard breaks the silence: "I'm terribly sorry, sir, about your father, especially out here. Being so far away and isolated like we are makes us feel even more helpless."

Colonel Huggins nods slowly. "You're right about that, Chaplain. Makes one feel pretty powerless," he says as his voice trails off, now looking away from Strom, a tear slowly meandering down his cheek.

There is another long, awkward silence. Richard slowly squats down in front of Huggins who now turns back face to face with his chaplain. He looks down at the deck, then back up, gathering his thoughts. "He's had heart failure for the past few years, but no matter how hard you prepare for it, the end is really hard to deal with. Guess you know all about that, huh, Chaplain?"

"Death lays us all low, Colonel, no matter how much we think we are prepared for it," Strom responds, "not being around family and friends makes us feel even more isolated and separate."

"I'm also facing a dilemma," the colonel continues slowly. "A part of me wants to go home and be with my family—I have six brothers and sisters. We're all pretty close. That's my natural instinct, to go home and be with my mom and family. But…" Huggins stops speaking, stands up and walks slowly around the ammo box and away from Richard. "I also don't want to leave my command, Chaplain." There is along, silent pause, then turns back toward Strom and continues. "First, since I'm relatively new to our outfit, it's not good for my staff and the troopers under our command to change again—not that Major Copeland couldn't handle the chore. This is an outstanding group of men but they need continuity and consistency."

Huggins turns back toward Richard and places his arm on his shoulder. "Chaplain, my guess is that you can understand my reluctance to go back home and leave the battalion, can't you?"

"Yes, sir, I certainly can," he replies.

Another long pause, then the colonel continues, "There is also another reason that creates an even heavier issue with me, one that you probably might have trouble understanding, having been in the military less than two years. Ah, that right, Chaplain?"

"That's right, Colonel." Strom nods in agreement. "About a year and a half."

"And I hear you're not going to make a career out of the naval service, that right as well?" he questions.

"That's correct, Colonel," he responds.

It is almost dark now and Richard is finding it difficult to see Huggins, so he steps closer to make out his face, a face whose affect shows sadness and consternation. "Chaplain, I graduated from the naval academy in 1948 and requested the Marine Corps for permanent duty, something I've wanted to do since I was a kid. My goal in life was to become an officer in the Marine Corps."

Richard can see Huggins is close to tears as he continues, "After graduation my first occupational choice was to become an infantry officer. That's all I wanted—the infantry! What evolved out of those first two choices," he now states convincingly, "was my strong desire, you might call it an obsession, to get command of an infantry battalion. Well, I have my life dream right in front of me, Chaplain, and I'm finding it extremely difficult making the right decision. I have equally competing forces inside of me."

He suddenly stops talking, shakes his head back and forth, a sad, painful look on his face, then begins to speak again, anger and frustration in his voice, "Which family do I respond to, Chaplain? Either way I'll get kicked in the ass. Go home and be pissed for the rest of my life because I gave up my life dream, or stay here and feel guilty until death us do part because I didn't respond to my family's needs! So what would you do, Chaplain, how do you get through that kind of a paradox? Attend to your dad's death or stay with your troops?"

Unnoticed because of the commanding dynamics and feelings of the moment, Major Copeland has silently approached the two men in dialogue, apprehensive lest he disrupt what he knows must be a riveting and very personal conversation going on with the colonel and chaplain.

There is an awkward silence, then Strom turns toward the ops officer and states indifferently, "Yes, sir, Major, what's up?"

"Colonel," Major Copeland begins, "I'm truly sorry to interrupt this conversation, sir, but the skipper of Hotel is waiting for your command to begin their move and Fox has made contact on the other side of the hill."

Lt. Col. Huggins takes a big deep breath, stares at Richard for a few seconds, then turns toward his ops officer. "Tell Sergeant Bailey to get the skipper back on the horn, then get me Fox 6. After that tell the rest of the staff we leave in five minutes."

With that the three men began walking toward the forward CP. The colonel suddenly stops and places his right hand on Strom's shoulder: "I guess I've answered my own question, Chaplain, how I responded just seconds ago. I believe this is where I need to be at this time." Huggins pauses for five seconds, then continues, "I think my dad would understand.

"Yes, sir, Colonel," Strom replies, "good choice. When I get I chance," he continues as they begin to walk, "I'll contact Father O'Hearn at regiment and have him say a mass of intention for your dad. Isn't that what you Catholic folks call it, a mass of intention?"

"Yeah, that's what we call it, a mass of special intention," he replies evenly. "Thank you for thinking of that. And, Chaplain, thanks for listening."

"No problem, sir," he says, then continues, "Ah, Colonel, about that message from Father McGinty, the one about your request? Well, ah, guess I'm here for the duration."

In the dark Richard is barely able to make out the face of Huggins who then states, "Good choice, Padre." They continue on when seconds later the colonel says lightly, "Hey, you know what, Chaplain Strom, you're all right, even for a Lutheran!"

"That's my line, Colonel," Strom quickly replies, aware again of how sardonic humor and laughter are used to cover over layers of emotional pain and apprehension.

Within five minutes battalion has their lines ready to move. Within fifteen they are crossing the open terrain around the mountainous finger to the north where Fox had earlier encountered enemy troops in the villages called Phu Phong. The fierce firefight has stopped and the VC has vanished into the darkness of the multiple villes and tree lines and bamboo groves as they always do—silent, inscrutable, elusive, and extremely dangerous for the Marines who are attempting to engage them.

There is nothing sane about a night move, especially when there is no moon to bring any semblance of light to the black night. American troops are very clear about the underlying reality of Vietnam and who controls the countryside. Daylight means tanks, jets, and the ever-present helicopter ferrying troops and supplies at will, promoting the illusion that the Americans are in charge and can control their environment. However, nighttime brings a paradigm shift in both perception and reality. Because after dusk the VC and NVA own the countryside. They decide when and where and how they will engage. And when they inevitably do, the deadly mixture of darkness and incoming usually means pandemonium no matter how disciplined or experienced the combatant is.

It is 0430 and the forward elements of battalion are now passing through the area secured yesterday when Echo was airlifted from An Hoa to join battalion. Silently the troops containing battalion forward headquarters, including the BAS and the chaplain, move on through the villages, Hotel strung out for almost a kilometer ahead. Beyond them, forward elements of Fox have reached the southern bank of the Son Vu Gai River and the notorious villages named Minh Tan that the Marines had bombed just before the night move begin. In back of them Golf has entered the villages of Nam An that Hotel and battalion had left behind yesterday.

Only four kilometers from Hills 52 and 100—those two coordinates of land that had destroyed so many Golf and Echo lives eleven months ago—Minh Tan is the area where recon lost two squads of Marines the past two months. That mountainous finger jutting into the flat plains of Arizona Territory is again becoming a major infiltration route into the villages that dot the landscape and also flow eastward all the way into Da Nang fifty kilometers away. *Two-five* will become the primary blocking force—as they always seem to be—and perhaps end up on Highway 4 or even Hill 52 again.

Although the whole area has been declared a free-fire zone for the past eighteen months, there are peasants still living in their ancestral homes, gradually, insidiously moving back to their home villages in spite of the perils this creates for them. Artillery and bombing strikes are permitted without regard to the safety and well-being of the civilian population and the peasants are also at the mercy of local VC or the Marines, depending on which outfit is present and what time of the day it is—Marines in charge during the day, the VC living in the villages at night.

The column has stopped next to a small stream that runs south from the main river and through the middle of the village. Exhausted beyond capacity from lack of sleep and anxiety, Richard is lying down against his pack, helmet and flak jacket still on, communion kit draped under his arm. He is feeling a level of depression and flatness that he has never experienced before, a disconnection that severs all his senses and thoughts except for a gnawing, anticipatory, anxious projection that something isn't right, that some kind of catastrophic experience is about to unfold. Quickly, quietly, word is passed that they are to line up and move out. Stop and go, lie down and get up, move out, sit down, stand still for minutes at a time, then move out again, not knowing what the next few minutes will bring, following orders blindly in true Marine Corps tradition, pretending that the night will hide the move but knowing full well the enemy is following every advance and will pick their time and place should they choose to engage.

All four line companies are strung out from the south end of the finger all the way north to the river, a stretch of about four kilometers. Battalion staff is now moving north with first platoon of Hotel, anticipating a hump of one more click before setting up a CP and operations center. Except for the occasional reciprocal exchange of small arms fire Fox is experiencing as the point company, the rest of the companies have not taken any fire nor have they tripped any booby traps—miraculous for a night move.

Finally after the incessant stop/go scenario of moving in the dark, word is passed to set in and dig holes, a hopeful sign the hump is over for now. Hotel and Fox are ahead, along the river in the villages collectively called Minh Tan. Across the river elements of the Seventh Marines are blocking Highway 4, past Hill 52 and two kilometers north to the mountains. The Marines will now wait in fixed positions to stop the movement east of enemy troops and supplies from the mountains and the labyrinth of sophisticated pathways and roadways called the Ho Chi Minh trail.

Light is beginning to show over the hills to the east casting crimson and orange colors broadly across the early morning sky. With light comes some relief but that too can be an illusion. Dusk and dawn are dangerous—Marines are usually setting into a new perimeter or arising from sleep, making them more vulnerable to attack.

For the past ten minutes battalion corpsmen have been digging holes and setting up their medical equipment, ready for an emergency should it arise. Richard is now asleep on the deck, disregarding orders to dig a hole for protection. Fifty meters away battalion staff has set up their radios inside a hooch adjacent to a bamboo grove and Huggins is speaking to the skipper of Hotel, a look of dismay on his face. He hands the phone to his radioman, then turns to Major Copeland: "Major," he begins slowly, "Hotel just came upon a pretty bad situation."

The S3 says nothing, waiting for the Colonel to continue. Huggins takes a deep breath, turns away from Copeland, and stares ahead, shaking his head as if he doesn't want to acknowledge what he was just told. Turning back to his operations officer, the colonel takes another deep breath and continues, "Last night our bombers hit the village of Minh Tan 2 because intelligence believed that a battalion of NVA was occupying the area."

Huggins stops again and turns away from Copeland and walks to his radioman and says quickly, "I want to talk to Hotel 6 again." As he is waiting for Sergeant Bailey to make the hookup, he turns back toward the major and says softly, "Instead of whacking some enemy soldiers, it looks like we destroyed a number of villagers."

Copeland winces as Huggins begins talking to the new skipper of Hotel, Captain Billy Gould. "This is six, Skipper, how many civilian casualties do we have on our hands?"

There is a long silence as the CO listens intently, then replies tersely, "I want that count as soon as possible, out!"

He quickly wheels around and yells to no one in particular, "Jesus Christ, what kind of insanity is this! We can't be blowing up civilians. Goddammit, this is awful!"

"What about the injured, sir, do we need to get a medevac fragged?" the major questions.

"Can't find any survivors," Huggins responds, "if there were any, they must have split. Get me Chaplain Strom on the double."

Two minutes later, Richard Strom is standing in front of his commanding officer, groggy and irritated that he has been awakened for what he assumes will be a discussion about when and where he is to have worship services. Shortly he is being briefed on the calamity Hotel has uncovered.

"Maybe fifteen or twenty dead at least, Chaplain, we just don't know," Richard hears Huggins say quietly, aware that he is presently devoid of any feelings of aversion or dismay brought on by the tragedy. "I'm going to get a squad from first platoon and I want you to go with them to the village where third platoon is located. Some of the troopers are pretty devastated by all the dead civilians. I want you to talk to them and if need be, maybe have church services as well."

"Yes, sir," Strom replies flatly, "I'll get packed and be ready to move in a few minutes."

"Chaplain Strom," Huggins responds quickly, "I sure appreciate what you're doing for those boys over there. And thanks again for staying with us."

"Yes, sir," the chaplain says quietly, then turns and walks back to his gear.

Within ten minutes the squad is moving through second platoon's perimeter and within twenty-five minutes they arrive at Minh Tan 2. The destruction in the small ville is unbelievable. The five-hundred-pound bombs have destroyed everything within three hundred meters—not a tree, not a hooch is left standing. The shock and dismayed looks on the faces of the young Marines is obvious. Richard is directed to a large mound of dirt overlooking a huge hole ten meters across. Standing next to the hole is the platoon leader, 1st Lt. Manuel Rios and the skipper, Captain Gould.

They both turn toward the chaplain, and salute. Richard does not return the salute but instead puts his arm out to shake their hand. He stopped saluting out in the field months ago. Off to the right about twenty meters away he sees the mutilated bodies of young children and women. Third platoon had been given the ghastly chore of gathering body parts and bodies and bringing them to this central location.

The skipper breaks the silence. "Colonel says we're to bury the bodies as best as we can and mark the area for later identification." Chaplain Strom says nothing, continuing to stare at the mass of bodies a few meters away.

The bulk of the platoon is now gathered within the devastated area. Thereupon the chaplain slowly walks toward the civilian bodies laid out neatly, most of them in various stages of dismemberment. The scene is absolutely abominable, a nauseating and horribly dehumanizing experience. All those innocent young children and women slaughtered by our bombs because they didn't understand the concept of free-fire zones and domino theories and economic assumptions. They just wanted to live in peace in their ancestral villages, that's all.

Richard James Strom slowly approaches the bodies. He is so shocked by the scene in front of him he can feel no outrage, no sadness, no guilt. More like being in a dream state, he is unable to grasp the enormity of this experience. Richard stands still for thirty seconds, then stiffly kneels in the mud in front of the bodies. After a minute that seems forever, two tears emerge from his eyes. No sobbing, no crying, just some tears slowly moving down his cheeks. Quietly, 1st Lt. Rios has walked up behind the chaplain. He crosses himself, stands quietly for a few moments, crosses himself again, and walks away from the kneeling chaplain.

Strom's thinking processes are silenced, he is mute, as if his spirit is smothered. But gradually, percolating up from way deep in his soul, there is a stirring. A single word slowly begins to ferment and solidify—only a single word—"Why… why… why?" He lingers for many seconds in that consciousness, those words rolling off his lips over and over again.

But another reality is tugging at him simultaneously, the reality of guns and Marines and living and dying and eating and sleeping. He slowly, willfully begins to withdraw from his reverie, becoming aware of another presence, of an energy that he can feel behind him. He slowly, stiffly stands up, turns to see that just about every Marine in the platoon has been standing still, observing the chaplain kneeling in front of the dead Vietnamese women and children.

Richard takes a deep breath, brushes the mud off his knees, and walks back to face that existence, questioning if there will ever, again be another reality.

Diary Entry—312 Days In-Country

Last night a Marine attempts to shoot his index finger clean off his hand and botches the job. Says he was just cleaning his gun. Starts a firefight as well. Hell of a way to get out of the bush. Shoot yourself and get your friends almost shot because of the ensuing firefight that starts between two different squads. Wonder how he is feeling about himself— can anyone feel anyway—getting medevaced to Da Nang? They'll just reroute him from the hospital to the brig to An Hoa and back to the bush again. He'll be back.

Today, I'm thinking about that Marine. Maybe he was still feeling and thinking straight, still alive inside, which made him choose to do what he did. No blocks of concrete in his head—yet—for that fellow. Quiet admiration / public disrespect is what I saw from most of the grunts who understood why:

> *Sometimes when the firing is greatest*
> *Primal fear screaming inside*
> *A shot is fired*
> *Who knows where*
> *Carefully aimed*
> *A moan is heard*
> *A ticket home*
> *War's end*
> *He shot himself*
> *To life*
> *Ha, ha, ha*

Counting the Days

The Marine helicopter does a quick pass over First Medical Battalion Hospital, executes a starboard bank and slowly spirals down to the helipad, cautiously setting down on the steel-matted deck. Instantly two passengers in full battle gear exit the back of the CH46 and are met by six stretcher bearers coming from triage, two of whom enter the chopper with a stretcher. Inside four seriously wounded Marines are lying on the deck being tended to by the crew chief and a chaplain who flew in with the wounded. The entering corpsmen cautiously roll a wounded Marine onto the stretcher, then exit the aircraft. This is repeated for the next three troopers. The injured are immediately rushed into triage where they are quickly undressed, their bandages carefully removed, then evaluated for x-rays, immediate surgery, or any other needed intrusive medical procedure. The process is quick and intense and requires total focus on the part of the attending doctors and corpsmen. Whatever expertise they lacked in training upon arriving in Vietnam, they gain in experience from the weekly, daily, hourly, minute-by-minute life-and-death struggle they face each time a Marine comes through the triage doors.

Within two minutes the LZ controller is signaling the helicopter to take off, having been informed another medevac is coming in for a landing. The chopper begins to rev up to full power just as the chaplain who came in with the medevac suddenly runs out of triage and back out to aircraft. He disappears inside the aft door for ten seconds, then reappears and runs back toward triage, backpack and communion kit carelessly slung over his shoulders. Slowly, the chopper lifts off, makes a port turn, then moves off to the north as another medevac slowly spirals in from the south.

Reaching the end of the tarmac the chaplain wearily flops down onto the bench adjacent to triage and next to the Rose Garden. He slings his gear on the deck, leans back against the corrugated metal wall, takes a deep breath and remains immobile for the next three minutes, oblivious to the next chopper coming in for a landing or the life-and-death struggle taking place next door. His boots are scruffy yellow, his utilities are dirty and muddy, as are his hands which also are stained with blood, he hasn't shaved for four days, and his eyes are dark and sunken. Were it not for the two silver bars on his right collar and the gold cross on his left, and the lack of a rifle or weapon, he could have been mistaken for any of the hundreds and hundreds of Marine grunts who have just come in from the bush.

There has been very little contact by any of the line companies for five days after the Minh Tan tragedy, so the colonel asked Chaplain Strom to catch a supply chopper into Da Nang to visit the troops and also stop by the division chaplain's office to check on when his field replacement was due. Marshall had also arrived back in the field after getting back from R&R in Bangkok, so he was left behind to work with the BAS should they need any help during Strom's absence.

After the morning supply had been brought in, the routine helicopter picked up the chaplain for his journey to division. However, three minutes into the flight the mission was changed. Instead of flying directly back to Da Nang, they were ordered to pick up some seriously wounded Marines who had been ambushed earlier that morning across the bridge from Phu Lac 6 and deliver them to First Hospital Battalion. When the crew chief yelled over to Strom about the change, Richard was incredulous that again; no matter where he went or what he did, he always ended up in harm's way.

With his eyes closed, the chaplain reaches into his breast pocket and pulls out the two letters he had just received prior to leaving the battalion thirty minutes ago. He remains motionless for a few seconds, then his eyes open. Slowly he opens the first letter from his wife and begins rereading the contents, holding in his other hand the latest two photos of his now fourteen-month-old son. When he finishes reading the letter, he stares for a few seconds at the pictures of his baby son, then carefully folds the letter with the photos, places them back in the envelope, then stuffs the envelope back in his breast pocket. The second letter from his dad he opens for the first time and begins to read its contents.

Dear Dick:

This is a quick letter. Sorry it can't be longer as I have to leave shortly for a meeting Mother wrote you last month that your cousin Georgia Gould was very ill with cancer back in Minnesota. We just got word this morning that she passed away last night. I know how close you were to her and how much she meant to you and your brothers. Sorry the news has to come to you this way. Mother will send you a letter soon to give you more details. If you have time send a note to Aunt Ruth and Uncle George.

Jimmy will be going to San Jose State again next semester. Fritz got into a fight with another dog; got bitten bad but the vet says he'll be okay.

We all miss you very much and are anxiously awaiting your return home soon.

Love,
Dad

Chaplain Strom slowly puts that letter back in the envelope and then into his pocket, leans back again, and closes his eyes. His mind is blank, as if the slate in his brain is wiped clean no thought, no feel, nothing.

Then slowly the forgotten images of his youth began to rise. Having grown up in a family with five boys and no sisters, Georgia, living close by in the next farm town, was designated by the Strom boys as their older sister. She was dearly loved and respected. When Mom and Dad Strom expected bucking by the boys on some issue, many times Georgia's presence would somehow seem to materialize.

Oppositional behavior would mysteriously disappear when she was part of the limit setting. She taught them how to drive years before they got their license and took them to baseball games, fishing, and the show at her family's local theater when their parents were too busy.

The images are there but there are no feelings attached to them—just images—as if Marilyn's death has as much impact on him as going to the park or driving the car or eating a hot dog. One of the most important people in his life has died and Richard Strom hasn't a sad feeling or a tear or a negative thought about her passing.

"Hey, buddy, what's happening?" Richard suddenly hears as he is jolted out of his reverie and sees his good friend the Monk next to him. "Good grief," he continues with a smile on his face as Richard stands, "don't you Lutherans ever bathe?"

They embrace. Strom picks up his gear and says, "What are you doing here, Monk? I thought you were out of here!"

"Leaving tomorrow, old buddy," he replies as Richard picks up his gear. "I have orders to the naval station in Corpus Christi, Texas. Enough of the Marines." Strom nods but says nothing in response to Vince's good news.

"Have you seen John Rietch? Need to get some clean clothes and a bed," Richard asks.

They both are heading toward the chapel back of the tarmac. Vince puts his hand out to stop Richard's advance, then quietly says, "Guess you haven't heard about John."

Chaplain Strom stares at Gerlitis for a few seconds, no expression on his face, then says, "What are you talking about? I mean, no I haven't heard. Is there something I should know?"

Vince begins walking again toward the chapel, Richard next to him. "You know how he liked to take a weekly ride out with a medevac chopper, to get out of the hospital and experience some action? Well, this time he ended up way back in the boonies, someplace out where a recon patrol was ambush near the Laotian boarder," Vince begins. "I think this happened about three days ago."

Strom is staring straight ahead, curious but not upset about the information he is hearing. Cautiously, quietly, because he is aware of the good friendship Richard has with the hospital chaplain, Gerlitis continues, "The chopper never got to the assigned coordinates to pick up the wounded patrol. Apparently they had no contact with the chopper and were unable to raise them at all after they were about twenty kilometers west of An Hoa."

Richard stops and turns toward the Monk and says, "So what are you saying, Vince? They haven't been heard from in three days?"

"Yeah," Vince responds as he opens the door to the chaplain and surgeon's hooch. "That's the deal. They've been out searching but because of the rain up in the mountains it very difficult to see anything."

They quietly enter John's hooch. Inside Gerlitis points to an empty bed and says flatly, "Phil's gone on R&R, you can use his bunk tonight. I'm staying here tonight and cover for John in his absence."

Strom drops his gear on the deck and wearily sits down on the bed, leans over placing his arms and elbows on his thighs, continuing to stare at the floor, and says flatly, "Another one bites the dust, huh?"

"Don't know for sure, they're continuing to look for them," the Monk replies.

There is a long silence, uncommon when these two are together. Finally Vince walks over to the bed, sits down next to Richard, and continues, "Hey, look, how about I round up some clean utilities, you get showered and cleaned up, get your visiting done with your troopers, then tonight we'll go over to division mess and have some barbecued steaks and beer. You look like you need some good food. You're getting skinny, old buddy!"

"Yeah, why not?" Strom responds after a long pause, continuing to stare at the deck.

"In the meantime, Rich, the Marines are continuing to search for the helicopter," the Monk continues, "and I'd like you to join me in saying a mass for their safe return."

Strom is silent for a long time, then responds cynically, "Hey, Vince, you know I'm not a Catholic priest, I belong to that renegade bunch. We do mass together and the Catholics will burn you at the stake and the Lutherans will make me live permanently with the Norwegians."

Vince puts his arm around Richard's shoulder and says quietly, "To hell with Lutheran and Catholic church polity, this is between the Lord, you, and I, okay?"

A smile slowly develops on Strom's face. He looks up and says with some animation, "How 'bout when I see McGinty this afternoon? I invite him to attend our ecumenical tryst. He can be our altar boy!"

The Benedictine monk suddenly howls with laughter, visualizing he and Richard celebrating the Eucharist together, the futsy division chaplain serving the two as their altar boy.

Two hours later Gerlitis and Strom are in the chapel just finishing the Eucharistic prayers, simultaneously appreciative of how much similarity there is in their respective liturgies, yet aware of the division and rancor that has existed for over four hundred fifty years between their denominations. The bread and wine having been consecrated, they then commune each other, repeating the ancient words of Christian unity with their Lord: "Eat and drink, this is the body and blood of our Lord and Savior, Jesus Christ."

The two clergymen then turn away from the altar toward the eight standing Marines who have attended the Eucharistic service, who now come forward and are communed. There is no awareness that these two chaplains in front of them represent two differing traditions or of the chasm that has continued to exist between their respective churches. Their consciousness is not dogma or theology or church polity but rather finding strength and sustenance and forgiveness in the sacrament, nothing more.

After church services Gerlitis and Strom leave the chapel and walk toward the motor pool to obtain a jeep for transportation to the division chaplain's office. After their visit with McGinty both of them will head over to NSA Hospital across the river to visit troops from their respective commands. This will be Vince's final visit to that hospital and his troopers before he boards his flight back to the United States tomorrow night. He also remained with his infantry battalion throughout his twelve months in-country.

Within five minutes they are walking into McGinty office where four chaplains are presently standing around the division chaplain's desk. McGinty is smiling broadly. He quickly gets up from his chair, walks toward the newly arrived chaplains, extends his hand and shakes theirs, then speaks quickly, "I've got very, very good news, men, but it is mixed with some sad news as well."

Richard looks immediately at Vince, who is standing stoically at McGinty side, then back at McGinty, assuming the chaplain has some innocuous comments about the chaplain corps or paperwork that he wants to share with his chaplains. "Oh yeah, what's up?" Strom questions.

"Chaplain Rietch has been found along with three others," he begins. "We are very thankful for this. The downside is that the crew chief was killed and the copilot was seriously wounded."

"Where's John?" is Strom's immediate response.

McGinty walks back to his desk, picks up some papers, motions for the six chaplains to sit down, then begins a monologue on what has transpired. "The CH-46 apparently had some engine problems while flying out to pick up an ambushed recon patrol. They set down into some trees, which broke the chopper apart. As the helicopter disintegrated the passengers literally fell out onto the trees and brush below. The crew chief died on impact and the copilot broke a wrist and both legs. The corpsman, pilot, the other gunner, and John all sustained light injuries. Their radio was destroyed, so for almost three days they waited in a clearing in the jungle for the overcast to lift and listened for a flyby, assuming the Marines were looking for them."

McGinty gets out of his chair, walks in front of his desk and sits down on it and continues, "Early this morning a helicopter flew over at about five hundred feet, they fired a flare, the chopper saw it, and the rest is history."

While McGinty is talking, Richard is looking around the room at the four other chaplains. Their uniforms are clean and starched; they are shaved and look happy, healthy and full of energy. He doesn't see a familiar face and realizes these guys must be the new replacements he had heard were due in shortly.

He turns back toward McGinty, interrupting the monologue: "Where's John? I want to see him right away."

The division chaplain scowls, not used to having his monologues disturbed. "He's, ah… he's at the, ah, I was attempting to come to that point before you interrupted me, Chaplain Strom," replies McGinty, an edge to his voice.

The newly arrived chaplains look at Strom as if he's out of his mind—which of course he is—having been in-country and with the infantry just over eleven months now. At this point he couldn't care less what improprieties he exhibits in spite of the fact the man is three ranks his senior. However, because of all his combat experience, the twenty-four days spent in the hospital, and his command's deference to him, there is no way McGinty is going to hassle Strom. Should he wish to show his displeasure, there are only two options the navy captain has—banish him back to the bush or send him home to the States.

The grungy battalion chaplain from An Hoa says nothing but continues to stare at McGinty, expecting an answer to his question. The division chaplain clears his voice, obviously distracted by Strom's apparent impertinence, walks back to his seat behind his desk and sits down. The silence is intense. Slowly a smile begins to cross Vince's face, that goofy-looking smile that materializes on his face when he is thoroughly amused by some situation but is unable to laugh out loud or make a comment. The other chaplains are frozen in place, like pillars of salt, anxious lest this situation somehow get out of hand.

"To continue what I was saying before I was interrupted," McGinty continues in a subdued voice, "they airlifted the injured back to NSA Hospital. It is my understanding Father Rietch will stay there for observation for twenty-four hours. He apparently cracked some ribs in the crash."

Upon hearing this, Strom pokes Gerlitis softly in the ribs with his elbow and declare, "Let's go, Vince."

They both turn to walk out the door as the division chaplain immediately stands, shakes his index finger at the two exiting chaplains, and says, "You two stay just where you are. We are having an orientation meeting for these new chaplains. When I'm done, I want to talk to Chaplain Strom—alone!"

The two chaplains stop, then slowly turn back toward the room as the Monk mutters under his breath, "The gestapo has spoken."

"What was that?" questions McGinnis as the two sit down in a chair, a stern look on his face. "What did I hear you say?"

"Oh, ah, I was just asking the, ah, chaplain here how his family is doing," Gerlitis responds.

The division chaplain stares at the Monk and Richard, dubious about the innocence of Vince's remark but unwilling to challenge the two respected combat-weary clerics. Concurrently the four recently arrived chaplains are riveted to their seats by the heavy tension they now experience. McGinty clears his throat to refocus attention once again on his agenda, like a court judge when he slams down his gavel to start proceedings.

"Okay, now… Ah, Chaplain Strom," he continues, "ah, after this meeting we need to talk about some matters that need to be resolved."

"With all due respect, Father McGinnis," Strom immediately responds, "my primary obligation is to my wounded troops in the hospital and the needs of my command. Colonel Huggins gave me a direct order that I am to be back in the field before dark, which means if I don't get out of here now, there's no way I can obey his directive."

Everyone in the room is now aware that Strom is walking a very thin line between duty to his command and just plain old insubordination toward a navy captain. Vince quickly clears his throat loudly, as if to signal Strom to pull back.

Richard pauses, then says, "It's very important that I get back out in the field. All my line companies are now out there operationally and I want to visit each one of them before my replacement comes." After another short pause he continues, "Don't you think it important, Father McGinty, that I see all my troops again before I depart?"

"Well, ah… yes, indeed," the division chaplain responds. "That's, ah, commendable. Certainly you need to do that as an important part of your, ah… ministry."

"Thank you, sir," Strom responds immediately, "your insight is greatly appreciated!"

He softly nudges the Monk in the ribs, then turns and begins walking out the door, saying, "Let's hit the road, Vince." The other chaplains sit stone-faced in shocked silence while Richard and Vince quickly sally out the door.

Walking toward the jeep, a smiling Vince stops Strom and says, "You know what, Lutheran, that guy just doesn't get it, does he?"

"Get what?" Strom questions."

"That being a chaplain and rank and all that crap doesn't mean diddlysquat with the Marines," he says emphatically.

They climb into the backseat of the jeep, the driver starts the engine and slowly motors down the driveway to the highway, then heads south for the twenty minute drive to NSA Hospital.

"The Marines will eat you alive and spit you out if you don't earn their respect," Gerlitis continues. "They must have McGinty for lunch every day. What a futz!"

"That's for sure," Strom responds. "That's for damn sure, Bucko!"

HEADING FOR THE LAST HURRAH

Chaplain Strom is lying on the deck next to the tarmac wearing his flak jacket, the top of his helmet under his head, attempting to get a few minutes of shuteye before the An Hoa Express arrives. It is late afternoon and he is going over the vicissitudes of the day's events—his chopper ride in this morning from the field, the "in your face" encounter at the division chaplain's office, his hospital visits at First Medical Battalion and NSA Hospital, the matter-of-fact goodbye to his best friend, Vince Gerlitis, just one hour ago. The day seems surreal. What he is aware of—again—is his lack of connection anymore to events, to people, to his work with Marines. Emotional disengagement now permeates his living experience. The fact that he is going home within two or three weeks inspires him no longer. Life has become shades of gray lacking the hues and intensity of color that resurrects life for the soul each waking day.

He chose not to return to see McGinty earlier that afternoon. He has neither the energy nor the presence of mind to interface anymore with the division chaplain, nor does he wish to talk to any of the new chaplains. His capacity for chitchat long ago left him. He dreads the thought that he will shortly be spending time with his new replacement helping him "snap in," hoping this is a chore he can somehow circumvent. "Let him get his feet wet on his own like I did," he broods, brushing away the ever-present flies from his face. What a contrast to eleven months ago when he would do anything, spend any amount of time to make his ministry meaningful and helpful.

A jeep slowly drives up to the tarmac and stops. A young Marine lieutenant jumps out of the backseat, grabs his valpack and seabag, walks to the tarmac, and drops them on the deck a few meters away from Strom. A .45 is strapped to his waist, his utilities are clean and starched and his helmet cover and flak jacket are brand-new.

The jeep slowly makes a U-turn, then heads back down the narrow road leading to the main highway one hundred meters away. Richard slowly opens his eyes as the young officer turns to face the prone chaplain. "Squared away and ready for action," Strom thinks to himself. Then as an afterthought, he thinks, "Poor bastard, doesn't know what's ahead of him." Then he shuts his eyes.

The lieutenant slowly walks the remaining five meters toward Strom so that he is almost on top of the chaplain, clears his throat, and says, "When's the chopper due, Marine?"

After a five-second pause, eyes remaining shut, the chaplain responds, "I haven't the slightest idea. Sit down and relax, Lieutenant, take a load off your feet."

The Marine is startled by the acerbic response, assuming the person lying on the deck is enlisted. "You're military courtesy stinks," he responds with irritation, then elevating the volume in his voice he continues, "You're talking to an officer!"

Richard opens his eyes, looks directly at the young lieutenant, slowly pulls his flak jacket open so the Marine towering above him can see his two lieutenant bars on his right collar and the cross on his left, then response caustically, "Yeah, and so are you, pal!"

There is a short, awkward pause. "Oh, ah, I'm sorry, sir, ah... Didn't know you were a chaplain, sir," responds the startled and embarrassed Marine officer. He then salutes the prone chaplain.

The chaplain does not return the salute. "Relax, have a seat and let go of any expectations that you can count on Sunshine Airlines to adhere to a schedule," he says as he sits up, rubbing his eyes. "You gotta name, Lieutenant?"

"Yes, sir, First Lieutenant Peter Gustafson, sir, everyone calls me Pete," the young Marine says nervously as he squats down and extends his hand.

Richard, still sitting, shakes his hand and says, "Chaplain Richard Strom, second battalion, Fifth Marines. Where you heading, Lieutenant?"

"*Two-five*, sir, like you," he quickly responds, "hopefully to a line company as soon as possible."

Not wanting to dampen the Marine's enthusiasm about his desire to get an assignment out in the bush, and hearing a helicopter off in the distance, Strom changes the subject. "Where you from, Pete?"

"I'm from Minnesota, Minneapolis to be specific," he answers quickly.

"No kidding," Strom responds smiling. "So am I. Grew up west of the Twin Cities near a small farm community. Ever hear of Glencoe?"

Smiling he replies quickly. "Yes, sir, my best friend in college had a girlfriend for a while from Glencoe, her name was Bernice Reed. Do you know her?"

"Don't know her but I know the Reed family," Richard states, feeling relaxed and aware of a sudden, momentary compassion for this young man from his home state. The sound of the chopper is getting louder, so Strom stands and says to the lieutenant who towers over him by six inches. "Looks like our ride is here. Welcome to Vietnam."

Within three minutes the aircraft is airborne heading west toward An Hoa, the two officers the only passengers aboard. Gustafson is seated across from Strom, gazing out the port side of the chopper, mesmerized by the fascinating, beautiful hues of green terrain below. The chaplain, seated directly across the aisle from the young officer, stares at the lieutenant, images of his first trip to An Hoa—full of enthusiasm, anticipation, and a low level anxiety driven by not knowing what lies ahead—streaming into his consciousness, experiences that seem like a millennium ago. There is only an inkling of nostalgia before the competing need to numb extinguishes any feelings. This need to numb is not a process he consciously works to implement. Rather it just happens, like breathing or walking or scratching one's head. Far too much life and death has been imploded into the past twelve months.

Fifteen minutes later the CH46 lands on the south tarmac. The two passengers pick up their gear and scramble out the aft door, then move quickly off the tarmac to the road heading south toward *Two-five*. The chopper immediately takes off and heads to the western area of the base where it will pick up ammo and food for delivery to one of the line companies in the field. "How far to battalion?" the young lieutenant questions, struggling with his gear.

"It's about half a click," Richard replies quickly, reaching to help Gustafson with his valpack. "Here, let me give you a hand."

Instead, he quickly places his gear on the deck and says, "Where can we get some transportation?"

Strom shakes his head slowly, then replies, "Lieutenant, if you have any expectation about getting ground transportation now or in the future, forget it!" The chaplain picks up the valpack and continues walking down the road ahead of Gustafson. "Lesson number one, out here or in the bush, your feet are the only transportation you can count on. Wheels are an illusion."

Gustafson slowly picks up his heavy seabag and follows the chaplain, gradually becoming aware of the sounds indigenous to a regimental field headquarters, especially late in the afternoon when the big guns are going off and the choppers are ferrying evening supplies to the Marines out in the bush. Switching the valpack to his other hand, Strom continues, "This isn't Quantico or the Marine barracks in Washington, DC. Lieutenant, there are no bellhops, you hustle your own gear."

Gustafson looks down at the crusty-looking chaplain walking next to him, smiles, and says, "Yes, sir, but I see you're carrying my valpack."

"This is different," Richard replies quickly, "I'm a dedicated servant of the Lord. Plus it's part of my duties as an infantry chaplain—page thirty-seven, Marine Corps Manual."

Walking due south now toward *Two-five*, a look of confusion on his face about the dubious and sarcastic remarks coming from his newly acquired battalion chaplain, Strom continues, "So what made you decide to leave the land of milk and honey back there in Minnesota and join the Marines?" Before he can answer the question, the chaplain continues, "Good pay, excellent food, or are you just a slow Swede like me that doesn't know any better?"

Gustafson scowls for a few seconds, then a smile slowly comes across his face. "Sir," he responds slowly, "are you sure you're a chaplain?"

Walking into the battalion compound, Richard points in the direction of the S1's office. "Sometimes I wonder what I am anymore," he replies softly, thoughtfully, then continues, "We'll head over there and you can get your assignment squared away, Lieutenant."

Reaching the steps of the office of H&S Company, Strom opens the door and walks in with Gustafson behind him, dropping the valpack on the deck in front of the seated S1—a straight-laced, by the book, up from the enlisted ranks first lieutenant that the chaplain briefly met only once before. Looking somewhat startled by this unannounced intrusion, he immediately stands at attention.

"Relax, Lieutenant," Strom says casually, pointing his thumb over his shoulder at Gustafson, "I just brought this new guy in here with me, name's Gustafson. I want you to cut him some orders so he can be my chaplain's assistant for the next two weeks." Turning back toward his new acquaintance, he continues, "Well, Pete, how about it? Wanna hang out with me for a couple of weeks? We can talk Minnesota together."

Gustafson is dumbfounded and says nothing while the S1 harrumphs loudly, then clears his throat and responds with a confused look on his face, "No, sir, ah, Chaplain, ah... First Lieutenant Gustafson is to be assigned to Echo Company," he responds, a very solemn tone to his voice. "With all due respect, Chaplain, Marine officers aren't trained for that kind of duty."

"Gee, that's too bad," Richard says, incredulous that Lieutenant Bush took him seriously. "I kinda thought that I deserved at least a first lieutenant to be my bodyguard since I have more time in the field than anyone else in the battalion."

Bush rigidly stands next to his desk, tongue-tied, unable to respond. Strom turns back toward Gustafson, disregarding the S1, shakes Pete's hand, and says warmly, "See you out in the field, my friend. I'm gonna see Echo one more time, maybe in a couple of days." With that said, he walks out of the office, back to his hooch, unlocks the padlock, and walks in. He dumps his gear by his rack, pulls three beers out of his refer, and gulps them all down within twenty minutes. Depressed that he will be returning to the field in the morning, he lies down and within fifteen seconds is asleep until 0600 the next morning, the most continuous sleep he's had in eleven months.

Diary Entry-339 Days In-Country

    They say time flies. Whoever coined that catchy phrase never served in a war zone, has not been ground up in combat day after day, crushing hope squeezing the life out of tomorrow's tomorrow:

> *Minutes become hours*
> *Months are years*
> *Days become a time machine*
> *That forces life*
> *Out of a future*
> *Only the present is infinite*
> *Shattering*
> *One's sense of balance*
> *When*
> *Past, present, future*
> *Are merged in endless combat,*
> *Faith, hope, love*
> *Are lost as experience*
> *Becoming only a fleeting*
> *Concept...*
> *How sad, how terribly sad...*
> *and hopeless.*

No More Left

The colonel is nervous again, reports having come from division intelligence that the Fifteenth North Vietnam Army Regiment has moved north into the foothills west of Arizona Territory and adjacent to *Two-five's* area of operations. This is the same outfit that created so much havoc with battalion four weeks ago at Hill 42 and blew up the ammo dump at An Hoa. Leaning against a tree, his helmet on the deck in front of him, Huggins just got off the radio to regiment. He is not a happy camper because Fox Company, over his protestations, is presently being lifted out of their position in the mountains east of Arizona this morning and assigned to regiment for security purposes. He is also holding a radio message slip in his hand.

He looks down at the piece of paper, then stares at Richard Strom standing in front of him. "I don't know what to tell you, Chaplain," he begins slowly, shaking his head. "The major and I really don't want you to go up to Golf and Echo. Losing Fox makes it pretty sketchy out there."

There is a long pause, then Copeland speaks. "You've got your orders now to go home, Chaplain. Don't be foolish and get into harm's way. You can take the resupply out this afternoon to An Hoa."

Richard says nothing as he adjusts his pack and communion kit, assuming he is to be on his way shortly. Huggins hands him the slip of paper he is holding and says, "You know this guy? He's your replacement and due in An Hoa this afternoon."

Strom looks quickly at the yellow message paper. "Nah, can't say that I do," he replies quietly, then continues, "Regarding Golf and Echo, they're the remaining line companies I haven't visited the past couple weeks. It's something I need to do, Colonel."

The two senior officers look at each other for a moment, then Huggins shrugs his shoulders and quips, "Okay then, do what you feel you must. I'm not happy with it but you gotta do what you gotta do. Be sure you take some security with you."

The battalion chaplain says nothing, turns to his assistant, and says, "Corporal Marshall, go get those three Marines you rounded up a few minutes ago, we're leaving now." He turns back to Copeland and continues, "Hopeful I'll be back tomorrow morning first thing, sir, so when I return, I'll be ready to get outta here, no doubt about that." He finishes with a big smile on his face.

"Sergeant Bailey, let Golf know that one-niner will be on his way shortly," Huggins replies, turning back toward his radio operator.

"Sir, they already know," Strom responds.

Lt. Col. Huggins turns back toward his chaplain, looks at Copeland, begins to say something, then shakes his head and walks away. He suddenly whirls around and points his finger at Strom. "That's pretty damn presumptuous of you, Chaplain, isn't it?"

Marshall fires a quick, nervous look at the chaplain. Richard says nothing for a few seconds, clears his throat, and replies, "Sir, with all due respect..." Then he hesitates a few more seconds before continuing. "You told me a few weeks back that you would support me in discharging my duties to the troops as battalion chaplain." Strom walks toward his commanding officer and continues, "You've been very supportive colonel and presumption was not in my thinking at all. Time is short. Just want to get all my bases covered before I leave."

Huggins slowly shakes his head in affirmation, places his hand on Richard's shoulder and answers, "You have my blessings, Padre, go take care of our troopers up there." He jerks his head in the direction of Golf. "And be careful out there, you hear?"

"You know what, Colonel, you sound more like a bishop than a commanding officer," Richard replies with a smile on his face. "Thanks for the special dispensation."

Within five minutes Marshall, Strom, and the three Marines secured from Hotel Company are walking past the BAS west into the foothills. Smitty, presently the corpsman in battalion with the most time in-country, is sitting on the deck playing cribbage with his best friend, Corry Nakamura, also a corpsman.

"Hey, Chaplain, you be careful up there and don't get hurt," Smitty says, slapping a card down on the ammo box in front of them. "I'm winning some cash." Don't want to have my card game interrupted and have to run up there to fix you guys."

"Ten percent of your winnings go to the Lord," Strom replies, slapping Smitty's outstretched hand as he walks by.

With a big smile on his face, he responds, "Yes, sir, I'm a believer in tithing!"

Leaving battalion behind and continuing west into the foothills toward Golf less than a kilometer away, two Marines walk ahead of the chaplain, followed by Marshall and a fourth Marine. Richard lacks his usual vigilance as he humps up the narrow, winding pathway toward Golf. Rather, he is distracted this morning by a collage of experiences that have transpired over the past few weeks, of faces and events and emotions that usually pull the need to shut down and go into no-think and no-feel. This morning he is finding it difficult to isolate and block off these experiences. He is especially focused on the three remaining people left in the battalion that have become like family surrogates, wondering what, if any, emotions will arise when he leaves to go back home tomorrow.

Lt. Col. James Huggins, a naval academy graduate from Virginia whose great-grandfather was a brigadier general for the Confederacy, has a quick wit and intelligence that reminds Richard of his own father. From the very beginning of their relationship back in Camp Pendleton, Huggins has always treated the twenty-nine-year-old Strom more like an equal than a subordinate. On occasion the colonel has sought out the chaplain to sometimes process stuff that is going on in his head. His father's death still weighs heavily on him and he continues to question the wisdom of remaining with the battalion. This morning Richard is feeling an empathy for Huggins, knowing how much he misses his dad.

"Hey, Bob," Strom says softly to his assistant following closely behind him, "how about you coming back to An Hoa with me tomorrow? I'll get you transferred to the battalion aid station until you get your orders to go home." The chaplain turns to face Marshall and continues, "That okay with you?"

"Yes, sir," his assistant replies.

The chaplain turns back, walks ahead for a few seconds, and says, "Don't want anything to happen to you. Understand, Bob?"

Strom turns back again and sees Marshall smiling. "Yes, sir. Anything you say, sir."

Since that very first day when Marshall came into his hooch to interview about the chaplain's assistant job, Richard has come to understand that selecting this kid was the best decision he would make in Vietnam—this young Marine who comes from Seattle blue-collar stock, the soft-spoken, very bright high school dropout who has beaten the chaplain in fifty straight games of chess the past nine months. "Marshall is with me so much, sleeping, eating, and dodging bullets together," Strom had commented to Dr. Grant, "that he feels like my kid brother—except I don't feel the need to kick his butt once in a while to keep him in line."

Within ten minutes the group is close enough to Golf's position to hear Marines ahead in conversation and also see four grunts walking down the trail toward them. The point Marine stops in front of the chaplain, salutes, then says nervously, "Sir, would the chaplain follow us back to the CP?"

"Relax, Corporal," Strom responds with a smile, then sticks out his hand to shake instead of saluting. "I'm here to have church services, not convene a court-martial."

Shaking Strom's hand, the Marine replies, "Yes, sir, the skipper wishes to see you immediately, sir." Then he turns and begins the walk back up the path.

The battalion chaplain turns toward Marshall and says casually, "Hey, Bob, I think he's got too much starch in his shorts. You guys in the Corps need to be more relaxed like your navy brethren." Bob smiles and says nothing as the group from battalion then follows the four Marines up the hill toward the CP.

Richard's mind quickly goes back over his recent encounter with Ronnie Smith, the ever-engaging, bright, courageous navy corpsman from south central Los Angeles whose singular purpose in life is to break through the invisible wall of prejudice indigenous to all of California's medical schools and become a physician. Upon completion of his time in the naval service, he is already planning his return to Long Beach State to finish his undergraduate work.

Always articulate and energized, Smitty is a free spirit who immediately puts everyone around him at ease with his bantering and genuine care for people. Unlike most of the Marines and Corpsmen who become jaded and withdrawn after a few months in-country, Ronnie Smith continues to dispense high quality medical care and project warmth and humor in spite of the urgency and pressure that comes with his job. He is a reminder to Richard of a part of himself that somehow got lost or has been crushed along the way.

The group finally comes into a small clearing next to a grove of trees. Adjacent to the trees a company CP has been set up and the new captain, the fourth Golf skipper since the chaplain's arrival almost twelve months ago, is squatting on the deck speaking with two of his platoon leaders. Strom and Marshall drop their gear, then Richard turns toward his security group. "Thanks a lot, fellows, for your help in getting me up here," the chaplain remarks as he shakes each Marine's hand. "Have a safe trip back." As the group turns to leave, he then says, "Tell Smitty I want an accounting of his gambling proceeds!" The four Marines disappear quickly down the trail.

Richard and his assistant then make their way slowly toward the three officers engrossed in conversation, stopping a short distance away staring at the squatting Marines. Suddenly the skipper looks up at the two people in front of him and says in a brusque, irritate voice, "What in the hell is so damn important that I need to be interrupted?"

Strom slowly removes his flak jacket exposing his collars. Immediately the three officers stand up, the skipper moves quickly toward Richard and says apologetically, "Sorry, Chaplain, I was busy here with some operational stuff." He salutes the chaplain, which Richard does not return but sticks out his hand and shakes the captain's hand instead. "I'm Captain Daniel Dugan, sir," he continues, turning then to his platoon leaders, "and these are Lieutenants Derrick Dobus and Rick Lano from our first and second platoons."

The battalion chaplain shakes their hands, then turns and introduces his assistant. "This is Corporal Bob Marshall. He's my assistant and a very important part of me getting anything done. He stays with me. No extracurricular activity for him, Captain."

"Oh, no problem, Chaplain," the captain replies, nervously looking at his officers. "I'm kind of new at this, Chaplain. The colonel says you want to have church services. Let me know what you want from us."

After the skipper informs Strom that the best time for services will be in about an hour, the two newcomers unpack their gear near the CP and next to the company corpsmen.

Marshall is on his knees pulling out his poncho liner and looks up at Strom. "Sir, what was that stuff about extracurricular activity?" he questions.

The chaplain is rummaging through his communion kit, looking for testaments and rosaries. "Remember back months ago when Goofy Golf was skipper and that butthead of a platoon sergeant attempted to put you out on the line?"

Marshall nods. "Yes, sir, I remember."

"Just a reminder to these new folks that it ain't gonna happen again, capish?" he answers.

Bob nods in acknowledgment. "You're different now, Chaplain," he begins quietly. "You don't take no crap from anybody anymore, even the colonel lets you have your way." The chaplain says nothing, gazing straight ahead lost in thought.

Within an hour Bob has set up a unique looking altar on a hillside overlooking battalion a kilometer away. Using two M-16 rifles with fixed bayonets inserted upside down in the dirt, he has attached a one foot by two foot PC-25 radio carrier on top of the rifle butts, then placed the cross, paten, candle holders, and chalice on top of the flat metal. Within fifteen minutes over one hundred Marines from Golf CP and first and second platoons are standing and sitting in a semicircle around the altar. Third platoon is further up the mountain two kilometers away on patrol, negating their attendance today. Five Marine sentries stand guard in back of the chaplain and to the rear of the assembled congregation.

Standing in back of the altar he makes the sign of the cross and begins: "In the name of the Father, and of the Son, and of the Holy Spirit." He slowly looks from left to right out at the assembly of Marines in front of him, flashing on those three communion services he held for Golf so long ago on Hill 87 while standing in the rain, astounded at the passage of time and the extraordinary, unimaginable life experiences that have thrust him into the present moment. Hands now folded, he bows his head slowly and remains silent for fifteen seconds, opens his eyes, and walks around the makeshift altar, finally standing almost on top of the seated Marines in the front row. Again his eyes slowly sweep the faces of the Marines in front of him, most of them still adolescents, kids who have been thrust into the machinations and politics of old men. They are the fodder of war—the ultimate squandering of the energy, resources, and idealism of youth. As his gaze locks onto these young men he sees anger, sadness, and fear but mostly vacant eyes that appear bereft of feelings. A profound sense of sadness begins to emanate from a place that Richard believed had been neutralized months ago. He swallows hard and takes a big breath, garnering his strength to keep those feelings locked into a tar pit of unrecoverable experiences. "Nice to see so many of you Marines out for church this afternoon," he begins. "Guess it's more fun being here than walking point." There is some scattered laughter as Chaplain Strom tugs on his ear for a few seconds stalling for time, still pushing down the sadness that came up so spontaneously moments ago. "Those of you that have been with battalion for more than a week—let's see, that's about ten of you, right?" Again laughter emanates from the Marines. "You've seen my mug around for quite a while and had to put up with the way I do things. I want all of you to know that I consider it a real privilege and an honor to have been your chaplain. The journey has been real difficult for all of you and I have the deepest admiration and respect for the Marines of this battalion and what you all have been through. Your courtesy and help and kindness will always be remembered. Within the next couple of days a new chaplain will be arriving. He is a Roman Catholic, so you Catholic guys will have a priest in your battalion for a few months, which helps to give balance to our religious coverage."

Richard pauses for a few seconds to shift gears, then speaks again. "I happen to come from the Lutheran denomination but that really doesn't mean anything out here. What is really important is that you pay close attention to your spiritual needs and to the dictates of your conscience because shortly I will be offering Holy Communion, or for some of you it is known as the Lord's Supper."

Richard takes a few steps back and continues, "All of you are welcome to receive communion. Whatever you decide is a choice between you and the Lord. He is looking into your hearts and at your needs now and that is all that is required."

The battalion chaplain turns and faces the altar and begins the ancient liturgy of the Eucharist. Fifteen minutes later communion has been served; again most of the Marines participate. Marshall and Strom place the paten and chalice back on the altar, then the chaplain turns again toward the standing Marines, bows his head, and begins a closing prayer: "Lord God, bring your protective love to these young men, who face life and death each day. Especially I commend them to your holy protective keeping—all who are far from home, friends, and loved ones; all who tonight must lie down hungry or cold; all who suffer physical or emotional pain; all who are kept awake by anxiety or suspense; all who are facing constant danger; all who keep the watch while others sleep. Please Lord, give them a sense of your presence, some semblance of peace, some respite from this terrible burden they bear. Abide with them, O Christ, our Lord, through all the days of their lives." Chaplain Strom now opens his eyes and slowly surveys the troopers of Golf for the last time. He lifts up both arms, palms out, and begins the blessing: "May the Lord save you while waking and defend you while sleeping, that when you awaken you will watch with Jesus Christ and when you sleep you may rest in his peace. Amen."

Soon after the benediction Strom and Marshall collect the small prayer books from the troops. Again, as always, the Marines linger for a minute or two before returning to their respective platoons and their daily routines. Richard always remains should any trooper wish to talk to him about a spiritual or personal matter. "Hey, Bob,"

Richard absently says, "aside from being the last time with Golf, did you know what was different about today?"

"No, sir," Bob responds as he packs the communion gear and cross into the kit.

Chaplain Strom gazes wistfully toward the Marines now leaving the area and continues, "Everybody is gone that I knew in this company. Just about every single face I saw at communion is new. Feels kinda weird, know what I mean, Bob?"

"Yes, sir," Marshall replies, "I sure do."

Their conversation is interrupted by Captain Dugan, who has been waiting off to the side. "Chaplain Strom," he begins, "thank you for coming up here and having mass for, ah, I guess you don't call it that in the Lutheran church."

Shaking the Captain's hand, Richard responds, "Whatever is comfortable for any of the Marines to call it, that's what it is. Keeps it simple and meaningful." Richard slings the communion kit over his shoulder and continues. "Captain Dugan, I need a favor from you. Any chance you can frag me and Marshall a bird for a ride up to Echo this afternoon?"

"Anything you want, Chaplain," the skipper responds, "although I was hoping you could maybe hang out with us tonight. Not much action going on around here. Third platoon will also be returning in the morning."

Marshall leaves to return the equipment used for the altar. The two officers turn and begin the walk back to the CP. "Thanks for the invitation, Captain," is Strom's reply. "Normally I would ask to stay overnight, get acquainted, visit with the troops, and show you how to eat well by avoiding C-rations. But tonight it's important I get up to Echo. Got some friends up there I want to see before I leave."

Approaching the makeshift CP, Richard drops his communion kit by his pack. Dugan walks to his radio operator and says, "Get me battalion, I need to get the chaplain here some transportation up the mountain to Echo."

The captain picks up his map, walks next to Chaplain Strom, unfolds it on top of some ammo boxes, kneels down, and motions for the chaplain to also kneel. "I'm going to show you where Echo is, at least this is where they were last night," he begins, pointing to an area on the map shaded dark green. "You know how to read coordinates, Chaplain?"

"Yeah, in an elementary way," Richard responds, bending over the topographical map. "First you locate vertical grid to left of point, then horizontal grid below point. That right, Skipper?"

"That's right," replies Dugan. "Here's the coordinates Chaplain—783502—where would that be on the map?"

The battalion chaplain scans the top carefully, then slowly his finger comes to rest on the far left side of the map. The skipper smiles, looks at Strom, and says, "Right on, Chaplain. That's exactly where they're supposed to be." He stands up and folds the map, placing it back in his case, then continues, "We'll get you up there as soon as we can."

The skipper's radio operator approaches the two officers with his PC-25. "Captain, sir," he begins with hesitation. "Ah, battalion six is on the horn. Got some news about Echo."

Dugan takes the phone and says, "Six, this is Golf, six, over." There is a long pause as the Captain listens to Huggins. He is looking directly at Strom. "Yes, sir, I'll tell him what their status is, then get back to you," Dugan replies, "out." Marshall has now joined Strom. The skipper walks closer to the chaplain and begins, "Sir, Echo has made contact and right now one of the platoons is engaged in some small arms fire." He pauses before he continues, "The colonel does not want you to go up there, he said that maybe you should come back to battalion."

Richard is quiet and looks at Marshall, then back at Dugan. "Captain Dugan, he said maybe. Was that a direct order or a permissive order from the colonel?" he asks.

"Chaplain," the skipper immediately replies, "you need to talk to Colonel Huggins about that."

"Unless there is a full-blown assault going on, I'm going up there, Captain," is Strom's answer. "So if you will, please get back on' the horn and tell them I still plan to go up there."

"There's one more thing, Chaplain," Dugan says somewhat ominously. "The new chaplain just arrived at battalion from An Hoa."

The chaplain scowls, kicks some dirt, and says with irritation in his voice, "What the hell is he doing out here?" Dugan shrugs his shoulders, then after a long twenty-second pause, Strom continues, "Here's what we'll do." He turns toward his assistant. "We'll have Corporal Marshall here go down to battalion with resupply so he can be with the new guy." He scratches his head and again kicks some more dirt. "Captain, I sure will appreciate it if you get that bird fragged for me," he says with authority, "and if the colonel doesn't like it, well hell, it's up to him to stop the process, right?"

"Sir," Marshall responds, "I respectfully request that I stay with you."

Captain Dugan walks away with his radio operator. Richard turns to his young assistant, places his arm on his shoulder, feeling relief that he will be sending Marshall to battalion. "I think the only way I'm going get past the Old Man on this one is to have you go back down and hang out with the new chaplain and take care of him. You might want to smack him around a little bit Bob so he can get used to being with grunts!"

Marshall smiles and responds like any good Marine does, "Yes, sir."

Two hours later Richard's assistant has been picked up by the resupply helicopter for return to battalion and he is awaiting a chopper to bring him to Echo four kilometers away up near the triple-canopy forests. The latest reports from battalion indicate that Echo second platoon has seen no further action. Awaiting his ride, the chaplain's thoughts are on the people remaining with Echo that he has continued to have a relationship with Sgt. Washington and L/Cpl. Martinez, the two young Marines who came into his hooch the day after Strom decked the inebriated and combatant Martinez; 1st Lt. Pete Gustafson, the young officer from his home state whom he met on the way back to An Hoa just days ago; and Staff Sergeant Mac, who may have already gone back to the States, Richard's good friend that taught him how to make C-ration stew so long ago and tutored him on so many things about staying alive and "comfortable" out in the bush. A touch, just a hint of nostalgia brushes his consciousness, but only for a moment. That's a dangerous place to go. In the background Richard Strom can hear a chopper getting closer. His only thought in the moment is that within three or four days he'll never have to ride in a helicopter again—ever!

ANOTHER FACE OF WAR

Chaplain Strom can hear the faint background sound of a helicopter in the distance as he and two Marines lift the badly mangled body of First Lt. Peter Gustavson into a body bag. The macabre act of placing arms and legs and smashed bodies into a plastic bag that will shortly be flown back to the next of kin is the single most distasteful, demoralizing act Richard has ever done in his life. On two different occasions he was given a direct order by the S3 that he was not to "bag and load," a task that was to be done only by selected enlisted personnel. However, at this point the chaplain passively disregards pretty much anything Major Copeland or anyone else directs him to do. Isolated with a line company and away from battalion, Strom has no constraints on how he chooses to function as the chaplain.

The NVA has disengaged just as suddenly as they started the fierce firefight followed in quick succession by mortar rounds. In the twenty-five minutes following the sudden, hellish onslaught, the Americans have focused their efforts first on getting the wounded immediate medical attention and medevaced back to a field hospital, then finally sending the dead back to Da Nang.

After getting the thirteen wounded lifted out, the four dead Marines are quickly loaded onboard a second chopper. The helicopter slowly lifts out of the small clearing, beating down the adjacent tree branches and brush underneath. Then in a slow-motion arc the chopper bears east, drops its nose slightly, and speeds off with the lifeless cargo of young men bound for a final journey back to their roots.

There will be no intermittent stop at the hospitals this time to unload a mixture of dead, dying and wounded Marines. This flight

419

goes directly to the morgue at III MAF where the four bodies—or what is left of them—will be prepared for burial, placed in a casket, then flown back to Hickham AFB in Hawaii. From there the bodies will be delivered to the military installation closest to their then shipped by plane, train, or hearse to their local hometowns.

The shrapnel that has ripped out the groin and lower intestines of Lcpl. Roberto "Bobby" Martinez has severed his main intestinal artery. There is no way in heaven or hell the terrible bleeding can be stanched in spite of the heroic efforts of Corpsman Jacobi. In deep shook, his life force eroding quickly, the battalion chaplain kneels in the mud next to Martinez. With his right arm under his neck and head, he gently pulls the young Marine next to his body while wrapping a rosary around Bobby's blood-drenched left hand. The breathing is now very shallow and becoming less frequent. Mindful of the fearsome firefight that is continuing less than one hundred meters away, Strom now leans over the dying Marine and whispers into his ear, "Jesus is your refuge and your strength. He is here right now in your heart and he is going to take you home with him." And just like that L/Cpl. Martinez gives up his last breath and dies.

Oscar and Lupe Martinez, Mexican American immigrants from the state of Durango, Mexico, are very typical of the people who came to America seeking to find a better life. They are hardworking, family-oriented folks whose singular purpose is to provide for their children the necessities and amenities that they had lacked or believed they would never get back in their home country. Oscar worked hard, day and night, at three jobs, monthly sending money back to Mexico to support Lupe and their three children. After three years he saved enough money to send for his wife and children, moved from Los Angeles to Santa Ana in rural Orange County. It was here Oscar found steady work as a farmhand with the largest property owner in southern Orange County, the giant Irvine Company, eventually becoming a crew foreman.

Roberto Martinez was born in 1950, the fourth of six children and first born in the United States. Although Spanish was the only language spoken in the home, his parents had insisted that Roberto and his brothers and sisters learn English by sending them to special classes taught by the church for the wave of post–World War II Mexican immigrants coming to Southern California. All six children were regularly sent every Wednesday and Saturday to St. Joseph's Catholic Church in downtown Santa Ana, each child receiving their first communion and confirmation from this old parish established in 1884.

However, in spite of their hard work, love of family, and dedication to church and country, assimilation into Orange County by the Mexican American community is difficult if not impossible. This politically conservative county considers itself the bastion of democracy and equality; however, only the Catholic Church practices what they preach and earnestly attempts to bring them into mainstream America. Mexican Americans are systematically denied access to the social, educational, and political structures of Southern California. A de facto social and political system of bigotry and financial disenfranchisement leaves their communities isolated and separate, especially the schools where the only thing that is true about "separate but equal" is the "separate" part. This de facto segregation keeps them down on the farm, isolated from good jobs and better schools, and with very few exceptions, treats them as outlaws rather than allowing them in as in-laws.

Bobby Martinez grew up in this milieu of social separateness and denied opportunity. Feeling the helplessness and hopelessness inherent when the social and economic structures implement racial barriers but then are vehemently denied, Bobby would sometimes verbalize his bitterness and anger to his parents. His parents would not allow him to speak unfavorable about their newly adopted country. Their message was always the same to Roberto and his siblings: "If you want to change things for our people, then you must work hard and study hard!"

His anger finally exploded one evening when he was hanging out with his girlfriend and two childhood friends. A car full of Anglos pulled up next to his, angry words were exchanged, a fight ensued in which one of his friends and an Anglo were seriously injured with stab wounds. Bobby went to jail—his second offense for assault and battery—and when he was released two days later, the public defender made a plea bargain with the judge. He was given a choice—join the Marine Corps and have the charges dropped or serve two years in prison and three more years on probation. Bobby knew in his heart this was no bargain. Should he opt for the Marines, he was well aware that this decision would be tantamount to a free trip to Southeast Asia. It was the same no-win offer that many young American men would be offered during the course of the war.

The dark blue sedan slowly turns off McFadden Avenue onto a small cul-de-sac. The driver is an enlisted Marine, a navy chaplain, and a Marine officer are seated in the backseat. They are looking out the windows, scanning the street for the address contained on the message given them earlier by the Department of Defense. The car comes to a stop at 241 S. Pardia Street.

The small homes and duplexes on this street and in this area referred to as the barrio are clean and well kept. It is late afternoon and people are beginning to arrive home after laboring hard in the fields or in the kitchens of the many restaurants in South County or in the yards and streets of the more affluent of Orange County. The driver gets out of the car and opens the back door and the two officers step out onto the sidewalk. Their car has attracted the attention of numerous residents who are quietly watching the unusual scene of military officers intruding into their neighborhood.

First Lieutenant Carl Abrahamson and Chaplain Vince Germano turn slowly toward each other, take a deep breath, then slowly proceed toward the light tan duplex, walking around two tricycles on the walkway, then stepping onto the porch. Abrahamson rings the doorbell, then turns and says softly, "Okay, Father Germano, this is your part."

Germano nods slowly and crosses himself as he turns toward the door. A young woman in her late teens, holding her two-and-a-half-month-old son, opens the door. For a few seconds that remains an eternity, she is completely immobile, unable to grasp the horrendous meaning of the presence of two military officers standing on her porch. Slowly she begins to shake her head back and forth, then blurts out, "What do you want? You have the wrong house, you don't belong here. Please leave!"

"May we come inside for a few moments," Chaplain Germano request softly.

"What do you want, go away!" Rosia Martinez begins to scream at the two officers who are now inside the door as she begins to back away, then quickly falls to her knees almost dropping the baby.

"No, no, oh please, no!" she screams as the young Marine officer grabs her by the arm to stop her fall. "Not Bobby, not Bobby, please not Bobby. He will be coming home in two weeks!"

*****

The Reverend Reynold J. Anderson slowly turns away from the ornate altar upon which rests the Thorwaldsen statue of Jesus with outstretched arms. He now faces for the final time a full sanctuary of twelve hundred mourners and the flag-draped coffin of his boyhood friend. In the front three pews are the grieving faces of the Marine's family and friends that have also been so much a part of the young cleric's life and direction. The newly ordained assistant pastor raises his arms and attempts to pronounce the ancient Hebrew blessing but is unable to vocalize the words. A tear slowly meanders down his cheek as he remains immobile, grief freezing his vocal cords and outstretched arms.

Pete Gustavson was bright, articulate, and popular. He was one of the kids who accomplished everything in his life with finesse and perfection, who went to the finest private schools, including Minnehaha Academy in affluent south Minneapolis. The summers of his youth were spent on the shores of Lake Vermillion and at Camp Ludsen among the pines and dark blue waters of northern Minnesota with the Andersons, Millers, Swansons, and other prominent members of Minneapolis financial and professional community.

As a high school all-American baseball player he had entertained the thought of signing a contract with the Minnesota Twins and playing on one of their farm teams. Instead, he went to St. Olaf's College in Northfield, Minnesota, majored in business economics, and graduated Magna Cum Laude.

The Gustavsons included four generations of Swedish Americans that had produced a governor, a US senator and two federal judges.

Bengt Gustavson, the family patriarch, arrived penniless with his new wife, Anna, from Sweden in the latter third of the nineteenth century. By 1925 he had made millions on lumber and mining interests in northern Minnesota and real estate dealings in the Twin Cities. He impressed upon his children and grandchildren the absolute need for a college education and inspired them with his hard word, dedication to family and a deep, abiding faith and love for his newly adopted country. "God made America for his angels, but he decided to give it to us humans instead," he would say time and again with a smile on his face.

The assumption then was that Peter Gustavson, this young man brimming with ability, personality, and talent, would throw himself into a promising graduate school program and become successful like his father and grandfather before him. It was with surprise and disappointment, when in the summer of 1966, Pete announced to his family that he would decline his acceptance into Stanford University School of Business and instead would be entering officer's candidate school at Quantico, Virginia. His father, a federal judge, was absolutely incredulous that his son, who faced such a bright future, would jeopardize his graduate school opportunities and maybe his life by becoming an officer in the Marine Corps. This talented young man had never discussed options about his future plans with anyone, so those who were family or close friends assumed he would follow in his father's or uncle's footsteps in a law or business career. The surprise and disappointment were attributable to his complete silence about military service. He was silent for a few moments after his parents articulated their concerns. Then softly, gracefully he disarmed them by saying, "I've decided to give back to my country first. When my service time is over, I will be ready to engage in my life pursuits." It was a decision his grandfather, Bengt Gustavson, would have heartily affirmed.

Pastor Anderson slowly drops his arms by his side, thoughtfully wipes away the tears running down his cheeks. He steps down from the area that contains the altar railing and walks the five remaining steps down to the main sanctuary floor that contains the casket of his friend. He then softly places both hands on the casket, then looks back up at the congregation in front of him. The silence is absolute and the milieu electrifying as he slowly begins his impromptu benediction, no longer fearful he will freeze in midsentence.

> Bless us Lord, we the living. So not to make this too
> much to bear:
> open our eyes to see the light,
> open our hearts to embrace the love,
> open our ears to hear the peace,
> open our spirit and be filled with your grace.
> Comfort us in our pain
> Somehow… somehow… somehow…
> Move us beyond the senselessness of dear Pete's death
> and all who suffer this terrible conflict we continue
> to endure… For greater love hath no man, then he
> lay down his life for another…

*****

It is early afternoon and the heat is almost unbearable as a hearse, followed by a row of twenty cars, slowly turns left off State Highway 3. The road into the cemetery is narrow and unpaved and the dust from the slow moving cars hangs like a heavy fog creating the illusion of peace and tranquility. There is stillness in the air that betrays the underlying tension of the grieving family and friends as the cars finally come to a stop at the only Negro cemetery in the area.

Although integration is the official policy of the United States, especially coming to the landmark 1964 civil rights legislation, Mississippi has hardly made a dent in relieving the heavy oppression and separation of the races that is indigenous to the culture, politics, and thinking of the Deep South, especially here in the middle of one of the poorest regions in the country—the Mississippi Delta. That cultural imprint of separation and racism is cast like steel reinforced concrete, disallowing the mixing of the races even in death. Because no black person, even if his name is Sergeant Marcel Washington, USMC, is going to be buried next to a white person in an all-white cemetery, even if he died a hero pulling four badly injured Marines to safety, three of whom were white, getting killed in the process, then posthumously awarded his second Purple Heart and the Silver Star.

The funeral procession slowly comes to a stop at the only visible open gravesite located thirty yards up a slight incline underneath two large elm trees. Although the area surrounding the gravesite has been trimmed and cut, the remainder of the cemetery is in various stages of neglect. This is in contrast to the "other" cemetery located on the other side of the county that is kept neat and manicured through funds budgeted yearly by the county commissioners. As family and friends slowly, sadly walk up the incline, an honor guard of six enlisted Marines and an officer assemble at the back door of the hearse, awaiting the casket as it is maneuvered out, each Marine patiently, reverently grasping the handle as it passes by them. With the six Marines in place facing the casket, First Lieutenant Jacob Feldman standing at the head gives a hushed command to a sergeant. Immediately, in complete unison, they face forward, slowly turn the casket toward the assembled folks, and in perfect step, walk the casket to the gravesite. Very slowly, in perfect unison, they again face the casket, carefully laying it on the caisson above the recently dug grave. There is a hushed silence broken only by the soft command of Sergeant Johnny Graham to the pallbearers, the Marines then retiring to an area behind the assembled mourners.

Mae Washington had collapsed screaming into the arms of the naval officer who had brought the terrible message of her son's death. She was inconsolable the remainder of that awful afternoon and evening, alternately collapsing into the arms of a friend or family member, sobbing uncontrollably, then become withdrawn, mute, as if she were in a deep trance. After that first day and night, Mae hardly said a word to anyone. She would sit in her favorite chair for hours, staring out the window wordless and tearless.

Ben, her husband, reacted as he always did in crisis, becoming stoic and mechanical, pushing the excruciating grief of his only son way down deep into a place that for now wouldn't tear him up and delete what little strength of spirit was left. As his wife sat in mute silence in her chair those days following the dreadful news, many times Ben would stand in back of her for hours, hands on her shoulders, unable to comfort or console her or himself. He was absolutely terrified when he thought about that day when his son would be brought home to be buried. He had confided to his oldest of five daughters that he didn't believe he had the strength and faith to get through the ordeal of losing his son.

The graveside ceremony lasts less than five minutes. The pastor of Mt. Zion Baptist Church has just pronounced the benediction. The silence is broken only by the sobbing of Sergeant Washington's sisters and their families. Mae and Ben Washington stare vacantly at the flag draped coffin in front of them. Sergeant Graham, the senior enlisted Marine, suddenly gives a simple, hushed command. In perfect unison the Marines bring their rifles to their shoulder and fire a volley three times. Within seconds, the mournful sounds of taps are heard, so penetrating surely the whole universe has stopped to listen.

Walking in their precise, orderly step the Marines move to the casket and began the sad, orderly, and final task of folding the American flag. When this is done, the flag is given to Lieutenant Feldman, who then walks slowly to the Washington's. He stops directly in front of Mrs. Washington, leans over with folded flag in hand, and says softly, "Mr. and Mrs. Washington, on behalf of the president of the United States and a very grateful nation..."

It is at this point Mrs. Washington stands up, pushes past the Marine officer, begins to sob, loudly saying, "My baby, oh God, why did you take my baby," then she falls to her knees, draping her body over the casket, repeating the sad refrain over and over again. Ben quickly gets up, goes to his wife, and kneels down with her, holding her sobbing body in his arms, tears of grief finally flowing from his eyes driven by the deep, horrendous loss they are both experiencing.

*****

Slowly the hearse makes its way up the windy road made muddy and nearly impassible by three days of rain. It is followed by a single vehicle, a somewhat battered, rusting 53 Chevy pickup truck. A gentle rain is falling softly as the vehicle carrying PFC Leroy Adrian comes to a stop. There will be no Marine honor guard this morning and no pallbearers for that matter. Rather, the mortuary has asked three cemetery workers who are digging graves that morning to help the Marine officer and the two mortuary employees in the hearse to offload the casket and carry the young Marine the twenty yards to the gravesite.

There has been no funeral or memorial service. Except for First Lieutenant Charles Freeman, the young officer assigned to accompany the casket to its final resting place, the only person in the world other than cemetery and mortuary employees who comes to the burial is Adrian's father, Jerome.

Leroy Adrian grew up in poverty in the coal mining district of southern West Virginia. His mother, Rose, an eighth generation of Scotch-Irish descendants who settled the area at the turn of the nineteenth century, had never been further than twenty-five miles from her birthplace. She died of cancer when Leroy was three. He and his three older sisters were passed around to various aunts and uncles throughout their childhood, the four of them never living in the same house or seldom in one place longer than a year. Their father was employed by the local coal mines when there was work and when he was sober, which was seldom since his wife's death. When Leroy did see his father the relationship was marred generally by complete indifference or physical violence brought on by his dad's alcoholism and the oppressive milieu of unemployment, poverty, and the lack of skills and aptitude necessary to explore other choices and lifestyles.

Leroy was a quiet, somewhat withdrawn kid who did not do well academically and dropped out of school when he was thirteen, never had a date, believed he had no choices except to work in the mines like his father and other family members, and, like his mom, had never been outside a twenty-five-mile radius of his birthplace. So when his Uncle Jesse, a miner and also a lay Baptist preacher who was the closest person Adrian had to having a mentor, suggested he go to the county seat and enlist in the navy, Leroy made the trip to Brinkley on his eighteenth birthday, experiencing both reluctance and a tad of excitement. However, instead of becoming a sailor as his uncle had suggested, the fast-talking recruiter convinced the reticent young man to join the Marine Corps instead.

Sheriff Garland Smallwood had been given the task of finding Jerome Adrian to let him know of his son's death in Vietnam. Smallwood found him drunk and passed out in the ramshackle house that had been in the Adrian family for three generations, woke the man up, and gave him the news of his son's death. The sheriff felt just terrible for Jerome, the news about his son coming just two months after his brother's death in a mining accident, because Smallwood was aware that his brother Jesse was the only person who had contact anymore with Leroy's father. When he finally sobered up and the reality of his son's death hit him, he stopped drinking and was still sober days later when they brought his son's casket to the mortuary in Brinkley. It was his longest period of sobriety since Rose's death fifteen years ago.

The soft, gentle rain continues to fall as the cemetery workers carefully, slowly maneuver the casket down into the earth. When the coffin reaches its final resting place, the workers pull up the heavy nylon belts that supported the casket. Next to the grave site the two mortuary employees and First Lieutenant Freeman stand silently with heads bowed, hands folded. In back of them and to their right, twenty feet away, Jerome Adrian stands alone, isolated, eyes riveted on the gaping hole left by the lowered casket, just beginning to comprehend the horrendous, empty void inside of him. The Marine officer quietly walks slowly to the father of the young Marine, hands him a folded American flag, and extends the condolences of the president. Jerome absently takes the flag and draws it to his chest, continuing to stare straight ahead.

An hour later the Marine officer and the workers and mortuary employees are gone. The grave has been filled in and a wreath has been placed over the spot where the casket once stood. Jerome Adrian is standing stationary in the same place. He hasn't moved since arriving, the American flag handed him by the Marine officer still tightly held next to his chest, rain slowly dripping off the old rimmed felt hat he put on before coming to the cemetery. He hasn't taken his eyes off the mound of dirt and is completely unaware of anything external going on in his world. However, he is aware that waves of emotions are beginning to push up—deep, primal feelings of sadness and grief brought on by the realization that he can never, ever say those words he wanted to express to his son so often but was never able to do: "Son, I'm real proud of you… and I love you."

You Can't Go
Home Again

"Chaplain Strom... Hey, Chaplain... Sir... you all right?" Richard hears dimly, like someone yelling far away in the distance. Gradually, as if pulling back from a distant dream state, a consciousness not of this place and time, Strom becomes aware of Gunnery Sergeant Carter standing in front of him, hand softly shaking his left shoulder.

"You're kinda spaced out there, sir," says the Hotel Company gunny, looking directly into Richard's eyes. "You gonna be okay?"

The chaplain is silent for a time as the concerned sergeant continues to stand in front of the dazed officer, aware of the activity again around him. "Yeah," Strom responds, reaching down to pick up his communion kit, unaware of how long he has been zoned out. "I'm okay. Just spaced out, lack of sleep, all that crap," he lies to the sergeant.

"Yes, sir," responds the seasoned Marine, "know what you mean, Chaplain." He is oblivious to what was really going on with Strom—a process that was far from just spacing out. Pointing over Strom's left shoulder he continues loudly over the sound of a chopper taking off, "We've got some more casualties over there, sir. I know the skipper would like you to talk to the wounded."

The battalion chaplain hesitates, flashing on the horrible experience last night with Echo Company and the death of his four remaining friends, quickly shutting the appalling pictures out of his mind's eye.

"Yeah, no problem, Gunny," he responds flatly.

Walking away from another landed helicopter, Strom comes upon Perkins kneeling on the ground, holding a body in his arms and against his chest, rocking back and forth. "Ah shit, don't die on me, Smitty, goddammit," he exclaims, tears of sorrow flowing down his face. He is cradling his good friend in his arms, his cheek pushed against the top of the dying corpsman's head, continuing his litany of anguish: "No... no... no... goddammit, Smitty, goddammit!"

Richard slowly kneels down next to the two young men—Perkins the quiet white kid from rural Louisiana and Smitty the gregarious young black man from south central Los Angeles. Although history has dictated centuries of separation and intolerance between the races, there is no dissonance or incongruity in this picture, only a coalescence of compassion and loyalty and love, a singular picture of a brother dying in another brother's arms.

The chaplain immediately sees the bullet holes in Smitty's abdomen and chest, observing the deep shock, the blank look in his eyes, and the slow but steady loss of consciousness as his life force dwindles. There is a quick gasp for a last breath, then quietly he slips away, leaving unfinished his legacy of hope and care and unfulfilled dreams. No '65 Mustang, no medical school, no infectious spirit, his boldness and magic squandered in a moment of unparalleled waste.

The chaplain does not move. Perkins continues to hold his dead friend rocking back and forth, now crying openly. "It's not fair, goddammit... It's just not fuckin' fair," he screams out, now looking at the kneeling chaplain in front of him.

Chaplain Strom stands and slowly walks around to the other side of the two, kneels next to Perkins, and places his right arm around his shoulder. "Yeah, I know, it's not fair." There is a long silence, then he continues, "I'm really sorry, Perkins... terribly sorry. He was the best of the best..." His voice trails off. He feels two tears meandering down his cheeks and yet is aware there are no feelings attached to his tears.

Strom gets to his feet, places his hand on Perkins's head, and says quietly, "I'll be back and we'll talk. I want to check on the rest of the wounded."

Perkins says nothing, continuing to hold his friend closely, weeping silently. Richard shakes his head slowly and walks away into another installment of this horrible, appalling milieu, redoing what he has done over and over again so many times the past year, comforting and praying for the wounded, talking to the survivors, endeavoring so many times to make sense out of nonsense and hope out of hopelessness.

Thirty minutes later, after having repeated numerous times the encounter he had earlier with Smitty and the other dead and dying Marines, the sixteen wounded and five dead Marines of third platoon cut down by the withering fire of an ambush have been medevaced back to Da Nang. One hour later the chaplain is standing in front of his commanding officer, packed and ready to head back to An Hoa.

"Good luck to you, Chaplain," Huggins begins, placing his hand on Strom's shoulder. "This must be a happy day for you, getting out of this place. It's the day all of us pray for."

The chaplain blankly looks at his CO and shakes his extended hand. "Yes, sir," he replies, not feeling happy or sad or anything at all, just empty and flat.

"You'll feel better once you're on that bird back to the States," Huggins continues in a soft, soothing voice, aware of Strom's weariness.

"One-niner chopper, inbound," announces a distant voice outside the CP.

Richard momentarily steps back and for a short few seconds he feels some sadness, wistfulness, as his eyes do a slow sweep of the five Marines in front of him but only for a moment. Quickly his feelings are layered over again by that flatness and disconnect that now permeates his day.

Each of the Marines step forward to shake his hand—the operations officer and his assistant, Major Copeland and Captain Ciribello, the brand-new intelligence officer, First Lt. Orly Lyle, and radio operators Sergeant Bailey and Corporal Werner Spizter. The ritual is quickly over, the preoccupied men focus back on their duties and Richard turns to begin his journey back to another reality. No ceremony. No rites of passage. Just a quick good-bye, then for the

Marines an abrupt refocus on the next encounter with the waste and decay brought on by combat.

Lt. Col. Huggins has personally fragged a special nonsupply helicopter to pick up Strom so he will not have to wait around all day. The CH46 is slowly dropping on the deck in an LZ less than one hundred meters away. The battalion chaplain doesn't run as he usually does when approaching a chopper ride but instead ambles slowly toward the landed craft. Along the way he notices that the twenty Marines nearby his walk to the chopper are all turned toward him, smiling, giving him the thumbs-up. He returns the smile and the gesture, remembering the many times this past year when he watched the Marines leave for the States. Although there is a deep desire to be that particular person going home on the "freedom bird," each homeward bound Marine is a reminder to all those left behind that there is a token of hope, a fragment of optimism that they too can perhaps survive the terrible daily onslaught and make it back as well—alive!

The battalion chaplain walks casually into the aft section of the aircraft, moves halfway down the passageway, slings his gear carelessly on the deck, then flops down heavily on a web seat next to the starboard-side machine gunner. The helicopter revs its engines, then softly lifts off the deck, slowly does a ninety-degree starboard turn south in the direction of An Hoa, then gradually picks up forward speed before lifting into the afternoon sky. Strom looks out the aft door and sees Perkins below and off in the distance waving at the aircraft. Lifting higher into the sky, the young corpsman disappears quickly into a collage of green below. There is a quick flash of guilt— that he didn't say good-bye to the grieving young man—but only momentarily. Quickly, the flatness returns as Richard closes his eyes and focuses instead on noise of the engines above him. There is no thought about going home to San Clemente, California, to his wife and son, to safety and three meals a day and normal routines. His consciousness is bereft of excitement or connection—to anything. He just sits, immobile, eyes shut, dark circles of stress and sleeplessness riming his eyes, his mouth taut and rigid, a mind-body set predicated by seeing too much the past twelve months.

Strom's chopper ride takes less than five minutes and lands on a seldom used, small LZ just to the west of the *Two-five* compound. The single passenger embarks quickly, then the aircraft lifts off and heads back toward the main landing strip to pick up supplies and passengers for the field. Slowly, the exhausted chaplain straps on his backpack, then slips the communion kit strap over his shoulder and walks the remaining one hundred meters to his hooch.

He walks up to the door and sees that it is padlocked, thinking this odd since the new chaplain and Bob are supposed to be in An Hoa. Dropping his gear, he digs in his pack for his wallet and retrieves the key. As he unlocks the door and steps inside, the company clerk from H&S Company quickly walks up to the hooch, knocks on the door, and says, "Sir, permission to come inside."

Richard wearily turns and faces the young Marine, motioning for him to come inside. "Come on inside, Corporal, and you can stop all the formality and sir crap while you're in here."

"Sir," he begins, "First Sergeant Rooney has your orders to go back to the States. He said he wants to see you when it's convenient for the chaplain."

"Thanks, that's good news," Richard responds flatly. "Have you seen Marshall and the new chaplain anywhere?"

"Sir, they just left for the field less than an hour ago," he says quietly. "They went out on a resupply chopper. The new chaplain was real anxious to get back out in the field as soon as possible."

Strom stands motionless, dumbfounded at what he is hearing. He places his hand to his forehead and sadly exclaims, "Oh God, no. I don't believe it." He slowly sits down while Corporal Lindemann stands stationary, uncomfortable and anxious at the battalion chaplain's anguish and also because he was the bearer of unintended bad news.

After a five-second pause, the young Marine clears his throat. "Sir," he says hesitantly, "is there something that I can help the chaplain with?"

There is another long pause, then Strom looks up at Lindemann. "I'm not a happy camper, Corporal, my best friend and companion that I've spent the last nine months with, well, I'm not going to see him again," he slowly reports to the young man standing in front of him.

"Yes, sir," he replies immediately.

Richard stands up slowly, walks to Lindemann, shakes his hand, and says, "Thanks for asking." Now smiling, he continues, "You know, that's my job, problem solving and all that stuff. But maybe there is a way you can help me out."

Directing him out of the hooch, they now quickly move toward H&S Company and walk up the two stairs and inside the hooch. First Lt. Jerry Bush immediately stands when he sees the chaplain enter and salutes. Richard does not return the salute but instead sits down in the chair in front of Bush's desk.

"I've got a big favor to ask you, Lieutenant," Richard says as Bush slowly sits down behind the desk.

The stiff-necked Marine officer sits rigidly in his chair and replies, "What is it that the chaplain wants?"

"Why do you use the word *the* when you address me, Lieutenant?" Richard responds rudely, shocking Bush.

"Well, ah… it's, ah, just a way of address the chaplain with respect," he now replies.

"See, there you go again," Strom says immediately, "like the dog, the head, the motor pool, the chaplain."

"Sir… I don't understand," Bush responds, confused by Richard's interaction with him.

Strom slowly shakes his head and says, "Well, I just don't get it. Anyway, my chaplain's assistant, Corporal Marshall, I need you to get him back here immediately."

Bush looks at Lindemann, who is standing directly in back of Strom. "What's this all about, Lindemann? Didn't you get Marshall hooked up with the new chaplain this morning?"

"Yes, sir," Lindemann responds.

"And how much time does he have left in-country before rotation back to the States?" he questions.

The corporal shoots a quick look at Strom, then back at the obviously irritated S1. "About twenty days, sir."

"With all due respect, Chaplain," he begins seriously, "your man cannot leave the field until five days prior to leaving for the States." He now leans over his desk, grabs a manila folder, and hands it to Strom. "May as well give these to you now. You're to report to the induction center at the Da Nang airbase twelve hours before leaving Vietnam."

Richard takes the folder, quickly examines the contents, then looks back up at Bush and says, "Marshall's been promoted twice since he's been in-country, has had his ass shot at for the past eight months assisting me and the corpsmen when he should have been pulled out of the field, as per Marine Corps regulations, because he has two Hearts." Angrily, the chaplain continues, "And you're telling me you won't cut him any slack? Is that what you're saying, Lieutenant?"

Bush's response is shocked silence. Then Strom continues, pointing his finger at the S1, "Your regulations suck, Lieutenant, and I'll tell you what I will do. I'm going to get his ass out of the field in spite of you!"

Richard whirls around almost knocking over the company clerk. He winks at Lindemann and walks quickly to the door. Then he stops, turns around to face the astonished S1, and says with a smile on his face, "You need to lighten up on the starch in your shorts, pal!"

The chaplain quickly walks directly to battalion combat center, hoping to find Major Cahill. Inside he sees two radio operators sitting in chairs, casually smoking cigarettes. They immediately stand when he enters, then he strides toward the two Marines. "Get me battalion six on the horn now," he says in a voice resonating irritation, disregarding the normal procedure of talking first to Major Cahill. Within two minutes Corporal Kerry has the commanding officer on the radio.

"Six, this is one-niner, sir," the chaplain begins, "I respectfully request one-niner assistant to be reassigned to me ASAP. He's been in the field longer than me, has two Hearts, and has less than two weeks left, sir, over."

There is a five-second pause, then Huggins responds, "You pull him out now and we have no one to help out our new 'outfit,' so I'm not inclined to do this, over."

"Sir," Richard continues, "I spent two months in the field on my own without any assistance. Besides, the regulations clearly state that—"

The chaplain is immediately interrupted in his communication. "I know what the regulations state," comes the irritated voice of Lt. Col. Huggins. "Right now you're tying up radio traffic in the midst of operational procedures. Out!"

Strom hands the receiver back to Corporal Kerry and walks slowly toward the door, turns back toward the standing Marines, and says quietly, "Thanks, guys, for your help. Guess the Old Man isn't very happy with me."

Both Marines smile at the chaplain, understanding the compelling reason the chaplain made the call, knowing the fierce loyalty he has for his young assistant and also the desire to protect him from becoming another casualty before shortly being rotated back to the States.

Richard Strom walks back to his hooch and begins packing his gear. When he finishes this chore, he empties the field issued communion kit and lays the contents on his cot. He is supposed to drop the kit off at the division chaplain's office. However, he made a decision two weeks ago that he would not follow through on the directive to bring his kit back to division or see McGinty again.

Slowly, he picks up the damaged cross and crucifix which had been hastily repaired that morning after the river crossing. A mosaic of geography and faces and circumstances and thoughts suddenly flash in his mind's eye. Laying aside his personal prayer book, his stole, and the four blood-stained communion linens given him long ago by two Vietnamese nuns, which he will take home with him, he carefully, mindfully repacks the communion kit he took possession of that first day he was assigned to recon. Sadly, he shakes his head in disbelief over his life events the past twelve months. Then quickly he shuts the images out of his consciousness, lest he be overwhelmed.

He will leave the kit on the desk. Let Porter decide what he wants to do with it.

His reverie is interrupted by a knock at the door. Still bent over the articles on his bed, he says, "Come in," not bothering to see who it is.

Corporal Kerry enters the hooch with a message slip in his hand. "Sir," he begins as Strom now looks up at the Marine, "this message just came from battalion."

Richard walks toward Kerry and takes the message. "One-niner, from Six: Your man left one hour ago for Golf. When returns, will send back for reassignment. Good luck," he reads quickly, somewhat relieved Marshall will be reassigned but also disheartened that he will not see his young friend again. "Thanks, Corporal, for getting this to me," Richard says to the messenger.

"Yes, sir, happy to bring it to you," Kerry replies, knowing the message will put the weary chaplain at ease.

At that moment, as Kerry leaves his hooch, Richard decides that he will leave this afternoon for Da Nang, now knowing that Marshall will not get back to An Hoa for at least another twenty-four hours. "I have no reason to stay out here any longer," he reasons to himself.

His gear packed, Richard now follows through on a decision he made after leaving the field this morning. He lugs his gear to the road fifty meters away from his hooch and hitches a ride from a passing jeep to the airstrip a few hundred meters away. His singular intent is to get transportation to Da Nang and be out of An Hoa as soon as possible.

There will be no disengagement process—no good-byes from anyone at battalion, the BAS, or even Bernie O'Hearn, who is also leaving shortly. His emotional disconnect now intact, he wishes no further upheaval caused by feelings.

Within an hour the C-130 airplane is circling Da Nang airbase. When it lands, he walks out the rear ramp and carries his seabag and valpack to the air terminal fifty meters away, the same building he first entered twelve months ago when he was full of energy and idealism and spiritual strength. Inside he walks past rows of inbound Marines awaiting their ride to III MAF or division. He looks past these young, fresh, eager faces, not wanting to process anymore thoughts or perceptions about the wasteland of innocence he sees spread about him. It is a consciousness he wants buried deep in a vault where it cannot ooze out and cause distress and anguish anymore.

The stark reality here is quite simple: for those who end up in combat this is a commencement exercise that will take them quickly into a reality they cannot even begin to imagine. Three weeks or four months or a full tour later—temporarily or permanently prone or sitting—there will be no "return of the native." Far too much will have happened. The combatant doesn't know this nor do those who await his return. Alive or dead, they can't go home again. Ever!

Twenty minutes later he has bummed a ride to division in a truck hauling medical supplies to First Medical Battalion. He has decided to stay there tonight, then in the morning go to the embarkation center for his flight tomorrow night back to Okinawa and then California. Exiting the base on the south end, the truck turns right and heads west around the base. Richard is sitting in the passenger seat of the transport truck gazing out the open window. For the first time he notices the many concrete reinforced revetments lined up on the south end of the base, looking like huge Quonset huts without front or back walls. Inside the structures the Marines and air force have parked their jet fighters and bombers to obviously protect their aircraft from rocket or mortar attack. It never dawned on Strom until this moment that none of the hospitals—both First Med and NSA—have no such protection from attack. Maybe some small bunkers here and there, but nothing at all like the elaborate structures protecting the expensive machines of war. Turning north on the west side of the base and heading toward division, as Strom processes this latest milieu issue, his disillusionment is now complete. Specific, concrete corroboration that bodies are expendable, the machines of war are not. He slowly, sadly shakes his head at this newest revelation, then places his head on the backboard, closes his eyes, and focuses on the sound of the diesel engine as the truck meanders up the crowded roadway full of mostly Vietnamese civilians riding bicycles and motorbikes or carrying their produce or crafts to market.

Twenty minutes later, baggage in hand, Strom is walking through First Med compound next to the mess hall. He turns left by ICU, slowly passing pre-op and the Rose Garden, three dynamic spheres of interfacing that will be forever, indelibly imprinted in his consciousness. Moving through this indispensable yet mostly horrifying domain, he is struck by the serenity and quiet of the place—no earsplitting sounds of choppers landing over and over bringing the maimed and bloodied Marines in from battle; no frantic activity by the medical teams to triage the living and dying; no bodies or green bags on the deck in the Rose Garden, awaiting transportation to their soon-to-be grieving families. For a moment, a rush of memories and feelings surges through his consciousness but only momentarily. His survival instinct immediately shuts this process down lest he be overwhelmed and crushed by the incredible tapestry of pictures and sounds and smells emanating from experiencing too much carnage and death. Shut down and go numb—the only possible way to make it back to "the real world."

Shortly he is entering the hooch where the hospital chaplain lives, hoping to find his good friend John Reitch, who has a month to go before rotating back to the States. Richard drops his gear, removes his helmet and flak jacket, and sits down heavily on a foot locker next to an empty bunk, placing his elbows on his thighs, face in hands. For many minutes he just sits and stares at the deck, an action that he finds himself doing more and more—a process of no thought and no feel.

"Hello there," Strom hears, breaking through his mute, withdrawn reverie, "is there something I can help you with?"

Unaware that anyone has entered the hooch, Richard looks up to see a smiling, clean-cut officer in freshly starched utilities standing in front of him. He recognizes the face as being one of the new chaplains he saw in McGinty office the day he and Vince left so abruptly.

"Yeah," Strom responds while remaining seated, "I need a place to crash tonight. Where's John?"

Richard hasn't bathed or shaved in a week and his clothes haven't been changed in days. Taken aback by the somewhat dour response of the person seated in his hooch, the newly assigned hospital chaplain suddenly recognizing who this grimy character is. "You're Chaplain Strom with the Fifth Marines," he responds while extending his hand. "I remember you from that day you showed up with that other chaplain at Father McGinty office."

"Where's John?" Richard replies tersely, continuing to sit on the foot locker while shaking his hand. "I thought he was still in-country?"

"He was assigned to First Tanks south of Da Nang," he responds with a smile. "I'm Father Gerald Keroack." Strom hasn't moved and is now staring at the new hospital chaplain. Sitting down on the bunk across from the thrashed chaplain, Keroack continues, "So what brings you to First Med, Chaplain?"

"I need a place to stay tonight, I rotate back home tomorrow," Richard continues as he does a slow sweep of the hooch. "Any empty bunks?"

"Yes, sir," he replies quickly, "the one you're sitting on now. You also look like you need some clean clothes and a shower. How about if we go get whatever you need from supply right now, get you squared away."

Immediately Richard feels irritation at Keroack's solicitous and eager attempt at kindness, feeling the need to just be left alone. "My name's Richard, and stop calling me sir for God's sake! I'm just a lieutenant, same as you," he mutters as he stands up. "Thanks for your offer, but I have what I need."

Keroack is immediately shocked by the brusqueness of Chaplain Strom but quickly recalls comments from Reitch and others about the flippant, brash, and impudent remarks emanating from those infantry chaplains with too much time in the bush. "I understand," he replies, "let me know if I can help." Then he walks out the door.

Within ninety minutes Richard has showered, changed into clean utilities, and eaten at the mess hall and is now nursing a beer in the officer club. During this period of time he has not engaged a single soul in conversation, content to isolate and be by himself. Shortly he is watching a movie, *The Sandpiper*, in the club. About forty-five minutes into the movie, he is bored and leaves. Twenty minutes later he is fast asleep.

An eerie quiet now permeates the area around division and First Med. No casualties have come through for the past ten hours. The sole noise in the compound is the steady hum of the generators located at the far east end of the compound. The only stirring is that of the duty corpsmen making their rounds, checking patients or playing cards in the OR waiting room. Even the Eleventh Marines and their artillery two kilometers away have shut down for the night. No choppers, no outgoing, no small arms or machine gun firing, no hustle and bustle indigenous to outlying combat operations—a deceptive, illusive calm has settle in.

Richard awakens from a restless sleep, sits up, and checks his watch. It is 0130. He can hear the soft snoring and breathing of the two doctors and one chaplain asleep in the hooch. He is thirsty and reaches for a canteen of water he placed by his bunk, aware of a gnawing anxiety, the kind that would come at times in the field when he felt something had was about to happen.

Kwaaap… Kwaaap—two rockets land in the rice paddy between First Med and the helicopter squadron down the road. Richard immediately jumps into his boots and reaches for his helmet and flak jacket. The other officers are now sitting up in their bunks, confused and agitated as their flight or fight immediately kicks in.

Kwaaap… Kwaaap… Kwaaap—three more rockets hit, each one landing closer to the compound as Strom is now heading out the door to find some kind of shelter, primal fear again permeating every cell in his body and mind.

Running straight west toward the chapel he hears an explosion rip into the motor pool, then another rocket slams in quickly into the area immediately back of the chapel. The next explosion Richard doesn't hear. His singular experience in that split second is seeing a huge, bright collage of orange flash in front of him.

EPILOGUE

A red and white civilian 707 makes a final directional adjustment, then bears northeast over the southern California coastal town of Laguna Beach toward El Toro Marine Corps Air Station. The hills between the ocean and the base this dry, fall afternoon are gold and brown, splashed with a smattering of green oak and manzanita. Continuing to slowly descend toward runway 2 in the distance, the aircraft flies a steady course over the newly developed retirement community of Leisure World, over Interstate 5 busily moving traffic between Los Angeles and San Diego, then past the eighteen-hole golf course located on the base's south end, softly landing fifty meters away from two F-4 Phantom jets awaiting take off.

A warm, mild Santa Ana wind is blowing out of the east as the airliner now bears left off runway 2, turns left again, and heads southwest toward a group of buildings five hundred meters away. Flight number 8249 from Okinawa bearing Marines from a tour of duty in Vietnam approaches the largest of the structures where four Marines await the aircraft and guide the pilot to a stop. Quickly a ramp is moved into place next to the aft door. The engines shut down, and except for the distant roar of the two Phantoms that just took off, there appears to be no other sound or activity on the base except at the terminal.

The aft door slowly swings open, then the ramp is pushed against the aircraft. A Marine officer quickly runs up the ramp and disappears into the airliner. For the next ninety seconds there is no movement. A Marine slowly emerges from the darkened pathway and promptly walks down the ramp and back into the terminal. Within seconds the first Marine appears in the doorway, squints at the bright sunlight, then slowly makes his way down the steps. More Marines now appear and make their way down the stairway, each of them reactive to the sunny afternoon light as they emerge from the doorway. Soon there is a steady stream of Marines moving casually into the terminal building. There is no commanding general to verbalize patriotic slogans, there are no prominent civilians to welcome them home, and family members haven't the slightest idea their husband or son or friend or boyfriend is finally back from Vietnam. Silently they continue to the terminal. There is no scoping out the surroundings, their eyes are focused straight ahead. Only the soft shuffling of feet can be heard as they make their way back to a reality that will never again exist for them. They are back home from the war but their eyes will be occluded and never see the same again, their voices will never articulate the innocence and idealism they left behind, and their hearing will forever be impaired and filtered. The real tragedy is that they don't even know it. Not yet anyway!

Ahead of them for months or years is the flat, dull, colorless boredom and disconnect from life events that clinicians call depression. A lifelong, exaggerated startle reflex will dog them, evoking questions and sometimes irritation from those who don't or won't understand. Year long, even decades long interfacing with the terrors of nightmares will bring years of disruptive, inadequate sleep. An overwhelming, seemingly irrational sense of dread and angst will create an obsessional need to control one's environment. Responding to an internal, constantly churning engine of negative thought, sad or angry feelings will rise up at inexplicable and inappropriate times and places.

When all of this becomes too much to bear, too much to handle, then medication with alcohol, marijuana, speed, heroin, and the like becomes the temporary solution to ease the pain. Or if the breadth and depth of the images and hopelessness creates too dark a hole and becomes too overwhelming, a gun can manifest a final resolution to the problem just like it did in combat.

Richard James Strom is one of the last passengers to step off the plane. He slowly, deliberately makes his way down the long stairway and steps onto native ground again. Looking like all the other passengers, he is wearing Marine-green dress pants, an open-neck khaki shirt, and a piss cutter on his head. Holding a small carry-on bag, he looks skinny and underfed, having lost thirty pounds the past year. His eyes have that vacant stare that is the hallmark of too many days in the bush.

"I wonder if I'll make it home in time for the evening news," is his only thought as he approaches the terminal door and walks inside to another reality.

ABOUT THE AUTHOR

Chaplain Lippert returning to
Battalion in rain after horrible
night with Hotel Company

Born and raised in the rich farmland of south central Minnesota, the family of five boys moved to Modesto, California, where the author attended Thomas Downey High School. He decided to go back to Minnesota and attend school at his parents' alma mater, Gustavus Adolphus College in St. Peter, Minnesota. After graduation he attended Augustana Lutheran Seminary for four years in Rock Island, Illinois, receiving his MDiv degree. Upon ordination he was directed to start a new mission church in New Orleans, Louisiana. During his tenure at St. Timothy Lutheran Church, he joined the naval reserve as a chaplain.

He was called to active duty and to report to officer's school in Newport, Rhode Island, on January 2, 1968. Two months later, he was on his way to Camp Pendleton, California, and within two weeks, on his way to Vietnam. Assigned to second battalion, Fifth Marine Infantry Regiment, First Marine Division, he was hit with shrapnel thirty seconds after stepping off a helicopter, his first foray into the bush, a precursor to the horror of sustained combat for the next year. His battalion sustained the highest casualties of any Marine battalion.

After returning to civilian life, he was assigned pastor of St. Matthew Lutheran Church, North Hollywood, California, for three years while concurrently enrolled in a graduate school program in Family Therapy at Azusa Pacific University. Licensed as a marriage and family therapist in 1974, he left the parish ministry and went into private practice as a family therapist for thirty-five years in Mission Viejo, California. During this same period Lippert functioned as a psychiatric social worker and therapist for Kaiser Permanente, Orange County, California.

Retired and living in the in the Dana Point–San Clemente area for the past fifty years, he continues to be astounded by his eight grandchildren and Trigger, his German shepherd, who daily teach him how to live in the present.